I0749094

LIBRARY OF TRANSLATIONS

FROM SELECT

FOREIGN LITERATURE.

Volume the First.

THE POWER OF THE POPE

DURING

THE MIDDLE AGES.

BY M. GOSSELIN,

DIRECTOR IN THE SEMINARY OF ST. SULPICE, PARIS.

TRANSLATED BY THE REV. MATTHEW KELLY,

St. Patrick's College, Maynooth.

VOL. I.

THE

POWER OF THE POPE

DURING THE MIDDLE AGES;

OR,

AN HISTORICAL INQUIRY

INTO THE

ORIGIN OF THE TEMPORAL POWER OF THE HOLY SEE,

AND

THE CONSTITUTIONAL LAWS OF THE MIDDLE AGES

RELATING TO THE DEPOSITION OF SOVEREIGNS.

WITH AN INTRODUCTION,

ON THE HONOURS AND TEMPORAL PRIVILEGES CONFERRED ON RELIGION AND ON ITS MINISTERS BY THE NATIONS OF ANTIQUITY, ESPECIALLY BY THE FIRST CHRISTIAN EMPERORS.

BY M. GOSSELIN,

DIRECTOR IN THE SEMINARY OF ST. SULPICE, PARIS.

VOL. I.

TRANSLATED BY

THE REV. MATTHEW KELLY,

Saint Patrick's College, Maynooth.

BALTIMORE:

J. MURPHY & CO., 178, MARKET STREET.

LONDON: C. DOLMAN, 61, NEW BOND STREET.

MDCCCLIII.

NOTICE.

In presenting to the Subscribers the First Volume of the Library of Translations from Foreign Literature, Mr. Dolman returns thanks for the encouragement which he has already received, but begs leave to impress upon them the expediency of their making the Series as generally known to their friends as possible; since upon the extent of subscription depends materially the success of the undertaking. The book now submitted to them, affords, it is believed, a very favourable specimen of the character and quality of the books which it is intended to be comprised in the Library. The Second Volume is already in the press, and will be produced as early as possible.

TRANSLATOR'S PREFACE.

No intelligent reader requires to be informed that there is not in the profane history of Europe any subject more comprehensive, or more deeply interesting, than the temporal power of the pope during the middle ages. For more than a thousand years, as intimately blended with the history of nearly all European states as the reigns of their own sovereigns, the papal power presents itself to the historian at every step, and is often a great, if not the chief agent in those memorable scenes which constitute epochs in national histories. An error in appreciating this great power is sure to involve false views and inferences, and in many cases grievous mis-statement of facts, not less injurious to the truth of national history itself than to the characters of popes. Acts of papal interference, imperatively required by the exigencies of the time and the voice of the people, and which were moreover in the strict sense of the terms, legal and constitutional, are made the themes of violent invective against priestly arrogance and usurpation; and occasional abuses (such as are inseparable from all human power), occurring once in a century, perhaps, in one particular country,—abuses for which no sober historian would venture to stigmatize the pettiest dynasty of a German principality,—are registered by modern historians as unanswerable evidence against that majestic moral power which, during so many centuries, ruled the destinies of Europe, moulding into civilized form its barbarous laws and institutions, and controlling with the same vigilance and fortitude the feuds of the baronial castle, and the tyranny of the imperial palace. The good effected by this power is forgotten; its occasional and accidental abuses alone are remembered. A pope aids the Norman conquest of England, and his name is hardly ever mentioned in connection with that event,—pregnant, if we believe a common opinion, with all the germs of the future greatness of England: another pope, a century later, aids the conquest of Ireland; and to this day, in the sad pages of the national historian, his name is identified with seven hundred years of almost unchequered misery.

It is fortunate, perhaps, that the first comprehensive inquiry into the origin, progress, and general influence of this power has come from the principal ecclesiastical college in France, — a country not suspected of undue partiality for the popes, but rather supposed by some English statesmen to have attained its undeniable greatness, notwithstanding its Celtic blood and Catholic creed, partly by its almost rebellious resistance to the popes. Our author, however, is not a Gallican; he agrees, in truth, neither with Bossuet nor Bellarmine; with Fleury nor with Orsi: if some of his theological opinions be identical with those of Bossuet, and with the oath of allegiance taken by British Catholics, his facts supply a vindication of the popes more likely to command respect than any yet produced by the advocates of ultramontanism. With the order and elaborate method characteristic of his countrymen, and totally free from that exaggeration of statement and intrusion of sentiment into the domain of fact, of which they are sometimes not unjustly accused by English practical sense, he arranges his materials, collected from the history of every Christian country in Europe, and estimates, or rather enables the reader to estimate, the papal power, not by isolated cases, but by its general results. For his own general views on the subject the reader is referred to the Preface. It is enough to state here, in general, the result of his inquiry; that the temporal power exercised by popes over sovereigns in the middle ages was required by the exigencies of the times; that it was no more than the application to sovereigns of principles then universally recognised; that it was not a usurpation, nor a practical error, founded on ignorance of the mutual independence of the temporal and the spiritual power each in its own sphere; finally, that whatever partial evils it may have occasioned, were amply compensated by its general beneficial influence. In its origin it was just; in its exercise, disinterested and prudent; in its general results, salutary.

This temporal power of the pope over sovereigns during the middle ages is the second and principal part of the work. It was published in 1839, and was very favourably received on the continent. An English version of it was prepared by the translator of the present volume before the announcement of the Library of translations; his principal object being to supply a corrective for very erroneous notions regarding the papal power, contained in some popular Irish works, and especially in one which he was editing for an Irish literary society. It can hardly be necessary to remind the reader that, during the protracted discussions on Catholic emancipation, these false views were, for very obvious reasons, popularized by some eminent advocates of that measure. While declaring on oath that the pope neither has nor ought to have any temporal power within this realm, they moreover recommended their loyalty by declaiming against the exercise of that power in other places and other times. To disarm or propitiate their oppressors, they denounced as unscrupulous usurpers that illustrious line of pontiffs whom the almost unanimous voice of impartial historians is beginning to recognise as having been the chief support of society and the regenerators of Europe. This mode of appeal answered well at the time, or it would not have been so frequently used; but it may be asked, if the popes were so unscrupulous during so many centuries, what security is there that they would not recommence the same formidable machinations against the independence of states wherever the Church is tolerated? In the present work that question is answered in a manner that must quiet the apprehensions of all rational men who propose it seriously. By tracing the real origin of the papal temporal power, it demonstrates that it was the natural growth of circumstances which no longer exist, and which cannot exist unless the world relapses into the same barbarism from which popes have delivered it. If, in the cycle of human affairs, the middle ages should again return, or if savages, worse than Hun or Vandal, issuing from the most polished capital in the world, should refute the fond prediction of proud philosophers, that barbarism could no more return on the earth; then, perhaps, disabused of false notions, and taught by the same experience, statesmen and philosophers, like the pious and enlightened men of the middle ages, might be among the first to turn to the chair of Peter as the last hope of civilization, and to thank Providence that in that chair was still to be found the same youthful energy which encountered the savage conquerors of the Roman empire, and which has left the impress of its creative and conservative power in the annals of almost every country in Europe.

The translation, it is hoped, will be found to be as literal as possible. When the author translates his authorities, he sometimes uses the paraphrastic latitude allowed by the taste of his countrymen. The English translation even of such passages is made from the author's text, not from the original authorities themselves subjoined in the notes, the first duty of the translator being to be faithful to his text, even though he does not approve of the author's translation. This remark is made principally because the translations made by the author, though substantially faithful, might, in a few cases, be exposed to cavilling.

AUTHOR'S PREFACE.

THE temporal power of the Church, and of the Pope, during the Middle Ages, and the influence of that power on political affairs during many centuries, present, it is admitted, one of the most astonishing phenomena in history, and one eminently worthy of the consideration of every reflecting mind.[1]

The uninterrupted persecutions which the world had raised during three centuries against the

---

[1] It may not be useless to explain here what is generally meant by the middle ages. That part of history embraces, we may say, the whole period from the establishment of the northern barbarians in the provinces of the Roman empire in the West in the fifth, down to the revival of letters in the fifteenth century: the middle ages, therefore, include a period of about 1,000 years. To fix their limits with more precision, a recent writer, who has made the subject his special study (but unhappily biassed by strong prejudices), dates the commencement of the middle ages at the establishment of the Franks in Gaul under Clovis, in 496, and assigns their close to the expedition of Charles VIII. to Naples in 1494. (Hallam, Europe in the Middle Ages, vol. i. Preface, p. iv.; vol. iv. p. 79.) See an account given of that work by M. Raoul Rochette, in the Journal des Savants, December, 1821. According to this division, the history of the Greek empire, at least since the fifth century, properly belongs to the middle ages; the history of the Greek empire, until the destruction of the Roman empire of the West in the fifth century, is generally considered as belonging to ancient history.

Church, had scarcely ceased, when she found herself suddenly invested with honours, wealth, and privileges. Constantine, and his most illustrious successors, not content with supporting her by their laws, superadded to her spiritual authority the splendour of temporal power, by inviting the bishops to take part in the administration of civil affairs, and by intrusting to their care interests most intimately connected with the welfare of the people, and with public order. This generosity of the Christian emperors was eclipsed by the sovereigns of the new monarchies, which arose after the fourth century on the ruins of the Roman empire. In these new states every succeeding year brought fresh accessions to the prerogatives and to the temporal power of the clergy. The princes of the hierarchy were summoned to the councils of kings, and to all political assemblies; the most honourable rank is assigned to them; they exercise an influence in all the departments of civil government, even in the election and deposing of princes; and so intimate was the union of the temporal and spiritual powers, during many centuries, that they appear completely identified in the government of Church and State.

While the temporal power of the clergy was establishing and extending itself in the different states of Europe, the temporal power of the Holy See was extending and consolidating itself throughout Italy, where the profound respect of the people for religion, aided by the gradual declension of the imperial power, gave rise insensibly to the temporal sovereignty of the popes. The influence of this new sovereignty was soon felt far and wide. In the midst of the disorders and anarchy of the middle ages, it created a new bond of union between nations the most distant, and the most opposed both by interests and character; it became a common centre and rallying-point for all society; it became, moreover, a supreme tribunal, which decided without appeal the controversies of kings, and whose decisions were equally respected by the prince and by his people.

By a revolution equally surprising, this temporal power of the clergy, which had exercised during many centuries so great an influence in all the states of Europe, insensibly declines and disappears. Princes and people, who had so long looked up to it as their most powerful resource and their firmest support, now regard it with jealousy and distrust; they vie with each other in diminishing, and even destroying it; in fine, at the present day, such is the general disposition of men's minds, that most people cannot contemplate without amazement, and almost without scandal, an order of things which to former times appeared so natural; nay, the clergy are often charged with the ancient power of their order as if it were a crime, a sort of usurpation and revolt against the legitimate authority of temporal princes.

An inquiry into this charge, and into the great revolution which has occasioned it, is undoubtedly a most interesting subject, not only in a religious, but also in a purely historical and philosophical point of view. With regard to religion, what subject is more entitled to consideration than one which affects so closely the honour of the clergy, and of a long succession of pontiffs? And with regard to history, or even philosophy, can there be a more engrossing subject than the rise and vicissitudes of a power, which, after having been for ages the mainspring of the political world, lost its energy insensibly, and is at present extinct and forgotten?

But however interesting the subject is in itself, prejudice and passion, as might well be expected, have influenced men's judgments regarding it, especially since the great change in the temper of the times, and the decline of religion and morality, have seduced so many writers to judge the history of the middle ages more by the standard of modern ideas and opinions than by a critical and attentive examination of facts in themselves. This is undoubtedly the principal cause of the very conflicting judgments pronounced in these latter times on so delicate a subject. On the one hand, a desire of excusing and vindicating men of commanding virtues and character, has made some persons invent theories, as dangerous as they are extravagant, on the rights of the ecclesiastical power in temporal affairs.[1] On the other hand, the extravagance of such systems, and the abuses which are supposed to have arisen from the temporal power of the clergy, and even of the pope, during the middle ages, have supplied a theme for the most scandalous declamations against the Church and against its

[1] An exposition of these systems is given at the end of this work,—Confirmatory Evidence, No. 8.

visible head. The reproach of "ignorance," "ambition," and of "fanaticism," has been repeated a thousand times, on this matter, against men whose learning and virtues had been the delight and admiration of their contemporaries. It is not from the tongues of heretics and infidels alone that these odious imputations proceed; we are surprised and shocked to find them stated, or at least confirmed, with more or less distinctness, by a great number of writers, in all other respects estimable and sincerely attached to religion;[1] and, most deplorable of all, so obscured has the history of the middle ages become by their reconcilable theories on this subject, that discerning writers have almost despaired of ever seeing it clearly understood. "A subject so interesting," exclaims a learned academician of our days, "a subject distorted by so many conflicting prejudices; a subject, in fine, of which no person has yet written, and of which we

---

[1] We shall cite, in particular, Fleury's and Bérault-Bercastel's Histoire Ecclésiastique; Velly's Histoire de France, and even Père Daniel's; Père Maimbourg's Histoire de la Décadence de l'Empire après Charlemagne; Michaud's Histoire des Croisades; Ferrand's Esprit de l'Histoire, &c. All these works, and an immense number of others, notwithstanding the religious principles professed by their authors, leave on the minds of their readers most unfavourable impressions against the popes and the clergy of the middle ages. In the course of our inquiry, the principal errors of those authors, and of many others, shall be pointed out. The Church History, recently published by M. l'Abbé Receveur, may serve as a very useful corrective, and it shall be often cited in this work in support of our views, especially on the origin of the temporal sovereignty of the Holy See, and on the constitutional laws of the middle ages, relating to the deposition of princes (part i. p. 243 et alibi passim).

may long expect in vain a complete and impartial history."[1]

In the mean time, as a prelude to some work which shall clear up this subject in all its details, it has been deemed useful to publish the following "Inquiry on the Origin of the Temporal Power of the Holy See, and on the constitutional laws of the middle ages, regarding the deposition of temporal princes." These two points are, in truth, the chief cause of the difficulties which perplex the history of the middle ages; if they could be cleared up, great light would be thrown on the principal events of that epoch, and especially on questions connected with the contest between the papal and imperial powers since the tenth century.

The first draught of this Inquiry was published in 1830, in the "Revue des quelques Ouvrages de Fénelon," which was intended as a supplement to the editorial notices prefixed to the different classes of his works.[2] The exposition given by us in the second article of that work,[3] of the opinions of Bossuet and of Fénelon on the authority of the sovereign pontiff in the temporal order, led us naturally to some inquiry into the "maxims of constitutional law," by which Fénelon believed he could explain the conduct of the popes who had formerly deposed temporal princes. We regretted

---

[1] Journal des Savants, December, 1821, p. 737; article by Raoul Rochette, on Hallam's Europe in the Middle Ages.

[2] This review, which was then published separately (212 pages 8vo.), was at the same time inserted in the last volume of Fénelon's works, entitled Table des Œuvres de Fénelon, précédées d'une Revue de ses Ouvrages: Paris, 1830, 8vo.

[3] Ibid. No. 84, &c.

at the time that our plan did not permit us to treat the subject at greater length; and we had good grounds for believing that more extensive researches would confirm more and more the opinion of the archbishop of Cambrai. Our hopes were not disappointed; the additional researches subsequently made, brought to light numerous and striking proofs of the existence of that constitutional law. Such at least was the opinion of enlightened judges, to whom we submitted the more extensive work published by us in 1839, under the title "Pouvoir du Pape sur les Souverains, au Moyen Age;"[1] and in corroboration of that first favourable judgment, we are now enabled to adduce the gratifying reception which the work has since that time met with, both in France and in other countries. Besides many periodical publications, deservedly held in high esteem for the solidity of the principles professed by their editors,[2] many eminent writers have spoken

---

[1] This work, which then appeared separately (Paris and Lyons, 8vo.), was republished as an appendix to the Histoire Littéraire de Fénelon (Paris and Lyons, 1842, 8vo.), to serve as a supplement to his History, and to the different editions of his works.

[2] See reviews of our first edition in L'Ami de la Religion, vol. cii. p. 419; vol. ciii. pp. 145, 257, 370, 387; vol. cv. p. 369; l'Université Catholique, Sept. 1840, p. 230; Bulletin Catholique de Bibliographie, April, May, 1840, p. 112; Journal des Villes et des Campagnes, Nov. 21, 1842; l'Union Catholique, Jan. 22, 1843; Annales de la Philosophie Chrétienne, May, 1843; l'Université Catholique, Nov. 1843; Bibliographie Catholique, vol. iii. p. 293; vol. iv. pp. 155, 168. Many foreign publications have also favourably noticed that first edition. We may cite among others the Cattolico, an Italian review, published at Lugano in Switzerland; the Mémoires of Modena; and the Annali dei Scienze Religiosi, published at Rome by l'Abbate de Luca.

in very flattering terms of the first edition of our work. Among the latter we may cite in particular, Mons. l'Abbé Jager, professor of ecclesiastical history in the Sorbonne, and the Abbate Palma, professor of ecclesiastical history in the Roman Seminary, and in the college of the Propaganda. Both these learned professors, specially qualified by the nature of their professional studies to appreciate our work, have approved it most warmly; the former, in his introduction to the histories of Gregory VII. and of Innocent III.;[1] the latter, in his Lectures on Church History, published at Rome,[2] where he has long enjoyed a very high reputation, which the extent of his erudition and the solidity of his judgment alone could secure for him, in the centre of Catholicity, in the bosom of that Church which is the mother and mistress of all others.[3]

---

[1] Voigt, Histoire de Gregorie VII., traduite de l'Allemand par M. l'Abbé Jager: Paris, 1838, 2 vols. 8vo. Hurter, Histoire d'Innocent III., traduite de l'Allemand, par le même et Th. Vial: Paris, 1840, 2 vols. 8vo.

[2] Prælect. Histor. Eccles. tom. iii. (Romæ, 1840-1842, 8vo.), part i. p. 7; part ii. pp. 5, 39.

[3] The first edition of our work has been cited with similar praise in the following works: Boyer, Défense de l'Eglise Catholique contre l'Hérésie Constitutionelle: Paris, 1840, 8vo. p. 15. Dumont, Hist. Rom. 2nd ed. Paris, 1840, 3 vols. 8vo. vol. iii. pp. 524, 649. Th. Nisard, Hist. de Charlemagne: Paris, 1843, 12mo. pp. 408, 433, &c. Pardessus, note in Bréquigny's work, Diplomata et alia Monumenta ad res Francicas spectantia, tom. i. p. 282. Artaud de Montor, Considérations Hist. sur les Papes qui ont porté le nom de Grégoire, pp. 75, 227, &c. Of foreign authors who have favourably noticed our work, we may mention Mons. Caddolini, archbishop of Edessa, secretary of the Propaganda, Rome. See his Discourse, read at the Academy of the Catholic Religion, Rome, Sept. 17, 1840. This discourse was published complete in the

Encouragement so flattering given to the first edition of our work was a powerful motive to us to spare no pains in completing and perfecting our plan. All possible care has been taken to make it still more deserving of public favour. We have earnestly solicited the criticisms of intelligent persons, and have profited by their advice in correcting and improving both the substance and the arrangement of our work. A glance at the order and plan adopted in this edition at once shows the very great difference between it and the two former in both these respects.

To elucidate more clearly the subject of our researches, and to point out the true origin of that temporal power with which the Holy See was invested after the fall of the Roman empire, we have deemed it advisable to extend our inquiry to a more remote period of history. It is one of the commonest errors of modern writers to attribute to the ignorance and superstition of the middle ages the honours and temporal privileges granted to the clergy in general, and to the pope in particular, in those ages, in every Christian country. Nevertheless, that order of things which appears so strange to-day, was indubitably the natural consequence of the customs and maxims even of pagan antiquity concerning the honours and privileges due to religion and its ministers. This fact is proved in

---

Ami de la Religion, vol. cx. p. 352, &c. (see particularly p. 373); also the Course of History of M. Cæsar Cantù, which was received so favourably in Italy, and which is now being translated into French,—Storia Univ. scritta da C. Cantù, vol. ix. p. 352: Torino, 1842.

our Introduction, now published for the first time, in which are detailed the honours and temporal privileges conferred on religion and its ministers by ancient nations, and especially under the first Christian emperors. The development of that subject naturally led us to refute, by the tradition and practice even of the primitive ages of the Church, the paradox maintained in our own times by some enthusiasts, who clamour for "the total separation of Church and state, as essential for the good of religion;"[1] a paradox justly condemned by Pope Gregory XVI. in his encyclical letter of the 15th of August, 1832, in which he thus expresses himself: "Nor could we hope for happier results to religion and to the state from the projects of those who wish that the Church should be separated from the State, and that the mutual concord of the priesthood and the government should be severed. For it is certain, that the partisans of the most licentious liberty dread that concord, which has ever been propitious and salutary to the well-being of Church and State."[2]

---

1 This was one of the paradoxes maintained with the greatest confidence and obstinacy by the journal L'Avenir. See propositions 51 and 53 of the Censure de divers Ecrits de M. de la Mennais et de ses Disciples, by several French bishops.

2 "Neque lætiora religioni et principatui ominari possemus, ex eorum votis qui ecclesiam a regno separari, mutuamque imperii cum sacerdotio concordiam abrumpi discupiunt. Constat quippe pertimesci ab impudentissimæ libertatis amatoribus concordiam illam, quæ semper rei sacræ et civili fausta extitit ac salutaris."—Greg. Papæ XVI. Epist. Encycl. Aug. 15, 1832.

In support of this opinion, see Conférences de M. Frayssinoüs sur les Principes Religieux, Fondements de la Morale et de la

From these preliminary observations it results, that the subject of our researches may naturally be divided into two parts; the first relates to the origin and foundation of the temporal sovereignty of the Holy See; and the second to the authority of the popes over sovereigns during the middle ages.

In the former, which is now published for the first time, we endeavour not only to assign the precise date of the origin of the temporal sovereignty of the Holy See, but also to explain its nature, and the titles which establish its legitimacy. An examination of these two points, besides its natural connection with our plan, has appeared moreover specially important, both to defend the memories of the popes of the eighth century against the attacks of many modern writers; and also to set in the clearest light the principal causes of the influence of the popes in the general concerns of Europe during the middle ages; and finally, to enable the reader to form his opinion on the principal events relating to the contests of the two powers during the same period. The sovereignty of Rome was in reality the principal point at issue between popes and emperors, principally from the time of Frederick Barbarossa, who maintained so haughtily and violently his pretensions on that

---

Société, et sur l'Union Réciproque de la Religion et de la Société, vols. i. and iii. Conferences. See also L'Examen d'une Opinion (of M. de la Mennais) sur les Traitements Ecclésiastiques, par un Prêtre du Diocèse de Paris (l'Abbé Delaconture): Paris, 1830, 8vo. Boyer, Défense de l'Ordre Social, vol. i. p. 173, &c.; vol. ii. p. 410, &c.

point.[1] Voltaire himself has been forced to acknowledge the fact. "To me it appears clear," he says, "that the real point of the dispute (between the popes and emperors) was that the popes and the Romans did not wish to have any emperor at Rome;"[2] that is to say, adds Comte de Maistre, "they did not wish to have a master in their own house."[3]

In the second part, which was published in 1839, we inquire by what right the popes formerly deposed temporal princes; and among the different solutions given to that question, we adopt and support the opinion of Fénelon and of many other modern writers, who explain and justify it by the maxims of constitutional law then universally admitted. In this edition we republish the substance of the former, but with many additions and important modifications. We may mention here particularly the details given in the first chapter of the second part on the temporal effects of public penance, which prepared the way for those of excommunication. Additions still more considerable are introduced in the third and fourth chapters, which are so developed, that they may be considered entirely new, expounding with greater perspicuity the principles which had been touched too lightly in the former editions. An interesting part of those additions comprises a discussion of the objections proposed to us in some periodical publications, whose

---

1 See below, first note, part i. ch. ii. art. 58.

2 Voltaire, Essai sur l'Histoire Générale, vol. i. ch. xlvi.

3 De Maistre, Du Pape, book ii. ch. vii. art. 3, p. 298.

editors, notwithstanding their favourable notice of our work, appear not to have seen the point of some of our arguments, and not inclined to adopt our opinion.[1] It is hoped that enlightened readers will be satisfied with our answers to these objections, and that, after following the discussion in all its details, they will conclude with us that the opinion of Fénelon on the constitutional law of the middle ages relating to the deposition of temporal sovereigns is perfectly borne out by facts, and that, in some measure, it supplies a key to the history of the middle ages, and to a great number of facts which have been too often represented in the most odious colours, from not having been regarded in their true light.

Besides the critical and explanatory notes which frequently accompany the text, we have placed at

[1] The periodicals referred to here are the Journal des Débats, Sept. 29, 1839; Revue Ecclésiastique, Jan. 1840; and Le Semeur, Sept. 8, 1841. All the objections proposed by the authors of these different articles may be reduced to three principal ones. The first disputes the fact, that is, the general belief of the middle ages on the subordination of the temporal to the spiritual power. The second maintains that this belief was founded in error, namely, on the theological opinion which attributes to the Church and to the pope a jurisdiction at least indirect over temporalities; whence it is inferred that neither the Church nor the pope could have any real right to temporal power, but merely a supposed or imaginary right, the exercise of which was still usurpation, though not intentional. The third is founded on the pretended incompatibility of the temporal with the spiritual power in the ministers of the new law, and the pretended opposition between the spirit of the Gospel and the enormous power attributed to them by the maxims of the middle ages. A satisfactory solution of the first objection is given, we trust, in ch. ii. part ii. of this edition; and of the two others, in ch. iii. See especially No. 274, et seq.

the close of the volume, under the title of Confirmatory Evidence, a discussion on some special difficulties, which could not be introduced without interfering too much with the unity of our work. Among these pieces, the most interesting are Nos. 7 and 8. The former regards the elevation of Pepin to the throne of France, and the usurpation of which that prince is commonly accused; the second contains a brief statement of the origin, progress, and vicissitudes of the opinion which attributes to the pope "a power of direct or indirect jurisdiction over temporal matters by virtue of Divine institution." The latter would admit, no doubt, of being treated at far greater length, especially by fuller developments of the opinions of the different authors whom we have cited; but the limits prescribed to us would not allow us to be more diffuse: brief though it be, we trust that it will not be uninteresting either in an historical or in a controversial point of view.

From the plan and even the very title of our work, it is obvious that we do not intend to revive the theological disputes on the "right divine" with regard to the distinction and reciprocal independence of the two powers. The mere statement of the facts which our plan includes, may contribute, no doubt, considerably to a solution of the questions agitated with so much noise on this topic in later times. In that controversy, as in many others, several important facts, from not being carefully examined with all their modifying circumstances, appear to have been cited without reason by the contending disputants; grave authorities have been adduced with equal confidence in favour of the most contradictory opinions; an attentive examination of history and of the true sense of the testimonies adduced on both sides must, of course, have the effect of elucidating the questions discussed. But this result is, in reality, quite foreign to the object of this work, which is purely historical; the sole end which we propose to ourselves being to prevent or to correct, by a simple statement of facts, the dangerous impressions produced on many heedless or prejudiced minds by a study of the history of the middle ages, principally in what relates to the temporal power of the Holy See during that period, and to the use which many popes made of it in their quarrels with sovereigns.

Far from wishing to revive theological discussions on this point, we carefully avoid, in the development of our plan, and of the facts which it comprises, everything that might give offence to the adherents of the different opinions. To the impartial reader himself we leave the task of deducing the objections which may result from our statement against the opinions of some divines, or, at least, against the arguments sometimes cited by them in support of these opinions.

The better to understand the principal facts which we may have occasion to cite, and also to guard against misstating them, or presenting them in false colours, we have made it a rule to cite none except on the testimony of contemporary authors, or of those who lived nearest to the time in which the facts are said to have occurred. Our limits do not always admit the insertion of the entire text of those authors; frequently we give only the substance, but as nearly as possible in their own words; but, to compensate for our brevity, we give in the notes faithful references to the principal passages of the authors adduced as authorities, having scrupulously verified each citation. All those passages which appeared most important for elucidating our subject, and dispelling the errors accredited by modern writers, are cited verbatim. With regard, however, to the texts of Greek authors, as they are intelligible in these days to only a small number of readers, our general rule is to cite them in the words of some generally approved Latin version; this Latin translation is also omitted whenever the original text is represented with sufficient fidelity in our own version.

Though the testimony of ancient writers is amply sufficient to establish the truth of our statements, it has been deemed advisable to confirm the most prominent facts, as well as their most remarkable consequences, by the testimony of modern authors by no means suspected of partiality for the clergy. It is, indeed, singular to find the principal facts which establish the legitimacy of the temporal power of the Church and of the pope in the middle ages confirmed by the admissions of authors the most opposed to ultramontane principles, and not unfrequently even by heretical writers imbued with the most pernicious prejudices against the Holy See and the Catholic Church. Among authors of the former class may be cited Bossuet, Defensio Declarationis; Fleury, Histoire Ecclésiastique, and Institutions au Droit Canonique; Velly and his Continuators, Histoire de France; Lebeau, Histoire du Bas-Empire;

Vertot, Origine de la Grandeur de la Cour de Rome; Gaillard, Histoire de Charlemagne; Bernardi, De l'Origine et des Progrès de la Législation Française; Ferrand, L'Esprit de l'Histoire; Michaud, Histoire des Croisades; Frantin, Annales du Moyen Age, &c. All those authors, even those who make the most earnest professions of respect for the Holy See and for the Catholic Church, express themselves in general with much liberty, some of them with very little moderation, on the subject which now engages us. Among Protestant writers, we shall often have occasion to cite, in support of facts most essential for the justification of the clergy and of the popes of the middle ages, some of the most eminent,—such as Liebnitz, Pfeffel, Gibbon, Hegewisch, Voigt, Hurter,[1] Eichorn, Hallam, Sismondi, &c. The two latter, in particular, are least liable to objection when they are in our favour, as they are habitually influenced by the most revolting prejudices against the Catholic Church, and especially against the Holy See.

Finally, to make our work more complete, and to enable the reader to find with greater facility illustrations relating to certain more important facts or personages, we have given, besides an index of chap-

---

[1] The History of Innocent III., written by M. Hurter long before his conversion to the Catholic Church, betrays in many passages traces of those prejudices from which the author had not at that time been able to emancipate himself. See below, note, part i. ch. ii. art. 99. Still the honesty and candour so manifest in every page of his work justified the hope that his prejudices should soon disappear. That hope has been realized; the printing of our work was nearly finished when we received the happy announcement of his conversion (L'Ami de la Religion, vol. cxxi. p. 688; vol. cxxii. pp. 21, 248, 465, &c.).

ters, "an alphabetical index of the principal facts and the principal personages" mentioned in the course of the work. The object proposed in the compilation of this latter index did not require a detailed enumeration of other subjects, which could easily be found by a glance at the index of chapters. Nevertheless, we have carefully indexed all those names, both ancient and modern, — such as popes, princes, or celebrated authors, whose actions or writings possess some peculiar interest, or present some special difficulties.[1]

Notwithstanding all the care bestowed on the object of our inquiry, we are very far from believing that it does not admit of a much more perfect elucidation; on the contrary, we are persuaded that researches more extensive and more profound would place the subject in a far clearer light. But however great the defects of this work may be, our wishes are more than realized, should this feeble sketch suggest more complete and more satisfactory discussions on a subject so deeply interesting in itself, so superficially treated even to the present day, and which is daily becoming more important since the study of the history of the middle ages, once confined to a small number of men of formed judgment and of solid erudition, occupies at present so considerable a place in the education of youth, and in the lecture-halls of our colleges.

---

[1] This observation applies particularly to the articles, Empire, Excommunication, Heresy, Public Penance, Pope, &c.

CONTENTS.

PART I.

CHAPTER I.

CHAPTER II.

CONFIRMATORY EVIDENCE.

INTRODUCTION.

HONOURS AND TEMPORAL PRIVILEGES CONFERRED ON RELIGION, AND ON ITS MINISTERS, BY ANCIENT NATIONS, AND ESPECIALLY UNDER THE FIRST CHRISTIAN EMPERORS.

1. *Plan of this Introduction.*

THE object of this Introduction, and the nature of the facts which it relates, suggest naturally that it should be divided into two parts. The first shall give a brief statement of facts anterior to the conversion of Constantine; the second gives those subsequent to that great event.

ARTICLE I.

HONOURS AND TEMPORAL PRIVILEGES CONFERRED ON RELIGION AND ITS MINISTERS BY ANCIENT NATIONS, AND ESPECIALLY BY THE ROMANS BEFORE THE CONVERSION OF CONSTANTINE.[1]

2. *Religion at all times regarded as the basis of Public Order.*

FROM the origin of society, religion has ever been regarded as the principal support of government and of laws, as the indispensable basis of morals, without which the wisest laws and the best governments would be of little avail. From the earliest

[1] Many interesting memoirs on this subject occur in the Histoire de l'Académie des Inscriptions et Belles Lettres. See especially the extract from the two memoirs of Burigny, Sur les Honneurs et les Prérogatives accordés aux Prêtres dans les Religions profanes, 4to. edit. vol. xxxi. p. 108; and the extract from another memoir by the same author, Sur le Respect des Anciens Romains pour la Religion, vol. xxxiv. p. 110. See also Petit-Pied, Traité du Droit et des Prérogatives des Ecclésiastiques, part i. Paris, 1705, 4to.

ages princes and people learned from experience, that attacks on religion were in reality rebellions against public order; that men capable of setting the Deity himself at defiance could not be restrained by any law; that their example was an encouragement to disorder, and to revolt against the most legitimate authority; in a word, that the scandal of their irreligion was the scourge and plague of society. Convinced of those great principles, governments felt that they ought to deny nothing to religion, which did everything for them; that they were bound to regard themselves as the visible representative of the Deity, and to secure for him the homage of the society subject to their control; that consequently a most rigorous obligation was imposed on them, of promoting the glory of religion, of honouring the Deity in the persons of his ministers, and of repressing by stringent enactments the public excesses of impiety.

3. *Honours conferred on Religion and its Ministers.*

This was the real motive of the honours and privileges conferred on religion and its ministers by all the nations of antiquity; thence more especially flowed the very considerable wealth, with which in every period of history we find the clergy endowed. To the wisest and most civilized, as well as to the most savage and barbarous nations, nothing appeared more natural and more becoming than to honour by rich offerings the Deity in the persons of his ministers. This liberality was generally regarded, not only as a mark of honour and respect for the august character with which the ministers of religion were invested, but also as a compensation due to them for the lucrative professions which almost invariably they were obliged to renounce, to devote themselves more unreservedly to the functions of their ministry. Natural equity, it was believed, demanded that every man whose life was devoted to the service of the public should be supported at the expense of the public; and that ministers of religion especially, consecrated by their profession to functions essential to the good of society, had a right to insist on such support as might both relieve them from the miseries of indigence, and enable them to discharge with dignity their sublime duties. From the mass of facts and authorities which ancient history supplies in support of these assertions, it is enough to cite here a few of the most remarkable.

4. *Opinions of Ancient Legislators on this point.*

Every one knows the importance attached by the most famous lawgivers of ancient times, even in pagan states, to the support of religion and of public worship. Lycurgus, Draco, and Solon, in regulating the first and most famous republics of Greece, made religion the basis of their institutions.[1] Romulus and Numa followed the same principle in the laws which they prescribed for their infant state.[2] In times more recent, Zaleucus and Charondas imitated these great authorities, placing at the head of their codes a series of maxims, which may be regarded as the foundations of religion and of morality.[3]

5. *Doctrine of the most celebrated Philosophers.*

The doctrine of the most celebrated philosophers was in conformity with the principles of these illustrious lawgivers. Aristotle and Plato, though widely differing in other points, agree in representing religion as the indispensable basis of government, and the principal source of the happiness and tranquillity of states; maxims from which they inferred that a wise government must ever make divine worship the first object of its solicitude.[4] The respect due to the Deity requires, they main-

---

[1] Voyage d'Anacharsis, vol. ii. ch. xxi.; vol. iv. ch. xliv.; vol. v. ch. lxvii. p. 481.

[2] See Mémoires de Burigny, cited above, p. 1, note. Also Terrasson, Histoire de la Jurisprudence Romaine, part i. § 2.

[3] Voyage d'Anacharsis, vol. v. ch. lxii. towards the end.

[4] "Quàm multæ autem sint res sine quibus civitas esse nequeat, videndum est. Primum igitur victus seu alimentum suppetere debet; deindè artes;.... tertio loco arma;...deindè aliqua pecuniæ vis et copia;...quintò, *quod etiàm primo loco ponendum est, rerum divinarum curatio, quam sacerdotium appellant.*"—Aristoteles, De Republicâ, lib. vii. cap. 8. Plato establishes, or supposes, manifestly the same principle in several passages. See especially De Republicâ, lib. iv. p. 391, 2nd col. near the end. De Legibus, lib. iv., ix. et x. pp. 535, 578, 589. Lyons edit. 1657. On the doctrine of Plato with regard to this subject, see Dacier, Œuvres de Platon, vol. i., Discours prélimin. p. 87.

tained, that his ministers should enjoy a distinguished position in the commonwealth, and that ordinarily the priests should be selected from the most respectable class of citizens.[1] Plato, moreover, required that private individuals should not be allowed to adopt gods of their own choice, nor to pay them divine honours privately in their own houses; but that all should follow the religion of their country, and fulfil its rites publicly with their fellow-citizens; finally, that the government itself had no right to regulate religious matters, but was bound to carry into execution the regulations made on that subject by the oracles of the gods.[2] He would have the magistrates, moreover, enact severe laws against crimes of impiety, especially against sacrilege and atheism, which should, he thought, entail in certain cases the penalty of death, and the privation of honours of interment.[3]

---

[1] "Nobilis quoque esse debet sacerdotum ordo; neque agricola, neque illiberalis artifex sacerdos instituendus est; à civibus enim deos coli oportet."—Aristot. De Republicâ, lib. vii. cap. 9. Plato, in his treatise entitled Politicus, sive de Regno, p. 148, 2nd col., cites, and strongly approves, the custom of the Egyptians, which was adopted by many Grecian cities, and especially by Athens, of investing the chief magistrates with the priesthood. "Apud Ægyptios," says he, "non licet regem absque sacerdotio imperare. Quin immò, si ex alio genere quispiam vi regnum usurpet, cogitur post regni assumptionem sacris initiari, ut rex denique sit et sacerdos. Præterea in plurimis Græcorum civitatibus, apud vos præsertim, reperies præcipua sacra à magistratibus summis institui."

[2] "Sacella nemo in privatâ domo habeat; cùm verò animum quis ad sacrificandum induxerit, ad publica sacrificaturus accedat, et sacerdotibus hostias præbeat, qui curam harum rerum castissimè gerunt, quibuscum et ipse oret, et quicumque cum eo simul orare velit."—Plato, De Legibus, lib. x. p. 597, col. 1. "Quid præterea restat nobis de legum constitutione (dicendum)? Nobis quidem nihil; Apollini autem Delphino *maxima, præclarissima, prima instituta.* Quænam ista? Templorum constitutiones, et sacrificia, cæterique deorum et dæmonum atque heroum cultus, sepulchra præterea et funera defunctorum, et quæcumque sunt ad eos placandos ministeria subeunda. Talia profectò neque ipsi scimus, et in ordinandâ civitate nulli credemus alteri, si sapiemus, nullove alio utemur interprete nisi patrio (deo); hic nempè deus, in rebus hujusmodi, cunctis hominibus patrius interpres, in mediâ terrâ super umbilicum sedens, exponit."—Plato, De Republicâ, lib. iv. p. 391, col. 2.

[3] "Si quis fortè sacrilegium committere audeat, legem de hoc feremus, quamvis onerosam nobis atque molestam.... Qui deprehensus in sacrilegio fuerit, si servus peregrinusve erit, in facie ac manibus calamitate ipsius litteris inustâ, verberatus prout judicibus videbitur, nudus extra fines pellatur; fortè enim hoc supplicio continentior factus, evadet denique melior.... Si verò civis quispiam aliquid tale in deos, aut in parentes, aut in patriam perpetrare, et ad maximam injuriam induxisse animum deprehendatur; hunc judex, quia ex puero benè doctus educatusque à maximo scelere non abstinuit, sanari non

After the example of those ancient philosophers, Cicero lays it down as an incontestable principle in the art of government, that religion must be its chief foundation; that magistrates and princes ought to give it the first rank among their institutions, and be ready to defend it even at the risk of their lives.[1] This profound respect for religion requires, moreover, according to him, that government should absolutely interdict new or foreign forms of worship, until they had been publicly authorized by law. He proves this point by the laws of the twelve tables.[2] He even goes so far as to express a wish that the government should invest the college of pontiffs with the power of appointing consuls and magistrates, of deposing them, and even of abrogating laws not approved by their suffrages.[3]

6. *Strict Union of Religion and Government under the Mosaic Law.*

History, both ancient and profane, proves that those principles were generally recognised and adopted in practice by all ancient governments. The political constitution of the Hebrews

---

posse existimet; pœna huic mors malorum minimum."—Plato, De Legibus, lib. ix. p. 578, col. 2. In the tenth book of the same work, speaking of the infidels, who by their licentious language weakened among the people the respect due to the gods, Plato adds, "Damnatus in mediterraneis carceribus vinciatur; nec ullus liber ad eum accedat, sed statutum illi à legum custodibus cibum servi afferant; vitâ denique functum extra regionis finis insepultum ejiciant; quem si quis liber sepelierit, à volente impietatis crimine accusetur."—Lib. x. p. 597, col. 1.

[1] Speaking of the duties of the chief magistrates of the republic, Cicero writes, "Hujus autem dignitatis hæc fundamenta sunt, hæc membra, quæ tuenda principibus, *et vel capitis periculo defendenda sunt: religiones, auspicia,* potestates magistratuum, senatûs auctoritas, leges, mos majorum.... Harum rerum tot atque tantarum esse defensorem et patronum, magni animi est, magni ingenii, magnæque constantiæ."—Cicero, pro P. Sextio, n. 46.

[2] "Separatim nemo habessit deos; neve novos, sed ne advenas, nisi publicè adscitos, privatim colunto."—Cicero, De Legibus, lib. ii. n. 8.

[3] "Maximum autem et præstantissimum in republicâ jus est augurum, et cum auctoritate conjunctum. Neque verò hoc, quià sum ipse augur, ita sentio; sed *quia sic existimare nos necesse est.* Quid enim majus est, si de jure quærimus, quàm posse à summis imperiis et summis potestatibus comitiatus et concilia, vel instituta dimittere, vel habita rescindere? Quid gravius, quàm rem susceptam dirimi, si unus augur *alio die* dixerit (esse agendam)? Quid magnificentius, quàm posse decernere ut magistratu se abdicent consules? Quid religiosius, quàm cum populo, cum plebe, agendi jus aut dare, aut non dare? Quid legem, si non jure rogata est, tollere?...Nihil domi, nihil foris per magistratus gestum, sine eorum auctoritate, posse cuiquam probari?"—Ibid. n. 12.

is entitled to special attention on this point, as well on account of its divine origin, as of its antiquity and long duration.[1] According to that political and religious constitution, God himself was the supreme monarch; the magistrates were but his ministers and representatives. Laws emanating from so sacred an authority could never be changed; to watch over their observance was the sole duty of magistrates and even of kings themselves. The transgression of those laws was both a political offence and a crime against religion. Idolatry, in particular, was regarded as a crime against the state, and as an act of revolt against the legitimate sovereign; it was accordingly punished with death, as were also magic and several other superstitious practices. As a natural consequence of such principles, the ministers of religion enjoyed great privileges; and God himself, as temporal sovereign of the nation, had conferred on them a part of his political rights. Hence the great power which they exercised even in purely civil matters, and especially in the administration of justice;[2] hence the wealth and revenues attached to their sacred character. In the partition of the land of promise, the tribe of Levi, which was consecrated to the functions of the sacred ministry, had not received a portion like that of the other tribes; but it was not on that account less rich than the others. Besides the tithes, first fruits, and the ordinary offerings which God had assigned to it, it possessed, moreover, forty-eight cities in the different tribes, with two thousand cubits of land around each city.[3] The high priest, even when he was neither judge nor prince in Israel, was one of the most wealthy in the nation; besides the special offerings which the people were bound to make to him on certain occasions, and the share

---

[1] Guénée, Lettres de quelques Juifs, vol. i. part ii.; Letter 3, § 1, 2. D. Calmet, Dictionn. de la Bible; art. Prêtres. Bible de Vence; Dissert. Sur la Police des Hébreux, at the end of Préface sur le Livre des Nombres. Jahn, Archæologia, n. 215, 219. Bossuet, Politique Sacrée, book vii. art. 5. Ryan, Bienfaits du Christianisme, ch. vi. n. 13.

[2] Deut. xvi. 18; xviii. 8, 9; Ezek. xliv. 24.

[3] Numb. xxxv.; Josh. xxi.

which he had in all sacrifices, the Levites gave him a tenth of all that they received.[1] Thus an ancient Jewish author, speaking of the revenues assigned to the priests by the law of Moses, does not hesitate "to compare the glory and majesty of the pontiffs to that of kings."[2] In consequence of this strict union established by God between religion and the state, the sacred books represent the care of the divine worship as the first duty of kings, and the chief object of their solicitude.[3] David, Solomon, Hezekiah, Josiah, and all good princes, are praised principally for their zeal in enforcing the observance of God's law, in prohibiting foreign religions, and in increasing the splendour of divine worship; neglect in these points being at the same time represented as the distinctive characteristic of bad princes, and as the source of misfortunes to themselves and to their subjects.

7. *The same Union with the Egyptians.*

This strict union of religion and the state is found differing only in degree in all ancient nations. We shall cite here none but the most famous and the most civilized.[4]

Egypt in particular presents an example so much the more entitled to attention, that country being generally regarded as the common source whence most of the ancient nations derived their principles of government and laws.[5] From the origin of that monarchy, and for many centuries after its establishment, religion was so highly respected, that the priests constituted the first order in the state, enjoyed enlarged privileges, and had a very great influence in all the parts of the civil administration. Kings themselves were invested with the priesthood in order

---

[1] Numb. xviii; et alibi passim.

[2] "Ex his rebus liquet, juxta legis judicium, sacerdotes æquiparari honore et majestate regibus."—Philo, De Præmiis et Honoribus Sacerdotum, Oper. p. 832, edit. 1640, fol.

[3] Deut. xvii. 15; Josh. i. 8, et alibi passim.

[4] See the authors cited above, p. 1, note 1.

[5] Goguet, Origine des Lois, des Sciences et des Arts, part i. book i. ch. i. art. 4.

to make them more venerable and august. The wisest among the clergy was selected to fill the royal throne ; and if a usurper succeeded in placing the crown on his head, he was obliged to assume the sacerdotal character, that he might be both the pontiff and king of the nation.[1] The priests held as their own property one-third of the lands of Egypt, and their estates were exempt from all taxes. They generally enjoyed the confidence of the king; and the most eminent of their order were habitually attached to his suite, to assist him by their councils. They filled the highest offices in the state, administered justice, superintended the levy of taxes, and the inspection of coins, weights, and measures, and by their reputation and their intelligence exercised over monarchs themselves a very great influence.

8. *Laws and Customs of Greece on this point.*

The laws and customs of Greece on this point are not less worthy of mention. One of the most ancient and most eminent institutions of that country was the Amphictyonic Council, composed of a certain number of deputies from the principal cities of Greece, and commissioned to decide with supreme authority all causes which concerned the general welfare of the nation.[2] The principal crimes of which this council had the right to take cognizance were those which violated the sanctity of the temple of Delphi. All the Amphictyons were bound by oath to discharge faithfully the obligations of their institution, and especially those which had reference to the honour and respect due to the temple of Apollo. The formula of that oath has been preserved: it contains the following singular words: "Should the impious carry away the offerings made to the temple of Apollo, we swear to exert against them and their accomplices our feet, our

[1] Plato, Politicus, sive de Regno, p. 148, 2nd col.; Strabo, lib. i. et xvii.; Ælian, Variar. Hist. lib. xiv. cap. xxxiv.

[2] Goguet, Origine des Lois, des Sciences et des Arts, part ii. book i. ch. iv. art. 1. Voyage d'Anacharsis, vol. iii. ch. xxxv. Memoir by M. de Valois, Sur les Amphictyons, in the Hist. de l'Acad. des Inscriptions et Belles-Lettres, 4to. edit. vols. iii. and v.

arms, our voices, and all our strength."[1] In consequence of this obligation, the principal states of Greece, either from zeal for the outraged honour of the god, or using that pretext as a cloak for their ambition, carried on war at several times against the Phocians. It was the occasion of the "sacred war," by which Philip of Macedon promoted so effectually the aggrandizement of his power, and which drew down on the impiety of the Phocians, by the sentence of the Amphictyonic Council, a punishment so terrible as might well prevent for a long time the recurrence of a similar sacrilege.[2] Independently of the motives, political and religious, which justified this severity, it was judged necessary to place some check on the avarice of the Phocians, which was too often tempted by the immense wealth of the temple of Delphi, situated in their territory.[3] This temple, it is well known, was the richest in Greece, and, according to the opinion of many learned writers, it is not exaggeration to assert that there was more gold and silver in its treasury than in all the rest of Greece. However surprising such an assertion may appear, it is by no means incredible, when we reflect that Diodorus Siculus estimates the gold and silver seized by the Phocians in the temple of Delphi before the second war at more than 10,000 talents of silver, that is, about £2,320,000 of our money.[4]

The profound respect of the Greeks for religion attracted to

---

[1] In the works which we have cited, the formula of this oath is given entire from the harangue of Æschines, De Falsa Legatione.

[2] See in vols. vii. ix. and xii. of the Hist. de l'Acad. des Inscript. (4to. edit.); several memoirs by M. de Valois, on the Guerres Sacrées. See also Voyage d'Anacharsis, vol. v. ch. lx. and lxi. pp. 92, 209, &c.; Rollin, Histoire Ancienne, vol. vi. book xiv. § 2.

[3] See in the Histoire de l'Acad. des Inscript. (vol. iii. 4to. edit. p. 78), an extract from the memoir by M. de Valois, Sur les Richesses du Temple de Delphos; Voyage d'Anacharsis, vol. ii. ch. xxii. p. 429.

[4] Supposing, with Paucton (Métrologie, pp. 292, 318, et alibi passim), that the Attic talent weighed 54,79 of our (French poids de marc) weight, and that the silver marc is valued now for 53,57, these 10,000 talents would be worth £2,320,000. This sum, which appears at first sight so enormous, is not at all improbable, when we remember the details certainly known from history of the wealth of many ancient temples. See on this subject, Documentary Evidences, No. 3, at the end of this volume.

its ministers great honours and considerable wealth.[1] In the earliest ages we accordingly find the priests enjoying universal respect, regarding themselves as independent almost as kings, and exercising great influence on temporal affairs both in peace and war.[2] At all times the character of minister of religion was one of the most honourable in the eyes of the whole nation, and was so distinguished in rank and privileges, that it was an object of ambition to families of the first order. No low profession could aspire to that dignity. Among the Greeks, as well as in many provinces of Asia, the office of some priests was regarded as a very elevated post, in consequence of the revenues and authority attached to it. Such, for instance, was the office of high-priest of Paphos, a dignity so exalted, that Cato promised it to the unhappy Ptolemy, as a compensation for the kingdom of Cyprus, of which the Romans had unjustly deprived him.[3] Even Roman tyranny itself never deprived the priesthood of that high favour in which it had always been held by the Greeks. From a letter of the Emperor Julian to the high-priest Theodore, it appears that the chief priest of each province had "the general superintendence of all that concerned religion; and also authority over all the priests of his

[1] Mémoires de Burigny, cited supra, p. 1, note 1. Eclaircissements généraux sur les Familles Sacerdotales de la Grèce.—Mémoires de l'Acad. vol. xxiii. p. 51.

[2] "Though thou art invested with supreme power," said Tiresias to Œdipus, "I have a right of reproaching you with what you reproach me; and I will do so without fear; for it is not you, but the great Apollo that I must obey."—Sophocles, Œdipus, v. 416.

At a much later period, about 200 years before Christ, we find the ministry of the priests employed by public authority at Athens, to excite the popular feeling against Philip, king of Macedon. A decree passed at that time, on the requisition of a public petition, was to the following effect: "Sacerdotes publicos, quotiescumque pro populo Atheniensi, sociisque et exercitibus et classibus eorum precarentur, toties detestari atque execrari Philippum, liberos ejus regnumque, terrestres navalesque copias, Macedonum genus omne nomenque."—Tit. Liv. Hist. lib. xxxi. cap. xliv.

[3] "Per Canidium amicum, quem præmisit in Cyprum, egit cum Ptolemæo ut sine certamine cederet, ostensâ spe neque inopem neque abjectum ipsum victurum; *sacerdotium enim ei Veneris Paphiæ populum daturum.*"—Plutarch, Life of Cato, n. 10. (Plutarch's Works, Antwerp, 1620, fol., vol. i. p. 776.). Crevier, Hist. Rom. vol. xii. p. 209.

district, with power to treat each one according to his deserts,"[1] which included the power of inflicting temporal penalties on all who discharged their duties badly, or were guilty of certain crimes, the cognizance of which was reserved to the college of pontiffs.

9. *Laws and Customs of the Athenians.*

The most civilized states of Greece adopted on this matter the customs of the rest of the nation. Amongst the Athenians especially, religion and its ministers enjoyed the highest honours.[2] In some ancient and powerful families the priesthood was transmitted from father to son, as the most honourable inheritance of their house. In addition to the revenues permanently assigned to most of the temples, the tenth of the spoils taken in war, and a considerable portion of the fines and confiscations, were ordinarily consecrated to the gods. In every temple there were, moreover, two officers called parasites, whose duty it was to raise an annual tax on all the lands in their district. The archons, or supreme magistrates of the nation, made the public worship their special care, and always presided at the religious ceremonies. The second of them, who was called the archon king, was bound to preside at the public sacrifices, to enforce the exact observance of all their established rites, and to punish all offences against religion. Of these, the one visited with the heaviest penalties of the law, was the introduction by private individuals of new forms of worship into the state, by their own authority; it was prohibited, under penalty of death, to admit any worship without decree of the Areopagus, on a public petition.[3] Neither the wise precautions of the law, nor

---

[1] Julian, Epistola lxiii. ad Theodorum Pontif. (Juliani Operum, p. 452, fol.). L'Histoire de l'Empereur Jovien, by Labletterie, p. 402.

[2] Voyage d'Anacharsis, vol. ii. ch. xxi. Mémoire où l'on examine plusieurs questions générales concernant les Ministres des Dieux à Athènes, by M. de Bougainville, vol. xviii. of the Histoire de l'Acad. des Inscript. et Belles Lettres, 4to. edit. Mémoire sur les Parasites, by M. Lebeau, jun. Ibid. vol. xxxi. p. 51.

[3] Josephus, lib. ii. contra Apion, chap viii. cites many remarkable examples of punishments inflicted on many eminent characters by the Athenians for

the vigilance of magistrates, could prevent, it is true, the commission of many offences against religion, especially after the depravity of morals had, as is commonly the case, weakened the religious principle. But any public manifestation of impiety hardly ever failed to excite general indignation. The wise as well as the simple accused the authors of such offences of revolting against the Deity, that they might the more freely indulge their passions; the government thought itself bound to inflict severe penalties on them; and the punishment of death was generally awarded to all who were convicted of having attacked, either by their words or their actions, the legally established worship. From many celebrated examples, it is clear that neither favour, nor dignity, nor merit, nor the most distinguished talents, could shield such culprits from the vengeance of the law. The accusations made against the poet Æschylus, and the philosopher Diagoras, for having revealed the secret doctrine of mysteries; the the condemnation of Protagoras and of Prodicus, who had publicly spoken against the gods acknowledged by the state; the inquiries instituted against Pericles and Anaxagoras, who were suspected of atheism; the sentence of death pronounced against Alcibiades, who was convicted of having ridiculed the mysteries of Eleusis; the verdict condemning Socrates to drink hemlock for the imputed crime of not acknowledging the gods of his country; all these, and many other well known facts, prove that, in the most brilliant period of the arts and sciences among the Greeks, impiety was not punished with less severity, than in the ages of primitive simplicity.[1]

10. *Laws of Romulus and of Numa.*

The same principles invariably inspired the government and

being merely accused or suspected of impiety. He then adds, "et quid mirum, si erga viros etiam eximios ita se gesserint, qui ne mulieribus quidem pepercere? Etenim sacerdotem quamdam interfecerunt, quoniam illam quidam accusaverat quod deos coleret peregrinos: decreto vero illud erat apud ipsos prohibitum, pœnaque mortis contra illos statuta qui deum introducerent alienum." Amsterdam, 1726; vol. ii. pp. 491—493.

[1] We merely refer to these facts. Their development may be found in the Voyage d'Anacharsis, ubi supra, p. 414.

the policy of the Romans.[1] The strict union established by Romulus and Numa between religion and the state, has been already mentioned.[2] Their legislation on this subject is the more worthy of attention, as it implies notions on the Deity, and on the worship due to him, far more perfect than might be expected in so barbarous and ignorant an age. Romulus ordered all his subjects to adore the gods whose worship was sanctioned by the state, and to avoid in that worship the absurd or ridiculous ceremonies with which the superstition of other nations had defaced it.[3] He ordered them never to commence any important enterprise without having previously consulted the will of the gods, through the ministry of the augurs and aruspices, of whom he had established a college at Rome.[4] Sacrifices and all religious ceremonies were to be celebrated in daylight; they were strictly forbidden in the night, lest they might become occasions of debauch and sedition.[5] In fine, the common people, and all who

---

[1] Memoires de Burigny, cited above, p. 1, note. Terrasson, Histoire de la Jurisprudence Romaine, parts i. ii. Rollin, Traité des Etudes, vol. iv. part iii. ch. ii. art. ii. sec. 7.

[2] For the laws of Romulus and Numa on religion, see, principally, Dionysius of Halicarn. Antiquit. Rom. lib. ii. cap. vii., xvi., etc.

[3] "A Deorum cultu exorsus,—omnia juxta optimos quosque Græcorum ritus instituit. Cæterùm fabulas de ipsis à majoribus traditas, probra eorum continentes ac crimina, improbas censuit, inutilesque ac indecentes, et ne probis quidem viris dignas, nedùm diis superis; repudiatisque his omnibus ad benè ac præclarè de diis sentiendum et loquendum cives suos induxit, nihilque eis affingi passus est quod beatæ illi naturæ parùm esset consentaneum....Etenim ne corruptis quidem his temporibus apud eos videas arreptos numine, aut furorem corybanticum,...*non Bacchationes* et *secretos mysteriorum ritus, non virorum cum fœminis in templis pervigilia*, non alia his similia prodigia; sed omnia quæ ad deos attinent, religiosiùs aguntur ac dicuntur quàm vel apud Græcos, vel apud Barbaros. Et quod omnium maximè miratus sum, quamvis innumeræ nationes in eam urbem convenerint, quibus necesse sit deos patrios domestico ritu colere, *nulla tamen peregrina sacra sunt recepta publicè*, quod multis jam urbibus accidit."—Dion. of Halicarnassus, ibid. cap. vii. n. 3; Leipsic, 1691, fol. vol. i. p. 90.

[4] "Romulus, acceptis à deo certis signis, advocatâ concione et indicatis auspiciis, rex omnium consensu declaratur, et morem instituit in posterum, ne quis regnum assumeret, magistratumve iniret, nisi et deus idem probaret, estque hæc auspicii lex apud Romanos longè observata, non solum sub regibus, verùm etiàm sublatâ monarchiâ, in consulum, imperatorum, cæterorumque magistratuum legitimorum comitiis."—Dionysius of Halicarnassus, Antiquit. Rom. cap. ii. n. 6 (p. 81 of the Leipsic edit.) Cicéro, De Divin. lib. i. n. 2 et 48.

[5] See the passage from Dionysius of Halicarnassus, cited above. It appears that this wise law of Romulus was not always observed afterwards; for it is

were not of noble race, were debarred from ever aspiring to the priesthood,[1] — a rule enforced in Rome, as well as in Greece, until the destruction of Paganism.[2]

On this, as on many other points, Numa Pompilius perfected the legislation of his predecessor. He augmented the number of priests and temples, granted them many immunities, and that they might make a deeper impression on the people, he added to the pomp and splendour of the religious ceremonies. During festival days all law proceedings were suspended; slaves were exempted from labour, that they might observe those days religiously; and that all might know the periods at which these festivals occurred, they were ordered to be inscribed on the public calendars.[3] By another law of Numa, it was prohibited to make any statue or image to represent the Deity, because it is a crime, the law declares, to imagine that God has the figure of a beast, or even of a man.[4] If it be true, as Plutarch asserts,

---

certain that it was often found necessary to revive it.—Codex Theodos. lib. ix. tit. 16, n. 7; lib. xvi. tit. 10, n. 5. Terrasson, ubi supra, p. 29, 30.

1 "Neque venalia esse voluit sacerdotia, neque sorte distribui; sed lege sanxit ut è singulis curiis legerentur bini annum egressi quinquagesimum, *qui virtute ac genere præcellerent cæteros, opesque haberent sufficientes*, et integro essent corpore. His non ad certum tempus, sed in omnem vitam eum honorem concessit, immunibus propter ætatem à militiâ, *et propter privilegium exemptis ab urbanis molestiis*."—Ibid. cap. vii. n. 7 (p. 92 of the Leipsic edition).

2 Prudentius, a Christian poet of the fourth century, alludes to this ancient custom in a hymn composed in honour of St. Lawrence, in which he thus describes the fruit of the death of the holy martyr:—

"Quidquid Quiritum sueverat
Ornare nænias Numæ,
Christi frequentans atria,
Hymnis resultat martyrem."
"*Ipsa et senatûs lumina,*
Quondam Luperci et Flamines,
Apostolorum et martyrum
Exosculantur limina."

Prudentius, Peristephanon, Hymn II. v. 517; Biblioth. PP. tom. v. p. 115, col. 1. Beugnot, Hist. de la Destruction du Pagan. vol. i. p. 389.

3 "Feriis jurgia amovento, easque in famulis, operibus patratis, habento. Itaque, ut ita cadat, *in annuis amfractibus descriptum esto*" (i.e. *in anni curriculis et fastis*).—Cicero, De Legibus, lib. ii. n. 8.

4 "Hic vetuit Romanis hominis vel bestiæ formam tribuere deo; neque fuit ulla apud eos antè vel picta vel ficta imago dei; sed primos centum sexaginta annos templa extruxerunt et cellas diis, simulacrum per id temporis nullum habuerunt, nefas putantes augustiora exprimere humilioribus, neque aspirari aliter ad deum quàm mente posse."—Plutarch, Life of Numa. (Plutarch's Works, Antwerp edit. 1620, fol. vol. i. p. 65.).

that Numa was the author of this law, there is every reason to believe that it was derived either from the Mosaic law, or from some of those primeval traditions which paganism had no doubt obscured, but never could totally obliterate. It is certain, at all events, that the legislation of Romulus and Numa, such as it is represented to us by historians, has so many points of resemblance to those of Greece, and of some Oriental nations, that the latter must evidently be regarded as the primitive sources of the ancient laws of Rome.

11. *Laws of the Twelve Tables.*

Whatever be the value of that conjecture, it must be observed that most of the laws of Romulus and of Numa, which we have cited, are found not only in the Papyrian code, attributed to Tarquinius Superbus,[1] but also in the laws of the Twelve Tables, which were always held in the highest esteem by the Romans, and which Cicero in particular preferred to all that had been written by the wisest philosophers on the subject of government.[2] We have only a few fragments of that code extant, and some few notices of it scattered through different authors; but even from that wreck it is manifest that religion was one of the principal subjects of its provisions.[3] It was divided into three parts; the first contained municipal or common law; the second, constitutional law; and the third, sacred law. The fragments of this third part which remain to us, regard principally oaths

---

[1] Terrasson, ubi supra, § 4 and 5.

[2] "Fremant omnes licet, dicam quod sentio: Bibliothecas, mehercule, omnium philosophorum unus mihi videtur xii Tabularum libellus, si quis legum fontes et capita viderit, et auctoritatis pondere, et utilitatis ubertate superare." —Cicero, De Oratore, lib. i. n. 44. Rollin, Hist. Romaine, book iv. an. de R. 306; vol. ii. edit. of 1769, p. 171, &c.

[3] Jacques Godefroy was the first that endeavoured to arrange those fragments in their proper order. He published the result of his labour with this title, Fragmenta Duodecim Tabularum, 1616, 4to. From the researches of this learned jurisconsult, it appears that the eight first tables regarded municipal or common law; the ninth, constitutional law, and the tenth, sacred law. The eleventh and twelfth were supplementary to the others. A more complete and more correct collection of those laws may be seen in Terrasson's work, already cited, second part; and in Bouchaud, Commentaire sur les Lois des Douze Tables, 1800, 2 vols. 4to.

and sepulture, which all ancient nations ranked next after sacrifices, as the principal acts of religion. It is therein enacted that after the example of their ancestors, all should observe an oath as an inviolable law, binding equally before God and man;[1] and that all luxury, extravagant grief, and many other practices either strange, or not in accordance with the spirit of religion, should be rigorously excluded from the mournful ceremonial of sepulture.[2]

12. *Permanence of those Laws even in the decline of the Republic.*

The whole series of their history proves the profound respect of the ancient Romans for religion, and the pride which they took in being considered the most religious nation on the earth. "Our city," Valerius Maximus observes, "has ever preferred religion to all other things, even to those which most nearly concerned her supreme dignity."[3] In the same spirit, Cicero declares in the senate-house, "The Gauls may surpass us in strength, the Carthaginians in craft, the Greeks in the fine arts, but in piety and religion we have surpassed all other nations."[4] Their profound respect for religion, they believed, was the cause of all their victories, and of that extraordinary degree of power which they attained over all kingdoms. Cicero introduces the pontiff Cotta expressing "his conviction that Romulus and Numa, by establishing the auspices and sacrifices, had laid the

---

[1] "Nullum enim vinculum ad adstringendam fidem *jurejurando* majores arctius esse voluerunt. Id indicant leges in xii Tabulis, indicant sacratæ, indicant fœdera, quibus etiam cum hoste devincitur fides, etc."—Cicero, De Offic. lib. iii. n. 31.

[2] "Jam cætera in xii (Tabulis), minuendi sumptus lamentationesque funeris translata de Solonis ferè legibus. *Hoc plus,* inquit, *ne facito: rogum asciâ ne polito...mulieres genas ne radunto, neve lessum* (i. e. ejulationem) *funeris ergo habento,* etc."—Idem. De Legib. lib. ii. n. 23, etc.

[3] "Omnia namque post religionem ponenda semper nostra civitas duxit; etiam in quibus summæ majestatis conspici decus voluit."—Valer. Max. De Dictis Factisque Memorabilibus, lib. i. cap. i. n. 9.

[4] "Nec robore Gallos, nec calliditate Pœnos, nec artibus Græcos;...sed pietate ac religione...omnes gentes nationesque superavimus."—Cicero, De Haruspic. Responsis, n. 9. "Si conferre volumus nostra cum externis, cæteris rebus aut pares, aut etiam inferiores reperiemur; religione, id est cultu deorum, multò superiores."—De Nat. Deor. lib. ii. cap. iii.

foundation of the Roman state, which never could have attained such a pitch of grandeur, but for its eminent piety to the immortal gods."[1] Valerius Maximus expressly adopts the same opinion in the work already cited: "What wonder is it," he exclaims, "that the constant favour of the immortal gods hath ever watched over the growth and preservation of our empire, which has complied so scrupulously with the smallest requirements of religion; for never has our state allowed its attention to be distracted from the most exact observance of religious rites."[2] So general was this persuasion among the pagans during the first centuries of the Christian era, that the philosopher Celsus inferred the superiority of the Roman gods over the God of the Jews, from the different destinies of both nations. "The Romans," he says, "are masters of the world; you have not one inch of territory; you are vagabonds, and obliged to hide yourselves from your exterminators."[3]

No doubt it may be not unreasonably supposed that some Roman, as well as Grecian philosophers, and all really intelligent men, in testifying this profound veneration for the established religion, were influenced much less by sincere piety towards the gods, than by the political motive of sustaining and turning to account the opinions of the people. It must moreover be admitted that, in the last days of the republic, and under the first emperors, the government, without ceasing to be in general attached to the national religion, allowed, at the same time, great latitude to individuals of speaking and writing against it.[4] It

[1] "Harum ego religionum (*religionum* scilicet *populi Romani*) nullam unquàm contemnendam putavi; mihique ita persuasi, Romulum auspiciis, Numam sacris constitutis, fundamenta jecisse nostræ civitatis, quæ nunquàm profectò, sine summâ placatione deorum immortalium, tanta esse potuisset."—Cicero, De Nat. Deor. lib. iii. cap. ii.

[2] "Non mirum igitur, si pro eo imperio augendo custodiendoque pertinax deorum indulgentia semper excubuit, quod tam scrupulosâ curâ parvula quoque momenta religionis examinare videtur; quia nunquàm remotos ab exactissimo cultu cæremoniarum oculos habuisse nostra civitas existimanda est."—Val. Max. lib. i. cap. i. n. 8.

[3] Origen, Adv. Celsum, lib. viii. n. 69.

[4] See, in support of this assertion, a memoir by Burigny, Sur le respect des Anciens Romains pour la Religion, 4to. edit. vol. xxxiv. p. 120--125. This

was insulted with impunity by poets in the theatre, by philosophers in their schools, and by orators in the senate; and even Cicero himself, while publicly pleading before the judges, treated the immortality of the soul as a foolish and groundless opinion.[1] This was indubitably a manifest consequence, and one of the most striking effects of the depravity of morals; but it is not the less certain, that with the Romans, as well as with all other ancient nations, the alliance of religion and of government was founded on the constitution of the state, and was generally regarded both by philosophers and by legislators as essential to the public good and to social order.

13. *Privileges granted to Ministers of Religion.*

Hence the honours and privileges granted in all ages by the Romans to religion and its ministers.[2] They were exempted from curial or municipal functions, which entailed considerable

---

inconsistency, which is so surprising, is found in many other periods of history among nations, who at the time prided themselves most on their philosophy. In modern times, and even in our own days, it is a maxim generally admitted by philosophers and politicians, that religion is the essential foundation of society, and the firmest support of public order. Machiavelli and Montesquieu are as strong on that point as Bossuet. Machiavel, Reflexions sur Tite Live, book i. ch. ii. Montesquieu, Esprit des Lois, book xxiv. ch. ii. iii. &c. Bossuet, Politique Sacrée. It is on this principle that all governments think it their duty (Ireland excepted, of course,—Ed.) to give a special protection to the dominant creed, whether they recognize it as the established religion, or only as the religion professed by the majority of the nation. Nevertheless, what is more common than to see that religion publicly attacked in the public chairs of our universities (by the Messrs. Quinet, Michelet, &c. in the days of King Louis Philippe,—Ed.) and even in the theatre, without the least means being taken by the government to check the scandal?

[1] In his oration for Cluentio, Cicero endeavouring to prove that the accused was not really guilty of the murder of Oppiniacus, his enemy, and that he could not have even any plausible motive to impel him to that crime, says: "Nam nunc quidem, quid tandem illi (Oppiniaco) mors attulit? Nisi fortè *ineptiis ac fabulis ducimur*, ut existimemus illum apud inferos impiorum supplicia perferre, ac plures illic offendisse inimicos quam hic reliquisse: a socrûs, ab uxorum, a fratris, a liberorum pœnis actum esse præcipitem in sceleratorum sedem atque regionem. *Quæ si falsa* sint, id quod omnes intelligunt, quid ei tandem (Oppiniaco) aliud mors eripuit, præter sensum doloris?"—Orat. pro Cluentio, n. 61. Cicero, it is well known, often maintains opposite sides of the same question, according to the system of the New Academicians, which he had embraced. This he does particularly on the immortality of the soul. Leland, Démonst. Evangel. vol. iv. part iii. ch. iv. § 7; ch. vi. § 3.

[2] See extract from the Mémoires de Burigny, cited above, p. 1, note. Gutherius, De Veteri Jure Pontificio, lib. i. cap. xxviii.; lib. ii. passim. (Tom. v. Grævius, Thesaurus Antiquit. Rom. p. 56.)

trouble and no slight expense.[1] The head priests, who were styled pontiffs, or flamens, were dispensed from taking an oath in trials; it was against law to demand it; whenever their evidence was considered nesessary in any judicial proceeding, a simple declaration alone was required, it being supposed that the word of a minister of the gods was worth the oath of other men.[2] The various colleges of pontiffs, in the principal cities of the Roman empire, constituted so many tribunals which adjudicated not only on matters relating to the worship of the gods, but also on last wills, on adoptions, on the emancipation of slaves, and on many other important concerns. All these colleges acknowledged as their head the sovereign pontiff, who exercised over them a very extensive jurisdiction, even in the temporal order. He was generally one of the most eminent men in the republic. He watched over the maintainance of the established worship, and prevented the intro-

[1] From the testimony of Dionysius Halicarnassus, cited above, p. 12, note 1, we learn that this immunity had been granted to the priests by Romulus. A law published by Constantine in 335, confirms to them the immunity which they had hitherto enjoyed. The following is the text of that law: "Quoniam Afri curiales conquesti sunt quosdam in suo corpore, *post flaminii honorem et sacerdotii vel magistratûs decursa insignia*, præpositos compelli fieri mansionum (*i.e.* annonarum), quod in singulis curiis, sequentis meriti et gradûs homines implere consuêrunt, jubemus nullum prædictis honoribus splendentem, ad memoratum cogi obsequium, ne nostro fieri judicio injuria videatur."—Cod. Theod. lib. xii. tit. i. n. 21.

The importance of this immunity is explained by Godefroy, in the preamble to his Commentaire sur ce XII. Livre.

[2] "C. Valerius Flaccus, quem præsentem creaverant (ædilem curulem) *quia flamen Dialis erat, jurare in leges non poterat.*"—Titus Livius, Hist. lib. xxxi. cap. 50.

Plutarch, in his Questions on the Customs of the Romans, not only records the fact of these exemptions, but also gives the reasons in the following terms: "Cur flamini Diali non licet jurare? Sive quia tormentum liberis est jusjurandum, sacerdotem vero quoad corpus et animam, oportet torturæ esse expertem; sive quia non convenit ei cui sacra, id est, maxima credimus, in minimis fidem non adhibere; sive quod omne jusjurandum in execrationem perjurii desinit, quæ quidem execratio funesta est atque exitiosa; unde aliis dira imprecari sacerdotes lege prohibentur;...sive quia perjurii discrimen omnibus commune futurum esset, si nefario et perjuro supplicationum sacrorumque urbis cura committeretur."—Problemata, n. 43. The passage of Livy, which we have cited, speaks only of the Flamen Dialis, or high-priest of Jupiter. But the motives of the exemption, as explained by Plutarch, suppose that the other pontiffs enjoyed the same privilege. See, in support of this explanation, Hansenius, De Jurejurando Veterum, cap. 30. (Grævius, tom. v. Thesaurus Antiquit. Rom. p. 863.).

duction of foreign rites. The regulation of the calendar was in his hands; and it was in his capacity as high priest that Julius Cæsar reformed that which had been in use before his time. The book of the Fasti[1] was intrusted to his keeping exclusively; a circumstance that enabled him to adjourn or accelerate the decision on the most important affairs, and frequently to thwart the designs of the chief magistrates of the republic.[2] So extensive, in a word, were his power and privileges, that the Emperor Augustus and his successors, in accordance with their system of concentrating in their own person all the authority of the chief magistrates of the republic, deemed it necessary to add the title of sovereign pontiff to the many others annexed to the imperial dignity: and it is remarkable, too, that in the announcement of their titles, that of "Sovereign Pontiff," was placed first, even before that of "Dictator."[3]

14. *Title of Sovereign Pontiff given to the first Christian Emperors.*

In consequence of this ancient usage, we find on many ancient monuments, the title of sovereign pontiff given to the first Christian emperors, until the time of Gratian, who formally refused to accept it.[4] Eminent critics, it is true, have doubted

---

[1] A sort of calendar, which prescribed the days on which it was lawful to plead.

[2] Censorinus, an author of the third century, attributes the defects of the calendar, before the time of Julius Cæsar, principally to the power which the priests formerly had of regulating it, and to the abuse which they frequently made of that power for their own private interests: "Quod delictum (defectum scilicet calendarii) ut corrigeretur," says he, "pontificibus datum est negotium, eorumque arbitrio intercalandi ratio permissa. Sed horum plerique, ob odium vel gratiam, quò quis magistratu citius abiret, diutiùsve fungeretur, aut publici redemptor ex anni magnitudine in lucro damnove esset, plùs minùsve ex libidine intercalando, rem sibi ad corrigendum mandatam, ultrò depravarunt; adeoque aberratum est, ut C. Cæsar, pontifex maximus,...quò retrò delictum corrigeret, duos menses intercalarios interponeret," &c.—Censorinus, De Die Natali, cap. xx.; Hamburgi, 1614, in 4to. p. 106.

[3] Gutherius, ubi supra, lib. i. cap. xi. Tillemont, Histoire des Empereurs, vol. i. p. 17. See also in the collection of Mémoires de l'Académie des Inscriptions et Belles-Lettres, many memoirs by M. de la Bastie, Sur le Souverain Pontificat des Empereurs Romains (vols. xviii. and xxii. of the edition in 12mo.). These Memoirs are analysed by Eckhel, Doctrina Nummorum Veterum, tom. viii. p. 380, &c.

[4] Quatrième Mémoire de M. de la Bastie, sur le Souverain Pontificat des Empereurs Romains. Annales de Baronius, anno 312, not. 93, &c. Bosius,

whether the Christian emperors ever did, or could, accept such a title: it is certain, nevertheless, that the pagans continued to give it; and it is highly improbable that they would have so long persisted in giving a title which the Christian emperors neither accepted nor wished to accept,[1] and which gave them so many opportunities of destroying paganism under pretence of reforming its abuses. It is much more natural to admit, with Cardinal Baronius and others, that reasons of state, and even the good of religion, concurred in removing every scruple on the matter. On the one hand, the title of sovereign pontiff invested them, in the temporal order, with a power which it was their interest to possess; on the other hand, their public profession of the Christian religion prevented any person from believing that by assuming that title, they wished in any way to favour or support idolatry. "Abstaining from every function of the pontificate contrary to Christianity, they believed themselves justified in conscience in retaining a title which they detested in their hearts, and which they had resolved to reject as soon as the interests of government allowed."[2]

15. *Privileges of the Pagan Priests maintained under Constantine and his successors.*

But whether the title of high-priest was assumed by the first Christian emperors or not, the pagan priests certainly continued to enjoy their ancient privileges long after the conversion of

---

De Pontificatu Max. Imper. Roman. (Græevius, Thesaur. Antiquit. Rom. vol. v. p. 271, &c.)

[1] Tillemont, Hist. des Empereurs, vol. iv. pp. 139, 635; vol. v. pp. 138, 705. Fleury, Hist. Eccl. vol. iv. book xvii. note 24. Pagi, Critica in Annales Baronii, anno 312.

[2] M. Labletterie, Vie de l'Empereur Julien, book iii. p. 232; idem, Vie de l'Empereur Jovien, p. 106. M. Beugnot, in his Histoire de la Destruction du Paganisme en Occident, looks upon it as an incontestable fact, not only that the title of Summus Pontifex had been given to Constantine, but that he even discharged some of its functions contrary to the spirit and to the principles of Christianity, vol. i. pp. 89, 92. This assertion of M. Beugnot is, however, very far from being established by decisive proofs. The Quatrième Mémoire of M. de la Bastie may serve as a corrective on this point to M. Beugnot's work.

Constantine.[1] Their exemption from curial offices was specially confirmed under the reign of that prince by two distinct laws promulgated in 335 and 337; the latter of these laws, however, restricts to perpetual flamens the immunity which all flamens, without exception, had formerly enjoyed.[2] Not content with confirming their ancient privileges, Valentinian I. granted new honours to such of them as had discharged their functions with credit; he raised them to the dignity of counts, a distinction conferred only on citizens eminent for the zeal and probity of which they had given proofs in the administration of public affairs.[3] Its privileges were very extensive. The pagan priests continued to enjoy these immunities even until the reign of Gratian and Theodosius, who gave the death blow to paganism in the empire; the former, by depriving the temples of their property; the latter, by totally prohibiting idolatry, or, at least, by executing with more rigour the laws enacted against it by the first Christian emperors.

16. *Prohibition of Foreign Religions by the ancient Romans.*

Another very remarkable effect of the veneration in which the religion of the state was held by the ancient Romans, was the

---

[1] Beugnot, Histoire de la Destruction du Pagan. en Occident, vol. i. pp. 33, 234, &c. 329, &c. 353, &c.

[2] We have cited above, p. 16, the first of these laws. The second runs thus: "Sacerdotes et *flamines perpetuos*, atque etiam duumvirales, ab annonarum præposituris inferioribusque muneribus immunes esse præcipimus. Quod ut perpetuâ observatione firmetur, legem incisam æneis tabulis jussimus publicari."—Cod. Theod. lib. xii. tit. v. not. 2.

[3] "*Qui ad sacerdotium provinciæ* et principalis (seu *primatis*) honorem gradatim et per ordinem, muneribus expeditis (non gratiâ emendicatis suffragiis) et labore pervenerint, probatis actibus, si consona est civium fama, et publicè ab universo ordine comprobantur, habeantur immunes, otio fruituri quod continui laboris testimonio promerentur;...*honorem etiam eis ex comitibus addi censemus*, quem hi consequi solent qui fidem diligentiamque suam in administrandis rebus publicis adprobarint."—Cod. Theod. ibid. tit. i. not. 75. Lebeau, Hist. du Bas Emp. vol. iv. book xvi. note 19. Fleury, Hist. Eccl. vol. iv. book xvi. note 29. This law of Valentinian I., and some other acts of his government, have made him to be suspected of indifference for the Christian religion. Tillemont thinks his conduct can be partly justified; nevertheless, he admits "that this prince has not always, either from true prudence or from false policy, manifested all that zeal which might be expected from a confessor of that faith which he had firmly professed under Julian."—Hist. des Emp. vol. v. pp. 10, 11.

general prohibition of all foreign religions not authorised by law.[1] Livy's words on this subject deserve especial attention: "Our wisest men, those who were eminently versed in laws human and divine, believed that nothing could be more destructive to religion than sacrificing, not according to the national, but a foreign rite."[2] The same historian cites a great number of decrees made by the senate on this subject at different times; many of which were not simply prohibitive, but inflicted also penalties more or less severe on persons transgressing the law.[3] It was by virtue of those decrees that the Prætor Cornelius Hispalus banished from Rome (A.U.C. 613) those who endeavoured to introduce the worship of Jupiter Sabasius;[4] and that the senate ordered the demolition of the temples of Isis and Serapis at Rome (A.U. 701), because their worship was not acknowledged by the laws.[5]

17. *This Prohibition in force under the Empire.*

This ancient legislation continued in force under the empire. Augustus, by the advice of Mæcenas, revived it, when an attempt was made to introduce the Egyptian paganism into Italy. The following is the discourse of Mæcenas to Augustus on the subject, as reported by Dion Cassius: "Honour the gods according to the customs of our fathers; and compel others to honour them. Detest all those who make innovations in matters of religion, and punish them, not only for the sake of the gods (for he who despises them respects nothing), but also because they who introduce new gods lead many persons to obey foreign laws; and hence arise societies bound together by oaths, leagues,

[1] See Mémoire before cited, of Burigny, Sur le Respect des Anciens Romains pour la Religion. Guénée, Lettres de quelques Juifs, vol. i. part ii. Letter 3, § 3.

[2] "Judicabant enim prudentissimi viri omnis divini humanique juris, nihil æquè dissolvendæ religioni esse quàm ubi non patrio sed externo ritu sacrificaretur."—Tit. Liv. Hist. lib. xxxix. not. 16.

[3] Many of those decrees are cited by Burigny and Guénée, ubi supra.

[4] Valer. Maxim. lib. i. cap. iii. § 2. Crevier, Hist. Rom. book xxvii. an de R. 613, vol. viii. in 12mo. p. 516.

[5] Dion Cassius, Hist. Roman. lib. xl. not. 47, Hamburg edition, 1750, vol. i. p. 257.

associations, and all other things dangerous to a monarchical government. Do not tolerate either atheists or magicians."[1] The example of Augustus, in this respect, was followed by Tiberius, who proscribed not only the Egyptian ceremonies, but also the Jewish, and ordered all the Jews who would not change their religion within a certain time, to depart from Italy, under pain of perpetual slavery. Four thousand freed men were on this occasion banished to Sardinia, according to Tacitus.[2]

18. *It was a Pretext for the Pagans for persecuting the Christians.*

This aversion of the Romans, and of all ancient nations, for foreign religions, was one of the chief causes of the opposition which Christianity encountered from the beginning in all parts of the empire, and of those cruel persecutions inflicted on it during three centuries by the emperors.[3] The most celebrated apologists of the Church have remarked it;[4] and the judges themselves not unfrequently assigned, as the grounds of their sentences against the Christians, their obstinacy in rejecting the gods of the empire, and introducing a new god.

19. *Injustice of this Pretext.*

It can hardly be necessary to observe that such a motive could not justify, even in the opinion of fair-minded pagans themselves, the edicts of persecution published against the Christians. For was it not evidently unjust to reject without inquiry, solely because it was new, a religion founded on miracles evidently divine, and whose pure morality naturally commanded the respect even of its greatest enemies, when they were every day changing

[1] Ibid. lib. lii. not. 36, p. 689.

[2] Tacitus, Annal. lib. ii. cap. lxxxv. Dion, Hist. Rom. lib. liv. not. 6, p. 735; lib. lx. not. 6, p. 945. Tillemont, Hist. des Empereurs, vol. i. p. 73.

[3] Naudet, Des Changements opérés dans toutes les Parties de l'Administration de l'Empire Romain sous les Règnes de Dioclétien, Constantin, &c., part ii. § 12. Fleury, Hist. Eccl. vol. ii. book viii. note 25.

[4] "Sed quoniam, cum ad omnia occurrit veritas nostra, postremò legum obstruitur auctoritas adversùs eam;...de legibus prius consistam vobiscum, ut cum tutoribus legum."—Tertull. Apolog. § 4. Also Lactantius, Instit. lib. ii. cap. vii. (Biblioth. PP. tom. iii.) Bossuet, Explic. de l'Apocal. ch. iii. note 4 (Bossuet's Works, vol. iii. p. 185, &c.).

without difficulty so many ancient laws, and sanctioning new forms of worship? This point was represented with great vigour and confidence to the magistrates of the Roman empire, and to the senate itself, by Tertullian, in the celebrated "Apology" which he addressed to them about the close of the second century.[1] "When," he says, "you have no answer to give to the truths which we oppose to you, you never fail to urge against us the authority of your laws. But if your law is wrong, it is because it is the work of men. Where is the wonder that a man should fall into error in making a law, or that he should acknowledge that error by repealing it? Have not the Lacedæmonians modified the laws of Lycurgus? and do not you yourselves, every day, by the light of experience, reform your ancient laws by new edicts and decrees?[2] I would ask those religious supporters of the laws of their ancestors, whether they have always the same respect for those ancient enactments? Whether they have never departed from them? Whether they have not even effaced from their memory those very laws which were most useful, and most indispensable for the preservation of morality? What has become of those laws which prohibited superfluous expenditure, ambition, luxury in dress, licentiousness in the theatre, sumptuous entertainments, divorce, and many vain and impure superstitions? And with regard to this very matter, the worship of the gods, have you not frequently abolished the wise laws made by your fathers? The consuls, with the consent of the senate, banished from Rome and from Italy Bacchus and his mysteries; they excluded Isis and Serapis, and Harpocrates and Anubis, from the Capitol, that is, from the temple of the gods; they threw down their altars, to prevent the disorders occasioned by vain and scandalous superstitions. You have, nevertheless, restored all those gods, and you have invested them once more with sovereign majesty. Where now is your religion?

[1] Fleury, Hist. Eccles. vol. ii. book v. note 4, &c.
[2] Tertullian, Apolog. § 4.

Where is this respect which you owe to your ancestors? You have abandoned their language, their simplicity, their modesty, their temperance: your are always praising old times, and always adopting new maxims; and while you are rejecting the noblest institutions of your fathers, those to which you ought to be most strongly attached, you retain those which you should be most anxious to abrogate.[1] ..... Every province, every city, has a god of its own; the Christians alone are deprived of that right; they are not allowed to call themselves Romans, because they adore a God not acknowledged by the Romans: you grant full liberty to adore everything except the true God; as if the God to whom all men belong, was not more than any other the God of all."[2]

20. *That Injustice often acknowledged by the Pagans.*

In support of these reflections, Tertullian cites the authority of everal pagan emperors, some of them renowned for wisdom, who, so far from thinking themselves bound by the ancient laws to persecute the Christians, publicly undertook their defence, and even threatened to punish their persecutors. "Tiberius, under whose reign the Christian name first appeared in the world, having been informed of the wonders which Jesus Christ had worked in proof of his divinity, made them known to the senate, and expressed a wish to have him admitted among the number of the gods: the senate rejected the proposal, but the emperor persisted in his resolution, and threatened to punish the accusers of the Christians. Consult your public registers; you will find that Nero was the first that persecuted the Christian religion, when it began to spread in Rome; but we deem it an honour that a prince of his character was the first of our persecutors; for whoever knows him, must admit that he never persecuted anything which was not a great good. Domitian, the worthy rival of Nero in cruelty, at first wished to follow his example; but he soon changed his mind, and recalled from exile those

[1] Tertullian, Apolog. § 6.

[2] Ibid. § 24.

whom he had banished. Such were our persecutors, unjust, impious, infamous men, whom you yourselves condemn, and whose injustices you endeavour to repair. Name, if you can, one really humane or religious prince who has persecuted the Christians. We can name one such character who declared himself their protector. Read the letters of Marcus Aurelius; you will there find that the prayers of the Christian soldiers obtained abundant rain which quenched the thirst of his army; and though he did not openly relieve the Christians from the penalties to which they were liable, he did it in another way, by condemning their accusers to still more severe punishments. What kind of laws, then, must those be which are enforced against us only by the impious, the unjust, the infamous, by savages, by fools, and by madmen; laws, which Trajan partly evaded, by prohibiting any search to be made for Christians; which were never enforced against us, neither by Adrian, the friend of literature; nor by Vespasian, the exterminator of the Jews; nor by Antoninus Pius, nor by Marcus Aurelius? Assuredly, if we be the monsters we are said to be, it is not men guilty of similar crimes, but all good men, that should have been our persecutors."[1]

21. *Obvious inference from all these facts.—Strict union of Religion and the State under the Christian Emperors.*

These details on the customs and maxims of antiquity relative to the strict union of church and state, have led us much farther than we intended. It is hoped, however, that they will not appear too tedious, when considered in connection with the design of this Introduction, which is to make known the honours and temporal prerogatives conferred on religion and its ministers after the conversion of Constantine. It is certain that the usage and maxims of pagan antiquity would of themselves explain the conduct of the Christian emperors on this point. On the fall of paganism, it would appear most natural to transfer to the

[1] Tertullian, Apolog. § 5.

Christian religion the favours which the national religion had hitherto enjoyed among the Romans, as well as amongst all other nations of the earth. That strict union of religion and of the state, which all ancient lawgivers had deemed so essential to the good of society, was held to be equally so after the establishment of Christianity; we shall see that it became even more necessary, in consequence of the deplorable condition of the empire. Far from meriting any reproach for adopting that principle, the Christian emperors would have evinced very little zeal or respect for the true religion, had they deprived it of the honours and privileges which a usage so ancient and so universal conferred on the religion of the state.

ARTICLE II.

HONOURS AND TEMPORAL PRIVILEGES CONFERRED ON RELIGION AND ITS MINISTERS UNDER THE FIRST CHRISTIAN EMPERORS.

22. *Origin of the Favours conferred on the Christian Religion by Constantine and his successors.*

THE wonderful conversion of Constantine to Christianity, and the general disrepute of the old religion, could not fail, as we have seen, to attract in a short time to the Church, not only the favour of the Christian emperor, but also the honours and temporal privileges which paganism had constantly enjoyed among the Romans as well as all other ancient nations. Still the origin and true cause of the temporal power with which the clergy were invested after the conversion of Constantine, would be but very imperfectly known, if we did not reflect on the deplorable state of the empire at the time, and on the powerful resources which religion and its ministers furnished against the innumerable perils which threatened to overwhelm it. A rapid glance at the state of Roman society, in this twofold view, will account very naturally for the numerous privileges which the emperors pressed on the acceptance of the Church, and which shall be detailed at length in the course of this introduction.

SECTION I.

Deplorable State of the Empire under the first Christian Emperors.—Powerful Resources of Religion and its Ministers.

23. *Seeds of Dissolution in the Empire long before Constantine.*

Long before the conversion of Constantine, the Roman empire carried within itself those seeds of dissolution, which were gradually weakening, and at last completely destroyed it.[1] The number of different nations which it contained, the infinite variety of their customs and characters, the relaxation of military discipline, the universal depravity of morals, all conspired to shake the constitution of the empire ; while the ceaseless irruptions of barbarian hordes aggravated the dangers resulting from the combination of so many different causes.

24. *Powerful Resources presented to it by Religion and its Ministers.*

In this wretched state of affairs, the Christian religion presented to the government one of the surest means of strengthening its authority and of securing the obedience of the people. The strong constitution of the Church, the beauty of its moral doctrine, the sublime virtues which it taught its children, the reformation which it everywhere produced in public morals, naturally pointed it out as the agent for the regeneration of the social system ; it alone could breathe a new life into that exhausted frame, by restoring morality, subordination, and all the other bonds of harmony between the different members of the state. The Christians were at once the most fervent servants of the Deity, and the most loyal subjects of the emperors. Submission to the powers of the earth, was one of their principal

[1] Essai Historique et Critique sur la Suprématie Temporelle de l'Église et du Pape, by M. Affre, ch. xiii. Montesquieu, Considérations sur les Causes de la Grandeur des Romains et de leur Décadence, ch. ix., x. &c. Bossuet, Histoire Universelle, part iii. ch. vii. Histoire de l'Église Gallicane, vol. i. années 407-409. Annales du Moyen Age, vol. i. book ii. p. 215, etc.

maxims and their most sacred duties. They had never been implicated in any of those seditions and revolts which so often deluged the Roman provinces with blood, and overturned the imperial throne. Constant and daily experience had proved to the emperors, that they could nowhere find more faithful subjects, more devoted soldiers, more upright magistrates, than in the bosom of Christianity.

25. *Eminent Virtues of the Clergy and especially of the Bishops.*

The clergy in particular were distinguished by virtues far beyond the standard of perfection known in preceding ages, and also above that then realised in the lives of the other classes of Christian society.[1] Nothing can be more striking than the picture of the virtues of the clergy, and especially of the bishops, during the first ages of the Church. "The most virtuous of our seniors," observes Tertullian, "preside in our assemblies; an honour which they attain, not by money, but by the suffrages of the Church, for holy things cannot be purchased."[2]

Hence the majority of the bishops mentioned in the history of those primitive ages were men of eminent sanctity, who preached evangelical sanctity much more by their example than by their words. In the exercise of their functions, they were assisted by priests and ministers of different orders, worthy of being proposed to the faithful as models, and selected from the most virtuous among them, often even from those confessors who had given proofs of the greatest constancy in persecutions.[3] The bishop selected them in presence of, and often at the request of the people, and was assisted by some intelligent priests in ex-

---

[1] Fleury, Mœurs des Chrétiens, n. 32, 48, 49. The same author confirms all that he says in this passage, in vol. viii. of his Eccl. Hist. 2nd Discourse, n. 4, &c.

[2] "Præsident probati quique seniores, honorem istum non pretio sed testimonio adepti; neque enim pretio ulla res Dei constat."—Tertullian, Apologet. cap. 39. Origen says the same thing, in other words, in his work against Celsus, book viii. n. 75 (Oper. tom. i. p. 798).

[3] St. Cyprian, Epist. 29, 38, &c.

amining whether they had the requisite qualifications. The bishop himself was chosen in presence of the people and with their suffrages, by the bishops of the province, convened for that purpose in the vacant church.[1] The bishops, no doubt, had the principal part in this election; nevertheless, the presence and suffrages of the people were considered necessary, that all being satisfied of the merit of the elect, they might yield him a more cordial obedience.[2]

The clergy selected for the service of a church, lived in complete subjection to the bishop, like disciples whom he was bound to instruct, to form, and to raise by degrees, to the different functions according to their talents and merits.[3] But this great authority of the bishops over the clergy, was by no means a despotic domination; it was a paternal government, distinguished by the mildness and charity which animated it.[4] The bishop

[1] Thomassin, Ancienne et Nouvelle Discipline, vol. ii. book ii. ch. 1—8. De Héricourt's abridgment of the same work, part ii. ch. xi.—Van Espen, Jus. Eccles. Univ. par. i. tit. xiii. cap. 1.

[2] Mosheim, and many other Protestant writers, have pretended that in the primitive ages of the Church her government was purely democratic, that all authority was then in the hands of the people, who alone had the right of making laws, and of appointing persons to govern in their name. Mosheim, Hist. Eccles. siècle i. part ii. ch. ii. § 6. In conformity with these principles, Jurieu maintained that "the election by the people was the sole essential required for the appointment of pastors." — Syst. de l'Eglise, p. 578. But nothing can be more opposed to the doctrine and constant practice of the Church than such pretensions. Even in those primitive ages, when the influence of the people was greatest in those elections, the principal authority was vested in the bishops of the province; the suffrages of the people were simply their petition or good wishes, subject to the decision of the bishops, who properly made the election. This is demonstrated clearly by the facts collected on this subject by the authors cited in the preceding note. (See also Fenelon, Traité du Ministère des Pasteurs, ch. xiv. xv. Bergier, Dict. Theol. art. Hiérarchie. Pey, De l'Autorité des Deux Puissances, vol. ii. p. 2, et seq.). Hence we may infer how incorrect and groundless is the assertion of M. Guizot, that "for a long time the bishops were chosen by their subordinates."—Hist. Générale de la Civil. en Europe, 5me Leçon, pp. 147, 149.

[3] Si quis presbyter, aut diaconus, aut alius è clericorum catalogo, relictâ parœciâ suâ, ad aliam abierit, et cum migraverit penitùs, in aliâ parœciâ præter episcopi sui voluntatem manserit; hunc jubemus non ampliùs sacris ministrare, præsertim si episcopo ad reditum hortanti non obtemperavit; illic tamen veluti laicus communicet. Sin verò episcopus apud quem versantur, pro nihilo ducens adversùm eos decretam cessationem à ministerio, receperit eos tamquàm clericos, segregetur ut magister interturbati ordinis." — Canon. Apost. 15, 16. See, on this subject, Thomassin, Ancienne et Nouvelle Discipline, vol. ii. book i. ch. i. ii. De Héricourt, ibid. part ii. ch. i.

[4] Saint Cyprian, Epistol. 5, 14, 29, 56, &c. Origen, in Matt. xx. 25. (Oper. tom. iii. pp. 722, 878.)

took no important step without the advice of the principal members of his clergy, and especially of the priests, who were in some degree the senate of the Church. He sometimes invested some of the oldest and most respectable among them with a kind of authority over himself, ordering them on every occasion to watch over his morals and conduct.

A great number of the clergy led very mortified lives, using nothing but herbs, fasting frequently, and practising the other austerities of the ascetical life, as far as was consistent with the functions of the sacred ministry. Chastity was the virtue most earnestly recommended to bishops, priests, and deacons.[1] It is true that in the early times, married persons were often promoted to those orders. For how could they find among Jews and converted pagans, persons who had preserved chastity to an advanced period of their lives? But all who were raised to the episcopacy, were bound thenceforward to perpetual chastity. In the greater part of the Church, this discipline extended to priests and deacons, who were prohibited to marry after their ordination.[2] To insure the more faithful observance of this discipline, unmarried clerics were forbidden to have any woman but a near relative living with them; a restriction which the Council of Nice extended to all, except mothers, sisters, and aunts.[3]

The bishops and clergy lived poorly, or at least with the simplicity common to persons in the middle ranks of life.[4]

---

[1] Thomassin, Ancienne et Nouvelle Discipline, vol. i. book ii. ch. lx. lxi. De Héricourt, ibid. part i. ch. xvi. Natal. Alexander, Dissert. 19 in Hist. Eccles. sæc. iv. Jager, Le Célibat Ecclés. dans ses Rapports Relig. et Polit. 2nd edit. Paris, 1836, in 8vo. Collet, De Ordine, tom. ii. cap. ix.

[2] "Placuit in totum prohiberi episcopis, presbyteris et diaconibus, vel omnibus clericis positis in ministerio, abstinere se à conjugibus suis, et non generare filios; quicumque verò fecerit, ab honore clericatûs exterminetur."—Concil. Eliberit. anno 301; can. 33 (Labbe, Concil. tom. i. p. 974). Concil. Ancyr., in 314, can. 9. (Ibid. p. 1467.) Epist. 1, Siricii papæ ad Himerium Tarraconensem (anno 385), cap. vii. (Ibid. t. ii. p. 1019.)

[3] Vetuit omninò magna synodus, ne liceat episcopo, nec presbytero, nec diacono, nec ulli penitus eorum qui sunt in clero, introductam habere mulierem, præterquàm utique matrem, vel sororem, vel amitam, vel eas solas personas, quæ omnem suspicionem effugiunt." — Concil. Nic. can. 3 (Labbe, Concil. tom. ii. p. 30).

[4] Thomassin, Ancienne et Nouvelle Discipline, vol. iii. book iii. passim. De Héricourt, ibid. part iii. ch. xv. &c.

Many of them, before receiving holy orders, had distributed their patrimony to the poor; others continued after their ordination to support themselves by manual labour, that they might not be a burden on the revenues of the Church, and might be better enabled to relieve the poor.

All the revenues of the Church were administered by the bishop; he had the sovereign control of them; and there was no apprehension that he would abuse them: the least suspicion of his integrity would have excluded him from the government of souls, who were valued infinitely more than treasures. To him accordingly all petitions for succour were addressed; he was the father of the poor, and the refuge of all the afflicted.[1]

To all these virtues, which rendered the clergy so respectable in the eyes of the people, the bishops and inferior ministers added a constant devotion to the service of the Church. The bishop presided punctually at public prayers, and at all the exercises of public worship. His ordinary occupations, like those of the other sacred ministers, were the instruction of the faithful and of catechumens, the visiting of the sick and of penitents, and the reconciling of enemies. He settled all disputes, for Christians were not allowed to plead before pagan tribunals; and they were themselves better pleased with the peaceful and disinterested arbitration of the bishops, than with the sentences of secular magistrates, who were almost always idolaters, and enemies of the Christian name.[2]

26. *How much they were respected by the Faithful and by the Pagans themselves.*

It may easily be conceived that such pastors must have enjoyed the heartfelt esteem and affection of the faithful. "It was remarked of St. Polycarp," Fleury observes,[3] "that they

---

[1] Saint Cyprian, Epist. 2, 34, &c. Canon. Apost. 39, 41, 59, &c. Thomassin, ubi supra.

[2] Thomassin, Ancienne et Nouvelle Discipline de l'Eglise, vol. ii. book iii. ch. ci. &c. De Héricourt, ibid. part ii. ch. xxix.

[3] Fleury, Mœurs des Chrétiens, note 32.

contended for the honour of unloosing his sandals. It was a common custom to prostrate themselves on meeting a priest and to kiss his feet, while he gave his benediction. It was considered a great honour to have even a deacon at their table or sleeping under their roof. No important affair was commenced without the advice of the pastor, who was the sole director of all his flock. He was regarded as the man of God, as the vicar of Jesus Christ. This respect and filial obedience were the only source of the power of the pastors, for they had no means except persuasion and spiritual penalties to insure obedience. The intimidation of the conscience was the sole coercion they could employ; and those who were impious enough to despise their censures, had no temporal penalty to dread." The pagans themselves could not refrain from respecting the character and the virtue of the ministers of the Christian religion. Their example was cited by the emperor Alexander Severus, as a model of the care to be taken in the election of public officers.[1] Origen, in his works against Celsus, composed in the third century, supposes as a certain fact, acknowledged by the pagans themselves, that the conduct even of very imperfect Christians, was far superior to that of the pagans, and that the virtue of the least perfect bishops and priests far surpassed that of the civil magistrates. "The assemblies of the Christians," he says, "compared with the popular assemblies of the cities which they inhabit, resemble those stars which illumine the world. For, can any one deny that the most imperfect portion of our assemblies is better than the popular assemblies. Compare the senate of the Christian Church with that of each city,[2] and it will be seen that among

[1] "Ubi aliquos voluisset, vel rectores provinciis dare, vel præpositos facere, vel procuratores ordinare, nomina eorum coràm proponebat, hortans populum ut si quis quid haberet criminis, probaret manifestis rebus; si non probasset, subiret pœnam capitis. Dicebatque grave esse, cùm id Christiani et Judæi facerent in prædicandis sacerdotibus qui ordinandi sunt, non fieri in provinciarum rectoribus, quibus fortunæ hominum committuntur et capita."—Lamprid. Vita Alex. Sever. (Historiæ Augustæ Scriptores, tom. i. p. 997; Lugd. Batav. 1671, in 8vo.) Baronii Annales, anno 224, n. 3.

[2] In this passage, by senators of the Church are meant bishops, priests, and deacons; the latter, it is known, had a share at that time in the govern-

the senators of the Church, there are men fit to govern a city of divine beings, if such could be found on this earth, whilst the others are entirely devoid of the morals required in the high dignity which they occupy. If you compare, moreover, the bishop of each church with the first magistrate of the city, you shall find that amongst the chiefs and governors of the Church of God, those least eminent for their virtues, are nevertheless better than the chiefs and governors of cities."[1] It must be remembered, that Origen expresses himself thus, in a work directed against pagans, who could manifestly overwhelm him with ridicule, if the facts which he states were not notorious and undeniable.[2]

27. *The Clergy distinguished by the same Virtues long after the Conversion of Constantine.*

After the times of persecution, and long after the conversion of Constantine, the clergy, and especially the bishops, maintained in general the same high character.[3] The ancient mode of electing bishops, from the most virtuous among the faithful, by the suffrages of clergy and people, was retained for a long time.[4] Many were taken from the monastic state, whose virtues they continued to practise in the episcopate, living in common with a certain number of monks, whom they attached to their person.[5] Several such examples occur in the East, whence the usage was imported to the West, about the middle of the fourth century, by Eusebius of Vercelli.[6] From that period even those bishops

---

ment of the Church under the direction of the bishop.—Note by Père Delarue, editor of Origen, on this passage.

[1] Origen, lib. iii. contra Celsum, n. 30 (Oper. tom. i. p. 466).

[2] Origen states, in the preamble to that work (note 6), that he did not intend it for Christians learned in the faith, but for pagans, or badly instructed Christians.

[3] Fleury, Mœurs des Chrét. n. 48 and 49. Hist. Ecclésiast. vol. viii. 2nd Discourse, n. 4.

[4] Thomassin, Ancienne et Nouvelle Discipline, vol. ii. book ii. ch. ix. &c. De Héricourt, ibid. part ii. ch. xii.

[5] Thomassin, Ancienne et Nouvelle Discipline, vol. i. book iii. ch. 2, 3, 4, 7, 13, &c. De Héricourt, ibid. part i. ch. 22—25. Theiner, Hist. des Instit. Eccles. vol. i. 1st period.

[6] "In Vercellensi Ecclesiâ, duo pariter exigi videntur ab episcopo (in sacer-

who had not been monks generally lived in common with their clergy, after the example of the faithful of Jerusalem, having no private property, living on whatever means their church might supply, sometimes even employed in manual labour, in order to lighten the burden on their Church, and to minister more abundantly to the wants of the poor. St. Augustine, who appears to have been the first who introduced those purely ecclesiastical communities into the West,[1] soon had many imitators, especially in France and Spain, where many councils published regulations to preserve and to extend a practice so eminently calculated to preserve the ecclesiastical spirit and morality.[2] The lives of St. Eusebius, of Vercelli; St. Augustine; St. Martin, bishop of Tours; St. Hilary, bishop of Arles; St. Gregory the Great, and of many other holy bishops, supply on this point details as edifying in themselves as they are honourable to the clergy of the principal Churches of the West at that time.

An admirable idea of the virtues of the clergy in that age may be gathered from St. Augustine's work on "the morals of the Catholic Church," in which he contrasts the virtues of that Church with those of the Manicheans. Having sketched in brilliant colours the virtues of the solitaries and of the monks, he describes in the following language the equally eminent virtues of the different orders of the clergy: "It must not be supposed," he says, "that the sanctity of the Catholic Church is confined to monks and to solitaries. What a number of excellent and holy

dotibus ordinandis), *monasterii continentia, et disciplina Ecclesiæ;* hæc enim *primus, in Occidentis partibus,* diversa inter se Eusebius sanctæ memoriæ conjunxit; ut et in civitate positus *instituta monachorum teneret,* et Ecclesiam regeret jejunii sobrietate." — S. Ambros. Epist. 63, n. 66 (Oper. tom. ii. p. 1038). Fleury, Hist. Eccl. vol. iii. book xiii. n. 14.

[1] It appears that the ecclesiastical communities before St. Augustine combined with the observances of the clerical life those of the monastic state: the members of those communities were both clerics and monks. The observances of the clerical state alone were preserved by St. Augustine in the community of clerics which he established in his own house after his elevation to the episcopacy. See on this subject Thomassin and De Héricourt, ubi supra. Tillemont, Mémoires pour servir à l'Histoire Ecclés. vol. xiii. p. 226, &c. 844, &c. D. Ceillier, Hist. des Aut. Ecclés. vol. xi. p. 23. Helyot, Hist. des Ordres Monast. vol. ii. ch. i. ii.

[2] See the authors cited above, note 2.

bishops, priests, deacons, and other sacred ministers, have not I myself known, whose virtue appeared to me the more admirable and deserving of all praise, as it is so difficult to preserve it in intercourse with the world and amid the agitations of ordinary life. For it is not healthy men, but invalids, that they have to govern; they are obliged to bear with the vices of the multitude, in order to cure them, and to tolerate the evil before they can eradicate it. In such circumstances, how very difficult it is to remain firm in virtue, in peace, and in tranquillity of soul: in one word, the clergy are in a place full of perils to their virtue; the solitaries are in the haven of virtue." [1]

28. *Remarkable Admissions of Julian on this point.*

Even the pagans themselves were struck with the imposing spectacle presented to the world in that admirable discipline which made the ministers of the Christian religion so venerable in the eyes of the faithful.[2] This appears particularly in a letter addressed by Julian the Apostate to Arsaces, pontiff of Galatia, about the year 362. After laying down the chief rules of conduct to be observed by the ministers of the pagan religion, which were manifestly borrowed from the Christian Church, the emperor cannot conceal his great annoyance on finding that on this, as on so many other points, the pagan priests are so decidedly inferior. "Let it never be said," he cries, "that those upstarts

---

[1] "Non ita sese angustè habent Ecclesiæ Catholicæ mores optimi, ut eorum tantùm vita quos commemoravi (*anachoretas* nempe et *cœnobitas*) arbitrer esse laudandos. Quàm enim multos episcopos, optimos viros sanctissimosque cognovi, quàm multos presbyteros, quàm multos diaconos, et cujuscemodi ministros divinorum sacramentorum, quorum virtus eò mihi mirabilior, et majore prædicatione dignior videtur, quò difficilius est eam in multiplici hominum genere, et in istâ vitâ turbulentiore servare! Non enim sanatis magis quàm sanandis hominibus præsunt. Perpetienda sunt vitia multitudinis ut curentur, et priùs toleranda quam sedanda pestilentia. Difficillimum est hìc tenere optimum vitæ modum, et animum pacatum atque tranquillum. Quippe, ut breviter explicem, hi (*anachoretæ* videlicet et *cœnobitæ*) agunt ubi vivere discitur, illi ubi vivitur." — St. Augustin, De Moribus Ecclesiæ Catholicæ, lib. i. cap. xxxii. (Oper. tom. i. p. 711).

[2] St. Greg. Naz. Oratio 4a (alias 3a) adversus Julianum, n. 3 (p. 138, edit. Bened.). Sozomen, Hist. Eccles. lib. v. cap. 16. Labletterie, Vie de Julien, p. 266, &c.

should rob us of our glory, and that, by imitating the virtues of which we have the model and the original, they should expose our negligence and inhumanity to obloquy: or rather let us not betray our religion: let us not dishonour the worship of the gods. To hear that you fulfil all those duties would fill my heart with joy."[1]

29. *The Empire sustained against its Foreign Enemies by the Christian Religion.*

The admiration and respect with which the greatest enemies of Christianity were inspired at the sight of so many virtues, proved clearly to the government what a powerful influence religion and its ministers could exercise in the regeneration of society, and in the maintenance of public order. But it was not against the internal causes of dissolution alone that Christianity strengthened the empire; it appeared not less adapted to defend that empire against its enemies from without. During the uninterrupted incursions of the barbarian hordes, the influence of the bishops was often the firmest bulwark of cities and of provinces.[2] The sacredness of their profession, the sanctity of their lives, their talent for business, their tender affection for the people entrusted to their care, won the esteem and veneration even of the barbarians themselves, who were frequently forced to yield to the ascendancy and interposition of men so respectable. In the year 350, the city of Nisiba, which was the principal barrier against the Persians, was saved from their assaults by the prudence and sanctity of St. James its bishop.[3] A few years later, in 383, the Empress Justina, when compelled to negotiate for the interests of her son Valentinian II. with the tyrant Maximus, thought she could not entrust the matter to safer hands than St. Ambrose; and so successfully did that holy bishop conduct his

---

[1] Juliani Epistola ad Arsacium Pontif. (Juliani Operum, p. 430.) This letter, which has been preserved by Sozomen, is translated entire by Labletterie, Vie de Jovien, p. 468.

[2] Fleury, Mœurs des Chrétiens, n. 58. Thomassin, Ancienne et Nouv. Discipl. vol. iii. book i. ch. xxvi. n. 14, 17, 19, 21; ch. 27, n. 6—9.

[3] Theodoret, Hist. Eccl. lib. ii. ch. xxvi. Philostorg. Hist. Eccl. lib. iii. n. 23. Fleury, Hist. Ecclés. vol. iii. book xiii. n. 2.

negotiation, that he arrested the usurper in his march, and concluded a treaty with him far more favourable than could be expected in circumstances so unfortunate.[1]

30. *Rome and many other Cities saved by the Influence of the Bishops.*

These remarkable examples of the salutary influence of the bishops occurred more frequently during the following century, when the irruptions of the barbarians became more frequent. Rome itself was twice saved from the most frightful calamities by the mediation of Pope St. Leo with the barbarian kings Genseric and Attila.[2] France, about the same period, found in the active zeal and inexhaustible charity of her prelates her most powerful resource against the scourges of war.[3] The city of Troyes in particular owed its preservation to the mediation of its bishop St. Lupus with the haughty Attila, who yielded in the same manner to the prayers of St. Aignan in favour of the city of Orleans.[4] When the emperor Julius Nepos wished to negotiate an arrangement with the Goths in 474, he could find no more efficient commissioners than the bishops, by whose mediation he succeeded in accomplishing his object.[5] Some years before, St. Germain of Auxerre, and St. Lupus of Troyes, while on a mission in Great Britain to oppose the Pelagian heresy, had saved that province from the invasion of Saxons and of Picts.[6]

31. *The temporal Power of the Clergy the natural Consequence of all these Facts.*

Similar benefits conferred by the clergy on the state in all parts of the empire,—the noble examples of virtue and fidelity which they generally gave to the people,—the extraordinary influence

---

[1] Fleury, Hist. Ecclés. vol. iv. book xviii. n. 28.

[2] Fleury, Hist. Ecclés. vol. vi. book xxviii. n. 39 and 55. Tillemont, Mém. sur l'Hist. Ecclés. vol. xv. pp. 750, 779, &c.

[3] Fleury, ibid. vol. vi. book xxix. n. 36, &c.

[4] Fleury, ibid. book xxvii. n. 50.

[5] Sidon. Apollin. Epistol. lib. vii. Epistola 6, ad Basil. (Tom. vi. Biblioth. Patrum, p. 1110.) Hist. de l'Église Gallicane, vol. ii. book iv. an. 474.

[6] Fleury, Hist. Ecclés. vol. vi. book xxv. n. 18. Lingard, History of England, vol. i. ch. i. p. 96.

of their example and doctrine on public morals,—the happy effects which government could reasonably expect from their concurrence in the support and defence of the empire, account at once and most naturally for the rapid increase of the temporal power of the Church under the first Christian emperors. The motives which had induced Constantine to lay the foundations of that power became every day more urgent in proportion as the empire approached its ruin, and as the causes of its dissolution became more active. The weaker the political authority became, the more it felt the necessity of enlisting the influence of religion and of its ministers in its favour, to hold the people to their duty, and to prevent, or at least defer, the total dissolution of the empire. Hence most of the Christian emperors—not excepting those who are most eminent in the art of government—far from seeking to diminish the temporal power of the clergy, laboured on the contrary to increase it; and to such a degree did they at length exalt it, that the bishops, though not invested with any political title, nor being in the strict sense a branch of the constitution of the state, were in some measure its first order, by their influence and their authority in all the departments of the civil administration.

32. *This Consequence acknowledged by unimpeachable authorities.—Admissions of Dupuy.*

In the sequel of this introduction, a great number of facts shall be produced in support of these observations. It may be mentioned here that long since, and even in our own days, they arrested the attention of many writers by no means favourable to the temporal power of the clergy, and much less so to the prodigious development of that power in the middle ages. Notwithstanding their well known prejudices on this subject, they have not hesitated to admit that the real origin of that power must be traced to the circumstances which we have mentioned. "As the bishops," observes the celebrated Dupuy,[1] "had dis-

[1] Dupuy, Traité de la Juridiction Criminelle, part i. ch. iv. p. 9. See also ch. viii. p. 19. This work is found at the end of vol. i. of Libertés de

tinguished themselves by their zeal, their justice, and their fidelity to the empire, the emperors entrusted to their care many temporal concerns:—first, jurisdiction in lawsuits even between laics who wished to submit to their arbitration; in the next place, the care of all those matters and regulations, the management of which could be best executed by men of piety and authority, and especially those which regarded the consolation of the afflicted,—such as widows, orphans, slaves, &c. &c., they had power to punish all disobedience to their rulers on these matters. They were associated with the magistrates in those affairs. In the course of time, the emperors having ascertained the fidelity of the bishops and their zeal for the empire, especially in the wars against the heretical nations, the Goths and the Vandals, &c. &c., entrusted them with the charge of cities, to hold them against the enemy,[1] and to punish all who should prove disloyal to their prince. At length they gave to the patriarchs, and especially to the popes, the same authority which the prefect of the prætorium[2] had in enforcing the laws, and in punishing those who violated them; they even were authorized to judge criminal causes of the laity."

33. *Admissions of M. Guizot.*

The opinions and admissions of M. Guizot on this point

---

l'Église Gallicane, edit. of 1731. In support of this testimony of Dupuy, see Fleury, Institution au Droit Ecclés. vol. ii. part iii. ch. i. p. 5. See also his 7th Discourse on Eccles. Hist. n. 4, last page (vol. xix. of the Hist. Ecclés.) Bossuet, Defens. Declar. lib. ii. cap. 36.

1 We shall cite in another place many remarkable facts in proof of this assertion. See ch. i. part i. note 13.

2 Under Constantine and his successors, all the provinces of the empire were divided into four prefectures: viz. the East, Illyria, Italy, and the Gauls. The office of prefect of the prætorium, though much curtailed of its privileges by Constantine, was still one of the most important in the empire. It had formerly combined the general superintendence of the finances with the highest jurisdiction both civil and military. The inconveniences of this extraordinary authority induced Constantine to restrict it to a purely civil administration, and to detach some departments even of that from it: the prefects of the prætorium thus retained of their former power nothing but the supreme administration of the finances, and of justice in civil cases, without any jurisdiction over the military. Tillemont, Hist. des Empereurs, vol. iv. p. 284. Notitia dignitatum Codicis Theodosiani (Ad calcem ejusdem codicis, Lipsiæ,

are equally remarkable.[1] However opposed to the prodigious, and, as he calls it, excessive influence exercised by the Church of the middle ages over European society in the political order, he willingly admits that, in the intellectual and moral order, her influence was very great and very salutary, as well by her doctrines as by her discipline and by the strong constitution of her government. " From the commencement of the fifth century," he observes,[2] " the Christian clergy had a powerful means of influence. The bishops and clergy had become the first municipal magistrates. Of the Roman empire there remained, strictly speaking, nothing but its municipal government; by the vexations of despotism, and the ruin of the cities, the curiales, or members of the municipal bodies, had fallen into apathy and discouragement. The bishops, on the contrary, and the body of the clergy, full of life and zeal, naturally came forward to superintend all and to direct all. It would be injustice to reproach them with it, to accuse them of usurpation; it was the natural course of things; the clergy alone had moral strength and energy; they became powerful everywhere; such is the law of the world.

" This resolution is manifest in all the legislation of the emperors in those ages. Open the Theodosian or the Justinian code, and you find an immense number of laws referring municipal affairs to the clergy and the bishops.[3] Thus the Christian Church has from that epoch powerfully influenced the character and the development of modern civilization. Let us sum up briefly the elements which she introduced into it.

" And, in the first place, in the midst of that deluge of

1743; in fol. tom. vi. par. ii. p. 1, &c.). Lebeau, Hist. du Bas Empire, vol. i. book v. n. 9, &c. Naudet, Considerations sur les Changements opérés dans l'Administration de l'Empire, vol. ii. part iii. ch. 7, p. 255—259.

[1] Guizot, Hist. Gén. de la Civilization en Europe, 3rd edit. Paris, 1840. 2me Leçon.

[2] Ibid. p. 55—58.

[3] In support of this assertion, M. Guizot cites particularly the Cod. Justinian, lib. i. tit. iv.; De Episcopali Audientiâ, n. 26 et 30, tit. 55; De Defensoribus, n. 8. The development of the succeeding paragraphs will prove that he could have cited many other authorities on this subject.

material force which at this period overwhelmed society there was an immense benefit in the presence of a moral influence, a moral power, a power which derived all its force from convictions, from belief, from moral sentiments. Had there been no Christian Church, the whole world would have been abandoned to mere material force. The Church alone exercised a moral power: she did more,—she kept up and diffused the conviction of a rule, a law, superior to all human laws. She professed that belief so essential to the well-being of mankind, that there exists, above all human laws, another law, at different times, and from a difference of morals, sometimes called reason, sometimes the divine law, but which everywhere and always is the same law under different names."

SECTION II.

The Divine and Ecclesiastical Laws sanctioned by the Authority of the Christian Emperors.—Origin of the Temporal Penalties against Idolatry, Judaism, Heresy, and other impious Crimes.

34. *Condition and Progress of Christianity in the Empire before the time of Constantine.*

Before presenting a summary of the numerous laws enacted by the Christian emperors in favour of religion, it will be useful to understand the condition of Christianity in the empire at the time of the conversion of Constantine. Notwithstanding the violent persecution to which it had been subjected during three centuries, it had long since formed a society not less imposing by its numbers than by its vigorous constitution.[1] Tertullian, in the commencement of the third century, asserted confidently, in his work against the Jews, that the kingdom of Jesus Christ was more extensive than the empires of Nebuchadnezzar, of Alexander, or of the Romans themselves.[2] His observations on

[1] See, on this subject, Bullet, Hist. de l'Etabliss. du Christian. 8vo. De la Luzerne, Dissert. sur la Vérité de la Rel. vol. iv. 3rd Dissertation. Frayssinous, Conferences sur l'Etabliss. du Christian.

[2] Tertullian, in this place, points out to the Jews the great difference between those great empires and that of Jesus Christ. The former could not go beyond

the same subject in his Apology are still more remarkable. "We are but of yesterday," he says, "and we fill your whole empire, cities, islands, castles, towns, councils, camps, tribes, decuria, the palace, the senate, the forum, — all except the temples. We could have fought you without arms and without rebellion, merely by retiring from your empire. Had this immense multitude of men retreated from you to some remote corner of the world, the loss of so many citizens would have shamed your tyranny; their retirement alone would have punished you. You would have been frightened at the solitude, — at the silence around you, and the stupor, as it were, of a departed world; you would look in vain for subjects; more enemies than fellow-countrymen would have remained with you; but now your enemies are a minority because of the multitude of the Christians."[1]

At the close of the same century, Arnobius, not satisfied with confirming this statement of Tertullian, urges against the pagans this rapid and universal propagation of Christianity as a manifest proof of the truth of that religion. "If," he asks, "the history of the facts in the Gospel be, as you say, false, how has it come to pass that this religion should have so soon filled the entire world? How have so many nations, in regions so far asunder, and under climates so different, united in the same spirit? Can you require

---

certain limits: his is diffused over all nations. "Nabuchodonosor cum suis regulis ab Indiâ usque Æthiopiam habuit regni sui terminos; Alexander Macedo nunquàm Asiam universam et cæteras regiones, postquàm devicerat, tenuit...Quid de Romanis dicam, qui de legionum suarum præsidiis imperium suum muniunt, nec trans istas gentes porrigere vires regni sui possunt? *Christi autem regnum ubique porrigitur, ubique creditur, ab omnibus gentibus suprà enumeratis* (scilicet, *barbaris etiam et ignotis*) *colitur, ubique regnat, ubique adoratur, omnibus ubique tribuitur æqualiter.*"—Tertull. Lib. adv. Jud. cap. 7.

[1] "Hesterni sumus, et vestra omnia implevimus, urbes, insulas, castella, municipia, conciliabula, castra ipsa, tribus, decurias, palatium, senatum, forum; sola vobis relinquimus templa.... Potuimus, et inermes nec rebelles, sed tantummodò discordes, solius divortii invidiâ, adversùs vos dimicasse. Si enim tanta vis hominum in aliquem orbis remoti sinum abrupissemus à vobis, suffudisset utique dominationem vestram tot qualiumcumque amissio civium, imò etiam et ipsâ destitutione punîsset; procul dubio expavissetis ad solitudinem vestram, ad silentium rerum, et stuporem quemdam quasi mortui orbis; quæsissetis quibus imperaretis; plures hostes quàm cives vobis remansissent; nunc enim pauciores hostes habetis præ multitudine christianorum." — Idem. Apologet. cap. 37.

any other motive for conviction but the rapid diffusion of our dogmas in so short a time through the whole earth, so that there is no nation, how barbarous soever, or removed from civilization, which, under the influence of the love of Jesus Christ, has not softened the rudeness of its manners, and exchanged its ferocity for sentiments more humane?"[1]

35. *These Facts admitted by Pagan Authors themselves.*

These testimonies, so decisive in themselves, are still further confirmed by profane historians, who describe the terror of the pagans at the ever-increasing progress of Christianity, the universal decline of their worship, and the immense multitude of victims that should be sacrificed if the edicts against the Christians were to be rigorously executed.[2] So incontestable is the prodigious diffusion of Christianity at the close of the third century, that it is generally admitted even in those latter days by the greatest enemies of religion. Most of the modern infidels pretend that the conversion of Constantine was not the result of conviction, but a stroke of policy to win over the Christians to his party.[3] We are very far from admitting this charge, which is irreconcileable, we believe, with all the monuments of history;[4] but those who maintain it do, by the very fact, acknowledge the

[1] "Quòd si falsa, ut dicitis, historia illa rerum est, unde tam brevi tempore totus mundus illâ religione completus est? Aut in unam coïre quî potuerunt mentem gentes regionibus disjunctæ, ventis, cœlique convexionibus dissitæ?... Nonne vel hæc saltem fidem vobis faciunt argumenta credendi, quòd jam per omnes terras, in tam brevi temporis spatio, immensi nominis hujus (scilicet, *nominis christiani*) sacramenta diffusa sunt? Quòd nulla jam natio est tam barbari moris, et mansuetudinem nesciens, quæ non, ejus amore versa, molliverit asperitatem suam, et in placidos sensus, assumptâ tranquillitate, migraverit?"—Arnobius, Adv. Gentes, lib. i. cap. 55; lib. ii. cap. 5. (Biblioth. PP. tom. iii. p. 438, 2nd col.; 446, 2nd col.)

[2] Plinii Epistol. lib. x. epist. 97, 98. Lamprid. Vita Alex. Sev. cap. 43. Lactantius, De Mort. Persec. cap. 11. Eusebius, Hist. Eccl. lib. viii. cap. 14; lib. ix. cap. 7—9. These authorities and many others are quoted by the Abbé Bullet, and by the Card. de la Luzerne; ubi supra.

[3] Voltaire, Dict. Philos.—arts. Christianisme, Julien, &c. Tableaux des Saints, by the B. d'Holbach, part ii. ch. 7, p. 90. De la Félicité Publique, by Chastellux, vol. i. sect. 2, ch. 4.

[4] See, on this point, Bergier, Traité de la Religion, vol. ix. p. 552. Labletterie, Vie de Jovien, p. 257, &c. Duvoisin, Dissert. sur la Vision de Constantin, part ii. § 14, 15.

important truth which we contend for here, namely, that before the conversion of Constantine, the Christians were so numerous and powerful in the empire, that it would have been the best interest of the emperor to declare for them, and that he could do so without having anything to fear from the pagans. Indeed, it is manifest that, had the relative numbers been otherwise, Constantine's act, as a measure of policy, would have been the most absurd and unwise imaginable.[1]

36. *The Triumph of Christianity over Paganism assured before the Conversion of Constantine.*

From these observations, we may infer that without plainly contradicting the monuments of history, no one can attribute the triumph of Christianity over idolatry[2] to the patronage of the Christian emperors and to their constitutions in favour of the Christian religion. That triumph was manifestly assured before the conversion of Constantine; and far from being the author of that movement of society, he merely followed the general

---

[1] It may be inferred, we think, from these observations, that at the conversion of Constantine, and for a long time previous, the Christians were in the empire, "a multitude at least equal in number to the pagans." The testimony of Tertullian, and of others whom we have cited, proves this fact clearly to the judgment of intelligent and impartial persons. Cardinal de la Luzerne even maintains with great appearance of probability that at the time of Constantine's conversion, the number of Christians exceeded that of the pagans (ubi supra, n. 19—25). But whatever may be thought of that opinion, we believe it may be confidently asserted, that the opinion of some modern authors who estimate the number of the Christians of the empire, when Constantine was converted, at the fifth, twelfth, or twentieth part of the population, is not only utterly destitute of proof, but evidently contrary to the monuments of history. M. Beugnot, in his Hist. du Décad. du Pagan. en Occident, goes so far as to assert that even about sixty years later, under the reign of Valentinian I., all the Christians throughout the whole empire did not constitute more than a twentieth of the population (book ix. ch. 13, et alibi passim). His conjectures on the subject are founded exclusively on isolated documents relating to certain cities, or to particular provinces, which cannot serve as a basis for calculating exactly, nor even by approximation, the number of Christians in the rest of the empire. It must be admitted, it is true, that notwithstanding the wonderful progress of Christianity before the conversion of Constantine, the pagans continued to be, long after that time, a considerable party, especially in the West, and above all in Rome, where a considerable number of senators persisted long in their adherence to idolatry. In support of these assertions, the reader may consult L'Hist. de l'Église, by M. l'Abbé Receveur, vol. iii. p. 38, note. See, also, some other observations on the work of M. Beugnot, in Documentary Evidences, No. 1, at the close of the work.

[2] De la Luzerne, ubi supra, n. 114, &c.

impulse, which had long since, in all parts of the empire, been attracting the people into the bosom of the Christian Church. His example, doubtless, supported by his edicts and by those of his successors, must have favoured the progress of Christianity and accelerated the ruin of idolatry; but it is nevertheless certain, that the triumph of the Christian religion over paganism was assured before his conversion, and that God's almighty power had clearly manifested itself in the establishment of the Christian Church, before the princes of the earth were called in to sustain it by their protection and their edicts. For as Bossuet observes, "God, who knows that the most energetic virtue grows up amidst sufferings, founded his Church by martyrdom, and kept her during three hundred years in that state, without allowing her even one moment of repose. Having demonstrated by so long a trial that he had no need of human succour, nor of the powers of the earth to establish his Church, he at length called on the emperors, and made the great Constantine the declared protector of Christianity.[1] .... It was God's decree, and if I may so speak, the destiny of truth, that she should be completely established in spite of the kings of the earth, and that in the course of time she should have them, first as her disciples, and next as her patrons. He did not call them when he built his Church; when he had laid the immovable foundations and completed the erection of that great edifice, then it pleased him to call them. "Et nunc reges."[2] He has called them, therefore, not from necessity, but as a favour. The establishment of the truth does not depend on their assistance, and the empire of truth is not a dependence of their sceptre. If Jesus Christ has made them defenders of his gospel, it was to honour them, not because he needed them; it was to honour their authority and to consecrate their power. His sacred truth ever sustains itself and maintains its independence."[3]

---

[1] Bossuet, Hist. Univer. part ii. ch. 20 (vol. xxxv. of his works, p. 311).

[2] Ps. ii. 10.

[3] Bossuet, Sermon sur la Divinité de la Rel. (vol. xi. of his works, p. 227).

After these observations, which have appeared to us very important to demonstrate the miraculous character of the establishment of Christianity against the assertions of some modern writers, we now proceed to state in detail the principal provisions of the Roman law in favour of religion, after the conversion of Constantine.[1]

37. *First Edicts of Constantine in favour of the Christian Religion.*

The first fruit and the principal result of that conversion, was the full and perfect liberty secured to Christians, of assembling, of building churches, and of practising all the exercises of their religion. That was the object of the edicts published by Constantine and Licinius, in 312 and 313.[2] The first of these edicts, which was addressed to the prefect of the prætorium, as we learn from Eusebius, has not come down to us; but that historian has preserved the second, of which the principal points are the following: "Having long been of opinion, that no person ought to be refused liberty in the choice of his religion, we have already ordered, that Christians, as well as others, should enjoy the free exercise of theirs. But since, in the rescript which gives them that liberty, there are certain clauses on which some disputes have been raised, some persons have thought themselves dispensed from observing it. Therefore we, Constantine Augustus and Licinius Augustus, having auspiciously met at Milan, and deliberating on the concerns of the public safety and interests, have felt that one of our first cares should be to regulate what regards the worship of the Divinity, and to grant to Christians and to all others, the liberty of following what religion they please, in order to draw down the favour of heaven on us and on our subjects. Be it known to you, therefore, [the emperors

[1] An analysis of Roman law on this point may be seen in the following works: Hist. des Aut. Ecc. by D. Ceillier, vol. iv. ch. 5, art. 4; viii. ch. 15; xvi. ch. 20. Domat, Droit Public, book i. tit. 19. Fleury, Hist. Ecclés. vol. iii. &c. passim. We shall, in another place, point out the principal passages to be consulted in that author.

[2] Euseb. Hist. Eccles. lib. ix. cap. 9.; lib. x. cap. 5. Fleury, Hist. Ecclés. vol. ii. book ix. n. 46. Hist. de l'Église Gallicane, vol. i. p. 171, &c.

continue addressing the officers to whom the edict is directed] that all clauses in the letters addressed to you concerning the Christians notwithstanding, it is our will to order absolutely and expressly, that all who wish to observe the Christian religion, may do so without being molested or disturbed in any manner whatsoever. And we have thought it our duty to make known to you this announcement, that you may know, that we have given to the Christians full and absolute liberty of observing their religion; allowing, nevertheless, to all others a similar liberty, in order to promote the tranquillity of our reign." The subsequent portion of this edict orders the restitution of all churches and places where the Christians used to assemble, as well as of all the property belonging to the churches, whether they had been confiscated by the state or acquired by individuals, giving, however, to the latter the right of applying to the governor of the province to obtain a suitable indemnity.

To these first edicts, Constantine and his successors afterwards added many others, to secure more effectually for the Christians the free exercise of their religion, and to protect them against the violence and the persecutions of their enemies. According to a law of Constantine, promulgated in 322, all who used any violence against Christians, on account of their religion, were condemned to be scourged if they were slaves, and to heavy fines if they were of better condition.[1] Honorius made it even a capital crime to insult a priest in the church, to attack the holy places, or to give any violent interruption to the divine service.[2]

---

[1] "Quoniam comperimus quosdam ecclesiasticos, et cæteros catholicæ sectæ (i.e. *societati*) servientes, à diversarum religionum hominibus (scilicet, *paganis*) ad lustrorum sacrificia celebranda compelli; hâc sanctione sancimus, si quis ad ritum alienæ superstitionis cogendos esse crediderit eos qui sanctissimæ legi serviunt, si conditio patiatur, publicè fustibus verberetur; si verò honoris ratio talem ab eo repellat injuriam, condemnationem sustineat damni gravissimi (i. e. *mulctæ pecuniariæ*), quod rebus publicis vindicabitur (i.e. *de civitatis redditibus exsolvetur*)."—Cod. Theodos. lib. xvi. tit. ii. n. 5.

[2] "Si quis in hoc genus sacrilegii proruperit, ut in ecclesias catholicas irruens, sacerdotibus et ministris, vel ipsi cultui locoque aliquid importet injuriæ;...deferatur in notitiam potestatum;...atque ita provinciæ moderator sacerdotum et catholicæ ecclesiæ ministrorum, loci quoque ipsius, et divini

38. *Their Exertions to bring Idolatry into disrepute.*

To promote the more efficiently the propagation and public exercise of Christianity, the first Christian emperors constantly endeavoured to bring the pagan superstitions into disrepute, and to restrict by degrees the exercise of idolatry, until circumstances should enable them to abolish it altogether. Constantine, in particular, during the whole course of his reign, never ceased from working by indirect, but very efficacious means, the ruin of the pagan worship.[1] On all occasions he manifested his high esteem for the Christian religion, and the great pleasure it would give him to see all his subjects ranged under its standard. He was lavish of his gifts and favours to the Christians; he had always in his company some bishops and priests eminent for their virtues and merits; they were his council and his usual attendants; he admitted them to his table, and to his intimate confidence, and honoured them more than any of his other advisers. Magistrates and governors of provinces were generally selected from the Christians, and those who still remained pagans were prohibited to worship their false gods. He omitted nothing to discredit among the people their old superstitions, throwing down an altar, or destroying an idol, wherever he could do so without exciting any tumult, stripping the pagan temples, carrying away their gates or roofs to expose them to speedy destruction, exhibiting in the public places the statues of the most famous gods, to expose them to the contempt of the people, or to use them as profane ornaments. When he made Constantinople the capital of his empire, he banished completely from that city the worship of idols and all pagan superstitions;

---

cultûs injuriam, *capitali in convictos sive confessos reos sententiâ noverit vindicandam.*" — Cod. Theod. lib. xvi. tit. ii. n. 31. Fleury, Hist. Ecclés. vol. v. book xx. n. 28.

[1] Euseb. Vita Constantini, lib. ii. cap. xliv.—xlvii. &c.; lib. iii. cap. xlviii.—liv. &c. Idem, De Laudibus Constantini, cap. viii. Fleury, Hist. Ecclés. vol. iii. book xi. n. 33 and 45. Lebeau, Hist. du Bas-Empire, vol. i. book ii. n. 27, and book iv. n. 5. Hist. de l'Église Gallicane, vol. i. p. 191, &c. Tillemont, Hist. des Empereurs, vol. iv. p. 200—211. Naudet, Des Changements opérés dans l'Administration de l'Empire, vol. ii. part iii. ch. ii. and iii. art. i.; et alibi passim.

he allowed no temple there not consecrated to the true God; and whatever idols were preserved in profane places, were maintained merely as ornaments and monuments to posterity of the ancient blindness of mankind.

These different measures, combined with the preaching of a number of holy bishops and zealous missionaries, in all parts of the empire, insensibly brought paganism into such disrepute, that multitudes of pagans were filled with shame and contempt for their ancient superstitions.

39. *Edicts against Secret Divination.*

Profiting by this happy revolution in the public mind, Constantine promulgated in the year 319, a law, which though not absolutely prohibiting idolatry, restrained it very much by proscribing, under very severe penalties, the practice of magic or secret divination, for purposes of libertinism or debauchery, or as a pretext for suspected assemblies.[1] It would even appear that the pagans, intimidated by this law, the first that had been made by Constantine against their worship, were afraid for some time to raise statues to their gods, to offer them sacrifices, or to exercise even in public the rites of divination. But the emperor lost no time in quieting their apprehensions, by a law published in the same year, whereby he guarantees to them the free exercise of their worship in the temples and in other public places. "All those," he declares, "who still adhere to the ancient worship, may go to the public altars and temples to celebrate the usual ceremonies; for we forbid no person, in daylight, to

---

[1] "Nullus haruspex limen alterius accedat; sed hujusmodi hominum, quamvis vetus, amicitia repelletur...Superstitioni enim suæ servire cupientes *poterunt publicè ritum proprium exercere.*"—Cod. Theod. lib. ix. tit. xvi. n. 1. D. Ceillier, Hist. des Auteurs Ecclés. vol. iv. p. 132. To understand the nature and character of these superstitious practices, which Constantine prohibited by that law, see the notes of Godefroy on this passage. Dissert. of M. Bonamy, Sur le Rapport de la Magie avec la Théologie Païenne,—(Mém. de l'Acad. des Inscript. vol. vii. of the 4to. edit. p. 25; vol. iv. of Hist. de l'Acad. edit. in 12mo. p. 34). Receveur, Hist. de l'Église, vol. ii. p. 5. Beugnot, Hist. de la Destruct. du Pagan, vol. i. p. 79, &c.

indulge in the practices authorised by ancient custom."[1] This law was not long after confirmed by a letter, addressed to the inhabitants of the province of the East, in which Constantine, while he plainly exhorts all his subjects to embrace Christianity, declares nevertheless that it is not his wish to disturb those who remain attached to the ancient worship, and that in that matter he leaves full liberty to all persons to act as they please.[2]

40. *His Leniency to the Pagans.*

Such was the moderate policy of Constantine to the pagans during the whole of his reign. It is true, there is reason to believe, that towards the close of his life, he promulgated a law, ordering the temples of the false gods to be closed, and generally prohibiting all idolatry in his dominions.[3] But, whether it is that this law was never promulgated in the East, or that the emperor never deemed it advisable to enforce it in the West, and especially at Rome, where idolatry still had, both in the senate and in many illustrious families, votaries, whom it was prudent not to offend, it is certain that until the close of his reign the pagans preserved the free exercise of their worship.[4]

---

[1] "Haruspices et sacerdotes, et eos qui huic ritui assolent ministrare, *ad privatam domum prohibemus accedere,* vel sub prætextu amicitiæ limen alterius ingredi, pœnâ contra eos propositâ, si contempserint legem. Qui verò id vobis existimatis conducere, *adite aras publicas atque delubra,* et consuetudinis vestræ celebrate solemnia; *nec enim prohibemus præteritæ usurpationis* (seu *consuetudinis*) *officia liberâ luce tractari.*"—Cod. Theod. lib. ix. tit. xvi. n. 2.

[2] "Nemo alteri molestiam facessat; quod cuique libitum fuerit, id agat. Illud tamen, apud eos qui rectè sentiunt, fixum ratumque esse oportet, solos illos sanctè castèque victuros, quos tu ipse (*omnium Domine et sancte Deus*) ad hoc vocavisti, ut sacrosanctis tuis legibus acquiescant."—Eusebius, Vita Constant. lib. ii. cap. lvi.

[3] Eusebius, Vita Const. lib. ii. cap. xlv.; lib. iv. cap. xxiii. et xxv. Theodoret, Hist. Eccl. lib. v. cap. xxi. Sozomen, Hist. lib. iii. cap. xvii. Orosius, Hist. lib. vii. cap. xxviii. (Vol. vi. of the Biblioth. des Pères, p. 442). See, on this subject, No. 1 of the Documentary Evidence, at the end of this work.

[4] Libanius states so expressly in his Oration for the Preservation of the Pagan Temples, in which he expresses himself thus regarding the conduct of Constantine towards the idolators: "Sacris pecuniis usus est, nihil verò de cultu solemni immutavit. Penuria quidem in templis erat; omnia autem alia impleta videre erat."—Oratio pro Templis Gentil. non exscindendis, § 3 and 9. This discourse was published for the first time, by Jacques Godefroy, Geneva, 1634, 4to. The above passage is given by the same Godefroy, Comment. in Cod. Theod. lib. xvi. tit. x. n. 3.

41. *His Prudence in this respect imitated by Constantius and Constans.*

The emperors Constantius and Constans, sons and successors of Constantine, followed his prudent policy in this respect. They persisted, it is true, in combating paganism by all the means which he had so successfully employed, and which the onward progress of Christianity made every day more efficacious. It appears even, that not content with renewing the edicts of Constantine against secret divination, they published another, prohibiting all acts of idolatry.[1] As a natural consequence of this edict, Constans, when he became sole emperor, cast out from the senate-house (in 357) the altar of Victory, on which it was the custom to burn incense at the opening of each session, even in presence of the Christian senators, who had hitherto been obliged to assist at this pagan ceremony.[2] It is, nevertheless certain, that the pagans continued to practise their religion in liberty under the reign of Constans, at least in the West. This fact is demonstrated evidently from the petition addressed by Symmachus to Valentinian II., in 384, for the

[1] The following is the text of the law published by the Emperor Constantius, in 341: "Cesset superstitio: sacrificiorum aboleatur insania; nam quicumque contra legem divi principis, parentis nostri, et hanc nostræ mansuetudinis jussionem, ausus fuerit sacrificia celebrare, competens in eum vindicta, et præsens sententia exeratur." — Cod. Theodos. lib. xvi. tit. x. n. 2. This law was confirmed not long after by that of the Emperor Constans, which prohibited the demolition of all temples outside the walls of Rome. "Quamquàm omnis superstitio eruenda sit, tamen volumus ut ædes templorum quæ extra muros sunt positæ, intactæ incorruptæque consistant."—Ibid. n. 3. It is to be remarked that these two laws, in as far as they prohibit idolatry, are merely a revival of those of Constantine, as the Emperor Constantius expressly states in the first. In the Theodosian Code (same title), two other laws of the Emperor Constans occur, one of which orders the pagan temples to be closed, and the other prohibits sacrifices under pain of death.—Ibid. n. 4, 6. But the date of these laws appears doubtful; and hence their authenticity has been contested. See the 4th Memoir of M. de la Bastie, Sur le Pontificat des Empereurs Païens. (Mém. de l'Acad. des Inscript. vol. xv. 4to.) Beugnot, ubi supra, vol. i. p. 141, &c.

[2] Symmachus clearly supposes this in several passages of his petition to Valentinian II. for the restoration of the altar of Victory. Relatio Symmachi, n. 5, 7. This petition may be seen in the Recueil des Lettres de Symmaque, lib. x. ep. 54, and among the Letters of St. Ambrose, after the 17th Letter, addressed to Valentinian II. on the same subject. (Oper. tom. ii.) It is translated into French in Beugnot's work already cited, ubi sup. p. 417; but we shall soon see that his translation is not faithful, even on the most important points. See infra, p. 48, note 4.

restoration of the altar of Victory. Therein he loudly condemns the Emperor Constans, for having removed that altar from the place in which the senate assembled; but he declares at the same time, that "this prince deprived the vestals of none of their privileges; that he gave the priestly offices to the nobles; did not refuse the Romans the sums necessary for their religious ceremonies; and that though he himself preferred another religion, he preserved, nevertheless, those of the empire; allowing to all their own customs and rites."[1]

This fact is moreover confirmed by many inscriptions still extant on monuments erected in Italy, and even in Rome, under the reign of Constans, which mention expressly altars and statues erected at this period in honour of the false gods.[2]

42. *Moderation of Jovian.*

The execution of the edicts against idolatry, promulgated by Constantine and his sons, having been suspended under Julian the Apostate, was again carried out by their successors; but it must be observed, that like the first Christian emperors, they combined so effectually firmness with gentleness, that the execution of those decrees against paganism excited no tumults in the empire. Themistius, a pagan philosopher, and one of the most illustrious magistrates of his day, praises the moderation of Jovian in this respect. "You have felt," he says, "that there are some points on which the sovereign cannot dictate to his subjects. Amongst the number, the principal are religion and piety to the gods. Hence, far from using violence, you have passed a law, allowing every one to honour the gods as may seem best to himself. A representative of the Divine being, you imitate his conduct; he hath placed in the heart of man a

---

1 "Nil ille (Constantius) decerpsit sacrorum virginum privilegiis; replevit nobilibus sacerdotia; Romanis cæremoniis non negavit impensas;...cumque alias religiones ipse sequeretur, has servavit imperio; suus enim cuique mos, suus cuique ritus est."—Relatio Symmachi, n. 8.

2 We find some inscriptions of this kind in Beugnot's work, ubi sup. p. 153. Nevertheless, many of those cited by him do not appear conclusive.

natural inclination to religion, but he doth not force him in the choice."[1]

43. The Altar of Victory sometimes replaced in the Senate-house, sometimes removed, according to circumstances.

The successors of Jovian adopted the same principles, and however attached they were to the Christian religion, all their measures against idolatry were confined to gradual restrictions on its exercise, according as circumstances permitted. The principles which guided their policy in this matter may be best learned from their conduct with regard to the altar of Victory, whose history may be said to epitomize the vicissitudes of paganism in the West, after the reign of Constantine.[2] This altar, which had been first removed by Constans, in 357, was restored by Julian the Apostate. Valentinian I., allowed it to remain in deference to the pagan senators, and in accordance with the general liberty which he considered himself bound to give all his subjects in the exercise of their religion.[3] Gratian not only ordered it to be removed in 382, but seized moreover, and confiscated at the same time, the revenues allotted for the support of the pontiff, and the expenses of the ancient worship.[4] The pagan senators, highly indignant at this measure, resolved to address a remonstrance to the emperor, and for that purpose deputed Symmachus, one of the most illustrious members, and generally considered as the first orator of his day. The Christian senators on the other hand, who were the majority of the senate,[5] also presented an address, in which they disclaim

[1] Themistii Or. V. (Inter ejusdem Orat. Paris, 1684, in fol. p. 68, &c.); Labletterie, Hist. de Jovien, p. 102; Beugnot, ubi sup. p. 226, &c.

[2] Hist. des Auteurs Ecclés, by D. Ceillier, vol. vii. p. 337, 339, 340, 522-527; vol. xviii. p. 74-76. Beugnot, Hist. de la Destr. du Pagan. en Occident, vol. i. p. 410, &c.

[3] Fleury, Hist. Eccl. vol. iv. book xvi. n. 29; Tillemont, Hist. des Empereurs, vol. v. p. 8, &c.; Lebeau, Hist. du Bas-Emp. vol. iv. book xvi. n. 19. See above, p. 19, our observations on that subject, note 3.

[4] Fleury, ibid. book xviii. n. 31; Beugnot, Hist. de la Destruction du Pagan. vol. i. p. 353, &c.

[5] St. Ambrose, and after him the majority of modern authors, state expressly that at this period the majority of the senate was Christian. (St. Am-

that of the pagans; they even protested publicly, as well as privately, that they would never assist at the senate, if the emperor assented to the pagan petition. Pope Damasus forwarded the Christian address to St. Ambrose, who presented it to Gratian. It produced on that prince the impression that might naturally be expected; when the pagan senators solicited an audience, the emperor would not receive them.

After the death of Gratian, about two years later, in 384, Symmachus, then prefect of Rome, presented his petition to Valentinian II., brother of Gratian; but this second attempt was

---

brose, Epist. 17, n. 9 et 10 (Operum, tom. ii. p. 825.). D. Cellier, ubi supra, vol. vii. Baronius, Annales, anno 384, n. 9. Fléchier, Hist. de Théodose, book iii. n. 30. Lebeau, Hist. du Bas-Empire, vol. v. book xxii. n. 27.—De la Luzerne, ubi supra, n. 76.) M. Beugnot supposes the contrary (ubi supra) p. 412, &c.), but he appears to have misunderstood the text of St. Ambrose, which he translates incorrectly (p. 426). We shall cite here the words of the holy doctor. After stating that the Christians had reason to think themselves persecuted if they were forced to assist at the deliberations of the senate in a place where they should be present at pagan sacrifices, and should take the oath of allegiance to the emperor before the altar of an idol, St. Ambrose adds, "that the pagans themselves are persuaded the altar of Victory was placed in the senate in order that the oath given before that altar should serve as the prelude for all their deliberations, *though the Christians were then a majority of the senate.*" *Propterea enim interpretantur* (*Gentiles*) *aram locatam, ut ejus sacramento, ut ipsi putant, unusquisque conventus consuleret in medium,* CUM MAJORE JAM CURIA CHRISTIANORUM NUMERO SIT REFERTA (n. 9)...."All the bishops," adds the holy doctor, "would join with me in imploring you not to sanction such an impiety, if the intelligence which attributes this incredible measure to your own council, or to that of the senate, had not been so unexpected. But God forbid that the senate should make such a demand; *it is all the work of a small number of pagans who abuse the name of that assembly. Absit, ut hoc senatus petisse dicatur;* PAUCI GENTILES COMMUNI UTUNTUR NOMINE. In fact, the pagans, ten years before, having made a similar attempt, the holy pope Damasus forwarded to me a petition from the Christian senators, a very great number indeed (*libellum Christiani senatores dederunt,* ET QUIDEM INNUMERI), in which they declare that they had made no such request, and that the demand of the pagans ought not to be granted. They declared, both in public and in private, that if it were granted they would appear no more in the senate" (n. 10). The language of St. Ambrose on this point is confirmed by that of Prudentius, a cotemporary poet, who in his books against Symmachus, states, as a notorious fact, that the senate and people of Rome are Christian, that all Rome is Christian, and, especially in the senate, *that you could scarcely find a few pagans tenaciously attached to the old superstition, and obstinately closing their eyes against the light.*

"Respice ad illustrem, lux est ubi publica, cellam (i. e. *curiam*);
Vix pauca invenies gentilibus obsita nugis
Ingenia, obtritos ægrè retinentia cultus;
Et quibus exactas placeat servare tenebras
Splendentemque die medio non cernere solem."

—Prudentius, contrà Symmach. lib. i. v. 570, &c. Rome, 1789, 4to. vol. ii. p. 749 (Bibliothec. Patr. vol. v. p. 1046).

not more successful than the preceding. Valentinian communicated the petition to St. Ambrose, who refuted it, in two letters addressed to the emperor himself.[1] These letters were read in the council, in presence of counts Banton and Rumoris, both military prefects, who signed the decision pronounced by the emperor against the pagan senators, notwithstanding their well-known bias in favour of the petition. The pagans were not yet discouraged; they made a last attempt under Theodosius, in 388, very probably through the same Symmachus.[2] But the emperor not only rejected the petition, but ordered Symmachus to be seized and carried off a hundred miles from Rome, in punishment of his obstinacy. He was recalled in a short time, that punishment being deemed sufficient to silence thenceforward the principal champion of paganism.

44. *Final blow given to Paganism by Theodosius.*

But, however decided was the firmness of Gratian, Valentinian, and of Theodosius, against the pretensions of the pagan senators, they yet believed themselves bound to tolerate idolatry at least in the West. St. Ambrose manifestly supposes that toleration, in his letter to Valentinian against the petition of Symmachus. "The zeal," he observes, "manifested by the pagans for their false religion, must teach you what you ought to have for the true faith. It is no injury to man to prefer God to him. The pagans are entirely free to hold their own private opinions, for you compel no person to adore what he does not wish. But keep the same liberty for yourself; and who can complain, because that he has not extorted from you a concession, which himself would not grant to you, should you happen to ask it?"[3]

---

[1] St. Ambrose, Epist. 17, 18, Oper. tom. ii.

[2] Fleury, Hist. Ecclés. vol. iv. book xix. n. 15.

[3] Taking occasion from the zeal of the pagans for their false worship, the holy doctor thus addresses Valentinian: "Sed proprio studio (*superstitionis suæ conservandæ*) docere et admonere te debet (*Gentilis*) quemadmodùm veræ fidei studere debeas, quando ille tanto motu veri vana defendit. . . . Nullius injuria est, cui Deus omnipotens antefertur. Habet ille (*Gentilis*) sententiam

It was reserved for Theodosius to give the final blow to idolatry throughout the empire; the universal contempt into which it had fallen enabled that great prince to prohibit it altogether, or at least to enforce more rigorously than had yet been done the edicts promulgated by his predecessors.[1] In the twelfth year of his reign (391), three years after the last petition of the pagan senators, he issued an edict, prohibiting any of his subjects to sacrifice to idols, or to enter any of their temples for the performance of any rite of pagan worship; the transgressors of this law, should they even be magistrates or governors of provinces, were condemned to a fine of fifteen livres of gold.[2] In the following year, another law prohibited the sacrifice of victims under penalty of death, and all other acts of idolatry, under penalty of the confiscation of the place in which they had been committed.[3] The enforcement of those edicts met with

---

suam. *Invitum non cogitis colere quod nolit;* hoc idem vobis liceat, imperator, et unusquisque patienter ferat, si non extorqueat imperatori, quod molestè ferret, si ei extorquere cuperet imperator."—St. Ambrose, Epist. 17, n. 6, 7.; Fleury, Hist. Eccl. vol. iv. book xviii. n. 32; Beugnot, ubi supra, p. 426.

[1] The principal edicts of Theodosius on this point are cited by Fleury, but not in strict chronological order. Hist. Ecclés. vol. iv. book xviii. n. 9, 38; book xix. n. 15, 32, 34, 50. The proper dates may be found from the Commentary of Godefroy Sur le Code Théodosien. See also D. Ceillier, Hist. des Auteurs Eccles. vol. viii. p. 611, &c.; Beugnot, ubi supra, p. 358.

[2] "Nemo se hostiis polluat; nemo insontem victimam cædat; nemo delubra adeat, templa perlustret, et mortali opere formata simulacra suspiciat (i. e. *veneratione prosequatur*); ne divinis atque humanis sanctionibus reus fiat. Judices quoque hanc formam contineant (i. e. *hanc legem in judiciis observent*), ut si quis, profano ritui deditus, templum uspiam, vel in itinere, vel in urbe adoraturus intraverit, quindecim pondo auri ipse protinùs inferre cogatur."—Cod. Theodos. lib. xvi. tit. x. n. 10.

"Nulli sacrificandi tribuatur potestas; nemo templa circumeat (*religioso cultu*); nemo delubra suspiciat; interclusos sibi, nostræ legis obstaculo, profanos aditus recognoscant; adeo ut si quis vel de diis aliquid contra vetitum sacrisque molietur, nullis exuendum se indulgentiis recognoscat. Judex quoque (i. e. *consulares et præsides*, juxta Gothofredi interpretationem), si quis, tempore administrationis suæ, fretus privilegio potestatis, polluta loca sacrilegus temerator intraverit, quindecim auri pondo, officium verò ejus (i. e. *officiales*), nisi collatis viribus obviârit, parem summam ærario nostro inferre cogatur."—Ibid. n. 11.

Supposing with Paucton, that the Roman livre was 10 ounces, 23-24ths of our avoirdupois, and that a marc of gold is worth 33*l.* 12*s.* 6*d.*, the fifteen livres of gold mentioned here would be worth about 690*l.* of our money.—Paucton, Métrologie, p. 291, 305. See, in support of this calculation, No. 2 of the Documentary Evidence, at the end of this volume.

[3] "Quòd si quispiam immolare hostiam sacrificaturus audebit, aut spirantia

slight obstruction in the East, where paganism had very few adherents in the higher classes of society. But the case was different in Italy, and especially at Rome, where a good number of senators, attached to the ancient worship, redoubled their zeal for its interests, in proportion as the numbers of its partizans diminished.[1] Theodosius, accordingly, deemed it prudent not to enforce so vigorously his laws against paganism in Rome, and he connived at their non-observance by individuals, in order not to excite any agitation prejudicial to the public interests. But after the defeat of Eugenius in 394, he summoned to his presence all the senators attached to the pagan religion, who had taken advantage of the usurper's brief triumph to restore the altar of Victory. He addressed them in an animated discourse, exhorting them to renounce their old superstitions, and to embrace the Christian faith. Not one, if we believe Zozimus, would listen to the emperor's exhortations; they answered unanimously that they never could renounce that religion under which Rome had been founded, and had lasted twelve hundred years; adding, that if they consented to such a change, they knew not what would be the consequences. Theodosius then declared to them that the public treasury was so heavily burdened, that it could not supply the expenses of the sacrifices and of the other pagan ceremonies, that the money required would be much better employed in supporting his armies. In vain the senators urged in reply, that the ceremonies could not be duly observed, if the expense was not borne by the state; their remonstrance was ineffectual. The sacrifices ceased, the pagan ceremonies were neglected, the priests and priestesses were dismissed, and all the temples consecrated to idols were

---

exta consulere; ad exemplum, *majestatis reus* (i. e. *velut majestatis reus*), licitâ cunctis accusatione delatus, excipiat sententiam competentem, etiamsi nihil contra salutem principum aut de salute quæsierit. . . . Si quis verò mortali opere facta, et ævum (i. e. *interitum*) passura simulacra imposito thure venerabitur; . . . . is, utpotè violatæ religionis reus, eâ domo seu possessione mulctabitur, in quâ eum gentilitiâ constiterit superstitione famulatum."—Ibid. n. 12.

[1] Beugnot, ubi supra, p. 411, &c. p. 489, &c.

abandoned. The historian Zozimus, who has preserved these details, deplored the catastrophe as the true cause of the ruin of the empire.[1]

45. *Laws of the Church confirmed by the Laws of the Emperors.*

In proportion as Christianity rose and became consolidated on the ruins of paganism, the emperors were not satisfied with merely protecting the public exercise of the Christian worship; they confirmed by their edicts the laws of the Church on faith, morals, and discipline. The general Council of Nice was confirmed by Constantine; the Council of Constantinople, by Theodosius the Great; the Council of Ephesus, by Theodosius the younger; and the Council of Chalcedon, by Marcian.[2] These four councils were placed by Justinian among the laws of the empire.[3] Other edicts confirmed specially particular points of faith, or morals, or discipline; such as the primacy of the Holy See,[4] the sanctification of the Sunday and of fes-

---

[1] Zozimus, Hist. lib. iv. p. 797; lib. v. p. 814. Prudentius, lib. i. contra Symmachum. Tillemont, Hist. des Empereurs, vol. v. p. 387. Fleury, Hist. Ecclés. vol. iv. book xix. n. 50. De Ceillier, Hist. des Aut. Ecclés. vol. viii. p. 630. In vol. ii. of Beugnot's work, already cited, there are interesting details on the decline of Paganism in the West, after the reign of Theodosius. These details are omitted here as not entering into our plan.

[2] Fleury, Hist. Ecclés. vol. iii. book xi. n. 24; vol. iv. book xviii. n. 9; vol. vi. book xxvii. n. 41; book xxviii. n. 34.

[3] "*Sancimus igitur vicem legum obtinere sanctas ecclesiasticas regulas, quæ à sanctis quatuor conciliis expositæ sunt aut firmatæ*, hoc est, in Nicænâ trecentorum decem et octo, et in Constantinopolitanâ sanctorum centum quinquaginta patrum, et in Ephesinâ primâ, in quâ Nestorius est damnatus, et in Chalcedoniâ, in quâ Eutyches cum Nestorio anathematizatus est. Prædictarum enim quatuor synodorum dogmata sicut sanctas Scripturas accipimus, et *regulas sicut leges observamus*."—Justiniani Novella 131, cap. i. (ad calcem Cod. Justin.) See also the Cod. Justin. lib. i. tit. i. n. 7, 8. Fleury, ibid., vol. vii. book xxxiii. n. 5. Lebeau, Hist. du Bas-Empire, vol. ix. book xli. n. 16.

[4] A constitution published in 445, at the request of Pope St. Leo (Epist. 10), by the Emperors Theodosius the younger and Valentinian III. gives us a remarkable testimony of the piety of these two princes, and of the public faith of that age in the primacy of the Pope. "Certum est et nobis et imperio nostro unicum esse præsidium in supernæ divinitatis favore, ad quem promerendum præcipuè Christiana fides et veneranda nobis religio suffragatur. Cùm igitur sedis apostolicæ primatum, sancti Petri meritum, qui princeps est episcopalis coronæ (i. e. *episcopalis dignitatis*), et Romanæ dignitas civitatis, sacræ etiàm synodi (*Nicænæ* scilicet) firmaret auctoritas, ne quid præter auctoritatem sedis istius inlicitum præsumptio attentare nitatur; tunc enim demùm Ecclesiarum pax ubique servabitur, si rectorem suum (agnoscat universitas) *fidelium*... Verùm ne levis saltem inter ecclesias turba nascatur, vel

tivals,[1] the celibacy of the clergy and of nuns,[2] the canons relating to the election of bishops, to residence, and to simony ;[3] and the canonical penalties decreed by the Church against the transgressors of her laws ;[4] so that in the course of time, there was hardly a single important article of faith or of discipline in the Church, which was not confirmed by imperial decrees.[5]

---

in aliquo minui religionis disciplina videatur, hoc perenni sanctione decernimus, ne quid tam episcopis Gallicanis quàm aliarum provinciarum contra consuetudinem veterem liceat, sine viri venerabilis Papæ Urbis æternæ auctoritate tentare ; sed illis omnibusque pro lege sit, quidquid sanxit vel sanxerit apostolicæ sedis auctoritas ; ita ut quisquis episcoporum ad judicium Romani antistitis evocatus venire neglexerit, per moderatorem ejusdem provinciæ adesse cogatur, per omnia servatis quæ divi parentes nostri Romanæ Ecclesiæ detulerunt."—Novell. lib. i. nov. 24 (ad calcem Cod. Theod.) The cause for this constitution is shown by Fleury, Hist. Ecclés. vol. vi. book xxvii. n. 5. Hist. de l'Eglise Gall. vol. ii. an. 445, p. 32, etc.

This constitution was published by Justinian in his Code and his Novellæ. "Sancimus," he says, "secundùm earum (prædictarum) synodorum definitiones, sanctissimum senioris Romæ Papam, primum esse omnium sacerdotum."—Justiniani Nov. 131, cap. ii. Cod. Justin. lib. i. tit. i. n. 8. Fleury, Hist. Ecclés. vol. vii. book xxxiii. n. 5.

[1] "Omnes judices, urbanæque plebes, et cunctarum artium officia, venerabili die solis (i. e. dominico die) quiescant. Ruri tamen positi agrorum culturæ liberè inserviant ; quoniam frequenter evenit ut non aptiùs alio die frumenta sulcis, aut vineæ scrobibus mandentur ; ne occasione momenti pereat commoditas cœlesti provisione concessa."—Cod. Justin. lib. iii. tit. xii. n. 3. Fleury, ibid. vol. iii. book x. n. 27 ; vol. iv. book xvi. n. 1 ; vol. v. book xxiv. n. 30 ; vol. vi. book xxix. n. 30 ; et alibi passim.

[2] A constitution published by Constantine in 320, abolishes the ancient laws which impose penalties on celibacy. "Qui jure veteri *cœlibes* habebantur, imminentibus legum terroribus (i.e. *pœnis*) liberentur ; atque ita vivant ac si numero maritorum, matrimonii fœdere fulcirentur ; sitque omnibus æqua conditio capessendi (i.e. *capiendi ex testamentis*) quod quisque mereatur (i.e. *de successione vel testamento lucrabitur*)."—Cod. Theodos. lib. vi. tit. xvi. n. 1. Fleury, Hist. Eccles. vol. iii. book x. n. 27.

Valentinian I. went farther, and declared virgins and widows exempt from the capitation tax. "In virginitate perpetuâ viventes, et eam viduam de qua ipsa maturitas ætatis pollicetur nulli jam eam esse nupturam, a plebeiæ capitationis injuriâ vindicandas esse decernimus."—Cod. Theod. lib. xiii. tit. x. n. 4. Fleury, ibid. vol. iv. book xvi. n. 1.

[3] Cod. Justin. lib. i. tit. iii. n. 31, 42 et 43. Justin. Novellæ, 123 et 127 (Cod. ad calcem Justin.). The text of these laws is omitted for brevity's sake. A summary of them may be seen in Fleury, ibid. vol. vi. book xxix. n. 30 ; vol. vii. book xxxii. n. 11 ; book xxxiii. n. 5.

[4] Cod. Theodos. lib. xvi. tit. ii. n. 27. Justiniani, Novel. 6, cap. i. § 10. Novella 123, cap. xx.—Ad calcem Cod. Justin.

[5] An analysis of these constitutions may be seen in the authors cited above, note 4, p. 60.

Many of these constitutions contain regulations on purely spiritual concerns, which in no manner belong to the temporal power. Such especially are those cited in the preceding note, whose provisions are sanctioned by canonical penalties. It is certain, however, that the emperors, in publishing this kind

46. *Temporal Penalties against the Transgressors of those Laws.*

The better to insure the observance of their edicts in favour of religion, the Christian emperors frequently added the sanction of temporal penalties against the transgressors of those laws. This was the origin of the temporal penalties with which the public excesses of heresy and impiety were long punished in all Christian states, and which have been so often stigmatized in the harshest terms by the philosophic spirit of these latter times. The importance of the subject compels us to enter into the details on the principal provisions of the Roman law regarding Jews, heretics, and apostates. But before we explain this ancient jurisprudence, so revolting to the customs and to the prejudices of our times, we must transport ourselves in spirit to the age and circumstances in which it was established, and form a true estimate of the principles by which governments were then guided in their relations with the Church.

47. *Principles of those Ancient Governments in their relations with the Church.*

Since total indifference on this subject has become the prevalent and almost universal opinion at present, it is very difficult, and even impossible, for some minds to judge impartially the conduct of a government which should regard such indifference as the greatest of evils, and the greatest of crimes. If we believe a host of modern philosophers and politicians, religion is, as it were, an alien in society; liberty of worship is for nations, as well as for individuals, a natural and inalienable right; the sole object of government is the temporal

---

of constitution, merely sanctioned the existing discipline; otherwise they would have clearly contradicted the principles professed by themselves on the independence of the Church in spiritual matters, as we shall soon see (infra, n. 51). In support of these views the reader may consult Godefroy, Commentary on the Code Theodos., and the work of Pithou brothers, Observationes ad Codicem et Novellas Justiniani, Paris, 1689, fol. These authors point out in detail the canons of councils, and the other monuments of ecclesiastical discipline, from which the emperors took their constitutions on spiritual matters. See also, on this point, Bossuet, Defens. Declarat. lib. iv. cap. v. Fleury, Hist. Eccles. vol. xix. Discourse vii. n. 4. Pierre Lemerre, Mémoires du Clergé, vol. vii. p. 397. Domat, Traité des Lois, ch. 10, n. 11. Idem, Droit Public, book i. tit. xix. Pey, De l'Autorité des deux Puissances, vol. iv. ch. iii. § 2.

happiness of the subject; or if it meddle at all with religion, it must be solely to secure for all the most complete liberty to say and do in that matter whatever they please.[1] Notions very different, and even diametrically opposed to those of modern philosophy, were held on this point, even by pagan legislators.[2] Religion they believed was the prime good, as it was the prime necessity of man and of society, and crimes of impiety were all opposed to the welfare and the tranquillity of states as they were injurious to the majesty of God; whence they inferred that the first duty of a sovereign was to repress, by severe penalties, these as well as other excesses contrary to public order.

As we have already remarked,[3] these principles derived additional force from the deplorable condition of the empire under the first Christian emperors. No society was ever a prey to more powerful causes of dissolution; and consequently, never had it been more necessary to maintain the influence of religion, which could bring to its aid such powerful resources against all the destructive principles to which it was exposed.

48. *The Edicts of the Christian Emperors in favour of Religion were founded on those Principles.*

These were the real motives of the decrees published by the Christian emperor in favour of religion. They are set forth by Constantine, with equal rigour and precision, in a letter written in 314, to Ablavius, governor of Africa, on the subject of the council of Arles, which was then assembled against the Donatists. "As I know," he says, "that you, like myself, adore and serve the Supreme God, I will declare to you that I do not think it lawful for us to tolerate those divisions and disputes,

---

[1] Belisaire, ch. xiv. Émile, vol. iii. p. 184, &c. Raynal, Hist. Phil. et Polit. &c. vol. x. p. 14, et alibi passim. The true principles on this matter are explained, and solidly established, in the Censures, published by the Theological Faculty of Paris, against these three works. See especially the conclusion of the censure of Bélisaire, and the Mandement, published in 1767, against the same work, by M. de Beaumont, Archbishop of Paris.

[2] See details given on this question in the first article of our Introduction, n. 2, &c.

[3] Supra, n. 29, &c.

which may draw down the anger of God, not only on my subjects, but also on myself, whom his divine goodness hath entrusted with the care and direction of all things on the earth. But I have every reason to expect most confidently from his goodness, all sorts of prosperity, when I shall see all my subjects honouring the Catholic religion as they ought, and offering their homage to God, in brotherly union and perfect concord."[1] Constantine's successors frequently refer to similar motives in their edicts against the heretics. This is particularly observable in a decree of Theodosius the younger against the Donatists and Manicheans, and in another of Justinian against all heretics, without distinction. These emperors assign as the motives of their edicts, "that whoever violates the religion established by God, sins against public order;" and "that the crimes which attack the Divine majesty, are infinitely more grievous than those which attack the majesty of the princes of the earth."[2]

49. *These Principles admitted by the most celebrated Modern Writers.*

It must be remarked that these ancient maxims, on the necessity of repressing by temporal penalties the excesses of impiety, are equally admitted by the most celebrated modern authors, even Protestants themselves. Grotius, Domat, and Montesquieu, prove as an incontestable maxim, that the civil power is bound by all means to repress crimes contrary to religion, because they are of such a nature, that they disturb both public order and the safety of individuals.[3] "Most important

[1] Constantini Epistol. ad Ablavium. (Labbe, Concilia, tom. i. p. 1422.) Fleury, Hist. Ecclés. vol. iii. book x. n. 14.

[2] Cod. Justin. lib. i. tit. v. n. 5, 19. We shall cite lower down the text of these laws (n. 63). Fuller extracts from the imperial constitutions on this point may be seen in the Droit Public, by Domat, book i. tit. xix.

[3] Grotius, De Jure Belli et Pacis, lib. ii. cap. xx. n. 51. Domat, Droit Public, book i. tit. xix. Montesquieu, Esprit des Lois, book xii. ch. iv. v.; xxv. ch. x. On this subject the following works may also be consulted with advantage;—Pey, De l'Autorité des Deux Puissances, vol. iv. part iv. ch. i. ii. De Maistre, Lettres à un Gentilhomme Russe, sur l'Inquisition Espagnole. Frayssinous, Conférences sur les Principes Religieux, fondements de la Morale et de la Société; sur la Tolérance; et sur l'Union reciproque de la Religion et de la Société, vols. i. and iii. of the octavo edition.

maxims," as Montesquieu observes; "we ought to be cautious in prosecuting magic and heresy. I do not say that heresy ought not to be punished; I say that we ought to be cautious in punishing it.[1] This is a fundamental principle of political laws, with regard to religion, when it is in the power of a state to receive or to reject a new religion (that is, as he explains himself, a false religion), it ought not to be received; it ought not to be established; if it be established, it ought to be tolerated."[2]

To this testimony may be added the judgment of a modern author, whose very enlarged views on government no one can contest. Comte de Maistre has the following reflections on the general law which formerly condemned obstinate heretics to be burned to death. "Without going back to the Roman laws which sanctioned this penalty, all nations have awarded it to those great crimes which violate the most sacred laws. In all Europe, sacrilege, parricide, and especially treason, were punished with death by fire; and as the latter was divided according to the principles of criminal law into two kinds, high treason against man and high treason against God, all crimes, or at least all enormous crimes against religion, were regarded as high treason against God, and of course should be punished as severely as treason against man. Hence the universal custom of burning heresiarchs and obstinate heretics. I think myself bound to add, that the heresiarch, the obstinate heretic, and the propagator of heresy, ought undoubtedly to be ranked among the greatest criminals. What leads us astray on this matter is, that we cannot prevent ourselves from judging of it according to the indifference of our own days on the subject of religion; whilst we should rather take as our standard that ancient zeal, which people may if they please call fanaticism, as a word makes no difference in the thing. The modern sophist dissertating at his ease in his cabinet, is not ruffled in the least by

[1] Montesquieu, Esprit des Lois, book xii. ch. v.

[2] Ibid. book xxv. ch. x. For the explanation of this passage, see La Défense de l'Esprit des Lois, part ii. art. "Tolérance."

the consideration that the arguments of Luther were the cause of the thirty years' war. But the ancient lawgivers, who knew well what dire evils could flow from those fatal doctrines, punished very justly with death, a crime capable of shaking society to its foundations and of deluging it in blood."[1]

50. *Application of these Principles often difficult.*

From these observations it clearly follows, that according to ancient principles, as acknowledged by the most famous modern authorities, the moderate use of temporal penalties against heresy and other impious crimes was essential alike to the good of religion and to the repose of society. Doubtless, on this, as on so many other matters, the application of the principle presents frequently great difficulties, because it depends on so many qualifying circumstances. The prince may err on this point by too much leniency as well as by too great rigour, but the difficulty of applying a well-established principle can never destroy its truth.[2]

But in fine, however difficult the application may be in many cases, the teaching of the Church, and the practice of the first Christian emperors, of those at least whose wisdom and piety have been praised by the Church, have not left us without some leading principles to be followed on this point.

51. *Rule* 1.—*The Church alone has the Power to regulate Spiritual Matters.*

The first and the most important is, that the Church alone has the right to regulate matters in the spiritual order, such as dogmas, morals, ecclesiastical discipline, and generally whatever regards the government of the faithful in matters pertaining to religion and to eternal salvation.[3] The duty of the temporal

---

1 De Maistre, Lettres sur l'Inquisition Espagnole, Letter ii. p. 53, &c.

2 These observations may serve as a corrective for those of Tillemont, on this subject, when speaking of the conduct of Valentinian I., who has been accused, not without reason, of a kind of indifference about religion. In his attempt to justify in some way Valentinian's conduct, Tillemont confuses the true principles on this matter. Tillemont, Hist. des Emp. vol. v. p. 10. See the passages cited above, note, art. 15.

3 For the development of this principle, see the work of the Abbé Pey,

power in those matters is confined strictly to protecting the Church, that is, to support her decisions, without even in any manner anticipating, extending, or modifying them. This principle, which has been so often inculcated by councils and by holy doctors, as part of the divine constitution of the Church, was also recognized by the Christian emperors, who repeatedly proclaimed it in their edicts,[1] and always repeated it in practice, unless when they were led astray by the suggestions of heresy or by perfidious councils. The language of Justinian on this point, in one of his Novellæ, is the most precise and formal that can be desired. "God," he says, "hath entrusted to man the priesthood and the empire; the priesthood to administer things divine, the empire to preside over things human; both proceed from the same principle." Whence the emperor concludes, that he does not presume of himself to regulate ecclesiastical affairs, but simply to sanction the rules of the Church and the canons of councils.[2]

52. *In what sense Princes are called Bishops exterior.*

By this principle, the title of "exterior" bishop, which the first Christian emperor sometimes assumed in presence of the bishops, must be explained. "God," he declared to them, "has appointed you bishops 'interior,' and me bishop 'exterior,'"[3] meaning thereby that, as the duty of the bishops was to teach and to conduct the people in the spiritual order, so it was the duty of princes to support their decrees and canons, by

De l'Autorité des deux Puissances, vol. ii. part iii. ch. i. § 1; vol. iii. ch. iv. § 5, 6; ch. v. § 1; vol. iv. ch. iii.

[1] The texts of many of those edicts are cited by the Abbé Pey, ubi supra, vol. ii. p. 43.

[2] "Maxima quidem in hominibus sunt dona Dei, à supernâ collata clementiâ, sacerdotium et imperium; et illud quidem divinis ministrans; hoc autem humanis præsidens, ac diligentiam exhibens. Ex uno eodemque principio utraque procedentia humanam exornant vitam. . . . Bene autem omnia geruntur et competenter, si rei principium fiat decens et amabile Deo. Hoc autem futurum esse credimus, si sacrarum regularum observatio custodiatur, quam justi, et laudandi, et adorandi inspectores et ministri Dei verbi tradiderunt apostoli, et sancti patres custodierunt et explanaverunt."—Justiniani Novella 6, Præf. (ad calcem Cod. Justin.).

[3] De Vitâ Constantini, lib. iv. cap. xxiv.

insuring for them the proper respect. This is the true meaning of that expression of Constantine, which princes have sometimes abused for the oppression of the Church, but which, rightly understood, and explained by Constantine's own conduct, conveys a most energetic admonition on the independence of the Church in the spiritual order, and on the protection which they are bound to give to her decrees and canons. "It is true," observes one of our most illustrious prelates,[1] "that the pious and zealous prince is called an exterior bishop, and the protector of the canons; expressions which we shall ever respect with joy, in the modest sense in which they were understood by the ancients. But the 'exterior' bishop ought never to usurp the functions of the 'interior' bishop. He stands, sword in hand, at the door of the sanctuary; but he takes care not to enter it. If he protects, he also obeys: he protects the canons, but he makes none. The two functions to which he must confine himself are: first, to defend the Church in full liberty against all her enemies from without, that she may be able within, without any molestation, to pronounce, to decide, to approve, to reform, to humble, in one word, every height that exalts itself against the knowledge of God; the second is, to support those decisions when made, without ever presuming, on any pretext whatsoever, to interpret them. This protection of the canons must, therefore, be directed solely against the enemies of the Church, that is, against the innovators, against the untractable and seducing spirits, against all those who spurn correction. God forbid that the protector should ever govern or not await in all things the judgment of the Church. He waits, he listens with docility, he believes without hesitation: he is obedient himself, and makes others obedient as much by the influence of his example, as by the power which he holds in his hands. In fine, a protector of liberty must not diminish it. His patronage would no longer be a protection, but a tyranny in disguise, if

[1] Discours prononcé au Sacre de l'Electeur de Cologne, first point, vol. xvii. of Fenelon's works, p. 147.

he attempt to prescribe to the Church instead of obeying her prescriptions."

53. *Rule 2.—Never to extort by Violence a Profession of the Faith.*

From the doctrine and practice of the Church in the primitive ages, it also may be inferred that the application of the temporal power ought never to proceed so far as to extort by violence a profession of faith, or a recantation of error. "It is not lawful for Christians," observes St. John Chrysostom, "to combat error by violence and compulsion, but solely by reason and mildness. For this reason, none of the Christian emperors has promulgated against paganism edicts similar to those which the pagan emperors had enforced against the Christians."[1] The sole object even of the severest edicts ought to be to punish the external acts of impiety; to prevent as much as possible the external profession of false religions; to deprive its adherents of certain honours and advantages dependent on the disposition of the laws, in order to induce heretics thereby to enter into themselves, and to dispose them to make sober reflections which might lead to a renunciation of their errors.

54. *Rule 3.—Never to inflict the Penalty of Death merely for Errors in Faith.*

It would be still more opposed to the spirit of religion to inflict on the followers of a false religion the penalty of death for their errors alone. This point is laid down by St. Chrysostom as an incontestable principle, in his commentary on that passage in St. Matthew, where the father of the family orders his servants not to pluck up the bad grain, lest they might pluck up the good grain with it. "God," he says, "speaks thus to his servants, in order to prevent wars and murders; for heretics ought not to be put to death: if they were, this earth would be a scene of never-ending war; besides, there are many who, by abandoning their heresy, may cease to be bad, and may become

[1] St. John Chrysos. Lib. in S. Babylam, contra Gentiles, n. 3. (Oper. vol. ii. p. 540.)

the good grain. God, therefore, does not prohibit us to repress heretics, to close their mouths, to deprive them of liberty of speech, to dissolve their assemblies, to break off all communication with them; he only prohibits us to shed their blood."[1] It is true that, in certain cases, the imperial edicts decreed that penalty against heretics, pagans, and Jews; but they do not inflict it for the errors alone; it is always for some other crime opposed to public tranquillity and ordinarily punished with death by the Roman laws; for example, the obstinacy of heretics in remaining in a place which had been forbidden to them or in preaching their doctrine notwithstanding repeated orders to the contrary.[2]

55. *Rule 4.—To oppose vigorously Heresy at its birth.*

In general, the prince was to use greater rigour against a rising heresy, than against one which he finds already established in his states, because it is both more easy and more safe to crush the evil in its birth, than to repress it when it has already made great progress. St. Jerome establishes the truth of this maxim in a few decisive words in his commentary on the epistle of St. Paul to the Galatians. "The spark," he says, "must be extinguished as soon as it is perceived, the leaven must be separated from the mass, the rotten flesh must be cut

---

[1] Idem. Homil. 46 in Mattheum, n. 1, 2. (Oper. vol. vii. p. 482.)

[2] Cardinal Bellarmin (Controvers. de Laïcis, cap. xxi. prob. 2, 4, Operum, vol. ii.) supposes "that the emperors Valentinian III. and Marcian enacted the penalty of death generally against all heretics who endeavoured to propagate their errors." This assertion is in many points incorrect. First, the law cited by Bellarmin was enacted, not by Marcian, but by the emperors Valentinian II. and Theodosius the Great (Cod. Theodos. lib. xvi. tit. v. n. 18). Secondly, that law does not order all heretics indiscriminately to be put to death, but the Manicheans only, who should refuse, notwithstanding express orders, to depart from Rome. Another law of Marcian against the Eutycheans, which we shall cite in another place (n. 64), does not enact the penalty of death against all heretics, but only against those who, notwithstanding repeated prohibitions, should persist in preaching their heresy, and in sowing in the state the seeds of revolt and insubordination. Hence Jacques Godefroy, in his valuable commentary on the Theodosian Code, carefully observes, that the Christian emperors never enacted the penalty of death against heretics "on account of their religion alone." Jac. Godefroy, Comment. in Cod. Theodos. lib. xvi. tit. v. n. 9, 34, et alibi passim. See also Bingham, Origines sive Antiq. Eccles. tom. vii. lib. xvi. cap. ii. § 4.

away, the diseased sheep cast out of the fold, lest the whole house be burned, the entire mass be corrupted, the whole body be putrified, and all the flock be destroyed. Arius was only a feeble spark at Alexandria; but because he was not promptly extinguished, his flame spread desolation through the whole earth."[1] It was on this principle that St. Leo the Great, who was raised to the popedom some years before the death of St. Jerome, was not content with using exhortations and ecclesiastical penalties, to bring back to the Church the Manicheans, who were discovered in Rome in his time, but moreover delivered up the most obstinate to the secular judges, lest, to use his own words, "the contagion of heresy should insensibly contaminate the rest of the flock."[2]

56. *The severe Provisions of the Roman Law on this point not approved by the Church.*

However valuable these observations may be to justify, in the opinion of impartial men, the moderate application of the temporal power in matters of religion, we are far from approving indiscriminately all the provisions of the Roman law on this point: we even acknowledge that it seems difficult to defend some of them. But to answer the objections which may be grounded on them, it must be observed, in the first place, that the Church has never approved them. She approved, it is true, in a general way, the zeal of the Christian emperors for the preservation of the faith, and the repression of heresy; but there is no evidence that she ever approved the severe provisions in

---

[1] "Scintilla, statim ut apparuerit, extinguenda est; et fermentum à massæ viciniâ semovendum; secandæ putridæ carnes; et scabiosum animal à caulis ovium repellendum; ne tota domus, massa, corpus et pecora, ardeat, corrumpatur, putrescat, intereat. Arius una scintilla fuit; sed quia non statim oppressa est, totum orbem ejus flammâ populata est."—Sancti Hieron. Comment. in Epist. ad Gal., cap. v. (Oper. tom. iv. parte i. p. 291.)

[2] "Aliquanti verò (*Manichæi*) qui ita se demerserunt (*in impietatis voraginem*), ut nullo his auxilii possit remedio subveniri, subditi legibus, secundum Christianorum principum constituta, ne sanctum gregem suâ contagione polluerent, per publicos judices perpetuo sunt exilio relegati."—S. Leonis, Epist. 8 (alias 2). Fleury, Hist. Eccles. vol. vi. book xxvi. n. 57.

some of their constitutions, and especially the penalty of death, enacted by them in certain cases, against the public acts of impiety. On the contrary, it is certain that in the person of her bishops and holy doctors, she invariably advised princes and magistrates to use great moderation in enforcing the laws enacted against heretics, and that she strongly denounced the conduct of her ministers whenever they rigorously pressed the execution of those laws.[1]

57. *Penal Laws generally severe in those Ages.*

In the second place, it must be observed that, in order to appreciate justly some provisions of the Roman law, which appear too severe to persons living in our days, we must go back in spirit to the times when they were established ; that is, to an epoch when penal laws were generally much more severe than they became after the mild spirit of Christianity had exercised its influence on public and private morals.[2] Is it then surprising that the Roman law should infuse into its provisions against heresy and against other impious crimes, some of that rigour which in those days characterized its whole penal system ? Was it not even natural that the Christian emperors should apply to crimes against the Christian religion, the penalties which had hitherto been invariably awarded against public acts of impiety ? "In all ages," observes Comte de Maistre, on this subject, "there are some general ideas predominant among men, and which are never called into question. They must be laid to the charge of all mankind, or of none." [3]

58. *The Severity of those Laws modified in their execution.*

Moreover the severity of the imperial constitutions on this

[1] Thomassin, Traité des Edits, vol. i. ch. xxx. &c. Observe in particular the details relating to the conduct of the holy doctors with regard to the heretics of their time ; for example, of St. Augustine to the Donatists, of St. Ambrose and St. Martin to the Priscillianists, &c.

[2] Ryan's Benefits of Christianity, ch. v. § 5. De Vouglans, Lois Crimin. de France, book ii. tit. iii. iv. et alibi passim.

[3] Lettres sur l'Inquisition Espagnole, Letter ii. p. 53.

matter was very much alleviated in practice, by the spirit of moderation and mildness in which they were generally enforced. We have already seen with what prudent circumspection Constantine and his successors had slowly progressed in their edicts against idolatry; at first, allowing to the pagans the free exercise of their worship, then restricting it by degrees, according as circumstances permitted, and not striking the final blow until it could be given without shocking public opinion, or causing any disorder in the state. The same prudence is generally observable in the conduct of the Christian emperors against the heretics.[1] Even a passing inspection of the succession and objects of the imperial edicts on this point proves that they varied in severity according to the different circumstances of time and place: and the moderation generally observed in the execution proves clearly that the object of the prince was much less to punish the heretics than to prevent the propagation of their doctrine, and to compel them, by salutary measures, to enter into themselves, and to confess their errors. This is the reflection of Sozomen, when speaking of the laws published against the heretics by Theodosius the Great. "This prince," he says, "promulgated severe laws against them, but he did not enforce them. His object was not to punish the heretics, but to bring them back to the true faith, by fear of chastisements; and he gave great praise to those who were converted of their own accord."[2] This moderation, recommended by the bishops themselves[3] to the emperors, deserves more especial notice, from the fact that the heretics were emboldened by it to commit more excesses against the Catholics. St. Augustine clearly supposes this fact in one of his letters;[4]

---

[1] Traité des Edits, vol. i. ch. xxxii. et seq. Bossuet, Politique Sacrée, book vii. art. iii. prop. 10.

[2] Sozomen, Hist. Eccles. lib. vii. cap. xii. Tillemont, Hist. des Empereurs, vol. v. p. 399.

[3] Note 1, art. 56.

[4] St. Augustin, Epist. 100, ad Donatum, n. 2. Epist. 133, ad Marcellinum, n. 1. (Oper. vol. ii.) The first of these letters is quoted by Fleury, Hist. Eccles. vol. v. book xxii. n. 18.

and it was frequently the cause why the emperors were obliged to revive the former laws which their leniency had allowed to remain a dead letter.[1] It was in particular the motive which obliged Honorius to revive the laws enacted by his predecessors against the different sects hostile to the Catholic Church. "Lest," he says, "the Donatists and the other heretical sects, as well as Jews and Pagans, should imagine that the former laws against them are abrogated, we order all our judges to enforce them rigorously, and to execute, without hesitation, whatever has been enacted against these different sects." [2]

After these observations, which we have deemed necessary to answer some objections on this delicate subject, we shall now state briefly the principal provisions of the Roman law on Jews, heretics, apostates, and persons guilty of sacrilege; provisions entitled to more attention as being on this, not less than on many other points, the model of the laws of all Christian states during the middle ages.[3]

I.—Laws against the Jews.

59. *Severity of those Laws.*

The first law of Constantine against the Jews was caused by the violence and public excesses of which many of them had been guilty. About ten years after his conversion, a certain number of Jews having presumed to insult the Christians publicly, so far as to cast stones at them, the emperor enacted, by public edict, that if any Jews should in future be guilty of a similar excess, he should be burned to death with all his accomplices. By the same law, he prohibits all persons from embracing Ju-

---

[1] Thomassin, Traité des Edits, vol. i. ch. xxxiii. n. 1, et alibi passim.

[2] "Ne Donatistæ, vel cæterorum vanitas hæreticorum, aliorumque error quibus catholicæ communionis cultus non potest persuaderi, Judæi atque Gentiles (quos vulgo Paganos appellant), arbitrentur legum antè adversùm se datarum constituta tepuisse; noverint judices universi præceptis eorum fideli devotione parendum, et inter præcipua, quidquid adversùs eos decrevimus, non ambigant exequendum."—Cod. Theod. lib. xvi. tit. v. n. 46.

[3] See the authors cited above, note 1, p. 48. Also Thomassin, Traité des Edits. vol. i. ch. xxx. &c.; vol. ii. ch. ix.

daism, which he describes as a sect of turbulent men, fired with a violent and inextinguishable hatred to Christianity.[1] In the same spirit Constantine forbad the Jews to circumcise their slaves who were not of their religion; the transgressors of this law were condemned to forfeit their slaves.[2]

This unhappy nation was not treated more leniently by the successors of Constantine; they were forbidden, under very heavy penalties to intermarry with Christians, to buy or circumcise slaves of a different nation or religion, and especially Christian slaves. A law of the emperor Constantius enacted, that in the last case the purchaser should be punished in the forfeiture not only of his slave, but of all his property; and that if he presumed to circumcise his slaves he should be even put to death.[3] By another law of the same emperor, a Jew marrying a Christian was condemned to death;[4] but the severity of this law was modified by Theodosius, who ordered that such marriages should

---

[1] "Judæis et majoribus eorum et patriarchis voluimus intimari, quòd si qui, post hanc legem, aliquem qui eorum feralem fugerit sectam, et ad Dei cultum respexerit, saxis aut alio furoris genere (quod nunc fieri cognovimus) ausus fuerit ademptare (i. e. impetere), mox flammis dedendus est, et cum omnibus suis participibus concremandus. Si quis verò ex populo ad eorum nefariam sectam accesserit, et conciliabulis eorum se applicaverit, cum ipsis meritas pœnas (*arbitrio nempe judicis*) sustinebit."—Cod. Theod., lib. xvi. tit. viii. n. 1. Fleury, Hist. Eccles. vol. iii. book x. n. 20.

[2] "Si quis Judæorum Christianum mancipium, vel cujuslibet alterius sectæ, mercatus circumciderit, minimè in servitute retineat circumcisum; sed libertatis privilegiis, qui hoc sustinuerit, potiatur."—Cod. Theod. lib. xvi. tit. ix. n. 1. Fleury, Hist. Eccl. book xi. n. 59.

[3] "Si aliquis Judæorum mancipium sectæ alterius seu nationis crediderit comparandum, mancipium fisco protinùs vindicetur. Si verò emptum circumciderit, non solum mancipii damno mulctetur, verùm etiam capitali sententiâ prematur. Quòd si venerandæ fidei conscia mancipia Judæus mercari non dubitet, omnia quæ apud eum reperiuntur protinùs auferantur; nec interponatur quicquam moræ, quin eorum hominum qui Christiani sunt possessione careant."—Cod. Theod. lib. xvi. tit. ix. n. 2.

This law was renewed in 384, by the emperors Valentinian II., Theodosius, and Arcadius, in these terms: "Ne quis omninò Judæorum Christianum comparet servum.... Quòd si factum publica indago compererit, et servi abstrahi debent, et tales domini congruæ atque aptæ facinori pœnæ subjaceant; addito eo, ut si qui apud Judæos adhuc Christiani servi... reperti fuerint, soluto per Christianos competenti pretio, ab indignâ servitute redimantur."—Ibid. lib. iii. tit. i. n. 5.

[4] "Illud in reliquum observari (placet), ne Christianas mulieres (Judæi) suis jungant flagitiis; vel, si hoc fecerint, capitali periculo subjugentur."—Ibid. lib. xvi. tit. viii. n. 6.

be punished only as adultery, and that all persons were at liberty to denounce them to the tribunals.[1] Several subsequent enactments disqualify the Jews for any civil office, prohibit them to give evidence against Christians, to build any new synagogues, or to pervert any Christian.[2] This last point was prohibited by Theodosius the younger, under penalty of the forfeiture of all the transgressor's property and perpetual banishment.[3]

60. *Motives of this Severity.*

Some of these enactments certainly appear very severe; but it must be remembered, in the first place, that the Jews often gave occasion to them by repeated excesses, opposed both to public tranquillity, and to the honour of the Christian religion. Their inveterate hatred against Christianity manifested itself on all occasions; sometimes by acts of violence and cruelty against the Christians, sometimes by the persecutions which they excited the pagans to inflict upon them, and not unfrequently by seditions and revolts which they raised in different parts of the empire.[4]

In the second place, the Jews had the less reason to complain of the edicts promulgated against them, as the emperors had at first treated them with great indulgence. Notwithstanding the excesses of which they had been guilty under the reign of Constantine, he had granted to all their chiefs, and to all the ministers of the synagogues, an exemption from all the personal or civil duties which could interfere with the free discharge of

---

[1] "Ne quis Christianam mulierem in matrimonium Judæus accipiat, neque Judæam Christianus conjugio sortiatur; nam si quis aliquid hujusmodi admiserit, adulterii vicem commissi hujus crimen obtinebit; libertate in accusandum publicis quoque vocibus relaxatâ."—Cod. Theod. lib. iii. tit. vii. n. 2.

[2] A collection of these edicts may be seen in the Cod. Justin., lib. i. tit. v. n. 21; tit. ix. n. 16, etc. Fleury, Hist. Eccl. vol. vi. book xxvi. n. 41.

[3] "Judæi et bonorum proscriptione, et perpetuo exilio damnabuntur, si nostræ fidei hominem circumcidisse eos, vel circumcidendum mandasse constiterit."—Cod. Justin. lib. i. tit. ix. n. 16.

[4] Fleury, Hist. Eccl. vol. iii. book xii. n. 28; book xiii. n. 15; vol. v. book xxiii. n. 25.

their functions.[1] This exemption they, in fact, continued to enjoy until the reign of Valentinian II., who revoked it in 383, not deeming it proper that the heads of the Jewish religion should retain a privilege which had been taken away from the ministers of the Christian religion by Valentinian I.[2] Finally, it must also be remembered, that while the Christian emperors were publishing those severe laws against the Jews, they at the same time strongly condemned and severely punished the arbitrary violence sometimes inflicted on them by the indiscreet zeal of their enemies. Numerous imperial edicts provide against the recurrence of such violence, and threaten to inflict severe penalties on the Christians who should presume, under pretence of religion, to throw down or plunder the synagogues, or in any manner to prevent the religious assemblies of the Jews.[3]

II.—Laws against Heretics and Apostates.

61. *Laws of Constantine.*

The same considerations which obliged the emperors to enact those severe laws against the Jews frequently obliged them to enact similar laws against the heretics. The first of those were promulgated about the year 316 against the Donatists, who were then afflicting the Church of Africa with all sorts of violence and pillage. Having tried, without effect, all gentle and conciliatory measures to bring them back to the Catholic faith, the emperor, at last, enacted a law depriving them of their churches, and confiscating their property, with the places in

---

[1] "Hieros, et archisynagogos, et patres synagogarum, et cæteros qui synagogis deserviunt, ab omni corporali munere liberos esse præcipimus."—Cod. Theod. lib. xvi. tit. viii. n. 4. Fleury, Hist. Eccl. vol. iii. book xi. n. 46.

[2] "Jussio quâ sibi Judææ legis homines blandiuntur, per quam eis curialium munerum datur immunitas, rescindatur; cùm ne clericis quidem liberum sit, priùs se divinis ministeriis mancipare, quàm patriæ debita universa persolvant."—Ibid. lib. xii. tit. i. n. 99. See also lib. xvi. tit. ii. n. 21.

[3] "Judæorum sectam nullâ lege prohibitam satis constat. Unde graviter commovemur, interdictos quibusdam locis eorum fuisse conventus. Sublimis igitur magnitudo tua, hâc jussione susceptâ, nimietatem eorum qui sub Christianæ religionis nomine inlicita quæque præsumunt, et destruere synagogas atque expoliare conantur, congruâ severitate cohibebit."—Cod. Theod. lib. xvi. tit. viii. n. 9. See also n. 21, 25, &c.

which they used to assemble; he also banished some of those who appeared to be the most obstinate and seditious.[1]

Some years later, that is, about 325, Arius having been condemned in the Council of Nice, Constantine published several edicts branding him as infamous, condemning him and the bishops of his party to exile, ordering all his writings to be burned, compelling his partizans to deliver them up, and threatening with capital punishment all who refused. All private persons, moreover, who persisted in this error, were condemned to pay, in addition to their capitation tax, the tax of ten other persons.[2] In the following year, a new edict restricted to the Catholics the immunities conferred on the clergy, and ordered that heretics and schismatics, instead of enjoying that immunity, should be subjected to heavier burdens than others.[3] From this law the emperor excepts the Novatians, whom, it would appear, he did not regard at the time as being absolutely condemned;[4] but, becoming afterwards better informed about that sect, he prohibited them, as well as the Valentinians, Marcionites, and all others, to hold any meetings, public or private; ordered that their churches should be given to the Catholics, that their other places of assembly should be confiscated, and that all their books should be diligently searched for and destroyed.[5]

---

[1] St. Augustin, Epist. 88, ad Januar. n. 3. Epist. 93, ad Vincentium (Oper. tom. ii. pp. 214, 236). Idem, contra Litt. Petil. lib. ii. n. 205 (Oper. tom. ix. p. 278). St. Optatus, De Schism. Donat. lib. ii. p. 47 (Paris edit. 1679, fol. Biblioth. Patr. tom. iv. p. 349, col. 1). Fleury, Hist. Eccl. vol. iii. book x. n. 19. Thomassin, Traité des Édits, vol. i. ch. xi.

[2] Socrates, Hist. Eccles. lib. i. cap. ix. p. 62, &c. Sozomen, Hist. Eccles. lib. i. cap. xx. etc. Fleury, ibid. book xi. n. 24.

[3] "Privilegia quæ contemplatione (seu *intuitu*) religionis indulta sunt, catholicæ tantùm legis observatoribus prodesse oportet. Hæreticos autem atque schismaticos, non tantùm ab his privilegiis alienos esse volumus, sed etiam diversis muneribus constringi et subjici."—Cod. Theod. lib. xvi. tit. v. n. 1. Fleury, ibid. book xi. n. 31.

[4] Cod. Theod. ibid. n. 2. Fleury, ibid. Thomassin, Traité des Édits, vol. i. ch. xxx. n. 67, &c.

[5] Eusebius, Vita Const. lib. iii. cap. lxiii.—lxvi. Fleury, ibid. n. 46. Lebeau, Hist. du Bas-Empire, vol. i. book v. n. 56.

62. *Laws of Theodosius the Great. Origin of the Inquisition.*

All these laws of Constantine were subsequently renewed by his successors, and applied with more or less rigour to the different heretical sects. By an edict published in January, 381, Theodosius the Great deprived heretics of all their churches, and annuls all edicts to the contrary into which preceding emperors had been surprised.[1] In this edict he condemns by name the Photinians, Arians, and Eunomians; he recommends the Nicene creed, and prohibits all assemblies of heretics within the walls of cities; adding, moreover, that if they attempted to cause any disturbance, they should be even banished from the cities. In the same year, he published a much more severe law against the Manicheans; he declared them infamous; deprived them totally of the power of making a will, or even of succeeding to their paternal or maternal property; and ordered all such property to be confiscated, except in the case of children, who were qualified, if they embraced a more holy religion, to inherit their father's or mother's property.[2] Another law of Theodosius treats still more rigorously those Manicheans who disguised themselves under the names of Encratides, Saccophori, and Hydroparastates; he subjected them to capital

[1] "Nullus hæreticis mysteriorum locus, nulla ad exercendam animi obstinatioris dementiam pateat occasio. Sciant omnes, etiamsi quid speciali quolibet rescripto, per fraudem elicito, ab hujusmodi hominum genere impetratum est, non valere. . . . Ab omnium submoti ecclesiarum limine penitùs arceantur, cùm omnes hæreticos illicitas agere intra oppida congregationes vetemus; ac si quid eruptio factiosa tentaverit, ab ipsis etiam urbium mœnibus, exterminato furore, propelli jubemus."—Cod. Theod. lib. xvi. tit. v. n. 6. Fleury, Hist. Eccl. vol. iv. book xviii. n. 9.

[2] "Si qui, Manichæus Manichæave, in quamlibet personam condito testamento, vel cujuslibet liberalitatis atque specie donationis, transmisit proprias facultates; vel quisquam ex his aditæ per quamlibet successionis formam collatione ditatus est; quoniam iisdem, sub perpetuâ justæ infamiæ notâ, testandi ac vivendi jure Romano omnem protinùs eripimus facultatem, neque eos aut relinquendæ aut capiendæ alicujus hæreditatis habere sinimus potestatem; totum fisci nostris viribus societur. . . . His tantùm filiis paternorum vel maternorum bonorum successio deferatur, qui, licet ex Manichæis orti, sensu tamen et affectu propriæ salutis admoniti, ab ejusdem vitæ professionisque collegiis, purâ semet dediti religione, dimoverint."—Cod. Theod. lib. xvi. tit. v. n. 7. Fleury, ubi supra.

punishment.[1] To insure the execution of this law, the emperor orders the prefect of the prætorium to appoint inquisitors, charged to discover heretics, and to inform against them. This is the first time that the name of an inquisitor against heretics occurs; but the inquisition itself was of older standing; for we have already seen Constantine institute one precisely similar against the Arians and the other heretics of his time.[2] These severe measures were provoked by the abominable doctrines of the Manicheans, which had drawn down on them, from the very origin of their sect, the severity of even the pagan emperors.[3] It is, in truth, well known that the errors of this sect attacked not only the dogmas of Christianity, but the foundations of morality itself, and tended to increase every day in society the greatest excesses of corruption and of depravity.[4]

Many other laws of Theodosius prohibit heretics to hold assemblies either in town or country, or to consecrate bishops.[5] The houses in which they assembled he ordered to be confiscated;

---

[1] "Quos Encratitas prodigali appellatione cognominant, cum Saccophoris sive Hydroparastatis, . . . summo supplicio, et inexpiabili pœnâ jubemus affligi. . . . Sublimitas itaque tua det Inquisitores, aperiat forum, indices denuntiatoresque, sine invidiâ delationis (i. e. *absque metu delationis*), accipiat; nemo præscriptione communi exordium accusationis hujus infringat."—Cod. Theod. lib. xvi. tit. v. n. 9. Fleury, ubi supra.

[2] See notes 2 and 5, p. 78.

[3] See on this subject, Fleury, Hist. Eccl. vol. ii. book viii. n. 25. Thomassin, Traité des Edits, &c. vol. i. ch. iii. n. 12.

[4] St. Augustin, De Moribus Manichæorum, passim. (Operum, tom. i.) Tillemont, Mémoires pour l'Hist. Ecclés. vol. xiii. art. 15, &c. Bossuet, Hist. des Variations, book xi. n. 7, &c.

[5] "Vitiorum institutio (seu *schola*), Deo atque hominibus exosa, Eunomiana scilicet, Ariana, Macedoniana, Apollinariana, cæterarumque sectarum quas veræ religionis fides sincera condemnat, neque publicis, neque privatis aditionibus (i. e. *conventibus*), intra urbium atque agrorum ac villarum loca, aut colligendarum congregationum, aut constituendarum ecclesiarum copiam præsumat; . . . neque ullas creandorum sacerdotum usurpet atque habeat ordinationes. Eædem quoque domus, seu in urbibus, seu in agris, in quibus passim turbæ professorum (i. e. *hæresim profitentium*) ac ministrorum talium colligentur, fisci nostri dominio jurique subdantur; ita ut hi qui vel doctrinam vel mysteria conventionum talium exercere consueverunt, . . . expellantur à cœtibus, et ad proprias unde oriundi sunt terras redire jubeantur. Quod si negligentiùs ea quæ serenitas nostra constituit impleantur, officia (i. e. *officiales*) provincialium judicum, et principales urbium, in quibus coitio vetitæ congregationis reperta monstrabitur, sententiæ damnationique subdantur."—Cod. Theod. lib. xvi. tit. v. n. 12. Fleury, ibid. vol. iv. book xviii. n. 27; book xix. n. 34.

their doctors, or public ministers, to be banished, or sent off to the place of their birth ; and he threatened to punish all magistrates who should neglect to enforce the observance of this law. In fine, an edict, published in June, 392, subjects to a fine of ten pounds of gold (£460) each, all heretics receiving or conferring ordination, and orders the place in which the ceremony took place to be confiscated ; but if the proprietor was not privy to this sacrilegious ceremony, the tenant alone was punished, by scourging or banishment if he were a slave, and by a fine of ten pounds of gold if he were a freeman.[1]

63. *Laws of Honorius and Theodosius the Younger. Heretics disqualified for all Civil Offices.*

Several edicts of the emperors Honorius and Theodosius the Younger declare heretics in general, and especially the Donatists and Manicheans, disqualified for all civil offices and rights, and subject to all the penalties enacted by preceding laws.[2] One of the most remarkable was published by Theodosius the Younger, about the year 407. "We punish," he declares, "the Manicheans and Donatists of either sex as their impiety deserves. Hence it is our will that they shall not enjoy the rights which custom and the laws confer on other men. We will that they be treated as public criminals, and that all their property be confiscated ; because *whoever violates the religion established by God, sins against public order.* Moreover, all persons convicted of those heresies are hereby deprived of the power of giving, of buying, of selling, and of making any contract. We will also, that their last will shall be null and void, in whatever form they

[1] "In hæreticis erroribus, quoscumque constiterit vel ordinasse clericos, vel suscepisse officium clericorum, *denis libris auri* viritim mulctandos esse censemus ; locum sanè in quo vetita tentantur, si conniventia domini patuerit, fisci nostri viribus aggregari. Quòd si id possessorem ignorasse constiterit, conductorem ejus fundi, si ingenuus est *decem auri libras* fisco nostro inferre præcipimus ; si servili fæce descendens, cæsus fustibus, deportatione damnabitur." —Cod. Theod. lib. xvi. tit. v. n. 21. These ten pounds are worth about 460*l.* of our money, supposing Paucton's principles for calculating the value of ancient coins to be correct : see n. 2, p. 48.

[2] Cod. Theod. lib. xvi. tit. v. n. 42, &c. Fleury, Hist. Eccl. vol. v. book xxii. n. 8, 15, 18, 26, 27 ; book xxiv. n. 54.

may have been drawn up, either as testamentary or by codicil, by letter or otherwise; and that their children shall not succeed as their heirs, unless they have renounced the errors of their parents." [1] Another law, by the same emperor, orders the Manicheans to be banished from the cities and punished with death, as being guilty of the worst excesses of depravity.[2]

64. *Laws of Marcian confirming and renewing the preceding.*

The Emperor Marcian, successor of Theodosius the Younger, was equally severe against the Eutychians, after their condemnation by the Council of Chalcedon.[3] His first edict against them, published in February, 452, forbids them to hold public disputations on religion, under penalty of deposition, if they were clerics; of the forfeiture of all their offices, if magistrates; and of banishment from Constantinople, and punishment according to their deserts, if they were private citizens. This first edict not being sufficient to quell some restless and turbulent spirits, the same prince published, some months later, another far more severe, ordering the Eutychians not to ordain bishops, priests, or other clerics, under penalty of banishment and confiscation against those who had received and conferred ordination.[4] The

---

[1] "Manichæos, seu Manichæas, vel Donatistas, meritâ severitate persequimur. Huic ergo hominum generi nihil ex moribus, nihil ex legibus sit commune cum cæteris. Ac primum quidem volumus esse publicum crimen; *quia quod in religionem divinam committitur, in omnium fertur injuriam;* quos bonorum etiam omnium publicatione persequimur. . . . Præterea, non donandi, non emendi, non vendendi, non postremò contrahendi, cuiquam convicto relinquimus facultatem. . . . Ergo et suprema illius scriptura irrita sit, sive testamento, sive codicillo, sive epistolâ, sive quolibet alio genere reliquerit voluntatem, qui Manichæus fuisse convincitur; sed nec filios hæredes eis existere aut adire permittimus, nisi à paternâ pravitate discesserint."—Cod. Justin. lib. i. tit. v. n. 4.

[2] "Ariani, Macedoniani, . . . *et qui ad imam usque scelerum nequitiam pervenerunt Manichæi,* nusquàm in Romanum locum conveniendi morandique habeant facultatem; Manichæis etiam de civitatibus pellendis, et ultimo supplicio tradendis; quoniam his nihil relinquendum loci est, in quo ipsis etiam elementis fiat injuria."—Cod. Justin. lib. i. tit. v. n. 5. Fleury, Hist. Eccl. vol. v. book xxiv. n. 54.

[3] Fleury, Hist. Eccl. vol. vi. book xxviii. n. 34.

[4] "Nulli Eutychiani vel Apollinaristæ publicè vel privatim convocandi cœtus, vel circulos contrahendi, et de errore hæretico disputandi, ac perversitatem facinorosi dogmatis asserendi tribuatur facultas. Nulli etiam contra venerabilem Chalcedonensem synodum liceat aliquid vel dictare, vel scribere,

same edict prohibited their assemblies, and the building of monasteries, under penalty of confiscation of the places, and of various punishments for the proprietors or tenants. The Eutychians were, moreover, incapacitated by this edict from receiving anything by will, from filling any public office, or remaining at Constantinople, or in any metropolitan city; the clergy and monks of the monastery of Eutyches were to be banished from the territory of the empire; their heretical books should be burned; the preachers of their doctrine punished capitally as disturbers of the state; and their disciples condemned to a fine of ten pounds of gold (£460).

65. *Similar Laws of Justinian in his Codex and Novellæ.*

Not satisfied with inserting these different contributions in his code, Justinian promulgated others to interpret and confirm the former. We have already noticed that of March, 541, which registers the four first general councils amongst the laws of the empire.[1] As a natural consequence of this principle, several other constitutions enact severe penalties on all heretics, without exception, as transgressors of the laws of the state. We shall notice particularly a law of Justinian, expressed in the following terms: "We declare for ever infamous, and deprived of their rights, and condemned to exile, all heretics of either sex, whatever be their name; their property shall be confiscated without hope of restoration, or of being transmitted to their children by hereditary succession, because crimes which attack the majesty of God are infinitely more grievous than those which attack the majesty of earthly princes. With regard to those who are strongly suspected of heresy, if, after having

---

vel edere atque emittere, aut aliorum dicta vel scripta super eâdem re proferre. Nemo hujusmodi habere libros, et sacrilega scriptorum audeat monumenta servare. Quòd si qui in his criminibus fuerint deprehensi, perpetuâ deportatione damnentur. Eos verò qui, discendi studio, adierint de infaustâ hæresi disputantes, decem librorum auri, quæ fisco nostro inferendæ sunt, jubemus subire dispendium. Ultimo etiam supplicio coerceantur, qui illicita docere tentaverint."—Cod. Justin. lib. i. tit. v. n. 8. Concil. Chalcedon. part. iii. n. 12 (Labbe, Concil. tom. iv. p. 868).

[1] See above, n. 3, p. 60.

been ordered by the Church, they do not demonstrate their innocence by suitable testimony, they also shall be declared infamous, and condemned to exile."[1] In consequence of those different laws, Justinian enacts, in one of his Novellæ, "that henceforward all governors of provinces, before they enter office, shall take an oath of fidelity to the emperor, in which they must formally declare that they are in communion with the Catholic Church, that they will never do anything against her, and that they will, with all their might, repress all the assaults of her enemies."[2] In consequence of those different laws, he gave the patriarch of Alexandria, about the year 540, full authority over the dukes and tribunes of Egypt, to deprive all heretics of such offices, and to substitute Catholics in their place.[3]

66. *Special Enactments against Sacrilege and Apostasy.*

The provisions of the Roman law were equally severe against sacrilege and apostasy. A detailed account of the various laws on this point is unnecessary, as they are merely the application of the penalties enacted against heresy.[4] We shall only remark, that the laws were much more severe against those who used

---

[1] "Omnes hæreticos utriusque sexûs, quocumque nomine censeantur, perpetuâ damnamus infamiâ, diffidamus atque bannimus: censentes ut omnia bona talium confiscentur, nec ad eos ulteriùs revertantur: ita quod filii eorum ad successionem eorum pervenire non possint; *cùm longè gravius sit æternam quàm temporalem offendere majestatem.* Qui autem inventi fuerint solâ suspicione notabiles, nisi, ad mandatum Ecclesiæ, juxta considerationem suspicionis, qualitatemque personæ, propriam innocentiam congruâ purgatione monstraverint, tanquam infames et banniti ab omnibus habeantur."—Codex Justin. lib. i. tit. v. n. 19. For the meaning of the words "diffidamus" and "bannimus," see Ducange's Glossary.

[2] "Juro ego, per Deum omnipotentem, et Filium ejus unigenitum Dominum nostrum Jesum Christum, et Spiritum Sanctum, et per sanctam gloriosam Dei genitricem, et semper virginem Mariam, etc. . . . Communicator sum sanctissimæ Dei Catholicæ et Apostolicæ Ecclesiæ; et nullo modo vel tempore adversabor ei; nec alium quemcumque permitto [ei adversari], quantùm possibilitatem habeo; etc."—Justiniani Nov. viii. (ad calcem Cod. Justin.).

[3] "Accepit [patriarcha Alexandrinus] ab imperatore potestatem super ordinationem ducum et tribunorum, ut removeret hæreticos, et pro eis orthodoxos ordinaret."—Liberati Breviarium, cap. xxiii. (Labbe, Conciliorum, tom. v. p. 777). Fleury, Hist. Eccl. vol. vii. book xxxiii. n. 1.

[4] Cod. Justin. lib. i. tit. vii. Digest. lib. xlviii. tit. xiii. Fleury, Hist. Eccl. vol. iv. book xviii. n. 27; book xix. n. 32.

violence or seduction to draw the faithful into apostasy. A constitution published in 435, by the emperors Theodosius the Younger and Valentinian III., makes that crime a capital offence.[1]

67. *The Roman Law on these points adopted by all the Christian States of Europe during the Middle Ages.*

All these details may serve as a corrective for the assertions of many modern writers; namely, "that Christian princes, and especially the Church, have made it a constant rule to use nothing but the arms of persuasion against errors which use only the arms of argument; that the Priscillianists were the first sect against which the secular arm had used the sword; that from the middle of the fifth century there is no record of imperial laws against heretics in the West."[2] On the contrary, from the facts and testimonies already cited, it follows manifestly, first, that from the conversion of Constantine, temporal penalties were inflicted on all heretics without exception; these penalties being more severe against seditious and turbulent heretics, and especially against the Manicheans and Donatists; secondly, that from the middle of the fifth century, and for a long time after, the imperial laws against heretics were in force in the West as much as in the East. In truth, most of the laws which we have cited were embodied in the Theodosian code, published in 438 by Theodosius the Younger; and it is certain, and generally admitted, that this code, which had been in force in all the provinces of the Western empire, where the barbarians established themselves after the middle of the fifth century, continued for a long time after that revolution to be observed at least by the ancient inhabitants. The new sovereigns

---

[3] "Eum qui servum sive ingenuum invitum, seu suasione plecteudâ [i. e. *culpabili et puniendâ*] ex cultu Christianæ religionis in nefandam sectam ritumve transduxerit, cum dispendio fortunarum capite puniendum esse censemus."—Cod. Justin. lib. i. tit. vii. n. 5.

[4] Bergier, Dict. Theol. art. Hérétique (edit. 1816), pp. 14, 15. Duvoisin, Essai sur la Tolérance, p. 357. Affre, Essai Historique, pp. 370, 372.

generally allowed the conquered people to retain these laws;[1] and it was with that view that Alaric II., king of the Visigoths, promulgated in 506, with the consent of the lords and bishops of his states, an "Abridgment of the Roman Laws," which was almost immediately adopted by most of the new monarchies, and which retains all the provisions of the Theodosian code against heretics.[2] These provisions were subsequently extended to all the subjects of the new monarchies, without distinction of Roman or barbarian. In all these states heresy was generally regarded as a crime, not less opposed to public order and to the good of society than to the honour of God and of religion. With such severity was it punished, that during many centuries its partisans or abettors dared not appear; and hardly a single example of it appears in the kingdoms of France, Spain, or England, from the conversion of these kingdoms to the Catholic faith until the close of the ninth century.[3] An obstinate heretic was immediately prosecuted by the two powers, and cut off from society as a rotten member; exile or perpetual imprisonment was the ordinary penalty of his impiety. It was thus that a Monothelite heretic was treated in France in the year 639; and some other innovators who endeavoured to pervert the people.[4]

---

[1] Thomassin, Traité des Édits, vol. i. ch. xxx. n. 2, 3. Jacques Godefroy, Prolegom. ad Cod. Theod. cap. iii. Terrasson, Hist. de la Jurisprudence Rom. part iii. § 8; part iv. § 1. Canciani, Barbarorum Leges antiquæ, tom. i. Præf. p. 13; tom. iv. Præf. in codicem Legis Romanæ, et in Wisigothorum leges. Heineccius, De Origine et Progressu Juris Germ. lib. ii. cap. i. Savigny, Hist. du Droit Rom. vol. i. ch. iii. et seq.

[2] It seems at first sight astonishing that Alaric II., who, together with all his nation, professed the Arian heresy, should have authorized as law those imperial constitutions, which prohibited, under severe penalties, Arianism as well as all other heresies. Of the fact, however, there is no doubt; for it is clearly proved by the express text of the Roman laws, published by Alaric.—Cod. Theod. lib. xvi. tit. v. n. 6, 8, 11, &c. This conduct will appear less surprising, if we reflect that, in publishing those laws, the prince did not intend to impose it on the Visigoths, but simply to recognise it as the Roman law, by which the ancient inhabitants of his conquered provinces were governed.

[3] Thomassin, Traité des Édits, vol. i. ch. lvii. n. 2; vol. ii. ch. xiii. n. 1, &c. Lingard, Antiquities of the Anglo-Saxon Church, ch. vi. p. 226. Daniel, Hist. de France, vol. iv. p. 153.

[4] Fleury, Hist. Eccl. vol. viii. book xxxvii. n. 40. Hist. de l'Église Gallicane, vol. iii. ann. 639.

The same means had been employed in England, about the close of the fifth century, to eradicate the remnant of Pelagianism.[1] Precautions not less rigid were adopted in Spain, as appears from the third canon of the sixth Council of Toledo, which binds the sovereign, among other conditions, to swear, in the ceremony of his election, that he will not tolerate heretics in his states.[2] "The law of the Visigoths," which was then in force in Spain, descends to very remarkable details on this point, "and expressly prohibits all persons from advancing anything against the Catholic faith, and the definitions of the ancient fathers;" all who violated this law, whether laity or clergy, were deprived for ever of their rank, their dignities, and their property; and if they obstinately refused to be converted, they were moreover condemned to perpetual exile.[3]

The legislation of all the Christian states of Europe during the middle ages presents similar provisions, as may be seen both from the texts of the laws then in force, and from the testimony of many councils, both general and particular, whose decrees on

---

[1] Bede, Hist. Eccles. lib. i. cap. xxi. Fleury, ibid. vol. vi. book xxvii. n. 7.

[2] "Quisquis succedentium temporum regni sortitus fuerit apicem, non antè conscendat regiam sedem, quàm, *inter reliqua conditionum sacramenta,* pollicitus fuerit, non permissurum eos [*subditos*] violare fidem [*Catholicam*]."—Concilium Toletanum vi. cap. 3 (Labbe, Conciliorum, tom. v.).

Instead of these words, *inter reliqua conditionum sacramenta, pollicitus fuerit,* another reading is, *inter reliquas conditiones, sacramento pollicitus fuerit,* which is the same in sense. This decree of the 6th Council of Toledo was renewed absolutely in the 8th, held in 653, which gives at greater length the conditions which the king at his coronation swore to observe.—Concil. Tolet. viii. can. 10.

[3] "Nullus itaque cujuslibet gentis aut generis homo ...., contra sacram et singulariter unam Catholicæ veritatis fidem, quascumque noxias disputationes, eamdem fidem impugnans, palàm pertinaciter aut constanter vel proferat, vel proferre silenter [i. e. *clam*] attentet ..... Nullus antiquorum Patrum impugnationibus suis, sacras definitiones irrumpat ...... Nam quæcumque persona in cunctis istis vetitis extiterit deprehensa, ex quâcumque religionis potestate vel ordine fuerit, amisso loci et dignitatis ordine, perpetuo reatu erit obnoxius, rerum etiam cunctarum amissione mulctatus. Si verò ex laicis extiterit, honore solutus et loco, omni rerum erit possessione nudatus; ita ut omnis transgressor sanctionis istius, aut æterno exilio mancipatus intereat, aut divinâ miseratione respèctus, à prævaricatione convertatur et vivat."—Lex Wisigothorum, lib. xii. tit. ii. n. 2. The Law of the Visigoths will be found in the fourth volume of Dom. Bouquet's Collection of the Historians of France; and in the 4th volume of Canciani, Barbarorum Leges Antiquæ. Venice, 5 vols. folio.

this point were published in presence of, and with the express or tacit sanction of the king.[1] The decrees of the third and fourth Council of Lateran, which we shall soon have occasion to cite, are conclusive on this point, and dispense us from the easy task of multiplying other authorities.[2]

68. *The Patronage of Princes insufficient for the Protection of the Church.—Necessity of the Divine assistance.*

In concluding this statement of the Roman laws in favour of the Christian religion, after the conversion of Constantine, it may not be useless to observe, that the protection generally given to the Church from that time by Christian princes, did not render unnecessary that Divine assistance, which alone had sustained her during three centuries of persecution. It were an error to attribute to the protection of princes, and to their edicts in favour of the Christian religion, the preservation of the Church after the conversion of Constantine. That protection was doubtless frequently useful to the Church, by supporting her against the attacks of heresy, schism, and impiety; and sometimes by even favouring her establishment among pagan nations. It is certain, nevertheless, that she had often to endure many persecutions from heretical princes, or partisans of heresy, who, in their blind zeal, turned against the Church herself the laws originally enacted for her defence. This was particularly the case with the heresies of Arius, Eutyches, and of many others, which caused such great disorder in the empire. Even Constantine himself, who had at first declared so sternly against Arianism, after its condemnation by the Council of Nice, suffered himself to be deceived so far by the Arians towards the close of his life, that he consented even to the condemnation and

[1] Decretal. lib. v. tit. vii. The analysis of this title of the Decretals may be seen in the Lois Ecclésiastiques de France, by De Héricourt, p. 148. For the development of the discipline of the middle ages on this point, see Alph. de Castro, De Justâ Hæreticorum Punitione, lib. ii. cap. v.—xiii.; Van-Espen, Jus Ecclesiast. Univ. tom. ii. part. iii. tit. iv. cap. ii. n. 41, &c.; Bossuet, Defensio Declar. lib. iv. cap. iii.; De Héricourt, Lois Ecclés. de France, part i. ch. xxiv.

[2] See subsequently, part ii. ch. ii. art. i. n. 87, &c.

exile of St. Athanasius.[1] His son Constantius, being involved in the same party, openly protected it by his edicts, and his persecution of the Catholics.[2] The Henoticon of Zeno in favour of the Eutychians;[3] the Ecthesis of Heraclius, and the Type of Constantius in favour of Monothelism;[4] the edict of Justinian in favour of the sect called the Incorruptibles, an offshoot of the Eutychians,[5] and many other facts, equally notorious in history, show what reason the Church frequently had to complain, even of those princes from whom she should naturally expect most protection.

To the persecution by heresy and schism was added, still more frequently, that by vice and scandals, which at different times introduced deplorable relaxations in morals and discipline, so that after, as well as before the conversion of Constantine, the Church was continually exposed to attacks which would inevitably have destroyed her, had she not been supported by the Divine assistance. Begotten in miracles, her life is a continued miracle; God alone gave her the victory over all the dangers which the world continually conjures up against her. "Scarcely does she commence," as Bossuet observes, "to breathe the peace given to her by Constantine, when Arius, that unhappy priest, causes her greater troubles than she had ever suffered. Constantius, son of Constantine, being deceived by the Arians, whose doctrines he sanctions, persecutes the Catholics throughout the whole earth: he was a new sort of persecutor of Christianity, and the more formidable, as he made war on Jesus Christ in the name of Jesus Christ himself. To fill up the measure of her afflictions, the Church, while in this divided state, fell under the hands of Julian the Apostate, who tried every means of destroying Christianity, and found

---

1 Fleury, Hist. Ecclés. vol. iii. book xi. n. 55, &c.
2 Fleury, ibid. books xiii. and xiv.
3 Fleury, ibid. vol. vi. book xxix. n. 53, &c.
4 Fleury, ibid. vol. viii. book xxxviii. n. 21 and 45, &c.
5 Fleury, ibid. vol. vii. book xxxiv. n. 8 and 9.

no plan more efficacious than to foment the dissensions with which it was torn. After him comes a Valens, as attached to the Arians as Constantius, and more violent. Other emperors protected other heresies with similar fury. By all this experience the Church learns that she has as much to suffer under the Christian emperors as under the Pagan emperors; and that her martyrs must bleed in defence, not only of the whole body of her doctrine, but also of each article in particular. There is in truth hardly one of them which has not been attacked by her children. Thousands of sects, and thousands of heresies rising from her bosom, have stood up against her. But if she has seen them rise, as Jesus Christ predicted, she has seen all of them fall, as he promised, though they were often supported by kings and emperors. Her true children, as St. Paul says, have been made known by their trials; truth only becomes more strong under persecution, and the Church has remained immovable.[1] This is manifest from the whole succession of her history. The world has threatened—truth remained firm; it has used wiles and flatteries—truth has remained upright. Heretics have caused confusion — truth has remained pure. Schisms have rent the body of the Church — the truth has remained entire. Many have been seduced; the weak have been troubled; even the strong have been shaken: an Osius, an Origen, a Tertullian, many others who seemed to be pillars of the Church, have with great scandal fallen — the truth has ever remained unshaken. What then is more sovereign, more independent than truth, which stands ever immovable, in spite of threats and of caresses; in spite of favours and of proscriptions; in spite of schisms and of heresies; in spite of all temptations and of all scandals; finally, in the midst of the defection of her faithless children, and of the fatal fall even of those who seemed to be her pillars?"[2]

---

[1] Bossuet, Hist. Univ. part ii. ch. xxi. vol. xxxv. of his works, p. 312.

[2] Bossuet, Sermon sur la Divin. de la Relig. 1st point, vol. xi. of his works, p. 278. See in support of these reflections the preface and conclusion of the

SECTION III.

Property and riches of the clergy during the primitive ages of the Church, especially under the Christian emperors. Holy use which they made of them.[1]

69. *Principles of the Primitive Church on the Renunciation of the Goods of the World.*

One should be utterly ignorant of the history of the first age of the Church not to know the unreserved detachment with which she generally inspired her children for riches and temporal honours.[2] Disciples of a God who in poverty and humiliation constantly preached, both by word and example, the renunciation of honours, of riches, and of pleasures, the primitive Christians were generally opposed to luxury and splendour; they esteemed no goods but virtue and piety; they placed all their perfection and security in living unknown to the world, and in not knowing it; still more they regarded the honours and the goods of this life as obstacles to that spirit of abnegation which they openly professed.[3]

Nevertheless, however careful the Church was to inspire all the faithful with the spirit of detachment, it is certain that she

---

Hist. de l'Église, by Lhomond; Feller, Catéch. Philos. vol. iii. n. 139; Massillon, Sermon sur la Vérité de la Rel. 1st point (1st Thursday in Lent).

[1] Thomassin, Ancienne et Nouvelle Discipline, vol. iii. book i. ch. i. ii. iii. xii. De Héricourt, ibid. part iii. ch. i. Natal Alexander, Hist. Eccl. sæc. iv. cap. v. art. xi.; sæc. v. cap. vi. art. v.; sæc. vi. cap. vi. art. vi. De Héricourt, Lois Ecclés. de France; Preliminary Dissertation on the 2nd and 4th parts. Muzzarelli, Dissertation sur les Richesses du Clergé. Idem, Dissert. de Origine et Usu Oblationum, Primitiarum, et Decimarum, 12mo. Dissert. sur la Grandeur Temporelle de l'Église in vol. i. of the Recueil de Pièces d'Histoire et de Littérature (by the Abbé Granet and Père Desmolets), Paris, 1731, 4 vols. 12mo. Bingham, Origines et Antiquit. Ecclesiasticæ, tom. ii. lib. v. cap. iv. Mamachi, Del Diritto libero della Chiesa di acquistare e di possedere Beni Temporali, si mobili che stabili, 5 vols. 8vo. Rome, 1769-70. Fleury, Mœurs des Chrétiens, n. 14 and 28. Petit-Pied, Traité des Droits et des Prérogatives des Ecclés. part i. Bellarmin, De Membris Ecclesiæ, lib. i. cap. xxvi. Bonnaud, Déclamation pour l'Église Gallicane, contre l'Invasion des Biens Ecclés. Paris, 1792, 8vo. p. 17—55. Carrière, De Justitiâ et Jure, vol. i. p. 137, &c.

[2] Duguet, Conférences Ecclés. 30th Dissertation. Fleury, Mœurs des Chrétiens, n. 11.

[3] Matt. v. 3; vi. 34; xix. 21; et alibi passim. Acts ii. 44, 45; iv. 34, 35. Tertullian, De Pallio, cap. v. Saint Cyprian, Epist. 1, ad Donatum (ed. Rigault, p. 6). Origen, contra Celsum, lib. viii. n. 75 (Operum, vol. i. p. 798).

never regarded the external and actual renunciation of the goods of this world as absolutely necessary for perfection even in her sacred ministers. To be convinced of this, we need only inspect those sacred books which from her first origin the Church gave to the faithful as the infallible rule of their faith and of their conduct. Far from representing riches as incompatible in themselves with the character and the perfection of sacred ministers, all the books of the Old Testament clearly suppose that character and perfection to be compatible with the greatest riches. Melchisedec, Abraham, Isaac, Jacob, Moses, and many other holy personages, who are proposed to us by the Scripture as models of consummate perfection, were both kings and priests, princes and prophets. Moreover, this union of riches and of the sacred character of the priesthood, was, as we have already observed, normal and permanent by the institution of God himself.[1]

70. *Practice conformable to those principles.*

The practice of the primitive ages proves clearly that the Church never regarded the possession of riches as incompatible with the character and perfection of ministers of the new law. One of the most affecting spectacles presented to us in the history of the infant Church is the first Christians selling their property, and laying the price at the feet of the apostles, to be disposed of at their discretion;[2] so that from that early period we find the first of all the churches, — one governed by the apostles themselves, and which should serve as a model for all others, possessing a considerable fund of wealth, intended for the support of the pastors and of the faithful.

In the churches, where this community of property was not established, the same principles of religion and of natural equity, which had secured so respectable an independence for the ministers of religion, even among pagan nations, did not fail to procure speedily similar advantages for the ministers of

---

[1] Supra, n. 3, p. 7.

[2] Acts ii. 44, 45; iv. 34, &c.

the Christian religion. This is the true origin of the tithes and first-fruits, and offerings and ordinary and extraordinary collections, which we find established in the days of the apostles, and which enabled many particular churches to provide abundant relief, not only for the poor of their own territory, but also for other churches which happened to be in greater necessities.[1] St. Justin and Tertullian mention the collections made regularly every Sunday in the assemblies of the faithful, and from which the pagans conceived the most exalted idea of the charity of the Christians.[2] The Apostolic Canons distinguish two sorts of collections as being then in use; the first, of corn, grapes, oil, and incense, was made at the altar; the other, consisting of milk, herbs, and animals, was made at the bishop's house, to be distributed partly to the deacons and the other clergy.[3] St. Irenæus, St. Cyprian, and all other ecclesiastics of this period, insist strongly on the obligation of making these offerings to the Church, from a motive not only of charity and compassion for the poor, but of justice to the sacred ministers who devoted themselves to the service of the holy altars.[8]

---

1 Acts xi. 29; 1 Cor. xvi. 1; 2 Cor. viii. ix.; Gal. vi. 6, et alibi passim.

2 St. Justin, Apologia, 1 (alias 2), towards the end. Tertullian, Apologet. cap. 39. We deem it unnecessary to cite the texts of these authors, and of others whom we have cited on this subject. A collection of these texts may be seen in the works of Thomassin and of Muzzarelli, cited above, note 1, p. 91.

3 Can. Apost. 3, 4, 5.

4 St. Irenæus, adversus Hæreses, lib. iv. cap. xxxiv. St. Cyprian, Epis. lib. i. ep. ix. Idem, de Unitate Ecclesiæ, versus finem. Constitut. Apostol. lib. ii. cap. xxv. xxxv.; lib. vii. cap. xxix. Origen, Homil. in Numeros (Operum, tom. ii.). Fleury, Hist. Ecclés. vol. ii. book ix. n. 19.

To understand the doctrine of the holy fathers on this point, it is important to remark, that the precept of the ancient law, which ordered tithes and first-fruits to be paid to the priests, belonged partly to the natural and partly to the positive law; to the natural law, inasmuch as it ordered the people to provide for the support of the ministers of religion; but to the positive law, inasmuch as it determined the mode of fulfilling that natural obligation. Under this latter respect alone the precept of the old law is abrogated in the new, but under the first respect it still is obligatory on Christians. Hence it happens that the holy fathers sometimes speak of the precept of paying tithes, as abolished under the new law, and sometimes as being still in force. St. Epiphanius (Hæres. viii. cap. vi.) and St. Chrysostom (Homil. lxxiv. in Matthæum) speak in the first sense; Origen (Hom. xi. in Num.) and some others speak in the second, which is supposed by St. Chrysostom also in many of his writings (Orat. v. adv. Jud.).

71. *Riches of some Churches during the persecutions.*

By means of these different contributions every church had a fund more or less wealthy for the relief of the poor, the support of the clergy, and the other expenses of the divine worship. The history of the persecution excited in Africa by Maximian Hercules in 303, may give us some idea of the wealth of the churches at that period. From the acts of that persecution we learn that Paul, bishop of Cirta, in Numidia, surrendered into the hands of the magistrates of that city two chalices of gold, six chalices of silver, six silver burettes, a cucumellum of silver,[1] seven lamps of the same metal, and many other valuable articles destined for the service of the Church.[2]

Besides the voluntary offerings of silver, of provisions, and other movable effects, the Church possessed moreover, even in the times of persecution, immovable property. The pagan emperors generally tolerated, and sometimes even protected this species of property against the injustice and violence of those who endeavoured to usurp it.[3] The last persecutions having frequently occasioned

The reader may consult on this point St. Thomas. Qq. quest. 86, art. 4; quest. 87, art. 1; Thomassin, Ancienne et Nouvelle Discipline, vol. iii. book i. chap. ix. n. 13; Van Espen, Jus Eccles. Universum, part. ii. tit. xxxiii, n. 1, &c. &c.; Bellarmin, Controver. de Clericis, cap. xxv.; Muzzarelli, Dissert. de Origine et Usu Oblationum, Primitiarum, et Decimarum; Cotelier, note on the Apostolical Constitutions, lib. ii. cap. xxxv.; Père De la Rue, a Benedictine, in his edition of Origen (ubi supra), transcribes that note of Cotelier, of which we give the substance. It may serve as a corrective for some exaggerated assertions of the Abbé Bonnaud on this point, in his work entitled, Réclamation pour l'Église Gallicane contre l'Invasion des Biens Ecclésiastiques et l'Abolition de la Dîme (Paris, 8vo.) pp. 100—163.

[1] The word "cucumellum," which occurs in this text, signifies properly a vase in the form of a cucumber, or *coloquinte* (cucumis colocynthis), which may be properly enough called an ewer or basin. It is well known, in truth, that the ewer was then used in the ceremonies of the Christian worship. It is surprising that Fleury, in this particular, translates the word a "chaudron," or kettle.

[2] The Acta, from which we learn these details, are given in the Annal. Baronii (anno 303, n. 6, &c. &c.), and in vol. ii. Miscellanies of Baluze. See also Fleury, Hist. Ecclés. vol. ii. book viii. n. 40.

[3] Lampridius, in his Life of Alexander Severus, cites some instances of this moderate conduct of some pagan emperors: "Cum Christiani quemdam locum qui publicus fuerat occupassent, contra popinarii dicerent sibi eum deberi, rescripsit [imperator] melius esse ut quomodocumque illic Deus colatur, quam

similar outrages, Constantine ordered all the churches which the pagans had destroyed to be magnificently rebuilt, and ordered, moreover, restitution to be made to the clergy of all the houses, possessions, fields, gardens, and other property of which they had been unjustly despoiled.[1]

Of all the churches in the world, Rome was both the richest and the most celebrated for her liberality.[2] Long before the time of Constantine she was able to provide for the support of a great number of clergy, of widows, of virgins, and of the poor. She supplied abundant succour to the faithful in the most distant provinces even of Syria and of Arabia.[3] She possessed also exceedingly rich vestments and plate for the celebration of the holy mysteries: chalices of gold and silver, embossed and set with diamonds; in a word, riches considerable enough to inflame the avarice of the persecutors, as we learn in particular from the history of the martyrdom of St. Lawrence.[4]

From these facts, it manifestly follows that, in the first ages, when the Church was generally poor, and even in the lifetime of the apostles, some particular churches possessed much more property than their own necessities required; that they were rich enough to support not only a great number of sacred ministers, but also to celebrate divine worship with splendour, to give abundant alms, and to relieve distant churches, whose resources were not equal to their wants.

---

popinariis dedatur."—Vita Alex. Severi (Hist. Aug. Scrip. Lugd. Batav. 1671, 8vo. vol. i. p. 1003).

Eusebius, in his Eccles. Hist., cites other facts of the same kind, in support of our assertion. See especially lib. vii. cap. xxx.—Fleury, Hist. Ecclés. vol. ii. book viii. n. 8.

[1] "Omnia ergo quæ ad ecclesias recte visa fuerint pertinere, sive domus ac possessio sit, sive agri, sive horti, seu quæcumque alia, nullo jure quod ad dominium pertinet imminuto, sed salvis omnibus atque integris manentibus, restitui jubemus."—Vita Constantini, lib. ii. cap. xxxix.; also cap. xxi. xxxvi. xli. of the same work. Idem, Hist. Eccles. lib. viii. cap. i. ii.; lib. x. cap. v. &c. Fleury, Hist. Ecclés. vol. ii. book ix. n. 46; vol. iii. book x. n. 2 and 40.

[2] Besides the authors cited above, note 1, page 91, see Alban Butler, Lives of Saints, August 10; Fleury, Hist. Ecclés. vol. ii. book vii. n. 39; St. Ambrose, De Officiis, lib. ii. cap. xxviii.; Prudentius, Hymn 2, de Corona.

[3] Eusebius, Hist. Eccles. lib. iv. cap. xxiii.; lib. vii. cap. v.

[4] See also note 2.

72. *Augmentation of Ecclesiastical Property after the Conversion of Constantine.*

But the increase of ecclesiastical property in all parts of the Church should naturally be one of the first effects of the conversion of Constantine, and of the liberty granted to her by that great prince. History, in truth, informs us that his munificence was in nothing more conspicuous than in his liberality to the Church. One cannot peruse without astonishment the accounts transmitted to us on this subject by contemporary authors, and especially by Eusebius, the most ancient of all, and who had the best means of acquiring accurate information. In all parts of the empire, principally in Rome, Constantinople, and Jerusalem, and in all the holy places of Palestine, Constantine erected magnificent churches and endowed them with considerable revenues, sparing no expense for the beauty of the edifices, the richness of the vestments and sacred vessels, the support of the clergy, and the maintenance of the different works of charity, which the zeal of the pastors and the piety of the faithful had prompted them to undertake.[1] In the same year in which he published, in concert with Licinius, the edicts authorizing the public exercise of the Christian religion, he resolved to make considerable grants to the Church. This may be seen especially from the letter which he wrote to Cœcilian, bishop of Carthage, to the following effect.[2] "Having resolved to give something for the support of the ministers of the Catholic religion in all the provinces of Africa, Numidia, and Mauritania, I have written to Ursus, treasurer-general of Africa, ordering him to place at your disposal 3,000 *bourses*.[3] When you have received that sum, distribute it among all those whom I have mentioned, according to the scale which

[1] Eusebius, Hist. Eccles. lib. x. cap. vi. Idem, Vita Constantini, lib. i. cap. xliii.; lib. iii. cap. xxvi. xli. l.; lib. iv. cap. lviii.; et alibi passim. See also Joan. Ciampini, De Sacris Ædificiis a Constantino Magno constructis; Rome, 1693, folio.

[2] Euseb. Hist. Eccles. lib. x. cap. vi. Fleury, Hist. Eoclés. vol. iii. book x. n. 2.

[3] It would be difficult, and perhaps impossible, to determine, at the present

Osius has sent to you. If you find that the sum is not sufficient to carry out my wishes, you need not have any difficulty in applying to Heraclidas, the superintendent of my domain; for I have given him orders to pay to you, without delay, all the money you may require of him."

The history of this period supplies many other equally striking evidences of the liberality of Constantine to the churches. He ordered the magistrates of Egypt, as we learn from St. Athanasius, to furnish annually a considerable quantity of corn to the patriarch of Alexandria for the support of the widows of Egypt and of Libya.[1] Theodoret adds that he, moreover, allowed all the churches a certain quantity of wheat for the support of the clergy, of the poor, of widows, and of virgins; that Julian the Apostate having revoked that grant, his successor, who was unable to restore it completely, granted at first one-third of it; and that from that third which the churches were enjoying in the time of Theodoret himself, some idea could be formed of the incredible liberality of Constantine.[2]

---

day, the value of those 3,000 *purses* (φόλλεις). The point has been much discussed by the learned; we give here what appears most probable.

Under Constantine and his successors, the word "follis" meant three different kinds of coin; a copper coin, otherwise called nummus, or tetrassarion, worth four assarions, or about one sou and a half of our money (French); secondly, the military follis, or purse, containing 175 denarii; thirdly, the balantion, another kind of purse, containing 250 denarii.

It is generally admitted, that the "follis" of which Constantine speaks, is not the tetrassarion; so small a sum would manifestly have been insufficient for the object which the emperor proposed in this letter. It is not more probable that he speaks of the military "follis," in a letter addressed to a bishop, on a point of the civil administration. It must, therefore, probably be the "balantion," which was worth 250 denarii. It is understood in that sense by Fleury, Hist. Ecclés. vol. iii. book x. n. 2; and by D. Ceillier, Hist. des Auteurs Ecclés. vol. iv. p. 151; and by the majority of critics.

Supposing with Paucton, that the denarius, in the reign of Constantine and his successors, was worth about 15½ sous of French money (*7d.*), this follis would be worth about 195 livres Tournois, and the 3,000 purses would be 585,000 livres Tournois. Fleury and Ceillier, who value the denarius much lower, reduce the value of 3,000 purses to 300,000 livres Tournois.—See Paucton, Métrologie, p. 424 and 765; Ducange, Dissert. de Nummis Imperii C. P. n. 90 (at the end of the Glossarium Infimæ Latinitatis); Pétau, Dissert. de Folle (at the end of the works of St. Epiphanius).

[1] St. Athanas. Apologia de Fugâ, n. 18; Epist. ad Solit. n. 31 (Operum, tom. i. part. i.).

[2] Theodoret, Hist. Eccles. lib. i. cap. xi.; lib. iv. cap. iv. Sozomen, Hist. lib. i. cap. viii.; lib. v. cap. v.

73. *His Liberality to the Church of Rome.*

Anastasius the Librarian, in his Lives of the Popes, published in the ninth century, from the archives of the Church of Rome, gives a still more surprising inventory of the offerings made by this great prince to the churches of that city, and to some other churches in Italy.[1] "During the pontificate of St. Sylvester," he says, "Constantine erected a great number of basilicas in Rome, and in many other cities in Italy, and decorated them magnificently. The following are the principal ornaments with which he enriched the Basilica of Constantine:[2]—

"1. A silver canopy,[3] having its front adorned with a statue of our Saviour, on a throne, about five feet high, seated on a chair, and weighing one hundred and twenty pounds.[4] On it were also the

---

[1] Anastasius, Vita S. Silvestri. Fleury, Mœurs des Chrétiens, n. 50; Hist. Ecclés. vol. iii. book xi. n. 36.

Fleury follows here the edition of Anastasius which is found in the collection of Councils by Père Labbe (vol. i. p. 1409). But it is well to remark, that since that edition, others more correct and valued have appeared. Among others, we shall cite that of Bianchini (Rome, 1718, 4 vols. fol.), and of Muratori, in the third vol. of Rerum Italicarum Scriptores (Mediolani, 1723, fol.). In some passages we have used these editions to correct the errors of Père Labbe.

[2] The Basilica Constantiniana, at present called St. John Lateran, was near the palace of Latran, formerly a residence of the emperors, which Constantine gave to Pope Miltiades and his successors. It seems that this palace, with its dependencies, was the first patrimony of the Holy See.—Baronii Annales, ann. 310, n. 80, &c. Lebeau, Hist. du Bas-Empire, vol. i. book ii. n. 29. Ciampini, De Sacris Ædificiis à Constantino constructis, Rome, 1693, fol.

[3] In the text of Anastasius, the word is "fastigium." It would be difficult to determine the precise sense of that word, as even Ducange himself has not ventured to do so.—Lexicon Infimæ Latinitatis, art. Fastigium. Fleury thinks that it is a tabernacle.—Mœurs des Chrétiens, n. 50. But the description given of it by Anastasius, the weight and dimensions which he assigns to it, incline us to believe rather that it must have been a canopy placed at the end of the choir or over the high altar. That is the sense which many learned writers give to the word "fastigium" in this passage (see among others, Macri, Hierolexicon, or Dictionarium Sacrum, verbo Fastigium), and this explanation has been inserted in Ducange, by his new editors (ed. 1733). Whatever may be said of this explanation, Anastasius tells us in his life of Pope Sixtus III., that this "fastigium" of which we are speaking, was carried off by the barbarians in the following century, but restored by Valentinian III. at the request of that pontiff. — Labbe, Concilia, tom. iii. p. 1258. However, it appears from the narrative of the same author, that the ornament given by Constantine was never restored in its old splendour; for the "fastigium" given by Valentinian weighed only 1,610 pounds, whereas that of Constantine weighed 2,025.

[4] The Roman foot was about 11½ inches of French pied de roi.—See Paucton, Métrologie, pp. 129 and 758.

twelve Apostles, with crowns of purest silver on their heads, each five feet high, and weighing ninety pounds. On the outside was another statue of our Saviour seated on a throne, and looking towards the apsis.[1] This statue is five feet high, and weighs one hundred and forty pounds. Near it are five angels in silver, five feet high, each weighing one hundred and fifty pounds. The whole canopy weighs two thousand and twenty-five pounds.[2]

"2. A lustre of the purest gold, adorned with fifteen dolphins, and weighing twenty-five pounds, with the chain that holds it suspended under the canopy.

"3. Four chandeliers in form of crowns, of the purest gold, adorned with twenty dolphins, and weighing fifteen pounds each.

"4. The roof of the basilica gilt, through its whole length, viz. five hundred feet.

"5. Seven silver altars, each weighing two hundred pounds.

"6. Seven patenas of gold, thirty pounds each.

"7. Seven patenas of silver, thirty pounds each.

"8. Seven cups of pure gold, ten pounds each.

"9. Another cup of metal, fretted with gold, adorned with coral, emeralds, hyacinths, and weighing twenty pounds three ounces.

"10. Twenty cups of silver, fifteen pounds each.

"11. Two sacred vases of the purest gold, fifty pounds each, and each containing three medimni.[3]

"12. Twenty sacred vases of silver, weighing each ten pounds, and each containing one medimnus.

---

[1] The word "apsis" is taken in various senses by the writers of the middle ages. In architecture it generally signifies an arch or vault, and it means sometimes the roof of a church, sometimes the end of the choir, terminating in a semicircle, sometimes the bishop's chair, set in that place. It would be difficult to fix the precise meaning of that word in the text of Anastasius; it would be equally difficult to determine the position of the two statues of our Saviour mentioned here. The first, it may be supposed, was placed under the canopy against the wall; the second, above and behind the canopy. The latter faced, perhaps, the vaulted roof of the church.

[2] For a valuation of the different sums mentioned here by Anastasius, see No. 2 of the Documentary Evidence, at the close of this work.

[3] Probably the Attic medimnus, which was equivalent, according to Paucton, to six Attic bushels, and three and a half Paris bushels, or forty-six pints and a half. See Paucton, ibid. pp. 239, 263, and 757.

"13. Forty chalices of the purest gold, one pound each.

"14. Fifty chalices of silver, two pounds each.

"15. A lustre, or chandelier, of the purest gold, placed before the altar, adorned with eighty dolphins, and weighing thirty pounds.

"16. A lustre, or chandelier, of silver, adorned with twenty dolphins, and weighing fifty pounds.

"17. Forty-five lustres, or chandeliers, of silver, placed in the nave, and weighing each thirty pounds.

"18. On the right side of the basilica, forty lustres, or chandeliers, of silver, twenty pounds each.

"19. On the left side of the basilica, twenty-five lustres, or chandeliers, of silver, twenty pounds each.

"20. Fifty other lustres, or chandeliers, of silver, placed in the nave, and each weighing twenty pounds.

"21. Three urns of the purest silver, each weighing three hundred pounds, and containing ten medimni.

"22. Two censers of the purest gold, each weighing thirty pounds.

"The principal ornaments of the baptistery were:—

"23. A porphyry basin, covered inside and outside with plates of the purest silver, weighing three thousand and eight pounds.

"24. In the centre of the basin, a column of porphyry supporting a lamp of the purest gold, weighing fifty pounds.

"25. On the rim of the basin a lamb of the purest gold, pouring in the water, weighing thirty pounds.

"26. On the right of the lamb, a statue of our Saviour, of purest silver, five feet high, and weighing one hundred and seventy pounds.

"27. On the left of the lamb, a statue of St. John the Baptist, holding in his hand the following inscription: 'Behold the Lamb of God, behold Him who taketh away the sins of the world.' This statue is five feet high, and weighs one hundred pounds.

"28. Seven harts of pure silver, pouring in the water, and weighing each eighty pounds.[1]

"29. A censer of the purest gold, weighing ten pounds, adorned with forty-two precious stones of emerald or hyacinth."

Summing up all these ornaments of gold and silver mentioned by Anastasius, we find that they amounted to six hundred and eighty-five pounds of gold, and twelve thousand nine hundred and forty-three pounds of silver, which, exclusive of the workmanship, amounted to more than £58,000 of our money.[2] And in this estimate is not included the gold required to gild the roof of the basilica, 500 feet long.

Constantine secured, moreover, for the same basilica and for its baptistery, considerable revenues in landed and house property, situate either in Rome or its environs, or in many distant provinces.[3] All these properties, mentioned by Anastasius, brought to the basilica a revenue of 14,604 denarii of gold, that is, about £9,266 of our money. The emperor also gave an annual supply of 150 pounds of aromatics for the divine service.

Besides these offerings to the Basilica of Constantine, he also made considerable presents to the churches of Rome which he had built or repaired, principally to those of St. Peter, of St. Paul, of the Holy Cross of Jerusalem, of St. Agnes, of St. Lawrence, of St. Peter and St. Marcellinus. His liberality was not less magnificent to another church in Rome built by St. Sylvester, and to churches erected by himself at Ostia, at Albano, at Capua, and at Naples. All the ornaments of gold and silver

[1] The harts placed in the baptistery were a symbol of the ardent desire which the catechumens should bring to the sacrament of regeneration. This symbolical type is founded on those words of the 41st Psalm, "Sicut desiderat cervus ad fontes aquarum, ita desiderat anima mea ad te, Deus."

Fleury supposes, according to the text of Père Labbe, that each of these harts weighed 800 pounds. The reading in Père Labbe appears, however, to be a typographical error, for it is found in none of the MSS. consulted by Bianchini and Muratori.

[2] See in support of this calculation, No. 4 of Documentary Evidences, at the end of this volume.

[3] On this subject, see 10th Dissertation of Padre Zaccharia, in his collection entitled De Rebus ad Hist. et Antiquit. Eccl. pertinentibus (Fulginiæ, 1781), tom. ii. p. 75.

given to those different churches, amounted to about two-thirds of the value of those given to the Basilica of Constantine. He also assigned to those churches considerable properties either at Rome or in Italy, or in the most distant provinces in Africa and Asia, and even on the banks of the Euphrates. The annual revenues of the properties belonging to the churches of Rome alone, exclusive of the Basilica of Constantine, amounted to 16,376 denarii of gold, worth about £10,500 of our money.

This inventory appears so prodigious, that it has been questioned by some modern critics, whether the ancient writer whose account Anastasius transcribes, has not attributed to Constantine all the offerings made by his successors.[1] This conjecture, as Fleury observes, is possible with regard to the offerings of gold and silver, but can hardly be admissible with regard to the properties, the titles to which would naturally be much more safely preserved.[2]

74. *Sources of this Liberality—Immense Revenues of the Empire.*

However surprising may be this detail of the liberality of Constantine, as described by Anastasius, it will nevertheless appear by no means incredible, when we consider the enormous sums of which that prince could dispose in favour of the Church, without deranging the resources of the state, or imposing any new tribute on his subjects. To form a correct notion on this point, we need only consider the immense revenues of the empire at this time, and the uses to which they were generally applied

---

[1] Fleury, Hist. Ecclés. vol. iii. book ii. n. 36; Mœurs des Chrétiens, n. 50.

[2] From not having made this reflection, Bingham goes so far as to regard the whole statements of Anastasius as fabulous, on the grounds that it appears to have been taken from a work falsely attributed to Pope Damasus. —Bingham, Origines et Antiquit. Eccles. tom. iii. lib. viii. cap. vii. § 5. But such a supposition appears absolutely untenable. Whoever the ancient author was from whom Anastasius learned that part of his statement, its truth cannot rationally be contested, with regard to the objects which he describes as existing in his own time. Hence Bingham's opinion on this point is generally abandoned by the learned. On the authority of Anastasius's work, consult Bianchini's preface. This preface is also given in Muratori's work, which we have cited. D. Ceillier gives a summary of it in vol. xix. Hist. des Auteurs Ecclés. p. 419, &c.

by Constantine's predecessors.[1] Both may be learned from the enormous sums expended by the pagan emperors, not only for the necessary expenses of government, but also in largesses to secure the attachment of the people and of the army. "After the civil wars," as a recent writer on this subject observes,[2] "there was no check on ambition, no shame in corruption, no limits to prodigality. When the Roman people were once detached from the cause of the republic, and when the armies were demoralized by the hope of gain, the candidature for the empire became literally an auction; to attain the government of the world, the generals promised its spoils to the soldiers and people. . . . Cæsar sometimes gave favours to his soldiers.[3] Octavius, on the field of Philippi, promised 5,000 drachmas each to all the Roman soldiers, though their numbers were twenty-eight legions.[4] More than 170,000 men, therefore, must have received each nearly £160 of our money.[5]

"Caligula, Nero, Didius Julian, Commodus, and all the tyrants who wished to gain the hearts of the soldiers and populace, augmented still more this rapacity and corruption by their follies. On one occasion, Commodus gave the people 725 denarii each, that is 2,900 sesterces, or nearly £23 of our money.[6] In the time of Augustus, 320,000 citizens were supported at the expense of the public treasury.[7] Severus boasted that he sur-

---

[1] Naudet, Des Changements opérés dans l'Administration de l'Empire Romain sous Dioclétien, Constantin, &c. vol. i. part i. ch. i. art. ii. and iii.

[2] Ibid. p. 177.

[3] Suetonius, De Duod. Cæsaribus, lib. i. (p. 40 of the Leyden edition, 1662, 8vo.).

[4] Appian, De Bello Civili, lib. iv. Justus Lipsius, De Magnitud. Rom. lib. ii. cap. xiii. (vol. iii. of his works, Antwerp ed. 1637, 4 vols. fol.).

[5] The value of 5,000 drachmas would be now £180, if we suppose with Paucton, that the drachma or Roman denarius was worth at that time 9*d.* of our money (18 sous). Paucton, Métrologie, p. 764.

[6] Lampridius, Vita Commodi (apud Hist. Script. tom. i. p. 519). According to Paucton, the Roman denarius, which was worth 18 (French) sous (about 9*d.*), before the reign of Claudius or Nero, was worth only 16 from Nero to Constantine.—Paucton, ibid. pp. 764, 765. In this supposition, the 725 denarii mentioned here would be worth about 580f. (£23. 4*s.* 2*d.*) of our money.

[7] Justus Lipsius, De Magnitudine Romanâ, lib. iii. cap. iii. (vol. iii. of his works, p. 424, 1st col.).

passed the liberality of all the emperors. Caracalla scattered in a few days the treasure amassed by his father during eighteen years. More ample details on this excessive prodigality may be seen in the work of Justus Lipsius, on the Greatness of Rome.[1] The good emperors were compelled to yield to a custom which had made the squandering of the revenues of the state a political necessity. From the reign of Claudius, the accession of a prince, or a birth, or an adoption into the imperial family, or the Decennalia, or anniversaries of an accession, which were celebrated every tenth year, victories, or the return of a prince to his capital, or other events recurring more or less frequently, were so many occasions on which largesses to the soldiers and people could not be omitted without exciting their hatred, and exposing the empire to a revolution."

The accounts transmitted to us by contemporary authors of the magnificence, or rather of the prodigality even of the best emperors, in feasts, in festivals, and in public shows, are equally marvellous. "Augustus," observes the author already cited,[2] "declared that he had celebrated public games twenty-four times in his own name, and twenty-three times for poor or absent magistrates.[3] Suetonius, Dion Cassius, and other writers on the history of the emperors, give almost incredible details of the magnificence and profusion of Caligula, of Nero, of Commodus, of Heliogabalus, and of others of the same class. All the days of their reigns were taken up between cruelties and feasts. Immense theatres glittering with gold, and hung with veils of purple; multitudes of ferocious beasts slain in the arena, with arms and lances adorned with silver; representations of naval battles given on lakes filled with wine; lotteries, for which the people received tickets, some for a horse, others for a vase of gold, or for a rich dress, or for a house; tables sumptuously laid out in every street; in fine,

[1] Justus Lipsius, De Mag. Rom. lib. ii. cap. xii. xiii. xiv.

[2] Naudet, Des Changements, pp. 178, 179.

[3] Suetonius, De Duodecim Cæsaribus, lib. ii. (p. 225 of the Leyden edition).

whatever the caprice of idleness, the insolence of unbounded wealth, the follies of dissipation, the contempt of all modesty and of all human feeling could suggest for the amusement of a sanguinary and frivolous people, was carried out in those extravagant and ridiculous Roman shows. Every day the very existence of the provinces was sacrificed to the amusements of that city. Abuses had become laws, and excesses necessities. Read in Dion, in Julius Capitolinus, the enormous outlay by Titus and Marcus Aurelius, for shows prolonged during whole months, and you may conjecture what must have been the morals of the Roman people, when such emperors were under the necessity of providing so liberally such amusements ; conceive if you can, an idea of the profusion of those other emperors, who imagined that they were masters of the world only to indulge their own desires, and to dissipate in foolish expenses the treasures wrung from the nations."

From these details, it may be easily inferred, that Constantine and his successors could well afford to be liberal to the Church and her ministers, without imposing any new tribute on their subjects, and even after diminishing the old tributes. The reforms effected in the government under Diocletian and Constantine, and more effectually still the ideas of order and propriety diffused by Christianity throughout all parts of the empire, diminished insensibly those abuses which we have mentioned, and left the Christian emperors more at liberty to employ on useful objects the enormous sums which their predecessors had lavished in ridiculous profusion. The application of that portion of the revenue of the state to the Church would appear the more suitable ; because, while it added nothing to the burdens of taxation, it contributed to the relief of the poor and to the support of a religion, whose influence over public morals appeared to point it out as destined for the regeneration of the whole frame of society.

75. Other sources of Wealth for the Church — Restitutions — Liberality of the Faithful.

It must be remembered, moreover, that the revenues of the empire were far from being the only source of the liberality of Constantine to the Church.[1] A resource, perhaps, still more abundant was found either in the properties unjustly confiscated during the persecutions, and of which the heirs could not be discovered;[2] or in the treasures and revenues of the pagan temples, many of which possessed enormous wealth;[3] or finally, in the large sums formerly allotted to the sacrifices, the games, and the different ceremonies of the pagan worship.[4] Thus it is manifest from history itself, that Constantine's liberality to the Church not only did not give any occasion to an augmentation of the public burdens, but did not even prevent him from publishing regulations most acceptable to the people, either reducing the taxation or checking the rigour and cupidity of the collectors.[5]

The Christian emperors were not only themselves liberal, but they encouraged by their edicts the liberality of private individuals.[6] The Roman laws generally allowed them to dispose of their property in favour of public establishments, and of communities authorized by the law.[7] In accordance with this principle, the law had at all times recognised donations and wills in

---

[1] Bingham, Origines sive Antiquitates Eccl. tom. ii. lib. v. cap. iv. Fleury, Mœurs des Chrétiens, n. 50; Hist. Ecclés. vol. iii. book x. n. 40; book xi. n. 36.

[2] Eusebius, Vita Constantini, lib. ii. cap. xxxvi.

[3] See the details which we have given on this subject in the first article of this Introduction, and No. 3 of Documentary Evidence at the end of this work.

[4] We have seen above that Gratian and Theodosius had seized and confiscated the revenues destined for the support of the pagan priests and worship, supra, art. 43, 44. See also Bingham, ubi supra, § 10.

[5] Naudet, Des Changements opérés dans l'Administration de l'Empire, vol. ii. pp. 207, 236, &c.

[6] Thomassin, Ancienne et Nouvelle Discipline, vol. iii. book i. ch. xviii.; De Héricourt, ibid. part iii. ch. ii.; idem, Lois Eccl. de France, part iv. p. 182, &c.; Bingham, Origines sive Antiquitates Eccl. tom. ii. lib. v. cap. iv. § 5, &c.

[7] Digest. lib. xxx. tit. i. n. 117, 122; lib. xxxiv. tit. v. n. 20. Domat, Lois Civiles, part ii. book iv. tit. ii. § 2, n. 13.

favour of the temples and the ministers of false gods.[1] It was natural of course that Constantine should allow the same right to the true religion and to its ministers; and accordingly he sanctioned it in the most formal manner, by authorizing all pious legacies to the Church.[2] Valentinian I., it is true, restricted this permission, by prohibiting in general all clerics and all those who professed continency, to receive anything from virgins and widows, either by donation or by will;[3] but there is every reason to believe, that so far from being injurious to the Church, this law was, on the contrary, most useful to her, by preventing the injury caused by the avarice of some of the clergy, who, by shameful artifices, turned to their own private benefit, the pious

---

[1] Digest. lib. xxxiii. tit. i. n. 20.

[2] This law of Constantine is found in the Cod. Theod. (lib. xvi. tit. ii. n. 4), and in the Justinian Code (lib. i. tit. ii. n. 1), with some slight variations which do not affect the substance of the enactment. The following is the text, of the Justinian code, which appears the more exact: "Habeat unusquisque licentiam sanctissimo, Catholico, venerabilique concilio [i. e. *sanctissimæ Ecclesiæ Catholicæ*] decedens bonorum quod optaverit relinquere; et non sint cassa judicia ejus. Nihil enim est quod magis hominibus debeatur, quàm ut supremæ voluntatis, postquàm jam aliud velle non possunt, liber sit stylus."

[3] "Ecclesiastici, aut ex ecclesiasticis [*nati*], vel qui *continentium* se volunt nomine nuncupari, viduarum ac pupillarum domos non adeant....Censemus etiam ut memorati [i. e. *jam dictæ personæ*] nihil de ejus mulieris [*viduæ* scilicet, *aut pupillæ*] qui se privatim, sub prætextu religionis, adjunxerint, liberalitate quâcumque, vel extremo judicio [i. e. *ultimâ voluntate*] possint adipisci; et omne in tantum inefficax sit quod alicui horum ab his fuerit derelictum, ut nec per subjectam personam valeant aliquid, vel donatione, vel testamento, accipere."—Cod. Theodos. lib. xvi. tit. ii. n. 20. Fleury, Hist. Eccl. vol. iv. book xvi. n. 41. D. Ceillier, Hist. des Aut. Eccl. vol. viii. p. 596.

The object of this law of Valentinian I. no doubt was, to prevent the indiscretion or the cupidity of some clerics who wished to abuse their ascendancy over virgins and widows, in order to obtain donations or legacies. Still St. Ambrose, when speaking of this law, expresses his surprise that the legislator had carried his precautions further in this matter against the Christian clergy than against the pagan ministers.—St. Amb. Epist. xviii. ad Valentin. II. n. 12. Fleury, Hist. Eccl. vol. iv. book xviii. n. 32. It was not very becoming that, under a Christian emperor, the ministers of the false gods should be more privileged in this matter than the ministers of the Christian religion. Hence Valentinian's law was modified soon after, and even entirely revoked by his successors, as we shall see lower down.

A modern author, who omits no opportunity of assailing the Catholic Church, infers, from this law of Valentinian I., "that avarice was then almost the characteristic vice of the clergy."—Hallam's Europe, vol. iii. p. 204. By a similar line of reasoning, we could infer, from the different laws published by Valentinian and other emperors against certain disorders in the magistracy, in the military, and in other departments, that these disorders were then "almost characteristics of these states." The sequel will demonstrate more and more the injustice of the assertion of this English writer.

gifts destined by the Roman ladies for religion.[1] Similar considerations appear to have suggested the law of Theodosius the Great, which prohibited deaconesses to make a will in favour of the Church, the clergy, or the poor.[2] It was apprehended probably, that some clerics, either from a spirit of cupidity or of indiscreet zeal for the support of the poor and of the Church, used improper influence to obtain legacies for the Church or for their own benefit. However, another law of the same prince and of the same year, modifies the severity of the former, and authorizes deaconesses to give to the Church, by donation, their slaves, their movable property, and very probably their immovable property.[3] Finally, the Emperor Marcian, either interpreting or reforming the preceding laws, authorized generally, widows, virgins, and all women consecrated to God, to leave their property by their wills to the Church, the clergy, and the monks.[4] About the same time the Emperor Theodosius the

---

[1] This conjecture appears to be founded on the words of St. Jerome, in his letter to Nepotian: "Non de lege conqueror, sed doleo cur meruerimus hanc legem. Cauterium bonum est; sed quò mihi vulnus, ut indigeam cauterio?.... *Sit hæres, sed mater filiorum,* id est gregis sui, *Ecclesia* quæ illos genuit, nutrivit et pavit; *quid nos inserimus inter matrem et liberos?*" — St. Hieron. Epist. ad Nepotian. (Oper. tom. iv. part. ii. p. 260).

[2] "Si quando diem obierit [*diaconissa*], nullam Ecclesiam, nullum clericum, nullum pauperem scribat hæredes; careat namque viribus necesse est, si quid contra vetitum, circa personas specialiter comprehensas [i. e. *modò designatas*] fuerit à moriente confectum."— Cod. Theod. lib. xvi. tit. ii. n. 27. Fleury, Hist. Eccl. vol. iv. book xcix. n. 24.

[3] "Legem quæ diaconissis vel viduis nuper est promulgata, *ne quis* videlicet *clericus, neve sub Ecclesiæ nomine, mancipia, supellectilem, prædia* (*velut infirmi sexûs dispoliator*) *invaderet, et remotis affinibus ac propinquis, ipse, sub prætextu Catholicæ disciplinæ, se ageret viventis hæredem,* eatenùs animadvertat esse revocatam, ut de omnium chartis, si jam nota est, auferatur; neque quisquam, aut litigator eâ sibi utendum, aut judex noverit exequendum."— Cod. Theod. lib. xvi. tit. ii. n. 28. There are some doubts regarding the landed property. The text of the law has "prædam" instead of "prædia," a reading which is adopted by many critics. Flechier, in his Hist. of Theodosius, book iv. n. 17, appears to have misunderstood this law. He must be corrected by the Commentary of Godefroy on this article in the Theodosian Code.

[4] This constitution of Marcian is the sixth in the Novellæ, in the collection of the Imperial Constitutions, placed at the end of the Theodosian Code (Legum Novell. lib. iii. tit. vi.). It was afterwards inserted in the Justinian Code in these terms: "Generali lege sancimus, sive vidua, sive diaconissa, vel virgo Deo dicata, vel sanctimonialis mulier, sive quocumque alio nomine religiosi honoris vel dignitatis fœmina nuncupata, vel testamento, vel codicillo suo (quod tamen aliâ omni juris ratione munitum sit), Ecclesiæ, vel martyrio [i. e. *templo martyribus dicato*], vel clero, vel monachio [i. e. *cœtui monachorum*],

Younger pubished an edict equally favourable to the clergy, transferring to the churches and monasteries the property of the religious and of the clergy who died intestate, and had no near relations.[1] This provision, however, merely extended to the Church a favour then enjoyed by many other corporations, which in similar cases inherited by law the property of their deceased members.[2]

76. *Tithes—First-fruits—Donations—Last Wills.*

The piety of the faithful, stimulated by the example and edicts of the emperor, increased every day the wealth of the clergy in all parts of the empire. Though there was no express precept of the Church before the sixth century, ordering the faithful to pay to the clergy the tithes and first-fruits of their property, the majority continued to pay voluntarily their offerings according to the custom established during the times of persecution.[3] In their writings and public exhortations, the holy doctors frequently urged the motives of charity and even of justice, by which the faithful were bound to this practice.[4] St. Jerome, among others, in his exposition of these words of our Saviour, "Render therefore to Cæsar the things that are Cæsar's, and to God the things that are God's," enumerates expressly among the things that belong to God, "tithes," "first-fruits,"

---

vel pauperibus, aliquid vel ex integro vel ex parte, in quâcumque re vel specie, crediderit relinquendum, id modis omnibus ratum firmumque consistat; sive hoc institutione, sive substitutione, seu legato aut fidei commisso per universitatem, seu speciali; sive scriptâ sive non scriptâ voluntate fuit derelictum; omni in posterum, in hujuscemodi negotiis, ambiguitate submotâ."—Cod. Justin. lib. i. tit. ii. n. 13.

[1] "Si quis episcopus, aut presbyter, aut diaconus, aut diaconissa, aut subdiaconus, vel cujuslibet alterius loci [seu *ordinis*] clericus, aut monachus, aut mulier solitariæ vitæ dedita, nullo condito testamento decesserit, nec ei parentes utriusque sexûs, vel liberi, vel si qui agnationis cognationisque jure junguntur, vel uxor extiterit, bona quæ ad eum pertinuerint, sacrosanctæ Ecclesiæ, vel monasterio cui fuerat destinatus, omnifariàm socientur." — Cod. Theodos. lib. v. tit. iii. n. 1.

[2] Godefroy, Comment. ad Cod. Theod. lib. v. tit. ii. n. 1.

[3] Thomassin, Ancienne et Nouv. Discipline, vol. iii. book i. ch. iv. et seq. De Héricourt, ibid. part iii. ch. i. et seq. Van Espen, Jus Eccl. Univ. tom. i. part. ii. tit. xxxiii. ch. i.

[4] See note 4, p. 93.

and the other kinds of offerings usual in the Church.[1] The same interpretation of these words of our Saviour occurs in a sermon attributed to St. Augustine, but which is more probably the production of St. Cæsarius, or some of his contemporaries.[2] These exhortations were certainly not without effect on the majority of the faithful; Cassian's writings manifestly imply, that in his time, tithes and first-fruits were paid to monasteries as zealously as to the Church.[3] There is every reason to believe that this universal custom of paying tithes to the clergy gave rise to the law on that point, which was generally established since the fifth century in the Latin Church.[4]

In addition to this kind of offerings, the Church saw her revenues gradually increased after the conversion of Constantine, by new donations of immovable property. Many persons of wealth and of the highest rank, after their conversion, or entrance into the Church or monastic state, renounced their patrimonies in favour of the Church or of the monasteries.[5] Others resigned a part only of their property during their life, and made their wills in favour of the Church or of pious institutions. The bishops especially and the other sacred ministers, made it almost invariably their duty to leave to the Church not only the property which they might have acquired in the service of the altar, but also their patrimonies, if they had not near relations.[6] The history of those ages supplies a great number of facts to

---

[1] "*Reddite quæ sunt Cæsaris Cæsari,* id est, nummum, tributum et pecuniam; *et quæ sunt Dei Deo,* decimas, primitias, et oblationes ac victimas sentiamus."—S. Hieron. Comment. in Matth. cap. xxii. (Operum, tom. iv. p. 105).

[2] "*Reddite quæ sunt Cæsaris Cæsari, et quæ sunt Dei Deo.* Majores nostri ideo copiis omnibus abundabant, quia Deo decimas dabant, et censum Cæsari reddebant."—St. Augustine, Operum, tom. v.; Append. Serm. lxxxvi. (alias xlviii. inter Quinquaginta), n. 3.

[3] Cassiani Collat. 14, 21, &c.

[4] See the authors cited in note 3, p. 109.

[5] Thomassin, Ancienne et Nouv. Discipline, book iii. ch. ii. iii. De Héricourt, ibid. part iii. ch. xv. n. 2.

[6] Thomassin, ibid. book ii. ch. 38, &c. De Héricourt, ibid. ch. xiii. n. 1. Le P. Thomassin gives the texts of most of the testimonies to which we refer in our notes, in support of the principal facts which prove our assertion. For brevity's sake we shall cite only the principal texts.

corroborate this assertion: we shall cite here a few only of the most remarkable.

The Empress Pulcheria, wife of Marcian, besides building and richly endowing a great number of churches, bequeathed to the Church and to the poor all her property, which must have been very considerable, after the high favour and authority which she had so long enjoyed; the emperor raised no objection to this pious munificence.[1] St. Ambrose, after his elevation to the see of Milan, resolved to renounce all in order to imitate the poverty of Jesus Christ. With this view he distributed all his money to the Church and to the poor; and moreover transferred to the Church the dominion of all his property, only reserving a life interest to his sister Marcellina.[2] St. Gregory of Nazianzen declares in his will that he leaves all his property to the Church, for the relief of the poor of the place.[3] St. Cyril of Alexandria bequeathed a considerable portion of his property to his successor, with a simple recommendation that he should take care of his nephew.[4]

77. *Liberality of the Faithful stimulated by the Exhortations of the Holy Doctors.*

The language and exhortations of the holy doctors at this epoch would of themselves be sufficient to give a great idea of the ordinary liberality of the faithful, and especially of the sacred ministers to the poor and to the Church. In several passages of his works, Salvian censures severely the conduct of deacons, priests, and especially of bishops, who having neither children nor near relations, left their property to strangers, rather than to the poor, to the Church, and to God himself.[5]

---

[1] Sozomen, Hist. Eccl. lib. ix. cap. i. Theodor. Lect. Fragm. Hist. lib. i. p. 552 (at the end of the History of Sozomen and Socrates). Fleury, Hist. Eccl. vol. vi. book xxviii. n. 42.

[2] Vita S. Ambros. à Paulino ejus notario scripta, n. 38 (at the end of the works of St. Ambrose). Fleury, Hist. Eccl. vol. iv. book xvii. n. 21.

[3] S. Greg. Oper. tom. i. p. 924—928. D. Ceillier, Hist. des Auteurs Eccl. vol. vii. p. 22.

[4] Concil. Chalced. act. iii. cap. v. (Concil. tom. iv. p. 405).

[5] Salvian, Epist. ad Salonium (Biblioth. Patrum, tom viii. p. 381, F).

He blames in like manner the virgins and the widows, who do not bequeath to the Church a good portion of their property, if they have no near relations. He exhorts even secular persons who have children, to make some such legacies, were it only to testify their attachment for the common mother of the faithful.[1] St. Augustine likewise recommends the rich who have many children to join to their number Jesus Christ, in the person of his poor, by leaving to them a portion equal to what they had bequeathed to each of their children. "If," he says, "a father has only one child, let him regard Jesus Christ as a second; if he has two, let him regard Jesus Christ as a third; if he has ten, let him regard Jesus Christ as the eleventh."[2] He moreover suggests, that if parents lose one of their children, they should leave to the poor the portion of property destined for that child.[3] St. Jerome addressed a similar exhortation to a rich and noble person, who had lost in a few days two of his daughters. "Instead," he observes, "of enriching their sister with the property designed for them, employ it in atoning for your sins and in relieving the poor."[4]

78. *They disapprove of excessive or indiscreet Donations.*

However urgent the exhortations of the fathers were on this

---

[1] Salvian, Ad Eccl. Cath. lib. iii. passim. See more particularly, p. 394, C.

[2] "Planè faciat quod sæpe hortatus sum; unum filium habet, putet Christum alterum; duos habet, putet Christum tertium; decem habet, Christum undecimum faciat."—St. Augustine, Serm. de Diversis, 355 (al. 49), (Operum, tom. v.).

[3] "Vivit filius tuus [scilicet, *in alterâ vitâ*]; interroga fidem tuam. Si ergo vivit filius tuus, quare invaditur pars ejus à fratribus ejus? Sed dices: Numquid rediturus est, et possessurus? Mittantur ergo illi quò præcessit ille [scilicet, *ad cœlum, mediante eleemosynâ*]. Ad rem suam venire non potest; res ejus ad eum ire potest [*ope eleemosynæ*]. Si in palatio militaret filius tuus, et amicus imperatoris fieret, et diceret tibi: Vende ibi partem meam, et mitte mihi; numquid haberes quod responderes? Modò cum imperatore omnium imperatorum, et cum rege regum est; mitte illi," etc.—St. Augustine, Serm. lxxxvi. (alias xliii.), n. 10.

[4] "Bona liberis pares, quæ te ad Dominum præcesserunt; ut partes earum non in divitias sororis proficiant, sed in redemptionem animæ tuæ, atque alimenta miserorum. Hæc monilia filiæ tuæ à te expetunt; his gemmis ornari capita sua volunt. Quod periturum erat in serico, vilibus pauperum tunicis servetur. Repetunt à te partes suas: junctæ sponso, nolunt videri pauperes et ignobiles: propria ornamenta desiderant."—S. Hieron. Epist. ad Julian. 92 (alias 34), (Oper. tom. iv. part. ii. p. 752).

point, it must be observed that they not only disapproved, but refused excessive and indiscreet alms, which were injurious to families, and which could give grounds to just remonstrances.[1] A rich citizen of Carthage, who had no children, and who was not likely to have them, had given all his property to the Church, reserving the life use to himself. It happened that he afterwards had children, and Aurelius, bishop of Carthage, restored, without any solicitation, all that the Church had received from him.[2] St. Augustine, who relates and praises highly this act, exhibited on several occasions the same disinterestedness. He refused absolutely all legacies which had their origin rather in the anger of a parent against his child, than in a sentiment of compassion for the poor; and he censured severely those parents, who by a false charity left their children or their near relations in destitution, or did not give them an inheritance suitable to their state. "Whoever," he declares, "wishes to enrich the Church by disinheriting his son, must look for some other person than Augustine to accept the donation; or rather, God forbid that he can find any person to receive it."[3] St. Jerome, St. Ambrose, St. Fulgentius, and many other holy doctors, testified both by their conduct, and by their discourses, the same spirit of moderation and of disinterestedness.[4]

---

[1] This point is solidly established by P. Thomassin, Ancienne et Nouv. Discipline, vol. iii. book i. ch. xvii.; ch. xx. n. 7. We think, however, that the author attributes to Salvian, without foundation, different sentiments on this point. See especially the passage of Salvian which we have cited above, n. 1, p. 112.

[2] "Quicumque vult, exhæredato filio, hæredem facere Ecclesiam, quærat alterum qui suscipiat, non Augustinum; imò, Deo propitio, neminem inveniat. Quàm laudabile factum sancti et venerandi episcopi Aurelii Carthaginensis! Quomodò implevit eos omnes qui sciunt, laudibus Dei! Quidam enim, cùm filios non haberet, neque speraret, res suas omnes, retento sibi usufructu, donavit Ecclesiæ. Nati sunt ei filii; reddidit ei episcopus, nec opinanti, quæ ille donaverat. In potestate habebat episcopus non reddere, sed jure fori, non jure poli."—S. August. Serm. 355 (alias 49 de diversis), n. 4.

[3] S. August. ibid.

[4] S. Hieron. Marcellæ Epitaphium, seu Epist. 96, ad Principiam (Operum, tom. iv. parte ii. p. 780). S. Ambros. Expos. in Lucam, lib. viii. n. 77 (Oper. tom. i.). Vita S. Fulgentii, per Ferrandum Diac. cap. 7 (among the works of S. Fulgentius). All these evidences are cited by P. Thomassin, ubi supra, ch. xvii. n. 7.

79. *Wealth of the Patriarchal Churches.*

The increase of the wealth of the clergy was especially remarkable in the patriarchal churches. St. Jerome, in a letter written to Pammachius, about the year 400, supposes that the Church of Jerusalem possessed at that period considerable wealth and revenues, in consequence of the great concourse of pilgrims flocking there continually from all parts of the earth.[1] The liberalities of St. John the Almoner, patriarch of Alexandria, in the seventh century, and all the details of his administration, manifestly imply that his church also had then immense resources for the relief of the poor.[2] On his accession to the patriarchal throne, he found in the treasure of his church eight thousand pounds of gold, which he proceeded to dispense without delay in good works.[3] He ordered, at the same time, a list of the poor of his episcopal city to be supplied to him; they amounted to more than seven thousand five hundred, to all of whom he daily supplied their food. In addition to these daily alms, the holy patriarch established in different parts of his diocese, houses of refuge for the sick, the old, and for strangers; and no pains were spared for the relief of the unfortunate, who were received in great numbers. His charity was not confined to the poor of his diocese and of his province; it provided, moreover, for the necessities of a number of churches, and of the poor throughout all Egypt and the East. The wealth of the Church of Alexandria in those days may be estimated from a single circumstance. During the pontificate of John the Almoner, thirteen vessels, each carrying

---

[1] St. Jerome, in a letter to Pammachius, against the errors of John, bishop of Jerusalem, thus apostrophizes that prelate:—"Tù, qui sumptibus abundans, et totius orbis religio, lucrum tuum est."—S. Hieron. Epist. 38 (alias 61), ad Pammachium (Oper. tom. iv. parte ii. p. 314).

Father Martianay, in a note on this passage, makes this reflection:—"Vides locupletatos, tempore Hieronymi, sacerdotes, ex Christianorum oblationibus, qui, religionis causâ, Jerosolymam pergebant."—Ibid.

[2] Vita S. Joan. per Leontium (apud Boll. tom. ii. Januar. p. 500). Fleury, Hist. Eccl. vol. viii. book xxxvii. n. 11, 12. Thomassin, Ancienne et Nouvelle Discipline, vol. iii. book iii. ch. xxx.; ch. xviii. n. 5.

[3] See note 3, among the Documentary Evidences, at the end of this volume.

10,000 bushels of wheat, the property of that church, were lost in one day.

80. *Wealth of the Roman Church—Its numerous Patrimonies.*

All this wealth was far surpassed by that of the Roman Church, which all Christians revered as the centre of Catholicity. Most of the nations enjoying the light of the true faith had received it from the zealous missionaries sent forth by that Church; they treasured up gratefully the memory of that great benefit, and looked upon respect for the Holy See as the characteristic mark of a true Christian. This sentiment, which was hereditary among all the children of the true Church, throbbed with fresh fervour at the news of the calamities inflicted by the invasion of the barbarians on the Holy See, and on the people of Italy placed under her protection. In all parts of the Christian world it was considered disgraceful that the head of their religion, and the vicar of Jesus Christ on earth, should suffer the inconveniences of want, or be paralyzed in his spiritual administration by the enormous sacrifices which he was under the necessity of making for the safety of the people intrusted to his care. In these views, princes and people emulously testified by rich offerings their profound respect for the successor of St. Peter, and contributed their property for the support and government of the universal Church. Hence the great wealth of the Holy See after the conversion of Constantine. At the close even of the fourth century, this wealth was so considerable, that Prætextatus, a Roman senator, when appointed consul of Rome, remarked pleasantly to Pope Damasus, "Make me bishop of Rome, and I will become a Christian on the spot."[1]

Nothing, however, gives a higher idea of the wealth of that Church, after the fourth century, than the number and extent of the patrimonies, that is, landed properties, which it possessed

[1] "Miserabilis Prætextatus, qui designatus consul est mortuus, homo sacrilegus, idolorum cultor, solebat ludens beato papæ Damaso dicere: *Facite me Romanæ urbis episcopum, et ero protinùs Christianus.*"—S. Hieron. Epist. 38 (alias 61), ad Pammachium (Oper. tom. iv. parte ii. p. 310).

in all parts of the Christian world.[1] The details already given from Anastasius the Librarian, on the liberality of Constantine to the Roman Church, leave very little doubt that she possessed, in the time of that prince, a great number of properties in the different provinces of the empire. Admitting even, what appears by no means probable, that the ancient biographer, whom Anastasius copied, was in error regarding the real origin of those properties, they must manifestly have been in possession of the Church long before that author was writing; otherwise the general belief would not have attributed them to Constantine.

But whatever may be the truth on that point, the monuments which remain to us of the history of the popes from the middle of the fourth century show the number of the patrimonies of the Roman Church increasing every day by the liberality of princes and of the people. "All the lives of the popes," as Fleury observes, "from St. Silvester and the commencement of the fourth century until the close of the ninth, are full of donations conferred on the Roman Church by popes, by emperors, and by private persons; and these donations were not merely vases of gold and silver, but houses in Rome, and lands in the country, in the different provinces of the empire, as well as in Italy."[2] It would be easy to prove, by a multitude of authorities, the truth of this assertion. A few selected from the most authentic sources will be sufficient for our purpose.

From the letters of St. Gregory the Great, we find that in his time the Roman Church had considerable patrimonies, not only in different parts of Italy, but also in Dalmatia, in Sicily, in Sardinia, in Corsica, in Spain, in the Gauls, in Africa, and in many other provinces.[3] Of these patrimonies some were

---

[1] On this point the reader may consult Dissertatio x. of P. Zaccaria, vol. ii. p. 68, of the collection entitled, De rebus ad Hist. et Antiquit. Eccles. pertinentibus Dissertationes. Fulginiæ, 1781, 2 vols. 4to.

[2] Fleury, Mœurs des Chrétiens, n. 50. Zaccaria, ubi supra, cap. 2, et seqq. Hallam's Europe, vol. iii. p. 296.

[3] S. Gregorii Vita, per Joan. Diacon. lib. ii. cap. 53, 55, &c. Ejusdem Vita recens adornata (auctore D. St. Marthe), lib. iii. cap. 9, n. 6 (Oper.

estates, the rent of which was paid to the Roman Church; others were real principalities, sometimes including cities and entire provinces, in which the pope exercised, through officers appointed by himself, all the rights of a temporal lord.[1] The number of those patrimonies was considerably increased in the course of time by successive donations of several princes and of the emperors themselves.[2] Authentic records prove that before the close of the seventh century the Roman Church counted among her patrimonies the territory of the Cottian Alps, comprising the city of Genoa and the whole neighbouring coasts to the frontiers of Gaul. The Lombards having usurped that territory about the close of the same century, *restored* it to Pope John (about the year 708), *as having been formerly a possession of the Roman Church.*[3] The patrimonies of that Church in Sicily and in Calabria, which were confiscated at the same time by Leo the Isaurian, were so extensive that they produced an annual revenue of three talents and a half of gold, or about £16,000 of our money, according to the most probable

---

tom. iv.). Fleury, Hist. Eccl. vol. viii. book xxxv. n. 15, 45. Zaccaria, ubi supra, cap. 3. Hist. de l'Égl. Gallic. vol. iii. p. 311.

[1] Zaccaria, ubi supra, cap. i. S. Greg. Epist. lib. i. epist. 44 et 75; lib. ix. epist. 19, 99, 100, &c. P. Dionysius de St. Marthe, in his Life of St. Gregory (ubi supra), Thomassin (Ancienne et Nouvelle Discipline, vol. iii. book i. ch. xxvii. n. 7), P. Zaccaria (ubi supra, cap. iii. n. 13), and many other learned men, are inclined to believe, that at the time of St. Gregory, the Roman Church had the dominion of the cities of Naples and of Nepi, wherein she exercised great temporal power; but they admit that this is only a conjecture. It can, in fact, be easily conceived, that the pope, in exercising temporal power in those two cities, as in many other cities and provinces in Italy, was only acting in the name and by the authority of the emperor. The details which we shall give in the first part of this work, on the temporal power exercised by St. Gregory, will confirm this observation.

[2] Thomassin, Anc. et Nouv. Discipline de l'Église, vol. iii. book i. ch. xxvii. n. 8, 17. Zaccaria, ubi supra, cap. 4.

[3] The following are Bede's words, in his Chronicle, A.D. 708:—"Aripertus, rex Longobardorum, multas cohortes, et patrimonia Alpium Cottiarum, *quæ quondam ad jus pertinebant apostolicæ sedis,* sed à Longobardis multo tempore fuerant ablata, *restituit juri ejusdem sedis;* et hanc donationem, aureis scriptam litteris, Romam direxit."—Vol. iii. of Bede's Works, edit. Cologne, 8 vols. folio.

The same fact is given, in almost the same words, by Paulus Diaconus, in his History of the Lombards, book vi. ch. xxviii. (Bib. Max. Patr. vol. xiii.). See also Baronius, Annales, A.D. 704, n. 1; Fleury, Hist. Eccl. vol. ix. book xli. n. 13; Zaccaria, ibid. cap. iii. n. 22-28.

conjecture.[1] At first sight this revenue may, no doubt, appear exorbitant; yet it will not appear incredible, when we reflect that, according to a very common and very probable opinion, the greater number of the patrimonies of the Church in Sicily and in Calabria had been given to her by the emperors after the reign of Theodosius, in exchange for those which she possessed in the East, where it was difficult to collect the revenues, in consequence of the frequent irruptions of the barbarians into the provinces.[2]

81. *Beneficial Influence of the Wealth of the Clergy on the good of Society.*

This continual increase of the wealth of the clergy from the fourth to the eighth century is sufficient evidence of the liberality of princes and people to the Church during that period. But what is equally certain and worthy of attention is, that the ecclesiastics and the religious generally deserved this liberality, and frequently excited it by the holy purposes to which they made it subservient. The increase of their temporal goods generally turned to the advantage of the poor, and to the relief of all the miseries of humanity. It may even be confidently asserted, that this invaluable result of the wealth of the clergy was one of the principal effects of the influence of Christianity on society, and especially on the poorer classes, so numerous at all times, and so universally neglected by the pagans.[3] From her very cradle the

---

[1] This fact is cited, in these terms, in the Chronicle of Theophanes, article on Leo the Isaurian: "Patrimonia Calabriæ et Siciliæ, quæ dicuntur sanctorum et coryphæorum apostolorum qui in veteri Româ coluntur, tria nimirum cum medio auri talenta, eorum ecclesiis ab antiquo assignata et pensa, in publicum ærarium conferri jussit."—Theophanes, Chronographia, Paris, 1655, fol. p. 344. For the value of those three talents and a half of gold, see No. 4 of the Documentary Evidence, at the end of this volume.

[2] Zaccaria, ubi supra, cap. ii. n. 9. Orsi, Della Origine del Dominio e della Sovranita de' Romani Pontefici (in Roma, 1788), cap. ii. The conjectures of these authors appear to be founded on the testimony of Theophanes, who supposes, when Leo the Isaurian seized the revenues of the patrimonies of St. Peter in Sicily and Calabria, that those provinces had been of old bound to pay it to the Holy See. It is difficult to suppose that the patrimonies of Sicily and of Calabria alone could have been so considerable *for a long time previous*, if they had not been given to the Holy See in exchange for many others situated in more distant provinces.

[3] Fleury, Mœurs des Chrétiens, n. 51. Ryan, Benefits of the Christian Reli-

Christian Church appeared raised up by God to call forth on that subject the feelings of humanity, and to inspire all men with a spirit of commiseration to which they had hitherto been utter strangers. To the pagans it was a spectacle altogether novel. When they witnessed that tender charity which united all the faithful together, they exclaimed, in astonishment, as we learn from Tertullian, "See how they love one another."[1] The Emperor Julian himself, that declared enemy of Christianity, was ashamed when he compared the conduct of the pagans in

gion, ch. iii. n. 29, &c. Thomassin, Anc. et Nouv. Discipline, vol. iii. book iv. ch. xlvii. &c. De Héricourt, ibid. part iii. ch. xix. n. 2. Bergier, Diction. Théol. art. Hôpitaux. Naudet, Des Changements opérés dans l'Administration de l'Empire, vol. i. p. 118. Some interesting details on this subject may be seen also in the work of M. de Gérando, entitled, De la Bienfaisance publique, vol. iv. part iii. pp. 271, 459, &c. The author, however, does not appear to be correct in the opinion which he gives on the services rendered to society by Christianity in the establishment of hospitals. He acknowledges, in fact, that nothing of the kind is found in ancient times before the fourth century of our era; and he thinks that Christianity founded these establishments precisely at the period when the necessity of them began to be felt. But he maintains also, that the want of them was not felt among the ancient nations, that want being supplied by three other institutions, which formed a part of ancient morals and customs; namely, hospitality, domestic infirmaries, and slavery, which bound the master to take care of the slave (pp. 271, 460, &c.). Now a very slight acquaintance with history is sufficient, in our opinion, to prove the utter untenableness of those opinions. In the first place, it is certain that the practice of primitive hospitality gradually relaxed, and even totally disappeared, among the ancient nations, especially the Greeks and Romans, in proportion as they departed from their primitive simplicity, which happened long before the origin of Christianity. Secondly, domestic infirmaries were not, as M. de Gérando supposes, ordinary family appendages with the ancient nations; they existed only in some rich families, and for their own private use. Thirdly, with regard to slaves, it is well known that they were generally treated with excessive severity, particularly by the Greeks and Romans, after the coming of Jesus Christ, and even a long time before. (See on this subject a Memoir, by M. de Bonamy, Sur les Esclaves Romains, in the Mém. de l'Acad. des Inscript. vol. xxxv. 4to. edit. p. 328, vol. lxiii. 12mo. edit. p. 102; Voyage d'Anacharsis, vol. ii. p. 108, &c.; vol. iv. p. 105, &c.; Leland, Demons. Evangel. vol. iii. pp. 100, 135, &c.) Facts are cited on this subject by M. de Gérando himself, which ought to have modified his decision (see p. 468, &c.). Indeed, he appears to admit the insufficiency of his proofs, by acknowledging "that the various charitable establishments found among the ancient nations supplied in a very imperfect manner the wants of the unfortunate in the then existing state of society" (p. 277). M. de Gérando would have avoided this sort of inconsistency, had he studied more attentively on this subject the authors whom we have cited in the commencement of this note.

[1] "Sed ejusmodi vel maximè dilectionis (mutuæ) operatio, notam nobis inurit penes quosdam. 'Vide,' inquiunt, 'ut invicem se diligant;' ipsi enim invicem oderunt. 'Et ut pro alterutro mori sint parati;' ipsi enim ad occidendum alterutrum paratiores."—Apologet. cap. xxxix.

this regard with that of the Christians. This appears particularly in his letter to Arsaces, pontiff of Galatia, in which he exhorts him to establish hospitals for the relief of the poor, after the example of the Christians, "who support," he says, "not only their own poor, but ours, whom we leave utterly destitute."[1]

82. *Charitable Establishments—Hospitals.*

The tender and universal charity of the clergy and of the faithful manifested itself not only in habitual almsdeeds, but also in the erection of a great number of public asylums destined for the relief of all the miseries of humanity. The Greeks and Romans, so eminent above all other nations for their civilization, their skill in government, and their success in the arts and sciences, either did not know or totally neglected this admirable means of relieving human miseries and infirmities. Their whole policy on this point was confined, as Fleury observes,[2] "*to the suppression of idleness and of able-bodied pauperism,*" or, at most, to some transitory measures of relief in times of unusual distress. Amongst them there was no permanent and public system devoted to the service of those poor creatures who can be of no use to society; there were none of those charitable institutions which Christianity has made so common in all the countries where it was established, and which it appears to have been the first to introduce. The ancient authors who have described in greatest detail the monuments of Rome and of Constantinople, and of the other celebrated cities of antiquity, describe palaces, and baths, and theatres, and temples; ports, and public granaries, and prisons, and other edifices of public utility; but they mention no establishment destined as an asylum for the sick and the unfortunate.[3] The first hospitals

---

[1] Julian, Epist. 49, ad Arsacium Pontif. (Operum, p. 430, fol.). This letter is given at the end of the Vie de l'Empereur Jovien, by Labletterie, p. 468.

[2] Fleury, Mœurs des Chrétiens, n. 51.

[3] Infirmaries (valetudinaria), of which there is question in Seneca, Columella, and some other ancient authors, were not public establishments, but apartments in or near the residences of the great, for such of their servants as lived

mentioned in history were founded by the charity of the Christians. In his discourse against Julian, composed in 363, St. Gregory of Nazianzen supposes as a fact, that a great number of those private asylums had been founded before the reign of that prince, who endeavoured in vain to found others on their plan.[1] From that period, we see this new order of establishments multiplied rapidly in all parts of the empire, and in all countries whither Christianity penetrated. St. Basil built an hospital for the poor in his episcopal city, about the year 372, and succeeded afterwards in building others in many towns and villages throughout his diocese.[2] Some years later, St. Pammachus established one at Porto, near Rome, for strangers; and another in Rome, with the aid of Fabiola, a Roman lady, who devoted herself in it with the most tender charity to attendance on the sick.[3] St. Augustine, about the same time, erected at Hippo, an hospice for strangers,[4] and St. Gallican another at Ostia.[5] From several constitutions of the emperor Justinian, it is manifest that in his time there were a great number of hospitals established in different parts of the empire, and that he conferred great privileges on these invaluable institutions.[6]

Ducange, in his description of the monuments erected at Constantinople under the Christian emperors, mentions thirty-five charitable institutions intended for the support of the different

with them. See the notes of Justus Lipsius on Seneca, De Irâ, lib. i. cap. xvi. et Epist. 27; Columella, De Re Rusticâ, lib. xi. cap. i.; Ryan, Benefits of the Christian Religion, ch. iii. n. 31.

[1] "Diversoria et hospitales domos, monasteria item et virginum cœnobia ædificare statuebat, simùlque et benignitatem erga pauperes adjungere, cùm in aliis rebus, tum in commendatitiis epistolis sitam, quibus eos qui inopiâ premuntur, ex gente ad gentem transmittimus; quæ videlicet ille in nostris rebus præsertim admiratus fuerat... Illius autem conatus inanis et irritus fuit, etc."—St. Greg. de Naz. Orat. 1, contra Julian. n. 111, 112 (edit. Bened. tom. i. p. 138).

[2] St. Basil, Epist. 94, 142, 143, 176, &c. (Oper. tom. iii.). St. Greg. de Naz. Orat. 43 (alias 20), n. 63 (Oper. tom. i. p. 817).

[3] St. Jerome, Epist. 54, ad Pammach. p. 586; Epist. 84, ad Oceanum (Oper. tom. iv. p. 662).

[4] St. Augustine, Serm. 356, n. 10 (Oper. tom. v.).

[5] Baronius, Martyrol. June 25.

[6] Cod. Justin. lib. i. tit. ii. n. 19, 22, et alibi passim.

classes of the poor.[1] Most of these houses were called by names which sufficiently indicated their destination. The Brephotrophium was an asylum for babes yet on their mothers' breasts ; the Orphanotrophium, for orphans ; the Nosocomium, for the sick ; the Xenodochium, for strangers or travellers ; the Gerontocomium, for old persons ; the Ptochotrophium, for all sorts of poor. These establishments were ordinarily placed under the superintendence of the bishop, who appointed some priest to represent him, and who spared no pains to procure all sorts of relief for the sick and for the poor.[2]

83. *Redemption of Captives, and Enfranchisement of Slaves.*

The bishops also devoted great care to the burial of the poor, and to the purchase of captives taken by the barbarians, as they frequently were in the decline of the empire. Even the sacred vessels were sold for charitable purposes of this kind. St. Ambrose sold them for the purchase of captives carried off by the Goths in the reign of Valens and Gratian.[3] About the same time, St. Exuperius, of Toulouse, reduced himself to such poverty, that he was under the necessity of preserving the body of our Lord in a case of ozier, and the precious blood in a chalice of glass.[4]

Another work of charity highly esteemed in the Church, and practised especially by the clergy, was the purchase and emancipation of slaves, principally of Christians, who belonged to Pagan or Jewish masters. From the origin of Christianity this had always been considered one of the most meritorious works of charity, and most conformable to the spirit of religion. To encourage it, Constantine at first, about the year 321, permitted

---

[1] Ducange, Hist. Byzant. part ii. Descript. Constantinopoleos Christianæ, lib. iv. § 9 (p. 113 edit. of Venice).

[2] St. Epiph. Hæresi, 75, n. 1. From these details we may correct the singular opinion of some modern authors, who refer the origin of hospitals to the time of the first crusades. See Peyrilhe, Hist. de la Chirurgie, book v. p. 421 ; Choiseul-Daillecourt, Influence des Croisades, p. 203.

[3] St. Ambrose, De Offic. lib. ii. cap. xi. xxviii. Fleury, book xvii. n. 39.

[4] St. Jerome, Epist. 95, ad Rusticum Monach. (Oper. tom. iv. p. 778).

these enfranchisements to take place in the churches, the mere presence of the clergy and of the faithful dispensing with all the formalities previously required for their validity. He moreover gave general permission to all clerics to enfranchise their slaves even privately, without any public act, and by the simple manifestation of their will;[1] and though it was generally prohibited to perform any judicial act on Sunday, he expressly exempted from that prohibition these enfranchisements, as being acts of religion most suitable for the sanctification of the sabbath day.[2] From that period enfranchisements became every day more common. Ecclesiastics, and especially the bishops, not content with recommending compassion for those slaves, generally enfranchised a great number that belonged to themselves. St. Gregory the Great frequently repeated that example of charity, and omitted no opportunity of recommending it to the bishops, and to all the faithful in general.[3] The principles and practice of the primitive ages on this point, being generally followed even by the barbarous nations, in proportion as Christianity penetrated among them, gradually effected the abolition of slavery throughout all Christian Europe.[4]

---

[1] "Qui religiosâ mente, in Ecclesiæ gremio, servulis suis meritam concesserit libertatem, eamdem eodem jure donâsse videatur, quo civitas Romana solemnitatibus decursis dari consuevit; sed hoc duntaxat iis qui sub aspectu antistitum dederint, placuit relaxari. Clericis autem ampliùs concedimus, ut cùm suis famulis tribuunt libertatem, non solùm in conspectu Ecclesiæ ac religiosi populi plenum fructum libertatis concessisse dicantur [i. e. *censeantur*], verùm etiam, cùm postremo judicio libertates dederint, seu quibuscumque verbis dari præceperint; ita ut, ex die publicatæ voluntatis, sine aliquo juris teste vel interprete, competat directa [i. e. *integra et plena*] libertas."—Cod. Theod. lib. iv. tit. vii. n. 1. D. Ceillier, Hist. des Aut. Eccl. tom. iv. p. 171. See on this subject a paper by Bouchaud, in the Mémoires de l'Académie des Inscript. 4to. edit. vol. xl. p. 119.

[2] "Sicut indignissimum videbatur (*vigente paganismo*) diem solis, veneratione suî celebrem, altercantibus jurgiis, et noxiis partium contentionibus occupari; ita gratum ac jucundum est, eo die quæ sunt maximè votiva [i. e. *quæ votis maximè expetuntur*] compleri. Atque ideo emancipandi et manumittendi, die festo, cuncti licentiam habeant, et super his rebus actus non prohibeantur."—Ibid. lib. ii. tit. viii. n. 1.

[3] Joan. Diac. Vita S. Greg. lib. iv. cap. xliv. St. Greg. Epist. lib. vi. Epist. 32, 33, et alibi passim.

[4] Ryan, Benefits of the Christian Religion, ch. iii. n. 32. L'Ami de la Religion, vol. lxxxviii. p. 17. Bibliographie Catholique, année 1, p. 221. De Maistre, Du Pape, vol. ii. book iii. ch. ii.

84. *Generous Charity of the Roman Church.*

The Roman Church in particular increased its alms and its beneficence in proportion as its revenues increased. From the time of the persecutions, history exhibits to us the Roman pontiffs invariably applying to the relief of the poor and to the support of the churches, the rich offerings presented to her from all quarters by the piety of princes and of nations. St. Jerome records this especially of Pope Anastasius, whom for that reason, he describes as a man "of the richest poverty and of apostolical solicitude."[1] St. Leo the Great devoted the revenues of his see with boundless generosity to repair the havoc which Italy had to suffer from the irruption of the Vandals, and especially to rebuild or repair the churches in Rome, which they had pillaged or destroyed.[2] Pope Gelasius I. voluntarily reduced himself to poverty for the support of a great number of destitute persons.[3] The pontificate of St. Gregory, especially, deserves to be cited as the most perfect model of pastoral charity.[4] That great pope was piously lavish of the property of the Church for the relief of the poor, not only in Rome and in Italy, but in all parts of the Christian world. The collection of his letters contains many addressed to the administrators or rectors of the patrimonies of the Roman Church, situate in

---

[1] "Vir ditissimæ paupertatis, et apostolicæ sollicitudinis."—S. Hieron. Epist. 97, ad Demetriad. (Oper. tom. iv. parte ii. p. 793).

[2] "Hic renovavit, post cladem Vandalicam, omnia ministeria [i. e. *ornamenta sive utensilia*] argentea, per omnes titulos (Ecclesiarum Romanæ urbis). . . . Renovavit Basilicam S. Petri apostoli, et fecit ibi cameram [i. e. *fornicem*] quam et ornavit; et beati Pauli Basilicam post ignem divinum renovavit; fecit et cameram in eâdem similiter, et in Basilicâ Constantinianâ, etc."—Anastas. Biblioth. Vita S. Leonis (Labbe, Concil. tom. iii. p. 1290).

[3] This fact is recorded by Dion. Exiguus, in the preface to his Code of Canons, addressed to Julian, arch-priest of St. Anastasia. The author of that preface passes a great eulogium on Pope Gelasius, especially for his charity to the poor: "Tantâ misericordiâ, cum animi alacritate, clarescebat, ut omnes ferè pauperes satians, inops ipse moreretur."—Dionys. Exig. Præf. in Can. (Labb. Concilior. tom. i. p. 4).

[4] Joan. Diac. Vita S. Greg. lib. ii. n. 24, &c. 51, &c. S. Greg. Vita recens adornata, lib. ii. cap. iii. n. 5; lib. iii. cap. ix. n. 2, &c. (vol. iv. of St. Gregory's works). Thomassin, Ancien. et Nouv. Discip. vol. iii. book iii. chap. xxix. n. 14, &c. Fleury, Hist. Eccl. vol. viii. book xxxv. n. 16.

different countries, exhorting them to increase their charities to the monasteries, to orphans, to widows, to all the poor, and especially to those who were ashamed to beg. To excite his subjects by his example, he distributed every day abundant alms in Rome, increasing them at certain times of the year, or on the first day of the month, at the approach of great festivals, and especially during the calamities which the incursions of the barbarians brought down so frequently in those days on Italy and on the other provinces of the western empire. Amongst the poor supported by him at Rome, there were, he tells us, three thousand nuns, to whom he gave annually twenty-four livres of gold, which is about £3,683 of our money.[1] So late as the ninth century, there was extant in the Lateran palace, a register of the poor of every age and sex whom this holy pope supported constantly in Rome, in Italy, and in cities beyond the seas, and an account of the stated sums which he allowed to them. So immense was the multitude of these poor, that the author who mentions them, could not give their number in detail, because it would be too fatiguing to the reader.[2] Long before the pontificate of St. Gregory, there existed in every place where the Roman Church had a patrimony, an hospital for the poor, called a Diaconia, from being generally administered by a deacon. St. Gregory not only preserved these valuable institutions, but frequently ordered the rectors of the patrimonies to devote all the revenues derived from them to the

---

[1] The following are St. Gregory's words in a letter to the princess Theoctista, sister of the emperor Maurice, who had sent to him thirty livres of gold (about £1,382. 10s. of our money), for the ransom of captives, and the relief of the poor: "Medietatem pecuniæ quam transmisistis, in eorum [*captivorum*] redemptionem transmisi. De medietate verò ancillis Dei, quas vos Græcâ linguâ *monastrias* (latinè *sanctimoniales*) dicitis, lectisternia emere disposui, quia in lectis suis gravi nuditate, in hujus hiemis vehementissimo frigore, laborant. Quæ in hâc urbe multæ sunt; nam juxta notitiam quâ dispensantur, tria millia reperiuntur; et quidem de sancti Petri apostolorum principis rebus, *octoginta annuas libras accipiunt.* Sed ad tantam multitudinem ista quid sunt, maximè in hâc urbe, ubi omnia gravi pretio emuntur?"—S. Greg. Epistol. lib. vii. epist. xxvi. (Oper. vol. p. 872). For the value of 80 pounds of gold, see No. 2 of the Documentary Evidences, at the end of this work.

[2] Joan. Diac. Vita S. Greg. lib. ii. n. 30.

support of the poor of the place; and in one of his letters, he declares expressly, that if he appoints clerics for the administration of those patrimonies, it is principally to make them, by a wise administration, available for the relief of a greater number of poor.[1]

Nor was it to the poor alone that he dispensed so liberally the revenues of the Church. We shall soon see him expending them with the same liberality in the defence of the empire, which was at the time fiercely assailed by the Lombards; and we shall find his generosity in the same cause adopted as the rule and principle by all his successors, until the complete extinction of the Roman empire in the West.

85. *The increase of the Wealth of the Church generally beneficial to Society.*

In drawing this description of the virtues and charity of the clergy at this period, we are far from supposing that there were not abuses in the use and administration of ecclesiastical property, or that all the members of the clergy were equally distinguished for their generosity and disinterestedness. One should be ignorant alike of human nature and of history not to know that ages most fruitful in heroic virtues were also sullied by many disorders. So long as society is composed of men, and not of angels, we may indeed wish, but can never reasonably hope, for the constant fidelity of all its members to the strict rules of evangelical detachment and abnegation. The increase of the wealth of the Church must therefore have been necessarily an occasion of luxury and of dissipation for some of its members, and many examples of these abuses are found, we admit, even in the best ages. But however certain were those abuses, which have been so often exaggerated by the malignant enemies of religion, it is certain that the errors of some individuals cannot

---

[1] "Non solùm frequentibus præceptionibus, sed etiam præsentem te sæpiùs monuisse me memini, ut illic vice nostrâ, *non tantùm pro utilitatibus ecclesiasticis, quantùm pro sublevandis pauperum necessitatibus, fungereris*, et eos magis à cujuslibet oppressionibus vindicares."—S. Greg. Epistol. lib. i. epist. lv. (Oper. vol. ii. p. 547).

sully, in the estimation of candid and impartial men, the splendour of the virtues generally produced by the body of which they were members. Even a superficial glance at the history of this period must extort the admission that the clergy were generally distinguished for their charity, as well as for all the other virtues of their state; that the increase of their wealth was for society at large, and especially for all classes of the unfortunate, a fruitful source of useful institutions, and of resources hitherto unknown; finally, that the Church, so far from forming in her minister a taste for luxury and superfluous expense, the natural concomitants of great wealth, firmly repressed them both by wise regulations and by the examples of a number of holy pastors; so that, notwithstanding the occasional abuses which she could not prevent, or which she was obliged to tolerate, the increase of her wealth was as beneficial to society as it was creditable to the religious feelings which had induced princes and people to be so generous to the clergy.

86. *Injustice of the Invectives against the Clergy on this subject.*

From these observations we can judge how misplaced and unjust are the invectives of some modern authors against the clergy of the most brilliant ages of the Church, because of the rapid increase of ecclesiastical wealth after the conversion of Constantine. "In that rapid transition from a state of misery and persecution to the summit of prosperity, the Church," says one of those authors, "soon degenerated from her primitive purity, and forfeited her title to the respect of future ages, in the same proportion in which she gained the veneration of her own. Avarice especially became the characteristic vice of the clergy."[1] Accusations so abominable made against the whole ecclesiastical body of that period are manifestly contradicted by history, which proves, on the contrary, that the clergy merited the liberality of princes and people by the practice of all Christian virtues, and especially by a tender and inexhaustible charity

[1] Hallam's Europe in the Middle Ages, vol. iii. p. 294.

for the poor. The law of Valentinian I., which we have cited above,[1] and which this author adduces in proof of his calumny, implies it is true that some of the clergy were then suspected, and perhaps guilty, of avarice and cupidity. But to assert that these vices were then dominant among the clergy, and formed their distinctive characteristic, is a supposition not only unfounded, but clearly refuted by history. In venturing such an opinion, this author contradicted the universal testimony of the most learned authors even of his own communion.[2]

But it is not in modern times alone that the wealth of the clergy exposed them to the reproaches and to the jealousy of their enemies, and that the irregular conduct of a small number of ecclesiastics gave occasion to slandering tongues to declaim against the whole body of which they were members. Even at this period of which we are speaking, there were found not only among pagans, but sometimes even among Christians, carping and malignant men, who condemned the clergy with excessive severity, and who, under the pretence of reminding them of the perfection of their state, loudly reproached them with their wealth and with their abuse of it, in securing for themselves all the enjoyments and luxuries of life. In this manner Ammianus Marcellinus, a pagan author, bitterly opposed to Christianity, exaggerates the disparity in respect of comfort and wealth between the pope and the provincial bishops, from the close of the fourth century;[3] "as if," observes Fleury, "it were surprising

---

[1] Supra, art. 75.

[2] Ryan, Benefits of the Christian Religion, ch. iii. n. 29, &c. This author cites many others who were members of his own church, the Anglican.

M. Beugnot, in his Hist. de la Destruction du Pagan. en Occident, is certainly far from admitting Hallam's odious declamations on this subject. Yet we must accuse him of favouring them, by the not very favourable character which he gives of the clergy in general at this time, and even of St. Ambrose, whom he represents as influenced by avarice under the cloak of disinterestedness (vol. i. pp. 429, 430, text and note). This opinion, like many others, is the result of that pernicious principle on which M. Beugnot composed his work; namely, that, in order to write a faithful history of the fall of paganism, we should distrust Christian authors, and study principally the writings of their adversaries (ibid. p. 4). See our observations on this subject in No. 1 of Documentary Evidence, at the close of this volume.

[3] This passage of Ammianus Marcellinus relates to the troubles occasioned

that the bishop of the capital of the world kept a coach to visit the different quarters of so large a city; that he was well dressed; and that he had a table fit to receive the first men in the empire."[1]

87. *Answer of St. John Chrysostom to those Invectives.*

But it is especially interesting to hear St. John Chrysostom, in defence of his clergy against the reproaches which their riches drew down upon them from certain laics.[2] The answer of the holy doctor is the more remarkable, because no person denounced more energetically luxury and worldly living among the clergy; and because his defence of the clergy of Constantinople on this point applies with still greater force to the clergy of the other cities of the empire, who were even less exposed to imbibe tastes for luxury and for superfluous expense than those of the capital.

In the first place, St. John Chrysostom observes that those who denounce the wealth of the clergy as a crime, prove themselves worse than the Jews, who made no such charge against the priests of the old law, to whom they punctually paid tithes and first-fruits, and many other sorts of revenues. He then reminds those accusers, that, living as they generally did in the

---

at Rome by the anti-pope Ursinus, who could not bear that Damasus had been preferred to him as successor of Liberius, in 366. Ammianus attributes the conflicting pretensions of the two parties to their desire of enjoying the immense wealth then attached to the popedom: "Neque ego abnuo," says he, "ostentationem rerum considerans urbanarum, hujus rei cupidos, ob impetrandum id quod appetunt, omni contentione laterum jurgari debere; cùm id adepti, futuri sint ita securi, ut ditentur oblationibus matronarum, procedantque vehiculis insidentes, circumspectè vestiti, epulas curantes profusas, adeo ut eorum convivia regales superent mensas. Qui esse poterant beati reverâ, si magnitudine urbis despectâ, quam vitiis opponunt, ad imitationem quorumdam provincialium viverent, quos tenuitas edendi potandique parcissimè, vilitas etiam indumentorum, et supercilia humum spectantia, perpetuo numini, verisque ejus cultoribus, ut puros commendant et verecundos." — Ammianus Marcellinus, Histor. lib. xxvii. cap. iii. (p. 481 of the Paris ed. 1681, folio). Fleury, Hist. Eccl. vol. iv. book xvi. n. 8; Mœurs des Chrétiens, n. 49.

[1] Mœurs des Chrétiens, n. 49, towards the end. See, in support of these reflections, Annals of Baronius, ann. 367, n. 8, &c.

[2] St. John Chrysost. Homil. ix. in Epistol. ad Philipp. n. 4, 5; idem, Homil. i. in Epist. ad Titum, n. 4 (Oper. vol. xi.). Thomassin, Anc. et Nouv. Discipl. vol. iii. book iii. chap. xxxvi. n. 13, &c.

lap of luxury and abundance, it was very bad grace in them to charge the clergy with luxury and sumptuous living, to which they were for the most part strangers; that it was absurd to call that wealth and abundance in a priest which was in reality nothing more than common decency,—such as to be well dressed, to take proper food, and to have a domestic to attend him; that the wealth of an ecclesiastic consisted in his knowing how to be content with little; while laics, on the contrary, are frequently poor in the midst of abundance. "If *you* have given the cleric the property which he holds, why," asks the holy doctor, "do you reproach him with it as a crime? It were better that you had given him nothing, than to be thus reproaching him with your own gifts. But if another has given it to him, you are still more guilty in presuming to censure the liberality of another; and your reproaches are the more unjust, because those whom you assail have voluntarily renounced all lucrative professions, to consecrate themselves to the service of God and of the Church. In truth, what does he gain by the exercise of his functions? Is he clothed in silks?—does he strut in public followed by a train of valets?—does he ride a charger?—or build a house, when he has one good enough to lodge him? If he does all this, I as well as you censure him; and, far from excusing him, I think him a disgrace to the priesthood; for how can he exhort others to despise superfluities if he cannot himself dispense with them? But if you think it a crime in him to provide himself with necessaries, do you wish, then, that he should beg? Now, candidly, would not you,—you, his disciple, be ashamed of that? Undoubtedly, if your father according to the flesh were reduced to that extremity, you would consider it a disgrace to yourself; and if your father according to the spirit were in the same state, will you not blush for it?"[1]

The accusers of the clergy pretended, moreover, that the spirit of the Gospel obliges all ecclesiastics to poverty. The holy

[1] St. Chrysos. Homil. ix. in Epist. ad Philipp. n. 4.

doctor answers that we must not be so sharp-eyed to the defects of others and so blind to our own; that the exhortation of St. Paul "to be content with food and raiment,"[1] was addressed not only to the clergy, but to all the faithful; that both may possess the goods of this world without being attached to them; and that St. Paul, in particular, made no difficulty in working at a lucrative trade, in order to provide himself with a decent support.[2] In support of these reflections, St. John Chrysostom adds, in another place, that the apostles themselves were served and relieved in their necessities by persons of the highest quality, gentlemen and ladies, who considered it an honour to expose their lives in defence of the ministers of Jesus Christ; whence he infers, that though delicacies and superfluities are censurable in a priest, it is but just that he be allowed to take reasonable care of his body, that he may be able to support the labour of his ministry, his journeys, pastoral visits, and so many other functions, equally fatiguing and necessary.[3]

SECTION IV.

Ecclesiastical Immunities under the Christian Emperors—Right of Sanctuary.[4]

88. *Origin of Ecclesiastical Immunities.*

Among the temporal advantages which the Church derived from the protection of the Christian emperors, must be remarked, in particular, those useful or honourable privileges afterwards called immunities. Their origin may be traced to a letter of

---

[1] 1 Tim. vi. 8.

[2] St. Chrysos. Hom. ix. Epist. ad Philipp. n. 5.

[3] Idem, Hom. i. in Epist. ad Tit. n. 4.

[4] Cod. Theod. with the Commentaries of Godefroy, lib. xi. tit. xvi.; lib. xvi. tit. ii. &c. Cod. Justin. lib. i. tit. ii. iii. iv. xi. xiv., et alibi passim. Thomass. Ancienne et Nouvell. Discip. vol. iii. book i. cap. xxxiii. xxxiv. De Héricourt, abridgment of the same work, part iii. ch. vii. Bingham, Origines et Antiquitates Ecclesiasticæ, vol. ii. lib. v. cap. ii. iii. Natal Alexander, Hist. Eccles. sæc. iv. cap. v. art. 12; Hist. sæc. v. cap. vi. art. 6; Hist. sæc. vi. cap. vi. art. 7. Naudet, Des Changements opérés dans l'Administration de l'Empire, vol. ii. ch. ii. p. 40, &c. Dupuy, Traité de la Jurisp. Crimin. part i. ch. ii. viii. &c. (at the end of the Traité des Libertés de l'Église Gallicane). Bergier, Diction. Théol. art. Immunités.

Constantine, in the year 313, to Anulinus, proconsul of Africa. "It being certain," observes that great prince, "that the contempt of the Christian religion, which honours God in so perfect a manner, has drawn down the greatest evils on the empire, and that fidelity in embracing and in preaching it is, by the divine mercy, a source of prosperity for the state as well as for individuals, I have resolved to reward those who consecrate themselves to the support of that august religion by the holiness of their lives, and by the assiduous discharge of their functions. My will is, therefore, that all those who are called clerics, and who are attached to the ministry of that religion in the Catholic Church, of which Cecilian is pastor,[1] be exempted from all public charges throughout the whole province under your jurisdiction ; lest, by a fatal error, or a sacrilegious exaction, they be diverted from the divine worship ; and that they may in perfect liberty consecrate themselves to the functions of their ministry ; for I am convinced that the homage which they shall thus give to the Divine Majesty will procure the greatest favours for the empire."[2]

Animated by the example of Constantine, and guided by the same spirit of religion, his successors confirmed and frequently extended the immunities which he had granted to the Church. At times, however, they thought it necessary to restrict them, either for reasons of state, or for some other considerations of public interest. We do not undertake to enter here into a detail of all the fluctuations of the Roman law on this point, a full history of which involves many difficulties, yet disputed among the learned.[3] For our purposes it is enough to point

---

[1] Cecilian was then bishop of Carthage, and in that capacity metropolitan of the province of Africa, that is, of Western Africa. See on this subject Baudrand, Geogr. Sacra, lib. iv. p. 79 ; Apparatus Concil. Append. Geogr. Episc. cap. xii.

[2] Euseb. Hist. Eccles. lib. x. cap. vii. Fleury, Hist. Eccl. vol. iii. book x. n. 2. D. Ceillier, Hist. des Auteurs Ecclés. vol. iv. pp. 150, 170. Comment. of Godefroy on the Theodosian Code, lib. xvi. tit. ii. n. 1.

[3] This subject appears to be treated with much care and solidity by Bingham, ubi supra. He may serve as a corrective on some points for Thomassin (ubi

out, in the Roman law itself, the origin of those ecclesiastical immunities which were subsequently so much extended by the liberality of Christian princes. We shall therefore only mention briefly the principal immunities, real or personal, conferred on the clergy by the Christian emperors.[1]

89. *Personal Immunities.*

The personal immunities then enjoyed by the clergy may be reduced to four principal heads.

First. *Exemption from curial or municipal charges.*[2] Constantine's letter, already cited, to Anulinus, proconsul of Africa, shows the origin and principal grounds of this immunity, which was subsequently explained and confirmed in a great number of edicts by Constantine and by his successors. This exemption, which the pagan priests had long enjoyed, was much sought for at the time, even by persons of high rank and fortune, principally on account of the trouble and expense entailed by a great number of curial or municipal functions. So great were the trouble and expense, that those who were selected by the cities or by the prince to discharge these functions frequently employed every means to evade them.[3]

Secondly. *Exemption from certain personal duties,* principally

---

supra), and even for the learned commentary of Godefroy on the Theodosian code.

[1] Personal immunities are those which directly affect the person ; real, are those which directly affect property.

[2] In the very year after his conversion to Christianity, Constantine enacted a law which supposes this immunity as already established by the emperor. The following is the text of that law, which was addressed to a governor of a province : "Hæreticorum factione comperimus Ecclesiæ Catholicæ clericos ita vexari, ut nominationibus [ad publica munera] seu susceptionibus aliquibus [eorumdem munerum] quas publicus mos exposcit, *contra indulta sibi privilegia prægraventur.* Ideoque placet, si quem tua Gravitas invenerit ita vexatum, eidem alium subrogari, et deinceps à supradictæ religionis hominibus [clericis nempe] hujusmodi injurias prohiberi."—Cod. Theod. lib. xvi. tit. ii. n. 1.

This law was confirmed in 319 by another law of Constantine, in the following terms : "Qui divino cultui ministeria religionis impendunt (id est, hi qui clerici appellantur), ab omnibus omninò muneribus excusentur, ne sacrilego livore quorumdam, à divinis obsequiis avocentur."—Ibid. n. 2. See on the same subject, n. 7, 9, 11, 16, 24, &c. of the same tit. ; Fleury, Hist. Eccĺes. vol. iii. book x. n. 2 and 40 ; book xi. n. 46.

[3] Godefroy, Comment. sur le Code Théodosien, book xii. ; Preamble of tit. i. Beugnot, Hist. de la Destruction du Pagan. en Occident, vol. i. pp. 77, 78, 93.

from those which were called *vile or sordid functions*, and from which citizens eminent either for rank or wealth were generally exempt.[1] Such were certain *corveés* generally imposed on private persons for the service of the state; as, for example, the repairing of the public roads, the service of the post-office, the lodging of troops or officers of the prince on their marches, &c. &c. Many of those *corveés* implied that those who were liable to them followed some trade or mechanical art, ordinarily confined to persons of low condition.

Thirdly. *Exemption from the capitation or personal taxes.*[2] This immunity, which was originally granted to the Roman Church by Constantine, was afterwards extended to all the Catholic clergy by that prince and his successors. Valentinian I. extended it even to virgins, widows, and deaconesses;[3] and what

---

[1] We find in the Cod. Theodos. many edicts of the emperor Constantius on this subject. We shall cite only a few of the most remarkable. The first, which was addressed to all clerics, is represented in the following terms: "Juxta sanctionem [seu *legem*] quam dudum meruisse perhibemini, et vos et mancipia vestra nullus novis collationibus obligabit; sed vacatione gaudebitis. Præterea neque hospites suscipietis; et si qui de vobis, alimoniæ causâ, negotiationem exercere volunt, immunitate potientur."—Cod. Theod. lib. xvi. tit. 2, n. 8.

This immunity was extended and confirmed by a subsequent constitution of the emperors Constantius and Constans, addressed to all the bishops of their territories in the following terms: "Ut ecclesiarum cœtus concursu populorum frequentetur, clericis ac juvenibus [i. e. *clericorum ministris*] præbeatur immunitas; repellaturque ab his exactio munerum sordidorum; negotiatorum dispendiis minimè obligentur, cùm certum sit quæstus quos ex tabernaculis atque ergasteriis colligunt, pauperibus profuturos. Ab hominibus etiam eorum qui mercimoniis student, cuncta dispendia [amovenda] esse sancimus. *Parangariarum* quoque [seu *cursûs publici*] parili modo cesset exactio. Quod et conjugibus, et liberis eorum, et ministeriis, maribus pariter et fœminis, indulgemus; quos à censibus etiam jubemus perseverare immunes." — Ibid. n. 10. See for a fuller development, lib. xi. tit. xvi. n. 15, 18, 21, 22.

[2] Cod. Theodos. lib. xvi. vol. ii. Besides n. 10, cited in a preceding note, see also n. 13 and 14. We suppose here, according to the common opinion, the existence of the capitation or personal tax under Constantine and his successors. Godefroy combats that opinion strongly in his Commentary on the Theodosian Code, but he is not generally followed by the learned on this point. Among others, Bingham appears to have solidly refuted him (Bingham, ubi supra, cap. iii. § i.). See also Naudet, ubi supra, vol. i. p. 345, &c.; vol. ii. p. 322.

[3] "In virginitate perpetuâ viventes, et eam viduam de quâ ipsa maturitas pollicetur nulli jam eam esse nupturam, à plebeiæ capitationis injuriâ vindicandos esse decernimus; item pupillos in virili sexu, usque ad viginti annos, ab istiusmodi functione immunes esse debere; mulieres autem, donec virum unaquæque sortitur."—Cod. Theod. lib. xiii. tit. x. n. 4. See also n. 6, same tit. Fleury, Hist. Eccl. vol. iv. book xvi. n. 1.

appears at first sight very surprising, it applied even to clergy engaged in commerce, to their wives, their children, and their servants.[1] The following were the occasion and grounds of this provision of the law. It is certain that the Church then allowed the clergy to procure for themselves, by commerce or labour, the means of subsistence, and of giving more abundant alms.[2] It was in accordance with those views of the Church that the first Christian emperors granted this immunity to the clergy. Nevertheless, to prevent the abuses which it might occasion, Constantius declared that it included none but the clergy who confined themselves to small traffic, but not to those inscribed on the list of great merchants.[3] Even this restricted exemption was in the end suppressed by Valentinian III. at a period when the increase of ecclesiastical property rendered commerce less necessary for the clergy, and when the Church herself deemed it advisable to prohibit it, on account of the abuses to which it might give birth.

Fourthly. One of the principal immunities of the clergy under the Christian emperors was *exemption* from *secular jurisdiction.* We shall discuss it at greater length in the following paragraph, in which we examine the question, what was at that time the jurisdiction or judicial power of the bishops in temporal matters.

The importance and the extent of these immunities soon gave rise to some abuses, which the emperors speedily repressed by their edicts. Persons sometimes embraced the clerical profession,

---

[1] Cod. Theod. lib. xvi. tit. ii. n. 8, 10, and 14. We have cited n. 8 and 10 in note 1, p. 134.

[2] Thomassin, Ancien. et Nouv. Discipline, vol. iii. book iii. ch. xvii. xviii. De Héricourt, abridgment of the same work, part iii. ch. xvii.

[3] "Clerici....ita à sordidis muneribus debent immunes, atque à collatione præstari [i. e. *à tributo negotiatoribus imposito*], si exiguis admodum mercimoniis tenuem sibi victum vestitumque conquirent. Reliqui autem, quorum nomina negotiatorum matricula comprehendit, eo tempore quo collatio celebrata est [seu *instituta est*], negotiatorum munia et pensitationes agnoscant; quippe postmodum clericorum se cœtibus aggregarunt."—Cod. Theodos. lib. xvi. tit. ii. n. 15.

[4] "Jubemus ut clerici nihil prorsus negotiationis exerceant; si velint negotiari, sciant se judicibus subditos, clericorum privilegio non muniri."—Valentiniani Novella 2, versus medium (ad calcem Codicis Theodos. ed. Ritter, vol. vi. p. 417). Thomassin, Ancienne et Nouv. Discipline, vol. iii. book i. ch. xxxiii. n. 5, &c.; ch. xxxiv. n. 4.

it was discovered, with the sole motive of enjoying the ecclesiastical immunities, and especially of avoiding the municipal functions to which they were liable by their rank or fortune. To check this disorder, Constantine prohibited more clerics to be ordained than were necessary for the service of the Church, or that they should be selected from those whose rank and fortune made them liable to public offices; "for it is just," observes the law, "that the rich should bear the charges of the world, and that the poor should be supported by the property of the Church."[1] Nevertheless, this law was modified afterwards by the emperor Constantius in favour of the bishops, and even generally in favour of such clergy as were called to the service of the Church with the consent of the municipal council, and by the universal suffrage of the people, which at that time had great weight in the election of the sacred ministers.[2]

90. *Real Immunities.*

The real immunities of the clergy underwent far more changes under the Christian emperors than those personal immunities. At first Constantine exempted all ecclesiastical property from public charges;[3] but this exemption did not last long; and there is every reason to believe that the chief cause of its being

[1] Cod. Theodos. lib. xvi. tit. ii. n. 3 and 6. "Opulentos enim," says this last law, "sæculi subire necessitates oportet, pauperes ecclesiarum divitiis sustentari."—Fleury, Hist. Eccl. vol. iii. book xi. n. 31. D. Ceillier, Hist. des Auteurs Ecclés. vol. iv. p. 175. Thomassin, Ancienne et Nouv. Discipline, vol. i. book iii. ch. lxi.

[2] "Solum episcopum facultates suas curiæ, sicut antè fuerat constitutum, nullus adigat mancipare; sed antistes maneat, nec faciat substantiæ cessionem. Sanè si qui ad presbyterorum gradus, diaconorum etiam seu subdiaconorum, cæterorumque [*clericorum gradus*] pervenerint, assistente curiâ, ac sub obtutibus judicis promente consensum (cùm eorum vitam insignem atque innocentem esse omni probitate constiterit) habere debet [*eorum unusquisque*] patrimonium probabilis institui [i. e. *patrimonium legitimè acquisitum*], ut retineat proprias facultates; maximè si totius populi vocibus expetatur." — Cod. Theodos. lib. xii. tit. i. n. 49, &c. See also Godefroy's Commentary on this part of the Theodosian Code.

[3] "Præter privatas res nostras, et Ecclesias Catholicas, et domum clarissimæ memoriæ Eusebii ex consule et ex magistro equitum et peditum, et Arsacis regis Armeniorum [*utpote, ab antiquo, Romanorum fœderati et amici*], nemo ex nostrâ jussione præcipuis [i. e. *immunibus*] emolumentis familiaris juvetur substantiæ."—Cod. Theodos. lib. xi. tit. i. n. 1. See for the exposition of this law, Godefroy's Commentary, and Bingham, ubi supra, cap. iii. § 3.

originally granted was the poverty of the churches. The gradual increase of that property under the reign of Constantine induced his successor Constantius to revoke the exemption, and to subject church property, as well as private property, to real taxes.[1] This regulation was invariably followed afterwards, with regard, at least, to ordinary taxes. The emperor Honorius, however, restored or confirmed the *real* immunities of the clergy from "*mean taxes and duties*,"[2] a provision which was adopted by Justinian in his Novellæ, wherein he points out, in great detail, *the extraordinary and mean duties* from which the property of the clergy was exempt.[3]

Besides those real and personal immunities enjoyed by the clergy in all parts of the empire, some particular churches, either on account of their dignity or their necessities, had received far more extensive privileges. Theodosius the Great, to honour the holy places in Palestine, ordered that even the laics who were in charge of those holy places should be exempt, like the clergy, from personal taxes.[4] Some years later, the emperors Honorius

---

[1] "In Ariminensi synodo, super ecclesiarum et clericorum privilegiis tractatu habito, usque eò dispositio progressa est, *ut juga* [i. e. *prædia*] *quæ videntur ad Ecclesiam pertinere, à publicâ functione cessarent* [i. e. *immunia essent*]; quod nostra videtur dudum sanctio repulisse....De his sanè clericis qui prædia possident, sublimis auctoritas tua, non solùm eos aliena juga nequaquam statuet excusare [i. e. *immunia facere*]; sed etiam pro his quæ ipsi possident, eosdem ad pensitanda fiscalia perurgeri."—Cod. Theodos. lib. xvi. tit. ii. n. 15.

[2] "Placet, rationabilis concilii [verisimiliter *Africani*] tenore perpenso, districtâ moderatione præscribere, à quibus specialiter necessitatibus ecclesiæ urbium singularum habeantur immunes. Prima quippe illius usurpationis contumelia depellenda est, ne prædia usibus cœlestium secretorum [i. e. *mysteriorum*] dicata, *sordidorum munerum fæce vexentur;* nullâ jugatione [i. e. *mensurâ pensitationis*] quæ talium privilegiorum sorte gratulatur, muniendi itineris constringat injuria; *nihil extraordinarium* ab hâc [*jugatione*] superindictitiumve flagitetur; nulla pontium instauratio; nulla translationum sollicitudo gignatur; non aurum cæteraque talia [*ad lustralem collationem pertinentia, sive ad censum negotiatoribus impositum*] poscantur. Postremò nihil præter canonicam illationem [i. e. *ordinarium tributum*] quod adventitiæ necessitatis sarcina repentina depoposcerit, ejus functionibus adscribatur. Si quis contravenerit, post debitæ ultionis acrimoniam, quæ erga sacrilegos jure promenda est, exilio perpetuæ deportationis uratur."—Cod. Theodos. ibid. n. 40. Fleury, Hist. Eccl. vol. v. book xxiii. n. 4.

[3] Justiniani Novellæ 37, 43, 131, &c.

[4] "Universos quos constiterit custodes ecclesiarum esse vel sanctorum locorum, ac religiosis obsequiis deservire, nullius attentationis [i. e. *oneris*, seu *muneris personalis*] molestiam sustinere decernimus. Quis enim capite censos

and Theodosius the Younger exempted the churches of Thessalonica, of Constantinople, and of Alexandria, from all real taxes, on condition, however, that they should not avail themselves of that favour to take under their protection the private property of individuals, whether laics or clergy, and thereby secure for them the same exemption to the injury of the state.[1] Justinian afterwards granted a new exemption of the same kind to the Church of Constantinople, in consideration of the great expense incurred by it, in the constant practice of providing gratuitous burial for a great number of the poor.[2] It does not appear that the Roman Church had then obtained similar exemptions. There is reason to believe that the great wealth which it enjoyed by the liberality of Constantine and of his successors, prevented the emperors from thinking of granting to it, with regard to public taxes, any other immunities than those generally enjoyed by all the churches in the empire.

91. *The Church always submissive to the Laws.*

But it is most important to observe here that, during the frequent changes of the law on ecclesiastical immunities under the Christian emperors, the Church never refused to submit even to

---

patiatur esse devinctos, quos necessariò intelligit suprà memorato obsequio mancipatos?"—Cod. Theodos. lib. xvi. tit. ii. n. 26. Fleury, Hist. Eccl. vol. iv. book xviii. n. 9. Bingham, ubi supra, lib. iii. cap. xiii. § 2.

It appears from this law of Theodosius, that there were a great number of guardians established in the holy places in Palestine, either as guards, or to maintain order among the great crowds of pilgrims constantly attracted there by devotion. There are interesting details on these pilgrimages in Gretser, De Cruce, tom. i. lib. i. cap. lxxiii. lxxvi. See also Michaud, Hist. des Croisades, 4th edit. vol. i. pp. 11, 546, &c.

[1] This exemption was granted to the church of Thessalonica by a law of the year 424, which fixed the amount of taxation for Macedonia, of which Thessalonica was the capital. The exemption is expressed in the following terms: "Sacrosancta Thessalonicensis ecclesia civitatis excepta; ita tamen ut apertè sciat propriæ tantummodò capitationis modum beneficio mei numinis sublevandum; nec externorum [seu extraneorum] gravamine tributorum rempublicam ecclesiastici nominis abusione lædendam."—Cod. Theod. lib. xi. tit. i. n. 33. A similar exemption had been granted some years before (in 415) to the churches of Constantinople and of Alexandria, by a law of Honorius and of Theodosius the Younger. We do not think it necessary to cite it at length. —Cod. Theod. ibid. tit. xxiv. n. 6. Bingham, ubi supra, lib. v. cap. iii. § 3.

[2] Justiniani Novella 43, cap. i.

the least favourable laws on that point. This appeared particularly after the law of Constantius, which revoked the real immunities granted to the clergy by Constantine. Far from protesting against that restriction, the bishops believed it their conscientious duty to submit on this, as on all other temporal matters, to the laws of their prince. Such is the character given of them by Valentinian I. in his letter to the bishops of Asia for the confirmation of the Council of Illyria. Among other eulogies on the bishops, he praises them "for being as obedient to the laws of temporal princes as to those of God himself, and for paying punctually the contributions established by law."[1] St. Ambrose expressly acknowledges the same fact in his "Discourse against Auxentius," in which he protests with so much energy against the demands of Valentinian the Younger, who asked a church for the Arians. To prove that he had no other motive for his refusal but the interests of the faith, the holy doctor declares that in all other matters he obeys the orders of the emperor, and that in particular he believes himself bound to pay the taxes commonly levied on the lands of the Church. "If," he says, "the emperor demands tribute, we do not refuse it; the church lands pay tribute. *We render to Cæsar the things that are Cæsar's, and to God the things that are God's. Tribute belongs to Cæsar; we pay it;* but the Church belongs to God; certainly it cannot be given to Cæsar."[2]

From not attending to the latter part of this text, which we have given in italics, Cardinal Baronius and some theologians and canonists thought that St. Ambrose speaks here not of a strict obligation, but of an obligation of mere propriety founded on that Christian meekness, which tells the faithful in certain cases, to consent to be unjustly deprived of their property rather

[1] Theodoret, Hist. Eccles. lib. iv. cap. viii.

[2] "Si tributum petit [imperator], non negamus: agri Ecclesiæ solvunt tributum.... Solvimus *quæ sunt Cæsaris Cæsari, et quæ sunt Dei Deo.* Tributum Cæsaris est, non negatur; Ecclesia Dei est, Cæsari utique non debet addici."—St. Ambrose, Serm. contra Auxentium, n. 33, 35 (ad calcem Epistol. 21, Oper. tom. ii.).

than to contend or dispute.[1] But an attentive and unprejudiced perusal of the words of St. Ambrose proves clearly that he speaks of a strict obligation founded on the precept of our Lord, "Render to Cæsar the things that are Cæsar's, and to God the things that are God's."[2]

St. Gregory the Great enounces the same principles in several of his letters.[3] However zealous he was for the immunities granted to the Church and its ministers by princes, he supposes and frequently acknowledges the obligation of paying the tributes, which, in accordance with the imperial constitutions, were then levied on the lands of the Church. In one of his letters to the "defensor" of Sardinia,[4] he advises him "to cultivate well the lands of the Church, that they might be able to pay the taxes."[5] He obliged, moreover, the religious of Palermo to pay the taxes demanded of them, according to the laws then in force.[6]

---

[1] Baronius, Annal. tom. iv. ann. 387, n. 11, &c.

[2] Matth. xxii. 21. This passage of St. Ambrose appears at first sight not easily reconciled with the language of one of his letters, in which he speaks of the tribute paid by our Lord, Matth. xvii. 26. When explaining this text of the Gospel, he appears to think that Jesus Christ and his apostles were exempt by the law of nature from the obligation of paying taxes, and that they paid them merely by condescension, in order not to give scandal to the Jews. —St. Ambrose, Epist. 7, n. 17, 18 (Oper. tom. ii.). But if we examine attentively the design and whole context of that letter, we shall find that the exemption of which the holy father speaks here, as applicable to the apostles, and to the ministers of religion generally, must be understood as being merely congruous and becoming, but still fully compatible with the rigorous obligation, which the holy doctor admits so clearly in his discourse against Auxentius, and which he proves by the literal sense of the words "Reddite quæ sunt Cæsaris Cæsari."

The difficulty of reconciling these two passages has made P. Thomassin speak so obscurely, that it is almost impossible to know what are the opinions which he attributes to St. Ambrose on the obligation of clerics to pay tribute. —Ancienne et Nouvelle Discipline, vol. iii. book i. ch. xxxiii. n. 10, &c.

[3] Thomassin, ibid. ch. xxxiv. n. 10, &c.

[4] Administrators of the patrimonies of the Roman Church in different countries were then called "*defensores.*" See Zaccaria, De Rebus ad Hist. et Antiquit. Ecclesiæ pertinentibus, tom. ii. dissert. x. cap. v. § 2; Ducange, Glossarium Infimæ Latin. verbo Defensor; S. Greg. Epistol. lib. v. epist. 29.

[5] "Ut possessiones Ecclesiæ . . . ad tributa sua solvenda idoneæ existant."— S. Greg. Epistol. lib. ix. epist. 64.

[6] St. Gregory writes thus on this point to Zittanus, militia-master of Palermo: "Epistolas vestras, Græco sermone dictatas, me indico suscepisse, in quibus dicitis quod quædam religiosa loca responsum [i. e. *satisfactionem* seu

92. *Error of Baronius on this subject.*

All these details on the origin and the variations of ecclesiastical immunities under the Christian emperors, may serve to correct a rather grave error of Baronius on this subject. That author asserts confidentially, that after the conversion of Constantine, no prince subjected the clergy to taxes, except Julian the Apostate, Valens the Arian, and Valentinian the Younger, who was under the influence of the empress Justina, a devoted adherent of the same sect.[1] It is clear, on the contrary, from the testimonies and the facts which we have cited, that all the Christian emperors, from Constantine to Justinian, subjected the clergy to more or less taxes; that even the most religious emperors, such as Gratian and Theodosius the Great, followed on this point the practice established by their predecessors; and that the holy doctors, far from protesting against the practice, believed themselves bound in conscience to submit to it.

93. *The Theological Question on the Origin of Ecclesiastical Immunities cleared up by these Facts.*

We may remark here in passing, the value of facts, in clearing up a question discussed by canonists and theologians *on the origin of ecclesiastical immunities.*[2] The common opinion of theologians is, that they are founded on human positive laws; canonists on the contrary hold generally that they are founded on the divine law, the natural law, and the positive law. Between these two opinions, Cardinal Bellarmine believed a mean could be found, which might in some measure reconcile them. Ecclesiastical immunities, that eminent controversialist maintains, are not founded on the divine law in this sense, that

---

solutionem] juri publico, de rebus ei competentibus, reddere contemnant. Quæ res me omninò contristavit. . . . Proinde Fautino defensori quæ scripserim Gloriæ vestræ transmisi, ut ipse religiosos quosque in Panormitanis partibus apud electos judices venire compellat, et suorum actuum rationem reddant."—S. Greg. Epistol. lib. x. epist. 27.

[1] Baronius, Annal. tom. iv. anno 387, n. 11, 14. This error of Baronius is harshly criticised by Bingham, ubi supra, lib. v. cap. iii. §§ 1, 4, pp. 227, 236.

[2] Bellarmine, Controv. de Clericis, cap. xxviii. xxix. (Oper. tom. ii.).

they rest on *any divine precept strictly so called, and formally expressed in the sacred writings;* but only in this sense, that they may be deduced by a natural inference from certain examples in the Scripture; such for example, as that of Joseph, who exempted the Egyptian priests[1] from all tributes, and that of Artaxerxes, king of Persia, who granted a similar exemption to the Israelite priests.[2] According to the same author, ecclesiastical immunities are prescribed by the natural law, not in the sense that they belong either to the primary principles, or the proximate and necessary consectaries of the natural law, but solely in this sense, that they are countenanced by, and based on, natural equity. "They are not," he adds, "evident and absolutely necessary dictates of the natural law, but remote and obscure inferences, which cannot be determined without human laws; and they are in reality so determined, substantially at least, by the laws of nations, or by the unanimous consent of all nations, which have always granted immunities in different degrees to the ministers of religion."

It does not belong to our plan to examine how far these explanations may serve to reconcile the conflicting opinions of theologians and canonists on this point; but from the facts already cited, it is manifest that ecclesiastical immunities are not founded on a divine precept properly so called, and that they are founded solely on positive human laws, at least in the sense explained by Cardinal Bellarmine. It is certain, in truth, that these immunities underwent several modifications under the Christian emperors; that the Church submitted without any difficulty to the different laws on the matter, even when they were least favourable to her; and that far from protesting against those laws which restricted her immunities, she considered herself rigorously bound to submit on this, as on all other points in the temporal order, to the edicts of the emperor. Now, it is clear that such facts cannot well be reconciled with

[1] Gen. xlvii. 22.

[2] 1 Esdras vii. 24.

the opinion of those who represent ecclesiastical immunities as prescribed by the divine law or the natural law, which all the princes of the earth are bound to respect, and which they never can dispense with. It is equally clear, on the other hand, that these same facts can easily be reconciled with the opinion which regards ecclesiastical immunities as founded solely on positive law, in the sense explained by Cardinal Bellarmine.[1]

94. *Right of Sanctuary—Its Origin.*

Among the real immunities of the clergy under the Christian emperors, may be ranked the right of sanctuary; that is, a right granted to persons accused, who take refuge in a church or in any other place, of not being prosecuted, at least during a certain time or by certain persons.[2] The origin and nature of this law are admirably explained in a memoir on the subject, read in 1711 before the Academy of Inscriptions, by Fr. Simon, one of the most eminent academicians of his day. "As soon," he observes,[3] "as men had commenced to invoke the Author of Nature, when they had erected altars to him and offered him sacrifices, to acknowledge him as the sovereign arbiter of their destinies and to implore his assistance, they regarded him as present in a special manner in the places where they celebrated his mysteries, and they dreaded to show themselves rigid towards others, when they sought to conciliate his clemency for themselves. This respectful fear disposed them to treat favourably those who took refuge there, and to prohibit all violence towards

---

[1] See, in support of these reflections, Pey, De l'Autorité des Deux Puissances, part iii. ch. iii. § 7, pp. 138, 525, et alibi passim. The same observations may serve as a corrective for some exaggerated assertions of the Abbé Bonnaud on this subject, in his work entitled, Réclamations pour l'Église Gallicane, pp. 308—347, et alibi passim.

[2] Cod. Theod. lib. ix. tit. xlv. Cod. Justin. lib. i. tit. xii. Thomassin, Ancienne et Nouvelle Discipline, vol. ii. book iii. ch. xcv.—ci. De Héricourt, Abridgment of the same work, part ii. ch. xxviii, § 2. Bingham, Origines, &c. tom. iii. lib. viii. cap. xi. Bergier, Dict. Théol. art. Asiles. Van Espen, Dissertatio de Immunitate Locali, seu de Asylo Templorum (Oper. tom. ii. ad calcem).

[3] Mémoire sur les Asiles, in the Hist. de l'Académie des Inscriptions, 12mo. edit. vol. ii. p. 52. The author of this memoir was F. Simon, conservator of medals in the king's cabinet. He died in 1719, aged 65 years.

them. This is properly what is called the right of sanctuary,"—as the author of the memoir proves solidly by the history of the sanctuaries admitted by the ancient nations. From the details of his history, it follows clearly, that the right of sanctuary was not established originally to protect criminals against the arm of justice, but to secure for the innocent a place of refuge; to save from violence and unauthorized punishment persons accused, and to give time to the judges to examine the charges dispassionately, before they proceeded to inflict the punishment which they deserved.

95. *It was maintained by the Emperors, but with wise Restrictions.*

These were the motives by which the emperors were induced to transfer to the churches the right of sanctuary hitherto enjoyed by the temples, and by some other places consecrated to the worship of the pagan deities. It would be difficult to decide whether this right was originally conferred on the churches by an express law, or whether it was regarded as the natural consequence of the right which the pagan temples had enjoyed in all ancient times. This last supposition, which is generally admitted by the learned, appears to be confirmed by the most ancient of the imperial constitutions on this subject, which was issued by the emperor Theodosius the Great.[1] It is in truth very remarkable, that neither that constitution, nor any of those subsequently published, establishes the right of sanctuary; they rather suppose it already established, and merely prescribe wise restrictions, to prevent the abuses which it might occasion, and to avert the injury which it might inflict on public order by securing impunity for criminals. With this view, the emperors ordered public debtors, homicides, adulterers, ravishers, and other notorious criminals, whose chastisement could not be

---

[1] "Publicos debitores [i. e. *tributorum debitores*], si confugiendum ad ecclesias crediderint, aut illico extrahi de latebris oportebit, aut pro his ipsos qui eos occultare probantur, episcopos exigi [i. e. *ad solvendum compelli*]. Sciat igitur præcellens auctoritas tua, neminem debitorum [*publicorum*] posthac à clericis defendendum; aut per eos ejus quem defendendum esse crediderint debitum esse solvendum."—Cod. Theod. lib. ix. tit. xlv. n. 1.

deferred without danger to public order, to be seized even in the church.[1]

96. *Zeal of the Clergy for the Maintenance of this Right.*

The right of sanctuary, under wise restrictions, was too much in keeping with the mild and merciful principles of the Christian religion, not to enlist in its defence the warmest sympathies of the clergy. Hence, we find the bishops and councils testifying generally great zeal for its preservation, and appealing to it with almost invariable success, sometimes in defence of persecuted innocence, sometimes to obtain the pardon of criminals who had taken refuge in the church, or to obtain at least a mitigation of the punishment which they had incurred; but above all, to prevent the rigour of human justice from depriving them, as was frequently the case, of the spiritual succours which religion never refuses to sinners, and which none need more than the greatest criminals.[2] These were the true motives of the zeal which bishops and councils invariably evinced for the maintenance of the right of sanctuary: they knew well, it is true, the authority vested in the magistrate for the repression and the punishment of crimes opposed to public order and to the rights of individuals; and far from wishing that guilt should go unpunished, they strongly acknowledged the necessity of inflicting in certain cases severe punishment on criminals;[3] but they wished that the severity of the magistrate, as well as of the government, should be tempered by clemency; and that in punishing sin, nothing should be left untried to save the sinner, in order that the temporal punishment of the criminals should contribute to their eternal salvation. St. Augustine explains all

[1] Cod. Theod. and Cod. Justin. ubi supra. Index of the Hist. Eccl. of Fleury, and of the Hist. des Auteurs Ecclés. of D. Ceillier, art. Asiles.

[2] Thomassin, ubi supra. The lives of St. Augustine, St. Basil, and St. John Chrysostom, contain many remarkable examples of this charitable interference of the prelates in favour both of criminals and of the innocent. See Fleury, and D. Ceillier, ubi supra.

[3] See our reflections, supra (n. 47, et seq.), on the moderate use of temporal penalties against heresy and other crimes of public impiety.

these views admirably in a letter to Macedonius, vicar of Africa, in which he treats the subject fully.[1] "Do you wish to know," says the holy doctor, "why we intercede as much as we can for all criminals? It is because all sin appears pardonable, so long as the guilty person promises to amend. That is your maxim; it is also ours. We are, therefore, far from approving sin, since we wish rather that people should refrain from it; and if we petition that it should not be punished, it is not because we love it, but because while we abhor the crime, we pity the criminal; and that the greater the horror we have of the evil, the more we dread that he who has committed it should die without having had time to amend. Our love for men, therefore, urges us to intercede for criminals, lest from that punishment which ends with their life, they fall into the punishment which never ends. You can have no doubt that religion authorizes our course, since God himself, with whom no injustice dwelleth, that God, whose power knoweth no limit, who seeth not only what each one is, but what he afterwards is to be, maketh nevertheless, as the Gospel says, his sun to rise on the unjust, and his rain to fall on the wicked, as well as on the just. But if amongst the wicked whom he spareth, and to whom he leaveth health and life, there be many whom he foreseeth will never do penance, and whom he beareth, nevertheless, with the same patience as the others; with how much greater reason ought not we to be touched with compassion for those who promise to amend, since, although we do not know that they will be faithful to their promises, we must, at least, always hope they will. The terrors of the law are, it is true, most usefully employed to repress the audacity and the lawlessness of the wicked: these terrors are useful not only to the good, who by that means live in security among the wicked, but to the wicked themselves, who, under the just punishments

[1] S. August. Epist. 153 (alias 54), ad Macedonium. Fleury gives an analysis of that letter, Hist. Eccl. vol. v. book xxii. n. 52. D. Ceillier, Hist. des Auteurs Ecclésiastiques, vol. xi. p. 245, &c. Thomassin, ubi supra, ch. xcv. n. 2, &c.

inflicted on them, may call on God and be converted. Nevertheless, the intercessions of the bishops are not contrary to the order established among men; nay, they exist only by that order; and the pardon which the intercessor obtains for the criminal is the greater, as the punishment was more deeply merited. It may happen, no doubt, that the pardon granted to a criminal who was about being condemned, may have consequences directly the reverse of what we expected. It may happen that the very person whose life we have saved by our intercessions, may yet deprive many others of their lives; and that his audacity, emboldened by impunity, may abuse the indulgence that has been given to him; or that if he profits by it for his own reformation, the hope of a similar impunity may seduce others into similar or perhaps greater disorders. These evils, which may result from our intercessions, must not, however, be imputed to us; nothing should be laid to our account but the good which we intend, and which we endeavour to effect; for in interceding for the guilty we wish to make religion amiable by examples of mildness, that those whom we deliver from a temporal death, may live so, that they shall not fall into eternal death, from which none can deliver them."

97. *Advantages of this Right when duly restricted.*

From these observations we may judge what value is to be attached to the opinions of some modern authors, who represent the right of sanctuary as the fruit of ignorance and superstition, as an abuse of ecclesiastical power; finally, as an encouragement to criminals, by promising to them impunity. Much declamation on this point might have been spared, if those writers had reflected that the right of sanctuary is coeval with society itself; that in a greater or less degree it has been admitted by all ancient lawgivers, and by all nations, even the most civilized; that God himself had sanctioned it, though under wise restrictions, in the law of Moses;[1] that at the epoch of the

[1] Numb. xxxv.

establishment of Christianity it was natural to apply to the churches a right founded on usage so ancient and so universal; finally, that this right, when restricted within just limits, tends of its own nature to keep alive among the people a profound respect for the holy place, and for the Deity himself, and to prevent a multitude of excesses fatal alike to public order and to the safety of individuals.[1] This right no doubt might be abused, as the most useful and legitimate institutions are every day abused; but those abuses should not prevent us from acknowledging the great advantages which it produced. In the infancy of society especially, and in general in all nations not much advanced in civilization, nothing is more useful than the right of sanctuary to supply the defect of laws and government; to check the revenge of individuals, who commonly imagine that they have a right to do justice to themselves; finally, to prevent or to moderate the first impulses of revenge, which are often unjust, and always dangerous.[2] Montesquieu himself, struck with these considerations, could not but admire on this point the wisdom of the laws of Moses, and approve generally the right of sanctuary, provided it were placed under proper restrictions, to prevent abuses. "As the Divinity," he observes,[3] "is the refuge of the unfortunate, and as none are more unfortunate than criminals, men have been naturally led to believe that the temples were an asylum for them; and this idea appeared more natural among the Greeks, among whom murderers expelled from their city and from the society of man, seemed to have no other home but the temples, no other protectors but the gods. This right regarded at first none but involuntary homicides; but when great criminals were included in it, there was a gross incon-

---

[1] Correct by these observations the Annales du Moyen Age, vol. vii. p. 337; Hegewisch, Hist. de Charlemagne, p. 176; Gaillard, Hist. de Charlemagne, vol. ii. p. 105, &c.; De Pouilly, Dissert. sur l'Origine et les Progrès de la Jurid. Ecclés. (Mém. de l'Acad. des Inscript. vol. xxxix. 4to. p. 576, &c.).

[2] See, in confirmation, Bernardi, De l'Origine et des Progrès de la Législation Française, book i. ch. ii. p. 76; Lingard, Anglo-Saxon Church, ch. iii.

[3] Montesquieu, Esprit des Lois, book xxv. ch. 3, versus finem.

sistency; for if they had offended men, much more had they offended the gods. The laws of Moses were very wise. Involuntary homicides were innocent; but they should be removed from the sight of the relatives of the slain; a sanctuary was therefore established for them.[1] Great criminals deserve no sanctuary: they had none. The Jews had only a portable tabernacle, which continually was changing its place; that excluded the idea of a sanctuary. It is true they were to have a temple; but the criminals who might flock thither from all parts would trouble divine service. If the homicides were expelled from their country, as among the Greeks, they might, it was to be feared, adore strange gods. All these considerations led to the establishment of cities of sanctuary, where the fugitives should remain until the death of the sovereign pontiff." An attentive perusal of history is enough to convince any person, that in the New as well as in the Old Law, the ministers of religion, and the sovereign pontiffs in particular, far from abusing their authority to extend the right of sanctuary to imprudent limits, have at all times co-operated with princes in correcting their abuses, and even in restricting them more and more in proportion as they became more liable to abuse, and less necessary for the maintenance of public order.[2]

SECTION V.

Judicial Power of the Bishops in Temporal Matters under the Christian Emperors.[3]

98. *Origin of Ecclesiastical Jurisdiction in Temporal Matters.*

As we have already remarked, one of the principal personal immunities of the clergy under the Christian emperors was

---

[1] Numb. xxxv.

[2] See, in support of this assertion, the authors cited supra, n. 2, page 143.

[3] Cod. Theod. lib. xvi. tit. ii. passim. Cod. Justin. lib. i. tit. iv. Thomassin, Ancienne et Nouvelle Discipline, vol. ii. book iii. ch. ci. &c. De Héricourt, abridgment of the same work, part ii. ch. xxix. Petit-Pied, Traité des Droits et des Prérogatives des Ecclésiastiques; Paris, 1705, 4to. part i. p. 62, &c. Bingham, Origines sive Antiquit. Eccles. tom. i. lib. ii. cap. vii.; tom. ii. lib. v. cap. ii. Fleury, Hist. Eccl. vol. xix. 7th Discourse, n. 4. Dupuy, Traité de la Jurid. Crimin. part i. ch. ii. viii. &c. (at the end of the Traité des Libertés de l'Église Gall.).

exemption from secular jurisdiction; that is to say, a privilege granted to the clergy of not being cited before secular tribunals, and of having their causes, even in temporal matters, judged by an ecclesiastical tribunal. But the power of adjudicating on disputes between clerics was only a part of the temporal jurisdiction of the bishops; in many cases they were invested with the same authority over laics. It is the more important to trace out here the origin and the progress of this temporal jurisdiction of the clergy, as the Roman law on this point has been the model for all the new monarchies which arose, after the fourth century, on the ruins of the empire.[1]

99. *The Bishops Umpires in Disputes from the time of the Persecutions.*

From the time of the persecutions, the custom of the faithful, founded on the doctrine and the exhortations of St. Paul,[2] was to take the bishops as arbiters of their differences. The august character of the first pastors, joined to the eminent virtues which then adorned the most of them, attracted generally the respect and confidence of the people, and made them be regarded as the natural arbiters of whatever differences might arise among the faithful. Their peaceful and disinterested arbitration was in truth far preferable to the judgment of secular magistrates, who were almost all idolaters, full of prejudice, frequently of hatred, against the Christians, and to whom consequently the faithful could not submit their differences without danger to themselves, and without scandal to the pagans.

100. *Reasons for retaining this Custom after the Conversion of Constantine.*

These considerations, which during the times of persecution had naturally introduced and maintained the arbitration of the bishops, lost no doubt much of their cogency after the conversion

[1] The complete elucidation of this matter presents, as we have already remarked (supra, n. 88, 89), very great difficulties, which it does not enter into our plan to discuss fully. A perusal of the authors cited in the notes may supply the omission.

[2] 1 Corinth. vi.

of Constantine; they became every day less strong, in proportion as Christianity became more diffused and better established in the empire. Nevertheless, the custom of taking the bishops as the arbiters of differences among the faithful had advantages so manifest that the Christian emperors should wish to maintain it. Sanctioned by the ancient laws of the empire, and by the customs of the most polished nations,[1] it was moreover conformable to the views of sound policy, in the then existing state of society. For not only was the judgment of the bishops more mild and more peaceable than the pomp of the secular law-courts, but it was in general more disinterested and less expensive for the parties, being given by men more eminent in virtue, more detached from the world, less exposed consequently to the seduction of bribes, and to all those interested motives which corrupt so frequently the decisions of secular tribunals.

101. *Still stronger Reasons for exempting the Clergy from Secular Jurisdiction.*

All those motives which should naturally incline the Christian emperors to favour the arbitration of the bishops in the case of the simple faithful, should of course influence them still more powerfully to exempt the clergy from secular jurisdiction. Very slight reflection must be sufficient to suggest the grounds of propriety on which such an immunity should be granted, and the serious injury inevitably resulting to religion and to society from making the clergy amenable to civil tribunals, even in purely temporal matters.[2] The natural result of such a practice would be to deprive the clergy gradually of that respect and veneration, without which the exercise of their ministry becomes absolutely impossible. For what can more effectually degrade a sacred minister in the eyes of the people than to see him dragged before a secular tribunal, where his real or apparent weaknesses shall be published before the world, and made the source of scandal?

[1] See the details on this subject in the first article of our Introduction.

[2] See our observations in the preceding section, "on the origin of ecclesiastical immunities," supra, n. 88—94.

How often will not the whole body have to suffer from the imprudence or the errors of individuals? How often will not these great inconveniences be occasioned by mere calumnies, and by the malignity of a certain class of men who are ever ready to believe all the evil that may be said of the clergy, and who are sometimes goaded on to defame them through a spirit of vengeance or of impiety? Even in the happiest ages of the Church men of that character were found, who never shrunk from the most absurd accusations, or the most odious calumnies, to defame the most saintly characters, and to involve the whole body of the clergy in the odium of accusations levelled against some individual? St. Augustine, in several of his writings, complains loudly of these odious proceedings of the enemies of the Church, and even of some bad Christians.[1] If such evils could happen in the best ages of the Church, how much more should they be apprehended in times of relaxation and disorder?

102. *Constantine and his Successors influenced by these Motives.*

Accordingly, we find that this was the motive which had the greatest influence on the emperors. Constantine especially was so forcibly struck by it, that he left no means untried of hushing up and deciding without much publicity all accusations against the ministers of the Church. Not long before the opening of the Council of Nice, as we learn from Theodoret,[2] some bishops, wishing to avail themselves of the emperor's presence in that city, to obtain his protection in the disputes which they had with their colleagues, forwarded to him some statements in support of their accusations. Constantine received them; folded and sealed without inspecting them, and ordered them to be preserved carefully until a certain day; he then proceeded to reconcile the prelates who were at variance. On the appointed day, peace being already made between the bishops, he ordered

[1] S. August. Epist. 77 (alias 136) ad Felicem et Hilarinum, n. 1; Epist. 78 (alias 137) ad Clerum Hippon. n. 5, 6 (Oper. tom. ii. pp. 181, 184, &c.).

[2] Theodoret, Hist. Eccles. lib. i. cap. xi. Sozomen, Hist. lib. i. cap. xvii. Fleury, Hist. Eccl. vol. iii. book xi. n. 8.

the documents to be produced and burned in his presence, declaring at the same time, on oath, that he had never read a word of them. He added, that the faults of priests should never be made known to the people, lest they might become a subject of scandal, and an occasion of greater evils. They say, moreover, that on that occasion he declared, if he saw a bishop committing a fault, he would cover him with his mantle, to conceal from the public the knowledge of such a scandal.

From an examination of the origin and the progress of ecclesiastical jurisdiction under the Christian emperors, it is clear, that those admirable sentiments of Constantine were the rules followed by his successors, and the source of most of the constitutions on this subject established by the Roman law.

103. *Judicial Power of the Bishops in Temporal Matters under Constantine.*

The first care of Constantine was to favour the arbitration of the bishops, and to give an additional authority to their decisions. "With this view," says Sozomen, "he gave general permission to all who had lawsuits to decline the jurisdiction of the civil judges, and to appeal to the judgment of the bishops; he even ordered that the sentence of the ecclesiastical tribunals should be more binding than that of secular judges; that they should have the same authority as those given by the emperor himself; finally, that the governors of provinces and their officers should be obliged to enforce their execution.[1] At the end of the Theodosian code there is a law of Constantine, addressed to Ablavius, prefect of the prætorium, which is considered by many learned writers to be that referred to by Sozomen. The emperor

[1] "Fuit hoc etiam argumentum vel maximum reverentiæ quam pius princeps erga religionem gerebat. Nam et omnes ubique clericos *immunitate* donavit, lege hâc de re specialiter datâ; et litigantibus permisit ut ad episcoporum judicium provocarent, si magistratus civiles rejicere vellent; eorum autem sententia rata esset, aliorumque judicum sententiis prævaleret, perinde ac si ab imperatore ipso data fuisset; utque res ab episcopis judicatas, rectores provinciarum eorumque officiales executioni mandarent."—Sozomen, Hist. Eccl. lib. i. cap. ix. Fleury, Hist. Eccl. vol. iii. book x. n. 27. Lebeau, Hist. du Bas-Empire, vol. i. book v. n. 57. Annales du Moyen Age, vol. i. book ii. p. 260.

orders "that all who have causes, whether as defendants or plaintiffs, shall be at liberty, either in the beginning, or in the giving of evidence, or in the pleading, or at the conclusion, to appeal to the judgment of the bishop, notwithstanding any opposition which one of the parties may give to such appeal."[1] The authority of this law is denied, it is true, by some writers;[2] but their objections have little weight with the greater number of critics, and the controversy is really of very little importance, since most of the provisions of that law are clearly expressed in Sozomen's text, which we have cited, and which is generally acknowledged to be authentic.[3] From that text of Sozomen it may, in truth, be clearly inferred, that the arbitration of bishops, which before Constantine's time was simply a work of charity, became then in the strict sense jurisdiction emanating from the sovereign himself; that the sentence of the bishop, which had no authority before, except from the consent of the parties, began thenceforward to have by law all the authority of a judgment pronounced by the secular tribunals, and even more than the judgments given by the ordinary judges; finally, that the secular tribunals could even then be declined *by all who had lawsuits*, and who wished to submit them to the ecclesiastical court.[4]

---

[1] "Quicumque litem habens, sive possessor, sive petitor erit, inter initia litis, vel decursis temporum curriculis, sive cùm negotium peroratur, sive cùm jam cœperit promi sententia, judicium eligit sacrosanctæ legis antistitis; illicò sine ullâ dubitatione, etiamsi alia pars refragatur, ad episcopum cum sermone [i. e. *cum allegationibus*] litigantium dirigatur."—Extravag. 1 (ad calcem Cod. Theodos.).

[2] See especially Godefroy, Commentar. on this Extravagant. which we have cited.

[3] Tillemont, in our opinion, proves solidly, against Godefroy's objections, the authenticity of the letter addressed to Ablavius (Hist. des Empereurs, vol. iv. pp. 295, 663). Tillemont's opinion is generally adopted on this point by the latest authors. See, among others, Thomassin, ubi supra, ch. 102, n. 2; Petit-Pied, ubi supra, p. 65; D. Ceillier, Hist. des Auteurs Ecclés. vol. iv. p. 176; Concilia Galliæ (Paris edit. 1789, vol. i. p. 755). It is to be observed that Bingham, though inclining to Godefroy's opinion, does not decide absolutely. (Origines et Antiquit. Eccles. tom. i. lib. ii. cap. vii. § 3.)

[4] We must correct or explain by those principles many modern authors who represent the bishops, in the reign of Constantine, as being mere umpires in the suits between laics, but not enjoying jurisdiction, properly so called, in temporal matters. (Fleury, Hist. Eccl. vol. iii. book x. n. 27; vol. v. book xx. n. 35; vol. xix. 7th Discourse, n. 2, 4. Idem, Instit. au Droit Ecclés. ch. i.

104. *This Power more or less restrained under the Successors of Constantine.*

It does not appear that this jurisdiction conferred by Constantine on the bishops was restricted by any of his successors until the close of the reign of Theodosius the Great. The conduct of the holiest prelates of that period clearly implies, as we shall see, that the bishops continued then to exercise a very extensive jurisdiction in temporal matters. After the reign of Theodosius, that jurisdiction, it is true, was sometimes restricted by imperial constitutions. We even find a law of Honorius and Arcadius, which appears to restrict the jurisdiction of the bishops to religious or purely spiritual causes.[1] But whether it is that these princes did not at first express themselves clearly, or that they afterwards changed their minds, both of them proved themselves subsequently very favourable to the temporal jurisdiction of the bishops. In the Justinian code we find two of their constitutions, which attribute to the bishops generally the power of judging definitely, even in temporal matters, like the prefect of the prætorium,[2] and of having their sentences executed by the ordinary officers of the secular courts. There were, however, two important restrictions on these rights; first, that the bishop could not exercise them, except in cases submitted to his tribunal by the consent of both parties; and, secondly, that they could be exercised in civil causes only, and not in criminal.[3]

---

p. 4. See also the note of Boucher d'Argis on this passage.) These authors do not reflect, that after the law of Constantine, addressed to Ablavius, the same probably of which Sozomen speaks, the bishops were not merely umpires, freely chosen by the two parties, but that in certain cases they alone could be judges, strictly so called, and established by law; thus they had real jurisdiction. See on this subject, Devoti, Instit. Can. tom. iii. tit. xvii. § 3. This state of things lasted, it appears, until Honorius's reign, who restricted, in some points, the jurisdiction granted to the bishops by Constantine, allowing, however, great authority to their decisions, as we shall see lower down.

[1] "Quoties de religione agitur, episcopos convenit judicare: cæteras verò causas quæ ad ordinarios cognitores [seu *judices*] vel ad usum publici juris [i. e. *juris communis*] pertinent, legibus oportet audiri."—Cod. Theod. lib. xvi. tit. xi. n. 1. See also Commentary of Godefroy on this law.

[2] On the duty of the prefect of the prætorium, see note 2, page 41.

[3] "Si qui *ex consensu* apud sacræ legis antistitem litigare voluerint, non vetabuntur; sed experientur illius, *in civili duntaxat negotio,* more arbitri sponte residentis, judicium."—Cod. Justin. lib. i. tit. iv. n. 7.

"Episcopale judicium ratum sit omnibus qui se audiri à sacerdotibus ele-

105. *This Power much more extensive with regard to Clerics.*

The judicial power of the bishops was much more extensive with regard to clerics. Many imperial constitutions exempt them totally from the secular jurisdiction, not only in purely ecclesiastical causes, but even in causes purely civil or pecuniary, and also in criminal causes, except certain enormous crimes, such as high treason, rebellion, homicide, and some others.[1] Nevertheless, Valentinian III., interpreting these constitutions, introduces important restrictions, which seem to evince on his part not much respect or regard for the clergy. He declares that bishops cannot judge even clerics without their own consent, and by virtue of an agreement to that effect; and he adds, that should a cleric have a suit with a laic, the latter shall be at liberty to cite his adversary before a secular tribunal, in civil and pecuniary as well as in criminal matters; the privilege of defending themselves by a procurator, being, however, allowed to bishops and priests in criminal cases.[2]

---

gerint; eamque illorum judicationi adhibendam esse reverentiam jubemus, quam vestris deferri necesse est potestatibus [i. e. *potestatibus præfecti prætorio*], à quibus non licet provocare."—Ibid. n. 8. Fleury, Hist. Eccl. vol. v. book xx. n. 35.

[1] Cod. Theod. lib. xvi. tit. ii. n. 23, 41, 47. We should remark especially the law of Honorius, which runs thus: "*Clericos non nisi apud episcopos accusari convenit.* Igitur si episcopus, vel presbyter, diaconus, et quicumque inferioris loci [seu *gradûs*], Christianæ legis minister, apud episcopum [*siquidem alibi non oportet*] à quâlibet personâ fuerint accusati, sive ille sublimis vir honoris, sive ullius alterius dignitatis; . . . noverit docenda probationibus, monstranda documentis [*crimina*] se debere inferre."—Ibid. n. 41. Fleury, Hist. Eccl. vol. v. book xxiii. n. 4; vol. vi. book xxviii. n. 54; book xxix. n. 30.

[2] "De episcopali judicio diversorum sæpe causatio [i. e. *mens* seu *opinio*] est. Ne ulteriùs querela procedat, necesse est præsenti lege sanciri. Itaque cùm inter clericos jurgium vertitur, et ipsis litigatoribus convenit, habeat episcopus licentiam judicandi, præeunte tamen vinculo compromissi. Quod et laïcis, si consentiant, auctoritas nostra permittit. Aliter eos judices esse non patimur, nisi voluntas jurgantium, interpositâ, sicut dictum est, conditione præcedat. Quoniam constat episcopos et presbyteros forum legibus non habere, nec de aliis causis, secundum Arcadii et Honorii Divalia constituta, quæ Theodosianum corpus ostendit, præter religionem, posse cognoscere. Si ambo ejusdem officii litigatores nolint, vel alteruter, agant publicis legibus et jure communi. Si verò petitor laïcus, seu in civili, seu [*in*] criminali causâ, cujuslibet loci clericum adversarium suum, si id magis eligat, per auctoritatem legitimam in publico judicio respondere compellat. Quam formam, etiam circa episcoporum personam, observari oportere censemus, [*ita tamen*] ut si in hujuscemodi ordinis homines actionem prævaricationis et atrocium injuriarum dirigi necesse fuerit, per procuratorem solemniter ordinatum, apud judicem publicum, inter leges et

106. *Enactments of the Justinian Code on this subject.*

Such was the state of ecclesiastical jurisdiction generally before the reign of Justinian, who collected in his code most of the preceding constitutions, adding, moreover, some new provisions to determine more precisely, and for the most part more favourably to the clergy, the limits between ecclesiastical and secular jurisdiction. The following are the chief provisions of the Justinian code on this point: [1]—

First. With regard to the causes of laics, Justinian adopts the law of the emperors Arcadius and Honorius, which we have cited above,[2] and, moreover, authorizes an appeal from the secular judge to the bishop, whenever the parties may think themselves aggrieved by the sentence of the former.

Secondly. In civil matters, clerics, monks, virgins, and widows must be brought under the episcopal jurisdiction in the first instance, and not before the secular judge, except in case of appeal. In criminal matters they may be cited either before the bishop or the secular judge, as the accuser may think fit.

Thirdly. The guardians of churches and the administrators of hospitals cannot be cited, except before the bishop, for things connected with official duties; and in case of appeal, their causes must be decided by the metropolitan or the patriarch.

Fourthly. The bishops cannot be prosecuted before a secular judge for any cause whatsoever, but only before the metropolitan or the patriarch, who is to decide the matter in a provincial council.

---

jura confligant. . . . Quod iis religionis et sacerdotii veneratione permittimus; nam notum est procurationem in criminalibus negotiis non posse concedi. Sed ut sit ulla discretio meritorum, episcopis et presbyteris tantùm id oportet impedi."—Valentiniani III. Novella 12 (ad calcem Codicis Theodosiani). Hist. de l'Église Gallicane, vol. ii. p. 76. Tillemont, Hist. des Emp. vol. vi. p. 254. Fleury, Hist. Eccl. vol. vi. book xxviii. n. 39. Baronius, Annals, tom. vi. anno 452, n. 52.

[1] We think it useless to cite all these provisions: a mere analysis of them seems sufficient for our purpose. See, for more ample development, the Justinian Code, lib. i. tit. iv. De Episcopali Audientiâ; Justiniani Novellæ 83, 86, 123, &c.; Thomassin, ubi supra, ch. ciii.; Fleury, Hist. Eccl. vol. vii. book xxxiii. n. 6; vol. xix. 7th Discourse, n. 4; Ceillier, Hist. des Auteurs Ecclés. vol. xvi. p. 470, 473, &c.

[2] Supra, note 1, p. 155.

107. *Decrees of many Councils explained by these Laws.*

These provisions of the Roman law being generally adopted by the new monarchies which arose in the West on the ruins of the Roman empire, supply a natural explanation of a great number of canons of councils from the close of the fourth century, prohibiting clerics, and in certain cases laics, from bringing their causes before secular judges.[1] The third Council of Carthage, held in 397, prescribes the penalty of deposition against bishops, priests, deacons, and other clerics, bringing their causes before lay courts, when it was in their power to bring them before the ecclesiastical courts. The reason assigned by the council for this prohibition is deserving of special attention: it is, that clerics, by acting thus, offer an insult to the Church by submitting to secular judges the disputes which the apostle St. Paul urged even the laics to bring before the ecclesiastical judges.[2] Hence the decree of the third Council of Carthage was re-affirmed by the general Council of Chalcedon in 451.[3] The fourth Council of Carthage, in 398, even excommunicates laics who shall bring their causes before heretical or infidel judges.[4] We find these regulations confirmed or renewed by a number of subsequent councils.[5]

---

[1] Thomassin, Ancienne et Nouvelle Discipline, ch. cii. n. 15. Muzzarelli, Dissert. sur les Immunités Ecclésiastiques, p. 14, &c.

[2] "Placuit ut quisquis episcoporum, presbyterorum et diaconorum seu clericorum, cùm in ecclesiâ ei crimen fuerit intentatum, vel civilis causa fuerit commota; si, relicto ecclesiastico judicio, publicis judiciis purgari voluerit, etiamsi pro ipso fuerit prolata sententia, locum suum amittat, et hoc in criminali judicio; in civili verò perdat quod evicit, si locum suum obtinere voluerit. Cui enim ad eligendos judices undique patet auctoritas, ipse se indignum fraterno consortio judicat, qui, de universâ Ecclesiâ malè sentiendo, de judicio sæculari poscit auxilium; cùm privatorum Christianorum causas apostolus ad Ecclesiam deferri, atque ibi determinari præcipiat."—Concil. Carthagin. iii. can. 9 (Labbe, Concil. tom. ii. p. 1168). Fleury, Hist. Eccl. vol. v. book xx. n. 25.

[3] "Si quis clericus habet cum clerico litem aut negotium, proprium episcopum ne relinquat, et ad sæcularia judicia ne excurrat; sed causam priùs apud proprium episcopum agat; vel de episcopi sententiâ, apud eos quos utraque pars elegerit, judicium agitetur. Si quis autem præter hæc fecerit, canonicis pœnis subjiciatur." — Concil. Chalcedon. act. 15, can. 9 (Labbe, Concil. tom. iv. p. 760). Fleury, Hist. Eccl. vol. vi. book xxviii. n. 29.

[4] "Catholicus qui causam suam, sive justam sive injustam, ad judicium alterius fidei judicis provocat, excommunicetur." — Concil. Carthagin. iv. can. 87 (Labbe, Concil. tom. ii. p. 1206).

[5] Some modern authors believed they could infer from these regulations,

108. *Temporal Penalties inflicted on Criminals by the Ecclesiastical Tribunals.*

A natural consequence of the temporal jurisdiction of the bishops was the right of inflicting on criminals temporal penalties, such as imprisonment, scourging, pecuniary fines, confiscation, and exile.[1] St. Augustine clearly supposes this usage, in a letter addressed about the year 412 to Marcellinus, exhorting him not to punish the Donatists with all the rigour of the laws. The holy doctor expresses a wish "that he should use against them neither the rack, nor iron nails, nor fire, but only rods, which are the instruments of punishment that fathers use with their children, masters with their scholars, and the bishops not unfrequently in their judgments."[2] The fifth Council of Carthage, held in 399 or 400, decrees pecuniary fines against certain crimes.[3] The fifth Council of Rome, held in 503, under Pope Symmachus, condemns to exile and to the forfeiture of all their

---

that the personal immunities of clerics were founded on the Divine law. (See, among others, Muzzarelli, Dissert. sur les Immunités Ecclés. p. 14, &c.) But the inference, as may be easily shown, is not logical. For it is easily conceived, that exemption from secular jurisdiction, being once granted to clerics by the civil law, the Church, by virtue of that concession, could bind her ministers to avail themselves of that privilege, founded as it was on so many considerations of propriety and congruity. This explanation of the ecclesiastical rules regarding the personal immunities of clerics is the more natural, as it must be apparently applied to those canons which in certain cases prohibit even laics to plead before infidel or heretical judges. Surely we may hold that this prohibition is not founded on the Divine law, but on the civil law alone; and yet it is expressed in terms not less absolute in many ancient councils than the prohibition against clerics pleading before secular tribunals. There is no reason, therefore, why both should not be taken as founded *solely* on the civil law, and on the mere consent of princes. See above, art. 93.

[1] Thomassin, Ancienne et Nouv. Discipline, vol. ii. book iii. ch. cii. n. 19. Devoti, Instit. Canon. tom. iv. lib. iv. tit. i. n. 10.

[2] "Imple, Christiane judex, pii patris officium; sic succense iniquitati, ut consulere humanitati memineris. . . . Noli perdere paternam diligentiam, quam in ipsâ inquisitione [*scelerum*] servasti, quando tantorum scelerum confessionem, non extendente equuleo, non sulcantibus ungulis, non urentibus flammis, sed virgarum verberibus eruisti; qui modus coercitionis à magistris artium liberalium, et ab ipsis parentibus, et *sæpe etiam in judiciis solet ab episcopis adhiberi.*" — S. August. Epist. 133 (alias 159), ad Marcellinum, n. 2 (Operum, tom. ii. p. 396).

[3] "Et illud statuendum, ut si quis cujuslibet honoris clericus, judicio episcoporum, pro quocumque crimine fuerit damnatus, non liceat eum, sive ab ecclesiis quibus præfuit, sive à quolibet homine defensari; interpositâ pœnâ damni, pecuniæ atque honoris, quâ nec ætatem nec sexum excusandum esse præcipimus." — Concil. Carthagin. v. can. 2 (Labbe, Concil. tom. ii. p. 1215). Fleury, Hist. Eccl. vol. v. book xx. n. 43.

property calumniators of bishops, *conformably to the ancient decrees of the fathers.*[1] Ecclesiastical history furnishes a great number of similar examples after the fourth century.[2]

The bishops having by law judicial power only, and not coercive, in the temporal order, were obliged for the execution of the sentences to apply to the secular magistrate. Nevertheless, from the close of the fourth century, they had prisons for the clerics condemned to imprisonment.[3] These prisons are mentioned in a constitution of the emperors Arcadius and Honorius, published in 396; in the acts of the Council of Ephesus, held in 431, and in a Novella of Justinian, dated in 539.[4] We shall soon see that the sovereign pontiff and the patriarchs began about the same period to have under their orders a corps of officers, whose duty it was to enforce their decrees.

109. *Great Labour and Embarrassment imposed on the Bishops by this Temporal Jurisdiction.*

An immense increase of business and of trouble, it may be easily conceived, was imposed on the bishops by the exercise of this temporal jurisdiction. The history of St. Augustine, of St. Ambrose, of St. Gregory of Nazianzen, of St. John Chrysostom, and of many other holy bishops, proves that they regarded this part of their functions as one of the most essential for the maintenance of peace and union among the faithful, and that they did not scruple to devote habitually a considerable portion of their time

---

[1] "Hi qui adversa eis moliuntur, sicut à sanctis Patribus dudum statutum esse, et hodie synodàli et apostolicâ auctoritate firmatur, penitus abjiciantur, et exilio, suis omnibus sublatis, perpetuo tradantur."—Concil. Rom. v. (Labbe, Concil. tom. iv. p. 1336 E.). This very remarkable decree is omitted by Fleury, D. Ceillier, and many others, in their analysis of this Roman council.

[2] See the authors cited in note 1, p. 159.

[3] These prisons were called Decanica, or Diaconica, because they were ordinarily situated near a diaconia, or sacristy, the care of which was usually intrusted to a deacon. See Ducange, Glossar. med. et inf. Latin. verbis Diaconicum et Decanicum; Bingham, Origines et Antiquit. Eccles. tom. iii. lib. viii. cap. vii. § 9; Devoti. Instit. Can. tom. iii. lib. iii. tit. i. n. 21; Godefroy, Comment. in Cod. Theod. lib. xvi. tit. v. n. 30.

[4] Cod. Theod. ibid. Concil. Ephes. part i. cap. xxx. n. 3 (Labbe, Concil. tom. iii. p. 429). Justiniani Novellæ, 79, cap. iii. ad calcem Cod. Justin.

to the administration of justice.[1] St. Augustine, especially, complains, in many of his works, that the care of temporal affairs deprives him of the power of devoting himself as exclusively as he wished to study and meditation on the holy books;[2] and about the same time Synesius, bishop of Ptolemais, in Libya, fatigued with these temporal embarrassments, earnestly solicited to be allowed to resign his see.[3] It is true that, in order to make this care of temporal concerns compatible with the other obligations of their state, the bishops ordinarily committed a share in the administration of justice to priests and deacons, and sometimes even to laics of approved integrity.[4] Nevertheless, the delegation was not so entire that they did not still take an active part either in superintending their officers, or in examining personally the more important affairs. However painful this increase of their labours must have been, they did not hesitate to sacrifice on this point their own private inclinations to the interests of their flock, to the good of religion, and to the canons of the Church, which compelled laics, in certain cases, as well as clerics, to submit their disputes to the ecclesiastical tribunals.

SECTION VI.

Influence of the Clergy in the Civil Administration under the Christian Emperors.[5]

110. *Extent of this Power according to the Roman Law.*

The judicial power of which we have spoken, constituted but a small portion of the temporal authority of the bishops under

[1] Thomassin, ubi supra, ch. ci. et seq. D. Ceillier, Histoire des Auteurs Ecclésiast. vol. xiv. p. 256.

[2] S. August. In Psalm. 118, Serm. 24, n. 3 (Oper. tom. iv.). Idem, De Opere Monachorum, cap. xxix. (Oper. tom. vi.). Fleury, Hist. Eccl. vol. v. book xx. n. 35.

[3] Synesii Epist. 57, p. 198, etc. Fleury, Hist. Eccl. ibid. book xxii. n. 45.

[4] Thomassin, ubi supra. Bingham, Origines et Antiquit. Eccles. tom. i. lib. ii. cap. vii. § 5.

[5] Thomassin, Ancienne et Nouv. Discipline, vol. ii. book iii. ch. ciii. n. 13; vol. iii. book i. ch. xxvi. xxvii. Fleury, Hist. Eccl. vol. xix. 7th Discourse, n. 4; Instit. au droit Eccles. vol. ii. part iii. ch. i.

the Christian emperors. A glance at the historical monuments of that period, and especially at the constitutions of the Roman law on episcopal jurisdiction, proves that the bishops were then invested with a great share in the civil administration, and that they were in some sense the trusted agents of government, which believed it a duty to impose on them the care of all business essential to the good of the people and to public order. The reader can form his own opinion on this point, from the details which we are now about to give on the temporal power with which bishops and patriarchs were then invested by the imperial constitutions.

111. *Powers of Bishops in general.*

I. With regard to bishops in general, the detail of their powers as given in the Roman law, cannot at this day be read without astonishment.[1]

1. In the year 368, a law of the emperor Valentinian I. and of Valens, charged the bishops to watch over merchants, in order to prevent or correct injustice, especially against the poor.[2]

2. A law of the emperors Honorius and Theodosius the Younger, promulgated in 409, and revived afterwards by the emperor Anastasius, orders that the defenders of cities should be

---

[1] Cod. Theod. lib. xvi. passim. Cod. Justin. lib. i. See especially tit. iv. De Episcopali Audientiâ. Justiniani Novellæ, passim.

Thomassin appears to think that, from the time of Constantine, "all good bishops were charged with the heaviest part of the civil administration." (Ancienne et Nouv. Discipline, vol. iii. book i. ch. xxvi. n. 19.) This assertion he thinks is proved by a passage from Theodoret, who represents St. James, bishop of Nisiba, and all the good bishops of his time, as the protectors and defenders of orphans, of widows, and of all miserable or oppressed people. (Hist. Relig. sive Solitar. cap. i.) It does not appear, however, that the bishops had at that time any other temporal power than that which we have explained in the preceding paragraph, and which regarded solely the administration of justice. The passage from Theodoret proves, it is true, the paternal solicitude of good bishops even for the temporal good of their flock; and the ascendancy which they acquired over the mind of the people, by the sanctity of their life and of their character, combined with the judicial power which they possessed; all this, however, by no means supposes that extraordinary power which Thomassin attributes to them "in the principal part of the civil government."

[2] "Negotiatores, si qui ad domum nostram pertinent, ne modum mercandi videantur excedere, Christiani (quibus verus cultus est adjuvare pauperes, et positos in necessitate) provideant episcopi."—Cod. Justin. lib. i. tit. iv. n. 1.

selected and installed by the bishops in a meeting of the clergy and chief citizens;[1] it adds, that none but Catholics are eligible.[2]

3. A constitution published in 428, by the emperors Theodosius the Younger and Valentinian III., allows young women, whether of free condition or slaves, whom their parents or masters attempted to prostitute, to implore the protection of the bishop to preserve their innocence.[3] The emperor Leo I. afterwards extended this right to females who were forced to appear on the stage against their will.[4] Justinian not only confirmed these different constitutions, by inserting them in his code, but moreover increased still further the temporal power of the bishops. The principal enactments which he added to those of his predecessors were the following:—

4. He charged the bishops with the protection of orphans, of slaves, of prisoners, and generally of all wretched or defenceless

---

[1] This is the text of the law published by the emperors Honorius and Theodosius the Younger: "Defensores ita præcipimus ordinari, ut sacris orthodoxæ religionis imbuti mysteriis, reverendissimorum episcoporum, necnon clericorum, et honoratorum, ac possessorum et curialium decreto constituantur; de quorum ordinatione referendum est ad illustrissimam prætorianam potestatem; ut litteris ejusdem magnificæ sedis earum solidetur auctoritas."—Cod. Justin. lib. i. tit. lv. n. 8.

The law published on the same subject by the emperor Anastasius may be seen in tit. iv. of the same book, n. 19.

In those times there was in every chief city of the empire a defender, charged, as his name indicates, with the protection of the citizens against all sort of oppression, either from the magistrates or from private citizens. An account of the functions and obligations of those defenders may be seen in the Cod. Theod. lib. i. tit. xi.; Cod. Justin. lib. i. tit. lv.; and in the Novellæ, especially the 15th.

These "defenders" of cities, who date from the fourth century, must not be confounded with the "defenders" of churches, instituted somewhat later, to support the cause of the Church and of the poor before the magistrates. On the origin and functions of those latter, see Godefroy, Comment. sur le Cod. Théod. lib. ii. tit. iv. n. 7; lib. xvi. tit. ii. n. 38; Thomassin, Ancienne et Nouv. Discipline, vol. i. book ii. ch. xcvii. &c.; De Héricourt's abridgment of the same work, part i. ch. xix. § 3; Bingham, Origines, &c. tom. ii. lib. iii. cap. xi.

[2] See supra, art. i. n. 63.

[3] "Si lenones patres et domini suis filiabus vel ancillis peccandi necessitatem imposuerint; liceat filiabus et ancillis, episcoporum implorato suffragio, omni miseriarum necessitate absolvi."—Cod. Justin. lib. i. tit. iv. n. 12.

[4] "(Magistratibus oppidorum et episcopis) curæ erit, ne etiam invitam mulierem, liberam aut ancillam, conjungi patiantur animis aut choris [i. e. *matrimonio jungi, aut choris profanis adjungi*], aut aliud spectaculum in theatro agere invitam."—Ibid. n. 14.

persons, whose age or condition renders them more liable to oppression.[1] By virtue of this commission, the bishop was bound, in conjunction with the civil magistrate, to interfere in the nomination of tutors and trustees, to watch over the liberty of children abandoned by their parents, to visit every week prisoners, whether freemen or slaves, to ascertain the causes of their detention, to admonish the magistrate of any disorder in that department, and to report to the emperor himself any negligence of the magistrates in reforming such disorders.

5. According to the Justinian code, the bishops were moreover charged with watching over the observance of the police laws with regard to gaming, and to repress, in concert with the civil magistrates, the transgressors of such laws.[2]

6. They were also charged, in conjunction with the chief citizens of the city, with the administration of its revenues, the inspection of public works, and with many other duties connected with the interests of the city.[3]

---

[1] Most of those imperial constitutions are collected in the first book of the Justinian code, tit. iv. n. 22, 23, 24, 30, 33. "Neminem volumus in custodiam conjici, absque jussu gloriosissimorum, vel illustrium, vel clarissimorum magistratuum hujus felicissimæ urbis [*Constantinop.*] vel provinciarum, aut defensorum civitatum. De his autem quicumque conjecti aut conjiciendi sunt, Deo amabiles locorum episcopos jubemus per unam cujusque hebdomadæ diem, . . . eos qui in custodiâ habentur visitare, et diligenter inquirere causam ob quam detinentur, et sive servi sint sive liberi, sive pro pecuniis, sive pro aliis criminationibus, sive pro homicidiis conjecti, illustrissimos, et spectabiles, et clarissimos magistratus admonere, tam eos qui sunt in hâc felicissimâ urbe, quam qui sunt in provinciis, ut ea exequantur circa ipsos, quæ divalis nostra constitutio, ad illustres præfectos eâ de re emissa, præcipit; licentiâ datâ Deo carissimis pro tempore episcopis, si quam negligentiam admissam cognoverint ab illustrissimis, et magnificentissimis, atque clarissimis pro tempore magistratibus, vel iis quæ illis parent officiis, talem ipsorum negligentiam indicandi, ut conveniens adversus negligentes animi nostri motus insurgat."—Ibid. n. 22.

[2] "Quæ de aleâ, sive (ut vocant) cottis [quâdam ludi aleatorii specie], ac de eorum prohibitione, à nobis sancita sunt, ea liceat Dei amicissimis episcopis et perscrutari, et cohibere si fiant, et flagitiosos, per clarissimos præsides provinciarum, et patres defensoresque civitatum, ad modestiam reducere."—Cod. Justin. lib. i. tit. iv. n. 25.

It appears that the kind of play called "cotta" in this passage, took its name from the little bones which were used in it, and which the modern Greeks call κότζι. (See the word "cotta," in Facciolati's Latin Dictionary, Padua edit. 1827.) Ducange, Glossarium Mediæ et Infimæ Græcitatis, verbo κοτζια.

[3] Cod. Justin. lib. i. tit. iv. n. 26. This constitution of Justinian enters into very considerable details on the powers of bishops in the administration of the revenues of cities; but however interesting, its length precludes its insertion here.

7. A constitution of Justinian, which is one of the Novellæ placed at the end of his code, intrusts to the bishops the superintendence of weights and measures.[1] With this view the emperor ordered the standard weight to be kept in the principal church of each city. It is worthy of remark, that this regulation was borrowed from the legislation of many ancient nations, and especially from the Jewish, the Egyptian, and even the ancient Romans, who ordered the standards of weights and measures to be kept in the temples as sacred and inviolable things.[2]

8. It was customary under Justinian and his successors, that the laws on ecclesiastical matters should be addressed by the emperors to the patriarchs, who were to transmit them to the bishops, through the metropolitans.[3] The same course was sometimes observed with regard to laws on civil affairs.[4] In both cases the bishops were charged with watching over the observance of the laws, and with reporting to the emperor the negligence of magistrates in observing his orders, especially in all that regarded the discovery and the punishment of heretics.[5]

---

[1] Mensuras et pondera in sanctissimâ uniuscujusque civitatis ecclesiâ servari [præcipimus,] ut secundum ea, et gravamen collatorum, et fiscalium illatio, et militares et aliæ expensæ fiant."—Justin. Novella 128, cap. xv.

[2] Exod. xxx. 13; Levit. xxvii. 25. Clem. Alex. Stromat. lib. 6. Fannius, De Amphorâ. D. Calmet, Dictionnaire de la Bible, art. Poids.

[3] A remarkable example occurs in the 6th Novella of Justinian, which regards ordinations and the temporal administration of churches. It concludes thus: "Sanctissimi patriarchæ uniuscujusque diœcesis hæc proponant in ecclesiis sub se constitutis, et manifesta faciant Deo amabilibus metropolitis, quæ à nobis constituta sunt. Illi quoque rursus etiam ipsi proponant ea in metropolitanâ sanctissimâ ecclesiâ, et constitutis sub se episcopis hæc manifesta faciant. Illorum verò singuli in propriâ ecclesiâ hæc proponant, ut nullus nostræ reipublicæ ignoret quæ à nobis, ad honorem et augmentum magni Dei et salvatoris nostri Jesu Christi, disposita sunt."—Justinian, Novella 6, Epilogus. De Marca, De Concordiâ, lib. ii. cap. xi. n. 9; cap. xv. n. 2.

[4] The 8th Novella of Justinian, which regards elections and the principal duties of magistrates, was addressed to patriarchs and to metropolitans, by an edict to the following effect: "Traditæ nobis à Deo reipublicæ curam habentes, et in omni justitiâ vivere nostros subjectos studentes, subjectam legem conscripsimus; quam tuæ sanctitati, et per eam omnibus qui tuæ provinciæ sunt, facere manifestam, bene habere putavimus. Tuæ igitur sit reverentiæ et cæterorum [episcoporum], hæc custodire; et si quid transcendatur à judicibus, ad nos referre; ut nihil contemnatur horum quæ sanctè et justè à nobis sancita sunt."—Justiniani Edictum (ad calcem Novellæ 8).

[5] Ibid. See also Cod. Justin. lib. i. tit. v. n. 18.

112. *These Powers much more extensive in the West, under the monarchy of the Lombards.*

Far from regarding with displeasure this increase of the temporal power of the clergy, the successors of Justinian extended it still more, especially in Italy, where the state of affairs rendered the co-operation of the clergy more necessary for the good of the state.[1] After the establishment of the monarchy of the Lombards, which gave so fatal a blow to the authority of the emperors in Italy, the ever-increasing weakness of the empire compelled them to place almost unlimited dependence on the bishops, so far as to abandon to them the defence of the cities in the provinces most exposed to the incursions of the barbarians. The letters of St. Gregory furnish indisputable proofs of this fact, which would appear incredible, if we did not know from other sources the deplorable state of the empire of the West at this period. So much did the emperor Maurice count on the co-operation of the bishops for the defence of the cities, that he earnestly implored the pope to depose a bishop who was prevented by his infirmities from using all the necessary vigilance in defence of his episcopal city. St. Gregory, not thinking it right to depose a bishop for such a motive, gave him, however, a coadjutor capable of superintending the defence of the city in case of attack.[2] Many letters of the same pontiff consist of appeals, exhorting the bishops to discharge that duty with zeal, to pay constant attention to the proper guard of the walls, to the state of the different fortified places, to their stores of provision,—in a word, to all those other cares, which in happier times would have been entirely abandoned to the care of the civil magistrates.[3]

113. *Powers of the Patriarchs after the close of the Fourth Century.*

In proportion as the emperors extended the temporal power of

---

[1] See supra, n. 30, 31.

[2] This is Justiniana prima, in the province of Illyria. S. Greg. Epistol. lib. xi. Epist. 47 (alias 41).

[3] S. Greg. Epistol. lib. viii. Epist. 18 (alias 20); lib. ix. Epist. 4, 6 (alias 2, 5); et alibi passim.

the bishops, they gave, as might naturally be expected, new accessions to that of the patriarchs. History supplies us with numerous proofs of these accessions after the fourth century. We believe it is the more important to collect the details preserved for us on this subject, because they appear to have totally escaped the notice of a great number of modern authors.[1]

It does not appear that, until the close of the fourth century, the patriarchs enjoyed, either by law or custom, a more extensive temporal power than other bishops.[2] The pontificate of St. Cyril appears to be the date of a considerable development of the temporal power of the patriarchate of Alexandria, and probably of the other patriarchates.[3] From the historian

---

[1] On this subject, see Thomassin, Ancienne et Nouv. Discipline, vol. iii. book i. ch. xxvi. n. 3, 4, &c.; ch. xxvii. n. 14, 16.

[2] Thomassin supposes, that before the pontificate of St. Cyril (that is, before the year 412), and even from the time of Athanasius, the patriarch of Alexandria had great temporal power, not only in his episcopal city, but in all Egypt. (Ancien. et Nouv. Discipline, ch. xxvi. n. 3, 9, &c.) In support of that assertion he cites, first, the accusations made against Athanasius by the Arians, of having imposed a tribute of linen on all Egypt, and of having wished to prevent the export of corn, which was annually sent from Egypt to Constantinople. (Socrates, Hist. Eccl. lib. i. cap. xxvii. xxxv. Fleury, Hist. Eccl. vol. iii. book xi. passim. Tillemont, Mémoires sur l'Histoire Ecclés. vol. viii. Vie de St. Athanase, pp. 71, &c.) Secondly, the conduct of Theophilus to the monks of Nitria, whom he expelled from Egypt by armed force. (Fleury, Hist. Eccl. vol. v. book xxi. n. 3. Tillemont, ibid. vol. x. p. 474, &c.)

These examples prove, it is true, that the patriarchs then had, by their sacred character, a great ascendancy over the minds of the people; but they do not, in our opinion, prove demonstratively, that the patriarchs then possessed, either by law or custom, a temporal power more extensive than that of the bishops. The answer of St. Athanasius to the charge of the Arians seems, in fact, utterly irreconcilable with the notion of that great temporal power which Thomassin ascribes to him; for his principal answer to these calumnies was, that he was but a poor and simple private citizen (Apol. contra Arian. n. 9), an answer which he could not give with any sort of plausibility had he enjoyed great temporal power.

The example of Theophilus is no better proof of Thomassin's opinion; for the truth is, that it was not temporal power attached to his see that Theophilus used in expelling the monks of Nitria from Egypt; he appealed for assistance to the governor of Egypt, who placed troops at his disposal to enforce against those monks the penalties which government at that time generally inflicted on all heretics, as we have proved in another place (n. 62, 63).

[3] There were four patriarchs in the East in the fifth century: Alexandria, Antioch, Jerusalem, and Constantinople. The two first had been founded by St. Peter himself; Constantinople was not erected until the close of the fourth century, in the general council of that name held in the year 381. Finally, Jerusalem was definitively acknowledged as a patriarchate by the Council of Chalcedon, held in 451. See Thomassin, Ancien. et Nouv. Discipline, vol. i.

Socrates, we learn, "that St. Cyril enjoyed far greater powers than Theophilus, his predecessor; and that from this time, the bishop of Alexandria combined with his spiritual power the government of temporal things."[1] The same author adds, a little further on, that Pope Celestine, a contemporary of St. Cyril and bishop of Rome, "had long before combined temporal dominion with spiritual authority."[2] From these words of Socrates, it may naturally be inferred that the bishop of Rome was the first of the patriarchs whose temporal power had received some unusual extension about the close of the fourth century; and that the generosity of Honorius, emperor of the West, to the sovereign pontiff, excited that of Theodosius the Younger, emperor of the East, to the patriarch of Alexandria. Whatever be the value of that conjecture, the historian Socrates, in those passages which we have cited, loudly complains of the use which the bishops of Rome and of Alexandria made of this new authority to prevent the public assemblies of the Novatians, to close their churches, to carry off their vestments and sacred vessels, and to deprive of his property their bishop Theopompus. Coming from Socrates, these complaints are not surprising, as he is known to have been favourable to the Novatians; but they prove clearly the extensive temporal power then enjoyed by the bishops of Rome and of Alexandria, and the use which they made of it for the support of the Church and for the destruction of heresy.

114. *Use made by St. Cyril of Alexandria of his Power.*

It would be difficult to determine the precise extent of the powers of the patriarch of Alexandria at this period. But it may be assumed as certain, that from the time of St. Cyril, these powers were extensive enough to excite the jealousy of the

---

book i. ch. vii. et seq.; De Héricourt's abridgment of the same work, part i. ch. iii.

[1] Socrates, Hist. Eccl. lib. vii. cap. vii.

[2] Ibid. cap. xi.

governor, who felt that his authority was dwarfed beside that of the patriarch. For this information also, we are indebted to the historian Socrates, when he is speaking of the conduct of St. Cyril to the Jews, whom he expelled from Alexandria, in punishment of the violent acts which they had committed against the Christians.[1] In carrying these orders into execution, the patriarch employed a body of men, called "Parabolani," whom he had at his disposal to support his authority and make his orders be respected.[2] This corps had been originally, it appears, only a pious association devoted to the care of the sick; but in the course of time, they became, with the consent of the emperor, the principal support of the authority of the patriarchs of Alexandria. This appears clearly from a law of Theodosius the Younger on this subject, and from the details supplied by Socrates himself on the conduct of St. Cyril in this business. For Orestes, governor of Alexandria, dissatisfied with St. Cyril's rigour against the Jews, complained to Theodosius the Younger, who appears to have disapproved of that patriarch's conduct; it is even believed that to this period ought to be referred the law of the same emperor, which reduces to five hundred the number of the Parabolani, and deprives the patriarch of their appointment.[3] It is certain, however, that the emperor, either because he was mollified or better informed afterwards, revoked this first law by another, which raises the number of the Parabolani to six hundred, all to be appointed and governed by the patriarch.[4]

---

[1] Socrates, Hist. Eccl. lib. vii. cap. xiii. Fleury, Hist. Eccl. vol. v. book xxiii. n. 25. Thomassin, ubi supra, ch. xxvi. n. 12, 13.

[2] On these Parabolani of Alexandria, consult the Theodosian Code, lib. xvi. tit. ii. n. 42, 43; Tillemont, Mémoires sur l'Hist. Ecclés. vol. xiv. p. 227; Fleury, ubi supra; Bingham, Origines sive Antiq. Eccles. tom. ii. lib. iii. cap. ix.

[3] Cod. Theod. ubi supra, n. 42.

[4] Parabolani (qui ad curanda debilium ægra corpora deputantur) quingentos esse antè præcepimus. Sed quia hos minùs sufficere in præsenti cognovimus, pro quingentis sexcentos constitui præcipimus; ita ut, pro arbitrio viri reverendissimi antistitis Alexandrinæ urbis, de his qui antè fuerant, et qui pro consuetudine curandi gerunt experientiam, sexcenti parabolani ad ejusmodi sollicitudinem eligantur (exceptis videlicet honoratis et curialibus, i. e. *extra horum corpus*). Si quis autem ex his naturali sorte fuerit absumptus, alter in

We shall observe here, that from not having sufficiently examined the origin and the progress of the temporal power of the patriarchs, some estimable authors have appeared surprised at the conduct of St. Cyril, with regard both to the Novatians and to the Jews.[1] But omitting that the eminent virtue of St. Cyril cannot permit us to believe that he had usurped to himself so great a power, the testimony already cited from the historian Socrates, supposes clearly, that at this epoch the authority of the bishops of Rome and of Alexandria had received a great increase by the consent of the emperors themselves.

115. *Use made of it by Dioscorus.*

The history of Dioscorus, successor of St. Cyril in the see of Alexandria, supplies new proofs of this great power, of which he made so deplorable a use in sustaining the party of Eutyches.[2] Among the different statements presented against him in the third session of the Council of Chalcedon, in 451, we find that of Ischyrian, a deacon, of Athanasius, a priest, and of Sophronius, a layman, who accused the patriarch of having desolated the country, seized and destroyed the houses of his enemies, of having banished many, of having confiscated the goods of others; in fine, of having acted in Alexandria, as if it had been his own dominion, and as if he enjoyed there an authority superior even to that of the emperor.[3] These accusations, it appears, were not unfounded, since Dioscorus, when cited by the council to defend himself, and having refused to appear, was condemned for contumacy, and for ever deposed from his dignity. We cannot judge, it is true, of the legitimate powers of the patriarch of Alexandria, by the violent extremes of which

ejus locum, pro voluntate ejusdem sacerdotis [seu *antistitis*] subrogetur; ita ut hi sexcenti, viri reverendissimi sacerdotis præceptis ac dispositionibus obsecundent, et sub ejus curâ consistant."—Cod. Theod. ubi supra, n. 43.

1 Fleury, ubi supra. Alban Butler, Lives of the Saints, January 28, p. 457.

2 Thomassin, ubi supra, ch. xxvi. n. 8, 9. Fleury, Hist. Eccl. vol. vi. book xxviii. n. 13.

3 Concil. Chalcedon. act. iii. n. 4 (Labbe, Concil. tom. iv. p. 399, &c.). Fleury, Hist. Eccl. vol. vi. book xxviii. n. 7, &c.

Dioscorus was guilty; but even in their excess, these acts imply that the patriarch must in those times have had powerful means at his command to influence the administration of temporal affairs.

116. *Extraordinary Power given by Justinian to the Patriarch of Alexandria.*

The historical documents of the sixth and seventh centuries supply much safer examples for ascertaining the legitimate authority of the patriarchs of Alexandria, and the use made of it by prelates most eminent for sanctity, and entirely free from all suspicion of violence or of ambition.[1] Liberatus, deacon of the Church of Carthage in the sixth century, informs us that the emperor Justinian invested the patriarch Paul, about the year 540, with full authority over the dukes and the tribunes of Egypt, that is, over the civil and military officers of that province, to exclude from these offices all heretics, and to substitute Catholics in their place.[2] This extraordinary measure was in reality only an application of the laws often promulgated against heretics, and revived by Justinian himself;[3] but it is remarkable that the execution of these laws, even against the heretical magistrates of all Egypt, should be intrusted to the patriarch of Alexandria.

117. *Temporal Power of St. John the Almoner.*

The history of St. John the Almoner, who filled the same see in the commencement of the following century, contains details equally interesting and edifying on the exercise of his temporal power.[4] He sanctified the commencement of his pontificate by the reform of weights and measures, and obliged all the merchants to conform to his regulations on this point, under pain of fine and confiscation. He employed a great corps of officers, to

[1] Thomassin, Anc. et Nouv. Discipline, vol. ii. book iii. ch. ciii. n. 10, &c.; vol. iii. book i. ch. xxvii. n. 14, 16.

[2] See above, notes, n. 66, 67.

[3] See above, notes, n. 62, 63.

[4] S. Joannis Vita, per Leontium scripta, cap. iii. v. xxxiv. &c. (apud Bollandum, 30 Januarii). Fleury, Hist. Eccl. vol. viii. book xxxvii. n. 12.

watch over the government and the morals of the city. These officers had authority to imprison criminals, to seize their property, and to inflict on them other temporal punishments. But to prevent the oppressions of which they might be guilty in the discharge of these duties, the holy bishop ordered a chair to be placed every Wednesday and Friday before the porch of the church, where he gave a public audience, and distributed impartial justice to all appellants.

118. *Influence of the Patriarch of Constantinople on the Election of the Emperor. —Oath required from the Elected.*

History has preserved few details of the powers of the other patriarchs. It is improbable, in our opinion, that they all had in the beginning the same power as the patriarch of Alexandria, who was always considered the first patriarch in the East, at least before the creation of the patriarchate of Constantinople. But it is certain that, since the close of the fifth century, the patriarch of the imperial city was often summoned to political councils, and especially to the election of emperors; and that his influence on these occasions was generally very great.[1] This is proved most clearly from the history of Anastasius, who was raised to the imperial throne in 491 by the suffrages of the senate and of the army. As he was attached to the Eutychian party, the patriarch Euphemius perseveringly refused to give him the imperial crown until he had promised on oath to preserve the Catholic faith, and to make no change in religion.[2] From that period we find the patriarch, and sometimes even the bishops, summoned to political councils on many important occasions, principally at the elections of emperors. The patriarch's consent was considered necessary for the coronation, a function which he

---

[1] Thomassin, Anc. et Nouv. Discipline, vol. ii. book ii. ch. iv. n. 1; book iii. ch. xlvi. n. 1—5.

[2] Evagrius, Hist. Eccl. lib. iii. cap. xxxii. Fleury, Hist. Eccl. vol. vii. book xxx. n. 22. Lebeau, Hist. du Bas-Empire, vol. viii. book xxxviii. Bossuet, Defen. Declarat. lib. ii. cap. vii. Idem, Défense de l'Histoire des Variations, n. 6.

never performed until they had sworn to preserve the orthodox faith, and to maintain the peace of the churches.[1]

119. *Reasons for exacting the Oath.*

This conduct of Euphemius and of his successors may no doubt appear at first sight extraordinary; and many readers will perhaps be astonished that these prelates should have prescribed in the coronation of the emperor a condition which had no precedent under the first Christian emperors. But it ought to be borne in mind, that at the time when the patriarch of Constantinople began to insist on this condition, circumstances were very different from what they had been before. Since the reign of Theodosius the Great several imperial constitutions had disqualified heretics for all offices and for all civil rights.[2] This enactment had been applied successively to the different heretical sects, and especially to the Eutychians, whose doctrines Anastasius had professed before his election to the empire.[3] Is it surprising that, in such circumstances, the patriarch of Constantinople, when invited by the confidence of the senate and of the people to take part in that political assembly which elected the emperor, should raise some difficulty against the coronation of an heretical prince? Could he act otherwise without compromising both the interests of religion and those of the empire? To raise a heretic to the imperial throne in the midst of a Catholic people, and in a state whose laws declared heretics incapable of any civil employment or of any civil right, would it not be exposing both Church and state to the most violent convulsions? The conduct of the patriarch Euphemius, therefore, and of his successors, so far from being reprehensible on this point, was on the contrary most wise and prudent; it must be regarded as the natural consequence of the laws then in force, and of the

---

[1] See the authors cited on this subject by Thomassin, ubi supra.

[2] See above, n. 62, 63.

[3] See on this point the constitutions of the emperor Marcian, which we have cited above, n. 64, 65.

measures which the emperors themselves had deemed it their duty to adopt for the maintenance of the Catholic religion in their states.

120. *Consequences of this Oath, with regard to the Deposition of an Heretical Emperor.*

The practice of exacting this oath from the emperors at the time of their coronation, ever since the fifth century, gave rise in after-times to a most momentous question in constitutional law; namely, whether by virtue of that oath an heretical emperor could be deposed? Without entering here into a speculative discussion of that point, which would lead us to the domain of theological controversies foreign to our subject, we shall make here only a few historical observations of great use to elucidate the question, and to place in a new light the doctrines of ancient times regarding it.

1. Before the establishment of the new empire of the West under Charlemagne, it does not appear that this important question was ever raised; at least, we have not, as yet, discovered in the authentic monuments of history any trace of such a discussion. Popular commotions there were, it is true, against heretical emperors, especially against Anastasius and Leo the Isaurian; but the clergy took no part in these commotions, nor do we find any serious discussion among doctors on the forfeiture of the rights of an heretical prince.[1]

2. The conduct of the clergy, and even of the sovereign pontiffs, to the emperors of Constantinople, from the fifth to the ninth century, appears invariably to imply that a prince even notoriously heretical did not forfeit his rights. This appears manifest enough from the details which history has preserved to us on the conduct of Pope Symmachus and of the clergy of Con-

[1] On the popular commotions excited in Constantinople against the emperor Anastasius, on account of his adherence to the Eutychian sect, see the authors cited above, p. 172, note 2. In another place we shall speak of similar commotions in Italy against Leo the Isaurian, on account of his adherence to the heresy of the Iconoclasts: they were suppressed by Gregory II. (infra, part i. ch. i.).

stantinople to the emperor Anastasius. The same conclusion appears to follow, from the accounts which we shall give lower down of the conduct of the popes of the eighth century towards heretical emperors, especially Leo the Isaurian.

3. To account for the difference in the conduct of the popes to heretical princes before the ninth century, and after that time, it is of great importance to mark the essential difference between the constitution of the Roman empire, and the constitutions of the new monarchies, which after the fourth century arose on the ruins of that empire in the West. Neither the custom nor the constitution of the Roman empire declared that an heretical prince forfeited his throne. Though the Christian emperors were bound by the natural law, and still more by their coronation oath (since the fifth century), to maintain and protect the Catholic religion, it does not appear that the obligation contracted by that oath was then considered *a condition strictly so called* in their election. There was no formal compact about that condition at the time of the election; nor is there any proof that usage supplies on this point the absence of such formal compact; whereas, in the new monarchies, or at least in most of them, the profession of the Catholic faith was, during many centuries, a strict stipulation in the election of the sovereigns.[1] This condition was formally prescribed sometimes by the fundamental laws of the state; sometimes in the form of the actual election; sometimes by the custom and general persuasion of princes and people; whence it naturally followed that an heretical prince forfeited his throne by the constitutional laws of the state; and that the sentence of an ecclesiastical tribunal declaring a prince a heretic did, by the very fact, declare that he had forfeited all his rights. In another place we shall give, in greater detail, the principal facts which establish the constitutional law of Europe during the middle ages on this point.

---

[1] We shall see, in another place, that this stipulation was formerly usual in England, in Germany, in Spain, and in many other states. (Infra, part ii. ch. iii.)

121. *Important Conclusions from the Facts developed in this Introduction.*

The succession of facts developed in this introduction shows not only the origin and progress of the temporal power of the Church under the Christian emperors; but it moreover shows the real origin of that power which she exercised in the different monarchies raised on the ruins of the Roman empire after the fourth century. Many modern writers represent that power as the creation of clerical ambition and intrigue, aided by the ignorance and superstition of the middle ages. From the facts already stated, it follows, on the contrary,

First. That the foundations of that power were laid by Constantine and by his successors at a period pre-eminent in civilization, in the arts and the sciences.

Secondly. That in conferring this great power on the clergy, the Christian emperors merely transferred to the Church the honours and privileges allowed at all times to the ministers of religion by the Romans, as well as by all nations of antiquity.

Thirdly. That the conduct of the Christian emperors was not less conformable to the principles of sound policy than to the customs and maxims of antiquity on the strict union which ought to exist between religion and the state.

Fourthly. In fine, that the clergy, so far from having ambitiously intrigued for this power, assumed it with regret; and that among all the bishops, those who exercised it in its greatest plenitude under the Christian emperors were the very men least subject to the imputation either of ambition or of avarice.

All these conclusions shall be illustrated more clearly by the details which we shall give in the first part of this work on "the origin of the temporal sovereignty of the Holy See."

POWER OF THE POPE

IN THE MIDDLE AGES.

PART I.

ORIGIN AND GROUNDS OF THE TEMPORAL SOVEREIGNTY OF THE HOLY SEE.

1. *Circumstances which remotely prepared the way for the Temporal Sovereignty of the Holy See.*

THE establishment of the temporal sovereignty of the Holy See was not one of those sudden and unforeseen revolutions which astonish the world by the rapidity of their progress. On the contrary, from an attentive perusal of history, we can trace the steps by which the establishment of that sovereignty was, from a remote period, almost insensibly prepared and conducted to its issue by a combination of circumstances, completely independent of the will of the popes ; circumstances, whose influence it was impossible for them to resist, and whose natural results they could not even counteract without compromising the interests both of religion and of society. A rapid review of these circumstances in this place, will at once convince the reader of the importance and of the difficulties of the subject which we are to treat in this first Part. The details which we have given in our Introduction on the honours and temporal prerogatives conferred on religion and on its ministers, under the first Christian emperors, disclose some of those events which remotely prepared the way for the temporal sovereignty of the Holy See. It is indeed manifest, that the same considerations which induced the emperors at that time to give to all the bishops, and especially to the patriarchs, so great an influence in civil affairs, should naturally lead them to give still greater authority to the Holy See, which was venerated by all the churches as the centre of Catholicity; it was certainly becoming that the see, which was distinguished above all others by its prerogatives in the spiritual order, should be equally so by its prerogatives in the temporal order.

But to this first cause of the temporal power with which the Holy See was invested after the conversion of Constantine, many others may be added, which arose from the deplorable state of the empire under the successors of that prince, especially in the West; and from the important services which the popes rendered to Italy in the difficult circumstances in which it was placed.[1]

2. *Deplorable Condition of the Empire of the West after the Fourth Century.*

Every person knows the deplorable condition of the empire, especially in the West, after the fourth century.[2] The continual irruptions of the barbarians gradually dismembered its fairest provinces, and involved the wretched inhabitants in the most frightful calamities. To such a degree had these invasions increased, that before the close of the fifth century, the empire was almost annihilated in the West, and Rome herself, subjected at first to the tyranny of the Heruli, and afterwards to the Ostrogoths, seemed to be for ever severed from her ancient masters. Under the reign of Justinian, it is true, the conquests of Belisarius and of Narses restored for some years the glory of the empire in Italy. But no sooner had these two great captains quitted that province, than the Lombards once more brought it nearly under subjection, and founded in the north a monarchy, which, during more than two centuries, was a source of calamities to the provinces of Italy still subject to the imperial dominion. In the midst of these calamities, which were constantly recurring, these miserable provinces were almost entirely destitute of any aid from the emperors, who were hardly able to make head against similar irruptions in the East, and

---

[1] Among the French authors who may be cited in support of this opinion, see especially Bossuet, Defens. Declar. book ii. ch. 36—39; Thomassin, Ancienne et Nouvelle Discipline, vol. iii. book i. ch. xxvii. n. 6, 9; ch. xxix. n. 2, &c.; Affre, Essai Historique sur la Puissance Temporelle du Pape et de l'Eglise, ch. viii.; Lebeau, Hist. du Bas-Empire, vol. xiv. book lxvi. n. 51; Annales du Moyen Age, vol. iv. book xiii. p. 40, &c.; De Maistre, Du Pape, book ii. ch. vi. p. 249, &c.

[2] Besides the authors cited in the preceding note, see Bossuet, Hist. Univ. part i. epoch ii.

were almost always obliged to refuse to Italy the succour for which she was constantly appealing: many of them even forgetting the principles and the examples of their predecessors on the submission due to the Church and to the Holy See, appeared to be endeavouring to destroy their authority in Italy, by the public assistance which they gave to heresy, and by the tyranny inflicted on the people in punishment for their attachment to the Holy See and to the Catholic faith.

3. *Powerful Resources for Italy in the Wisdom and Virtue of the Popes.*

In this wretched situation of affairs, Providence had provided a powerful resource for Italy in the wisdom and virtue of the popes who then occupied the Holy See. From the conversion of Constantine to the reign of Charlemagne, they were almost all distinguished by their learning, their prudence, and their eminent sanctity. Their great wealth, and the general respect in which they were held, far from being the ruin of their virtue, served only to give it the greater lustre. The augmentation of their patrimonies was constantly turned to the benefit of the poor, in all parts of the Christian world;[1] and Italy especially, more than once owed to the prudence and to the generosity of the popes, the alleviation, or the prevention, of the calamities to which she was exposed from the neighbourhood of the barbarians.

All these motives combined should naturally make the protection of the popes every day more beloved and more esteemed; they should at the same time give them an ever-increasing influence in the temporal government; an influence the more legitimate, as it was the inevitable result of circumstances and of events entirely independent of their will. Hence authors, the least favourable to the Holy See, are compelled to acknowledge that this combination of circumstances was the principal cause of the prodigious increase of the pope's power after the

[1] The properties possessed by the Church for her own support and for the relief of the poor were then called "patrimonia." Most of the great churches had patrimonies more or less extensive; the richest by far in that respect was the Roman Church. See Fleury, Mœurs des Chrétiens, n. 49, 50, 58, &c.; Hist. Eccl. vol. viii. book xxxv. n. 16; Thomassin, Anc. et Nouv. Discip. vol. iii. book iii. ch. xxix.; Zaccaria, De rebus ad Hist. et Antiq. Eccles. pertinen. Fulginiæ, 1781, tom. ii. Dissertatio x.

fifth century.[1] Nevertheless, though agreeing with us on this point, they do not agree with us on the nature of the power exercised by the popes in Italy before Pepin's donation, nor on the precise epoch from which we ought to date the origin of their temporal sovereignty, nor on the real grounds of that sovereignty.

4. *Object and Plan of this First Part.*

The importance of these questions as bearing on the object of our inquiry, the great variety of opinions to which they have given rise among modern authors, and the pretext which they have too often supplied for odious declamations against the Church and against the Holy See, oblige us to spare no pains in clearing up the matter, and in treating it in all the detail consistent with the object and the plan of our work.

For this purpose, we shall divide Part the First into two chapters. In the first, we shall state the principal facts relating to the power of the popes in Italy from the conversion of Constantine to Charlemagne's elevation to the empire. This statement will serve as a basis for the discussion in the second chapter, of the questions raised by modern authors on the origin and foundations of the temporal sovereignty of the Holy See.

CHAPTER I.

STATEMENT OF THE FACTS RELATING TO THE TEMPORAL POWER OF THE POPES IN ITALY, FROM THE CONVERSION OF CONSTANTINE TO CHARLEMAGNE'S ELEVATION TO THE EMPIRE.

5. *Temporal Power of the Popes before the close of the Fourth Century.*

FROM the reign of Constantine to that of Theodosius the Great, that is, until the close of the fourth century, we find very little difference between the temporal power of the pope and that of the other bishops. The generosity of the emperors to the Holy See was often manifested, it is true, by rich offerings even of

---

[1] Besides the authors already cited, note, n. 1, part i. see Vertot, Origine de la Grandeur de la Cour de Rome, pp. 10, 11 ; Daunou, Essai Hist. sur la Puissance Temporelle des Papes, ch. i.

landed property;[1] but it does not appear that at that period they invested her in the temporal order with a power more extensive than that which was then generally possessed by bishops and patriarchs in the other parts of the empire.

6. *Pretended Donation of Constantine.*

It was long believed that the emperor Constantine, to testify his respect for the Holy See, had granted to it for ever by a solemn act "the city of Rome, with Italy, and all the provinces of the empire of the West."[2] The deed of this pretended donation, which appears to have been published for the first time in the ninth century among "the spurious decretals," was afterwards confidently cited by a great number of authors, and was even generally regarded as authentic from the tenth to the fifteenth century. But after the revival of learning many critics demonstrated that it was spurious;[3] and at the present day it is generally admitted that the donation of Constantine, both as it appears in the collection of the spurious decretals, and in the principal collections of councils, is an apocryphal document.

7. *Proved from History to be spurious.*

It is, in fact, certain that during the lifetime of Constantine, and long after his death, the city of Rome, as well as all the provinces of the empire of the West, remained constantly under the dominion of the emperors. In the partition made by Constantine of the empire among his sons, he assigned Italy, Africa, and Illyria to Constans, the youngest, who took possession of them, and exercised his sovereign authority without the concurrence or participation of the pope.[4] All the successors of Constantine exercised the same authority in Rome and Italy until the eighth century, except during the short period of the domination of the Heruli and the Ostrogoths, from the year 475

---

[1] See the details which we have given on this subject in the Introduction to this work, n. 71, 72.

[2] This act is in Labbe's Concilia, vol. ii. p. 1530. See also No. 5 in Documentary Evidence at the end of this work.

[3] We have cited among the Documentary Evidence the principal advocates of this opinion. See Nat. Alexander, Dissert. xxv. on the Ecclesias. Hist. of the fourth century, art. i. prop. 1, 2, 3.

[4] Eusebius, Vita Constantini, lib. iv. cap. li. Fleury, Hist. Eccl. vol. iii. book xii. n. 1.

until the year 553; nor is there any evidence that the popes ever protested against this conduct of the emperors, or that they ever assumed to themselves sovereign authority at Rome, or in any part of Italy before the eighth century. They had, it is true, a considerable share in the government of that province since the fourth century, and especially after the establishment of the Lombard monarchy in 572. But however extensive their temporal power was at this epoch, we shall soon see that it was always exercised in subordination to that of the emperors, whose representatives the popes were in Italy. In all their acts, whether as temporal lords in the administration of the patrimonies of the Holy See, or in the general concerns of Italy, the popes always acknowledge the sovereignty of the emperor; they used their authority to sustain his, and to keep in submission the people when they were disposed to revolt.

8. *Increase of the Temporal Power of the Pope under Honorius.*

The reign of the emperors Honorius and Theodosius the Younger may be considered as the first date of a considerable development of the temporal power of the pope as well as of the other patriarchs.[1] From that period we frequently find in history the holiest popes exercising their authority to prevent the meetings of heretics, to close their churches, to deprive them of their property, and even to condemn their ringleaders to exile. Thus the heretic Celestius was banished from Italy by order of Pope St. Celestine,[2] and the Manicheans, by the orders of Popes Gelasius and Symmachus.[3] For the execution of these measures there is every reason to believe that the pope, as well as the patriarch of Alexandria, had at his disposal a corps of officers.[4] Certainly the civil magistrates must have been obliged to cooperate efficiently with him to enforce the acts of his authority; this is manifestly implied by the fact of St. Augustine imploring

---

[1] See the details on the temporal power of the patriarchs in the Introduction to this work, art. ii. § 6, n. 113.

[2] St. Prosper, Contra Collat. cap. xxi. n. 138 (Operum S. Augustini, tom. iv. Appen. p. 195). Fleury, Hist. Eccl. vol. vi. book xxv. n. 2.

[3] Anastas. Bibliothec. Vitæ SS. Gelasii et Symmachi (Labbe, Concilia, vol. iv. pp. 1144, 1297). Fleury, Hist. Eccl. vol. vii. book xxx. n. 41, 55.

[4] We have seen above that the patriarch of Alexandria had at his disposal a body of men, called Parabolani, to maintain his power, and make his acts of authority respected. Supra Introduction, art. ii. § 6, n. 114.

Pope Celestine not to employ an armed force to restore to the see of Fussala, in Africa, Bishop Antonius, who had appealed to the Holy See against a sentence of deposition pronounced against him in a provincial council.[1]

9. *This Increase authorized by the Emperor—Doctrine of Pope Gelasius on the Distinction of the two Powers.*

History, which has preserved these details, does not make known to us the date and precise origin of the various developments of the temporal power of the Holy See during the course of the fifth century. But the eminent sanctity of the popes who then governed the Church, and the principles which they professed on the submission due to the temporal power, cannot allow us to doubt that the Holy See was then authorized by the emperor to exercise those acts of power. The doctrine of the distinction and mutual independence of the two powers was then certainly professed clearly by the Holy See, as founded on the divine institution and on the constant tradition of the Church. We know with what precision and clearness this doctrine is professed by Pope Gelasius in a letter to the emperor Anastasius, a declared protector of the Eutychians. This passage is the more remarkable, as it was subsequently adopted by the sixth Council of Paris, and inserted in the capitularia, which, during so many centuries, were the basis of all legislation in France, in Italy, and in Germany.[2] In order to convince the emperor of the impropriety of his conduct, he addresses him in the following terms: "August emperor, this world is governed by two powers,—by bishops, and by kings; of these, the responsibility of the priests is the weightier, since they have to render an account to God even for kings themselves. You know, my dear son, that though your dignity exalts you above other men, you devoutly bow your head to the bishops who are charged with the administration of holy things; you address yourself to them to be conducted in the ways of salvation; and in all that regards the reception and the administration of the sacraments, you acknowledge that far from having any power to command, you are bound

[1] S. Augustin. Epist. 209, alias 261 (Operum, tom. ii.). Fleury, Hist. Eccl. vol. v. book xxiv. n. 34. Tillemont, Mémoires sur l'Hist. Eccl. vol. xiii. art. 315, 316.

[2] See on this subject part second of this Inquiry, ch. iii. art. i. n. 178.

to obey them. You know that in all such concerns you depend on their judgment, and that you have no right to subject them to your will. *For if the ministers of religion obey your laws in all that belongs to the temporal order, because they know that you have received your power from above,* with what affection ought not you to obey those who are charged with the dispensation of our august mysteries?"[1]

The distinction and mutual independence of the two powers cannot assuredly be expressed in clearer terms; for they are represented here as having each its own proper object and distinct functions, according to divine institution; still more in being equally sovereign in all that belongs to their own order, because they are equally subjected one to the other in all that belongs to the order not their own. How could they be truly sovereign each in its own sphere? how could their functions be really distinct, if one could regulate concerns belonging to the jurisdiction of another, annul its acts, and even depose it by virtue of a superior jurisdiction either direct or indirect? In the principles of Pope Gelasius, it is true that in one sense the spiritual is superior to the temporal power; in this sense, namely, that "the bishops must render an account to God of the souls even of kings." It is manifest, however, that, in the opinion of that pope, this superiority does not authorize the spiritual power to regulate matters appertaining to the jurisdiction of the temporal power, much less confer the right of deposing it; such a right would manifestly be incompatible with the distinction of two powers, each sovereign in its own sphere. The superiority attri-

---

[1] "Duo sunt, Imperator auguste, quibus principaliter mundus hic regitur, auctoritas sacra pontificum, et regalis potestas; in quibus tantò gravius est pondus sacerdotum, quantò etiam pro ipsis regibus in divino reddituri sunt examine rationem. Nosti enim, fili clementissime, quòd licèt præsideas humano generi, dignitate, rerum tamen præsulibus divinarum devotus colla submittis, atque ab eis causas tuæ salutis expetis; inque sumendis cœlestibus sacramentis, eisque, ut competit, disponendis, subdi te debere cognoscis, religionis ordine, potiùs quàm præesse. Nosti itaque inter hæc ex illorum te pendere judicio, non illos ad tuam velle redigi voluntatem. *Si enim, quantùm ad ordinem pertinet publicæ disciplinæ, cognoscentes imperium tibi supernâ dispositione collatum, legibus tuis ipsi quoque parent religionis antistites,* . . . . quo, rogo, decet affectu eis obedire, qui pro erogandis venerabilibus sunt attributi mysteriis?"—S. Gelasii Papæ Epist. ad Anast. Aug. (Labbe, Concil. tom. iv. p. 1182). Fleury, Hist. Ecclés. vol. vii. book xxx. n. 31. For a more ample development of this passage, see Bossuet, Defens. Declar. lib. i. § 2, cap. xxxiii. &c.

buted by Pope Gelasius to the spiritual power consists solely in the right of directing the temporal power by wise counsels, by paternal advice, and if necessary, by the use of spiritual punishments.[1]

10. *This Doctrine inculcated by Pope Symmachus.*

The obstinacy of the emperor in supporting heresy compelled Pope Symmachus some years later to remind him of this fundamental doctrine. "Do you imagine," he says,[2] "that because you are an emperor it is lawful for you to despise the ordinances of God, and to exalt yourself against the power of St. Peter? . . . Compare the dignity of emperors with that of pontiff. Between them there is as much difference as between an administrator of earthly things and of celestial. Prince though you are, you receive from the pontiff baptism and the sacraments; you ask his prayers; you desire his benediction; you petition for penance; in a word, while you have charge of human things only, he dispenses to you the goods of heaven. His dignity, then, is at least equal, not to say superior, to yours. You will say,

---

[1] Many ultramontane divines cite those words of Pope Gelasius as well as ourselves, to prove that the Church has no direct power over temporal affairs. (Bellarmin, De Summo Pontifice, lib. v. cap. iii. Roncaglia, Animad. in Dissert. 2, Nat. Alex. ad Hist. Eccles. sæc. xi. § 1.) But they think that these words do not exclude an indirect power over such matters, by virtue, namely, of that authority which the Church has of doing all that the greater good of religion requires. Such an explanation, however, appears manifestly contrary to the words of Gelasius. What difference, in fact, does it make whether the power which the Church has of regulating temporal matters be direct or indirect, if she holds such a power really independent of all concurrence of the civil power, and even against it, for the greater good of religion? In both cases, that distinction between the two sovereign powers, which is so clearly marked by Gelasius, becomes useless and chimerical. On this question of direct temporal power and of indirect, see No. 8 of Documèntary Evidence at the end of this work.

[2] "An, quia imperator es, divinum putas contemnendum esse judicium? . . . An, quia imperator es, contra Petri niteris potestatem? . . . Conferamus autem honorem imperatoris cum honore pontificis; inter quos tantùm distat, quantùm ille rerum humanarum curam gerit, iste divinarum. Tu, imperator, à pontifice baptismum accipis, sacramenta sumis, orationem poscis, benedictionem speras, pœnitentiam rogas. Postremò, tu humana administras, ille tibi divina dispensat. Itaque, ut non dicam superior, certè æqualis honor est . . . Fortassis dicturus es scriptum esse, *omni potestati nos subditos esse debere.* Nos quidem potestates humanas suo loco suscipimus, donec contra Deum suas erigant voluntates. Cæterùm si *omnis potestas à Deo est,* magis ergo quæ rebus est præstituta divinis. Defer Deo in nobis, et nos deferemus Deo in te. Cæterùm si tu Deo non deferas, non potes ejus uti privilegio, cujus jura contemnis." —Symmachi Papæ Apologia ad Anast. (Labbe, Concil. tom. iv. p. 1298). Fleury, ibid. n. 55. Bossuet, ibid. lib. ii. cap. vii.

perhaps, that, according to Scripture, we ought 'to be submissive to every power.'[1] Certainly we obey the powers of the earth when they confine themselves to their sphere, and do not oppose their will to that of God. Besides, if all power comes from God,[2] that which is established to regulate divine things, with much greater reason comes from Him. Respect God in us, and we will respect Him in you. But if you do not obey God, you cannot use his gifts whose rights you abuse, nor exact from us a submission which you refuse to God himself."[3]

Thus Pope Symmachus, after the example of Gelasius, not only marks with precision the distinction between the two powers by the nature of the objects on which their authority is exercised, but binds the popes themselves, by virtue of a divine ordinance, to obey the powers of the earth in all that regards the temporal order, as princes are bound to obey the Church in all that regards the spiritual order. The only case in which he thinks disobedience lawful is when the prince, exceeding the limits of his authority, "opposes his own will to that of God." To maintain, after this, that the popes of the fifth century attributed to themselves, of their own authority, direct or indirect jurisdiction over temporal things, would be not only an evidently gratuitous supposition, but one directly opposed to history, and to the constant doctrine of the popes.

11. *Motives for the Generosity of the Emperors to the Popes.*

The generosity of the emperors to the Holy See at the time of which we are speaking is by no means surprising, when we reflect that there were very powerful motives for securing the papal influence by new liberalities; and that the popes were necessitated by the exigency of the times and by the interest of the empire itself to take a very prominent part in public affairs. Italy, continually harassed by the barbarians, had no firmer bulwark against them than the authority of the Holy See. It is well known that, about the middle of the fifth century, Pope St. Leo

---

[1] Rom. xiii. 1. [2] Ibid.

[3] These last words allude apparently to the danger which Anastasius had already incurred of losing his crown by the revolts occasioned by his adherence to the Eutychian party.

twice saved the city of Rome by his mediation with the barbarian kings Attila and Genseric.[1] In the following century, Pope Agapitus endeavoured, with the same zeal, but not with the same success, to negotiate a peace between Theodatus, king of the Goths, and the emperor Justinian.[2] Pope Vigilius was more fortunate in his negotiations with the same emperor for the interests of Italy; for he obtained from that emperor a constitution, or "*pragmatica*," the principal object of which was to confirm the donations made to the Romans by the Gothic kings Athalaric and Theodatus.[3] Cassiodorus, a Roman senator, alludes, no doubt, to this great influence of the popes in public affairs, when, after his promotion to the dignity of prefect of the prætorium,[4] in 534, he applied to Pope John II. requesting his prayers and advice for the exercise of his new dignity. "You are," he says, "the guardian of the Christian people; and your character as pastor does not exclude the care of temporal concerns; all the interests of the people are in your hands; you are bound to defend them with the zeal and the affection of a father."[5]

12. *These Motives still more powerful under the Monarchy of the Lombards.*

However perceptible the increase of the power of the Holy See was during the fifth and sixth centuries, it becomes much more so after the establishment of the monarchy of the Lombards in 572. After this new revolution, the ever-increasing weakness of the empire, and the defenceless state in which most of the

[1] Fleury, Hist. Ecclés. vol. vi. book xxviii. n. 39, 55. Tillemont, Mém. sur l'Hist. Ecclés. vol. xv. pp. 750, 779. Thomassin, Anc. et Nouv. Discipline, vol. iii. book i. ch. xxvi.

[2] Cassiodorus, Epist. lib. x. ep. xix. xx. Lebeau, Hist. du Bas-Empire, vol. ix. book xliii. n. 20, 25. Fleury, Hist. Ecclés. vol. vii. book xxxii. n. 53.

[3] Baronii Annales, anno 554, n. 9, &c. Fleury, Hist. Ecclés. vol. vii. book xxxiii. n. 52.

[4] On the office of prætorian prefect, see supra, Introduction, note to n. 32.

[5] "Vos enim speculatores Christiano populo præsidetis; vos patris nomine omnia dirigitis. Securitas ergo plebis ad vestram respicit famam, cui divinitùs est commissa custodia. Quapropter nos decet custodire aliqua, sed vos omnia. Pascitis quidem spiritualiter commissum vobis gregem; tamen nec ista potestis negligere, quæ corporis videntur substantiam continere; nam sicut homo constat ex dualitate, ita boni patris est utroque refovere."—Cassiodorus, Epist. lib. xi. ep. ii. (Operum, tom. i.). Ejusdem Vita, part. i. n. 31 (at the beginning of the same volume). Thomassin, Ancienne et Nouv. Discipline, vol. iii. book i. ch. xxvii. n. 10.

Italian provinces subject to the imperial dominion were left, made the power of the sovereign pontiff every day more indispensable for those provinces.[1] Harassed incessantly by the Lombards, they were always appealing, and almost always without success, for succours from the emperor, sometimes through the voice of the popes, sometimes through the exarchs, who then governed those provinces in the name of the emperor.[2] In so deplorable a

---

[1] Besides the authors above quoted, p. 178, n. 1, see also Annales du Moyen Age, vol. iii. pp. 191—198; Montesquieu, Considérations sur les Causes de Grandeur et de la Décadence des Romains, ch. xix. &c.

[2] The civil exarchs who are mentioned so frequently in the history of the empire of Constantinople must not be confounded with the ecclesiastical exarchs occurring in the history of the primitive ages. The dignity of the latter resembled very much that of the patriarchs and primates (see Thomassin, Anc. et Nouv. Discip. vol. i. book i. ch. xvii. &c.; De Héricourt's abridgment of the same work, part i. ch. iv.). In the civil order, the exarch was a magistrate placed by the emperor as governor over certain provinces. History mentions more frequently exarchs of Italy, of Africa, and of Sicily. But the most distinguished of all was the exarch of Italy, who was sometimes called exarch of Ravenna, because that city was his ordinary residence. He was invested over his own province with almost absolute authority both in the civil and in the military administration. He gave the title of "duke" to the governors of Rome, of Pentapolis, of Naples, and of the other cities of Naples which were still subject to the emperor's sceptre. The only check on his independence was the liability to be recalled, and the obligation of paying annually a certain sum to the emperor, who made that a condition when conferring the office of exarch. The first exarch of Italy was Longinus, who was sent over in 568 by Justin II. to defend that province against the Lombards. The authority of these exarchs was however but a feeble barrier against the progress of these barbarians, who desolated Italy with continual ravages, until the people, through the popes, implored the intervention of the French. The exarchate of Ravenna, after having lasted 184 years, disappeared with Eutychius in 752. Its authority immediately devolved on the popes, who, being invited to that post by the wishes and the confidence of the people, had already been governing with sovereign authority for some years the greater part of the provinces of the empire in Italy. (On the origin of the exarchs, see Lebeau, Hist. du Bas-Empire, vol. xi. book l. n. 21; vol. xiii. book lxiv. n. 18; S. Greg. Magni Epist. lib. i. ep. xxxiii. nota b; Ducange, Glossarium Infimæ Latinitatis, verbo Exarchus.) We have also, in the Art de Vérifier les Dates, the chronological succession of the exarchs of Italy. Everything connected with their history is carefully treated by Beretta, De Italiâ Medii Ævi Dissert. Chorograph. § 16, 20, apud Muratori, Rerum Italicarum Script. vol. x.

With regard to the names and geographical situation of the provinces subject to the jurisdiction of the exarch of Italy, it is important to observe that the word exarchate is taken by ancient authors in two different senses from the establishment and during the whole period of the Lombard monarchy. In its more general sense it includes all the provinces of Italy then subject to the imperial dominion; that is, principally, Venetia, a part of the coasts of Liguria, the eastern part of the ancient Emilia, Flaminia, the western part of the ancient Picenum, and the duchy of Rome. In its more restricted sense, it included only the eastern part of the ancient Emilia and Flaminia, corresponding very nearly with the modern Romagna. In this latter sense the exarchate is distinguished from Pentapolis and from the duchy of Rome. Pentapolis corresponds nearly with the western part of the ancient Picenum; it is at present

situation, the principal and frequently the only resource of Italy, was the authority of the Holy See, whose patronage was necessary for the exarch himself, sometimes to defray the expenses of government; sometimes to appease the people when inclined to revolt; sometimes to negotiate with the barbarians, who respected the dignity, and especially the word, of the pope, much more than those of the exarch; so that the popes, by interposing, as they frequently did at that time, in public affairs, were only yielding to the absolute necessities of circumstances, and to the combined wishes of prince and people.

13. *Temporal Power of St. Gregory the Great.*

The history of the pontificate of Gregory the Great, which was contemporary with the first period of the Lombard monarchy, supplies a number of facts in support of those positions.[1] No man could have a greater aversion than that great pope for the embarrassment and tumult of secular affairs, nor a greater love for that life of retreat and recollection, which he had so long led in the cloister before his elevation to the popedom.[2] So great

---

called the duchy of Urbino and part of the March of Ancona. The duchy of Rome included a part of Etruria or Tuscany, with Sabina, a part of Umbria and Campania; a territory nearly co-extensive with what is now called the patrimony of St. Peter, with part of Umbria, and the Campagna di Roma. For these geographical details, see Beretta, ubi supra, § 16, &c.; Baudrand, Geographia Ordine Litterarum Disposita, verbis Exarchatus, Æmilia, Pentapolis, Romanus Ducatus, &c.

[1] Thomassin, Ancienne et Nouv. Discipline, vol. ii. book iii. ch. cvi. n. 7; vol. iii. book i. ch. xxvii. n. 6—9. S. Gregorii Vita recens adornata (Oper. tom. iv.), lib. ii. et iii. passim. See especially lib. iii. cap. ix. n. 6. Fleury, Hist. Eccl. vol. viii. book xxxv. n. 15, 25. Annales du Moyen Age, vol. iv. book xiii. pp. 37—58. Orsi, Della Origine del Dominio et della Sovranità de' Romani Pontefici: prefazione.

[2] Gibbon, Hallam, and some other Protestant writers, accuse St. Gregory of a spirit of ambition and intrigue, utterly opposed to his character (Hallam, Europe in the Middle Ages, vol. iii. pp. 326—328; Gibbon, Decline and Fall, &c. vol. viii. ch. xlv.). The least knowledge of the writings of St. Gregory, especially his letters (Opera, tom. ii.), and of the ancient authors who wrote his life, must convince every impartial mind of the injustice of such a reproach. Hence the most eminent Protestant writers agree with the Catholics in representing St. Gregory as a pontiff, not less distinguished for his eminent virtues than for his large and enlightened views, and for the wisdom of his government. This is the opinion of Cave especially, in his Historia Litteraria. His praise of the virtues and talents of St. Gregory is the less liable to suspicion, because he censures him severely on other points, particularly for the testimony of respect given by him to the usurper Phocas, and also on the accusation made against him of having endeavoured to destroy all the writings and monuments of pagan antiquity. For the first charge, see Alban Butler, Life of St. Gregory;

was his repugnance for that dignity, that he employed all possible means to escape it, and constantly persisted in refusing it, until the will of God had been manifested even by miracles.[1] Nevertheless, he assures us himself, that in his time, the bishop of Rome, "in consequence of his pastoral charge, was so occupied with external cares, that he had often reason to doubt whether he was filling the office of pastor, or that of a temporal lord.[2] In fact, a sovereign of Rome and of Italy could not have been more burdened than he was with the cares of temporal government." Independently of the care imposed on him by the administration of the patrimonies and the seignories of the Roman Church,[3] the proximity of the Lombards, and their continual incursions into the provinces still subject to the emperors in Italy, involved him in a multiplicity of cares, which wrung from him in his grief the exclamation, "that in punishment of his sins, he had been made bishop, not of the Romans, but of the Lombards."[4] We find him constantly discharging the duties of a temporal lord and almost of a king, in the administration and defence of the cities most exposed to the incursions of the enemy. He sends a governor to Nepi, with directions to the people to obey him as the pope himself.[5] He sends the tribune Constantius to Naples to command the troops of that city, when

---

and on the second, the Eclaircissements, by M. Emery, in vol. ii. of the Christianisme de Bacon, p. 332, and following.

[1] S. Gregorii Vita recens adornata, lib. i. cap. vii. n. 2, &c.; lib. ii. cap. i. n. 5, &c. Fleury, ubi supra, n. 1.

[2] "Hoc in loco quisquis pastor dicitur, curis exterioribus graviter occupatur, ita ut sæpe incertum fiat, utrùm pastoris officium, an terreni proceris agat."—S. Gregorii Epistol. lib. i. Epist. 25 (alias 24), p. 514, c. (Oper. tom. ii.) The last editors of St. Gregory (note on the fifth letter of the same book, p. 491) suppose with Thomassin (ubi supra, vol. iii. book i. ch. xxvii. n. 6), that St. Gregory in this passage speaks of the temporal cares with which all the bishops of the West were then charged. But it appears very certain that St. Gregory speaks of the bishop of Rome only. The passage is so understood by Orsi (ubi supra, n. 2).

[3] See the details which we have given on this point in the Introduction, art. ii. § 3, n. 80.

[4] "Sicut peccata mea merebantur, non Romanorum, sed Longobardorum episcopus factus sum."—S. Gregorii Epistol. lib. i. Epist. 31 (alias 30).

[5] "Leontio curam sollicitudinemque civitatis [Nepesinæ] *injunximus*; ut in cunctis invigilans, quæ ad utilitatem vestram vel reipublicæ pertinere dignoscet, ipse disponat. . . . Quisquis congruæ ejus ordinationi restiterit, *nostræ resultare dispositioni cognoscetur*." — S. Gregor. Epistol. lib. ii. Epist. 11 (alias 8).

it was menaced by the enemies of the empire.[1] In several of his letters, he excites and animates the zeal and vigilance of the bishops for the defence of the cities, the manning of the walls, and the provisioning of the strong places.[2] He issues orders on the same subject to military officers;[3] he treats in person for peace with the Lombards, and facilitates the success of the negotiations, sometimes by his liberalities, and sometimes by his repeated solicitations to the exarchs, the emperors, and even the Lombards themselves. His authority, in a word, equally respected by princes and by people, by Romans and barbarians, became the centre of government and of all the political affairs of Italy.[4]

14. *Embarrassments and Difficulty of his Position—His Prudence.*

The embarrassments and difficulty of his position were augmented especially by the perversity of the exarchs, who, far from uniting with him for the protection of the people, the victims of so many calamities, frequently abused their authority, to inflict all sorts of rapine and tyranny. "I cannot express to you," he writes to a bishop, "how much we have to suffer here from your friend the exarch Romanus. In two words, I may tell you that his wickedness is more injurious to us than the arms of the Lombards; so that we prefer the enemies who kill us to the officers of the armies who devour us by their fraud and their rapine. To be charged with the care of the bishops, of the clergy, of the monasteries, and of the people;—to be continually on our guard against the surprises of the enemy, as well as against the treachery or malice of the governors, this will give you

---

[1] "Devotio vestra, sicut et nunc didicimus, epistolis nostris, quibus *magnificum virum Constantium tribunum custodiæ civitatis* [Neapolitanæ] *deputavimus præesse,* paruit, et congruam militaris devotionis obedientiam demonstravit."—S. Gregorii Epistol. lib. ii. Epist. 31 (alias 24).

[2] Ibid. lib. viii. Epist. 18 (alias 20); lib. ix. Epist. 4 et 6 (alias 2 et 5).

[3] Ibid. lib. ii. Epist. 3 et 29.

[4] "Sicut, in Ravennæ partibus, dominorum pietas apud primum exercitum Italiæ sacellarium habet [i. e. *ærarii dispensatorem*], qui, causis supervenientibus, quotidianas expensas faciat; ita et in hâc urbe, in causis talibus, sacellarius eorum ego sum."—S. Gregorii Epistol. lib. v. Epist. 21 (alias lib. iv. Epist. 34); paulò post medium. S. Gregorii Vita recens adornata, lib. ii. cap. viii. n. 3; lib. iii. cap. ii. n. 1, &c.; lib. iv. cap. i. n. 1, et alibi passim. Lebeau, Hist. du Bas-Empire, vol. xi. book liii. n. 47, &c. Fleury, Hist. Eccl. vol. viii. book xxxv. n. 40, &c.; book xxxvi. n. 4.

some idea of the labours and anxieties to which I am daily exposed in the discharge of my duties."[1] In so delicate and laborious a position, the wise pontiff conducted himself with so much prudence and disinterestedness, that his authority, far from being prejudicial to that of the emperor in Italy, served rather to maintain and make it be respected. So far was he from arrogating to himself the title or rights of sovereignty, that he openly professed, in all things appertaining to the temporal order, his submission to the orders and instructions of the emperor.

15. *His Principles and Conduct with regard to the Submission due to the Emperor.*

A very remarkable proof of this occurs in his conduct towards the emperor Maurice, when that prince enacted a law, excluding from the monastic state all who occupied posts in the civil administration or in the army.[2] The last provision of this law was, in the opinion St. Gregory, contrary to the good of religion, because it closed up, so to speak, the way to heaven against a class of men who might need very much a place of retreat to work out their salvation. Nevertheless, when, according to the usual custom,[3] the emperor addressed the law to him to be promulgated in the western provinces, the holy pope did not hesitate to send it to these provinces, *in obedience to the orders of the prince*, but contented himself with remonstrating with him on the propriety of modifying or retracting his law.[4] "Being subject to your authority," said he, "I have sent your law to the different parts of the world; but, as it is not in accordance with the law of Almighty God, I have considered it my duty to remonstrate with you. *I have thus discharged the double duty of obeying the emperor, and of declaring my sentiments for the honour of God.*"[5] Would St. Gregory have thus expressed him-

---

[1] S. Gregorii Epistol. lib. v. Epist. 42.

[2] Fleury, Hist. Eccl. vol. viii. book xxxv. n. 31. Bossuet, Defensio Declar. lib. ii. cap. viii. D. Gregorii Papæ Vita recens adornata, lib. ii. cap. x. n. 1, 4.

[3] We have already remarked, that the custom of the emperors was to address all laws on ecclesiastical matters to the patriarchs, who were to send them to the bishops through the metropolitans (supra, Introduction, n. 3).

[4] It appears, in fact, that the emperor soon modified this law, on the representation made by St. Gregory.—S. Greg. Epistol. lib. iii. Epist. 65, 66 (alias 62, 65). Fleury, Hist. Eccl. vol. viii. book xxxv. n. 35, 50.

[5] "Ego quidem jussioni subjectus, eamdem legem per diversas terrarum

self, had he believed that the divine law gave him *either direct or indirect jurisdiction over temporal things*; that is, had he believed himself to enjoy the right of regulating matters of this nature to advance the interests of religion? Holding such principles, would he have felt himself bound in conscience, in obedience to the emperor, to promulgate a law pronounced by his own judgment prejudicial to religion?

To weaken the strength of this argument, some modern authors have pretended that St. Gregory, in promulgating the law in question, modified it, or, at least, gave directions to have its execution suspended.[1] Others maintain that the *obedience of St. Gregory*, on this occasion, was not *an obedience de jure*, to which he thought the divine law bound him, but *an obedience de facto*, to which he was reluctantly driven by a fear of the trouble his resistance might occasion.[2] Both these explanations are quite irreconcilable with the text of St. Gregory; in fact, the text clearly supposes that the pontiff, despite his repugnance, considered himself bound in conscience to promulgate the law just as he had received it from the emperor, and consequently without any modification or any diminution of its authority. The same text supposes his obedience to have been really *an obedience de jure*, founded in the natural and divine precept, which obliges all subjects, pontiffs themselves included, to obey their lawful sovereign in everything appertaining to the temporal order.

A letter written by him about this time to the empress Con-

partes transmitti feci; et quia lex ipsa omnipotenti Deo minimè concordat, ecce per suggestionis meæ paginam serenissimis dominis nuntiavi. Utrobique ergo quæ debui exolvi, qui et imperatori obedientiam præbui, et pro Deo quod sensi, minimè tacui."—S. Greg. lib. iii. Epist. 65 (alias 62).

[1] Baronii Annales, ad ann. 593. De Marca, De Concordiâ, lib. ii. cap. xi. n. 9. Thomassin, Ancien. et Nouv. Discipline, vol. i. book iii. ch. lxi. n. 12. Rohrbacher, Des Rapports Naturels entre les deux Puissances, vol. i. ch. xix. The advocates of this opinion rely principally on a letter of St. Gregory to many bishops and metropolitans of the West, which makes some modifications in the provisions of this law (Epistol. lib. viii. Epist. 5). But on attentively perusing that letter, it will be seen that St. Gregory does not modify that law by his own authority, but in the name of the emperor, who had yielded to his remonstrances. It is in this sense that St. Gregory's letter is generally understood by critics, and especially by his latest editors (Vita S. Gregorii recens adornata, ubi supra; D. Ceillier, Hist. des Auteurs Ecclés. vol. xvii. p. 280).

[2] Bellarmin, De Potestate summi Pontif. adversus Barclaium, cap. iii. n. 10 (Oper. tom. vii.). Mamachi, Origines et Antiquit. Christ. tom. iv. p. 125, text and note.

stantina, wife of Maurice, places in a clear light his real sentiments. In this letter he represents himself as a mere officer of the emperor, commissioned to watch over imperial interests in the Italian capital. "I am living here," said he, "in the city these twenty-seven years, amidst the swords of the Lombards. But for the permission to live here, I cannot tell you what sums the Church daily pays them. To give you, in a few words, some idea of it, I will merely say that, as the emperor stations a treasurer in the province of Ravenna, near his principal Italian army, to supply the daily wants of the troops, so am I at Rome *the emperor's treasurer*, supplying the necessities of this city, incessantly attacked by the Lombards."[1]

16. *His Example on this Point followed by his Successors.*

The successors of this great pope, with his power, inherited his generosity.[2] The same circumstances which had obliged him to take such an active part in the political affairs and in the temporal government of Italy, imposed the same obligation on the majority of his successors; but their conduct, like his, was characterized by so much moderation and prudence, that they seemed to have had no other object in exercising their authority than to support and consolidate that of the emperor; and even when they had the greatest reason to complain of him, they generously employed their credit and their treasures to defend the empire, to preserve the walls and fortifications of Rome, to repair her aqueducts and public establishments, and, above all, to save Italy from the fury of the Lombards. It is remarkable, too, that the emperors, far from being offended at the conduct of the popes, and the increase of their temporal power, continued to maintain with them the most friendly relations; and nothing could disturb this pleasing harmony but the obstinate attachment of some emperors to heresy, which betrayed them—particularly in the eighth century—into measures the most imprudent, and the best calculated to effect the complete destruction of their authority in Italy.[3]

---

[1] S. Greg. Epistol. lib. v. Epist. 21 (alias lib. iv. Epist. 34). We have already cited the latter part of that text, Introduction, note 14.

[2] Thomassin, Ancien. et Nouv. Discipline, vol. iii. book i. ch. xxvii. n. 8; ch. xxix. n. 2, &c. Fleury, Mœurs des Chrétiens, n. 58, versus finem.

[3] See the authors cited above, note 1, first part.

17. *Imprudent Conduct of the Emperors with regard to Italy and the Holy See.*

In truth, about this period, the emperors, in contempt of the rules of ordinary prudence, instead of cautiously managing the people of this province, retained in obedience by love of duty alone, were constantly weakening their authority over them by openly attacking the Catholic religion, which they loved, and persecuting the Holy See, the object of their most cherished affections. They sent to Italy, and even to Rome, magistrates who cared nothing for the people, often even heretics, whom the laws then in force pronounced incapable of holding any civil employment.[1] These magistrates, naturally odious to a people deeply attached to the Catholic faith, instead of soothing them by conciliatory measures, frequently so irritated them by their annoyances, that they drove them to revolt, and rendered subjection to the emperor every day more intolerable.[2] Similar acts of imprudence necessarily hastened the fall of the Western empire, not only abandoned but persecuted by its own sovereigns: and, as a natural consequence, daily increased the power of the popes in Italy, which had been long accustomed to consider them as her only resource amidst her innumerable calamities.

18. *This Imprudence increases the Authority of the Pope.*

This was the natural result of the conduct of the emperors. Italy, unable to obtain from them the assistance she needed, became more and more attached to the Holy See, and showed her willingness to defend it even by open force against the annoyances of the emperor and of his officers. The army of Italy gave proof of this disposition, towards the end of the seventh century, when the emperor Justinian II. attempted to convey Pope Sergius by force to Constantinople, to procure his subscription to the acts of the *Quinisext Council.*[3] It defeated the design of the messen-

[1] We have cited in the Introduction the principal provisions of the Roman law on this point, art. 2, § 2.

[2] Anastas. Bibliothec. Vitæ SS. Pontif. Sergii, Joannis VI., Constantini, Gregorii II. &c. (Labbe, Concil. tom. vi.). Baronii Annales, tom. viii. anno 711, n. 12. Annales du Moyen Age, vol. vi. book xx. pp. 80—85.

[3] The Council Quinisextum, which was convoked by the emperor Justinian II. in 692, was so called because it was intended as a supplement to the fifth and sixth general councils. It was also called Trullanum, or in Trullo, because it was held in the dome of the palace called in Latin Trullus. The Greeks regard it as a general council, but the Latins rejected it; and Pope

gers of this prince, and would have put them to death, had not the pontiff interposed his authority, and taken them under his protection.[1] In 701, John VI. was similarly defended against the exarch, who was suspected of the intention of offering the same violence to him that Justinian had designed for his predecessor Sergius.[2]

Such was, at this time, the authority of the popes, that they alone could suppress the commotions frequently occasioned at Rome and in Italy by the vexatious annoyances of the emperor, and preserve a remnant of authority for him in a country which he was unable to defend. This has been just now clearly established; for none other than the pontifical authority could save the messengers of the emperor from paying the penalty due to their attempts on the liberty of Sergius and John VI.[3] An occurrence of the same kind happened during the pontificate of Constantine, when, in 713, the Romans revolted against the emperor Philippicus, who had become an avowed abettor of the Monothelite heresy.[4] This prince having sent the duke Beta to Rome as governor of the city, the people refused to acknowledge him, and even undertook his expulsion by force of arms; a combat which ensued would have been attended with fatal consequences, had not the pope sent the bishops with gospels and crosses to quell the commotion. "The case of the governor was hopeless, and his life in imminent danger; but the Catholics, in obedience to the pope, gave up the contest, and thus allowed their adversaries the honour of apparent victory."[5]

Sergius never could be induced to subscribe to it by all the entreaties of the emperor; he declared that he would rather die than consent to the errors and the innovations which it had introduced. It is certain, moreover, that the pope had no part in the convocation of this council, and that he did not assist at it, either in person or by his legates. See D. Ceillier, Hist. des Auteurs Ecclés. vol. xix. p. 785; Fleury, Hist. Eccl. vol. ix. book xl. n. 49.

[1] Anastas. Bibliothec. Vita Sergii, pp. 1290, 1291. Fleury, Hist. Eccl. vol. ix. book xl. n. 54. Annales du Moyen Age, ubi supra, p. 80, &c.

[2] Anastas. Vita Joannis VI. p. 1382. Fleury, Hist. Eccl. vol. ix. book xli. n. 5. Annales du Moyen Age, ubi supra, p. 84.

[3] Anastas. ubi supra.

[4] Anastas. Vita Constantini, p. 1305. Fleury, Hist. Eccl. vol. ix. book xli. n. 23.

[5] "Pars Petri [ducis Romani] ita angustiata [erat,] ut nulla illi esset spes vivendi; verùm, ad pontificis jussionem pars alia, quæ et Christiana vocabatur, recessit; sicque defensoris hæretici pars valuit Petri, ac si illa attrita recederet."—Anastas. ubi supra.

19. *Revolution in Italy under the Pontificate of Gregory II.—Its true Causes.*

The great power of the pope more clearly appeared, about the year 726, under the pontificate of Gregory II., the real epoch of that extraordinary revolution, which prepared the way for the temporal sovereignty of the Holy See, by completing the destruction of the Roman empire in the West. We will relate the principal circumstances of this important revolution, as we find them in the most trustworthy authors.[1]

The undisguised protection afforded by the emperor Leo the Isaurian to the Iconoclast heresy, and the violence offered by him to Catholics, and even to the sovereign pontiff, were, these authors tell us, the real cause of this revolution. Paul, deacon of Aquileia, in the eighth century, gives the following brief account of it, in his History of the Lombards:[2] "The king of the Lombards," said he, "besieged Ravenna, took possession of the imperial fleet, and destroyed it. Then the patrician Paul sent emissaries from Ravenna, with orders to put the pontiff to death; but the conspiracy was defeated by the resistance of the Lombards, who, in conjunction with the inhabitants of Spoleto, and the other Lombards of Tuscany, undertook the defence of the pope. It was at this time the emperor Leo burned at Constantinople the images of the saints, which he had plundered from the churches; he even commanded the pope, if he wished to recover his friendship, to follow his impious example. But the pope despised his orders. All the troops of Ravenna and Venice were unanimous in their opposition to Leo; *and had they not been restrained by the pope, they would have chosen another emperor.*[3] Luitprand, on his side, took possession of

[1] Of ancient authors, see especially Paul. Diacon. De Gestis Longobard. lib. vi. cap. xlix. (Bibliothec. Patr. tom. xiii. p. 198, &c.); Anastas. Bibliothec. Vita Gregorii II. (Labbe, Concil. tom. vi. p. 1430).

Of modern authors, see Bossuet, Defens. Declarat. lib. ii. cap. xi. &c. xxxvi. &c.; Thomassin, Ancien. et Nouv. Discipline, vol. iii. book i. ch. xxvii. n. 8; ch. xxix. n. 2, &c.; De Marca, De Concordiâ, lib. iii. cap. ii.; Orsi, Della Origine del Domin. de' Romani Pontefici, cap. i. &c.; Observations sur l'Hist. de la Seconde Race de nos Rois, by P. Griffet, in vol. iii. of Daniel's Hist. de France, p. 250.

The principal events relating to this revolution were well understood and presented in their true bearings by Alban Butler, in a note on the life of the emperor Henry II. (Lives of the Saints, July 15), and by the Abbé Pey, De l'Autorité des deux Puissances, vol. i. part ii. ch. i. p. 106, &c.

[2] Paulus Diaconus, De Gestis Longobard. ubi supra.

[3] "Omnis quoque Ravennæ exercitus vel Venetiarum talibus jussis unanimi-

several cities of Emilia. . . . He also took the city of Sutri, in Tuscany, but soon after restored it to the Romans. Meantime, the emperor Leo commanded the inhabitants of Constantinople to plunder the images of our Saviour, of the Blessed Virgin, and of the saints, wherever they found them, and to burn them publicly; and many, having disobeyed his orders, were, in punishment of their resistance, killed or mutilated. It was on this occasion that Germanus, patriarch of Constantinople, was driven from his see, and replaced by the priest Anastasius."

20. *The Account of Paul the Deacon confirmed by Anastasius.*

All the facts here briefly related by the historian of the Lombards are detailed at much greater length by Anastasius the Librarian, in his Life of Pope Gregory II., composed from the archives of the Roman Church, in the middle of the next century. "The king of the Lombards," says he, "having raised a large army, advanced towards Ravenna,[1] which he besieged for many days; and having obtained possession of it, he also took the fleet, with an immense booty. Soon after, the duke Basil, and some other officers of the emperor, conceived the design of putting the pope to death. Marin, who then governed the duchy of Rome, and who received similar orders from the emperor, favoured the conspiracy. But God did not permit them to succeed. Paul having been afterwards sent to Italy, in the capacity of exarch, they contemplated again the execution of their criminal intention; but the conspiracy was detected by the Romans, and two of the principal conspirators put to death. . . . In the mean time the exarch Paul, in obedience to the orders of the emperor himself, sought an opportunity of putting the pope to death, *under pretence of his preventing the levying of imposts in the province.*[2] . . . He even sent emis-

---

ter restiterunt; et nisi eos prohibuisset pontifex, imperatorem super se constituere fuissent aggressi."—Paul. Diac. De Gestis Longobard. ubi supra.

[1] Anastas. Bibliothec. Vita Greg. II. (Labbe, Concilia, tom. vi. p. 1430). Fleury has inserted the greater part of this narrative in his Hist. Ecclés. vol. ix. book xlii. n. 6; but he has changed its order, for what reason we know not. The order of the facts narrated by Anastasius is better observed by Lebeau, Hist. du Bas-Empire, vol. xiii. book lxiii. n. 40, &c. See also Annales du Moyen Age, vol. vi. book xxiii. p. 384, &c.

[2] "Paulus verò exarchus, imperatoris jussione, eumdem pontificem conabatur interficere, *eò quòd censum in provinciâ ponere præpediebat.*"—Anastas. ubi supra, p. 1434. A little further on we shall defend the meaning assigned by us to the words in italics.

saries from Ravenna, and some other cities, to perpetrate the horrid crime; but the Romans and Lombards, uniting to defend the pontiff, prevented the consequences of this conspiracy. Soon after, the emperor commanded the destruction of the images of the saints and martyrs in all parts of Italy, threatening with his anger all those who should dare to disobey, promising favour to the pope in the event of his submission, and threatening him with deposition as the penalty of his resistance. When the holy pontiff received these impious orders, he armed himself against the emperor as against a professed enemy, openly condemning his heresy, and writing to the faithful in all places, to caution them against such an impiety.[1] The inhabitants of Pentapolis, and the troops of Venice, moved by the exhortations of the pope, also refused to obey the emperor, declaring their determination to permit no attempt on the life of the pontiff, and their willingness to become his avowed defenders. They anathematized the exarch Paul with all his adherents; and in contempt of his authority, the people everywhere through Italy selected leaders for themselves,[2] to secure their own independence and the pontiff's. Besides, when the evil intentions of the emperor became known, *all Italy resolved to choose another emperor, and to send him to Constantinople; but the pope, expecting the conversion of the prince, opposed this resolution.*[3] ... Shortly after, the emperor sent to Naples the eunuch Eutychius, who had formerly been exarch, for the purpose of executing the wicked project which the exarch Paul and his adherents had failed in accomplishing; but

[1] "Respiciens ergo pius vir profanam principis jussionem, jam contra imperatorem quasi contra hostem se armavit, renuens hæresim ejus, scribens ubique cavere Christianos, eò quòd orta fuisset impietas talis." — Anastas. ubi supra, pp. 1433, 1434.

[2] "Spernentes ordinationem ejus, sibi omnes ubique in Italiâ duces elegerunt, atque sic de pontificis, deque suâ immunitate cuncti studebant."—Anastas. ubi supra, p. 1434.

We have already seen that, after the establishment of the exarchate in Italy, the principal cities still subject to the emperor were governed by dukes subordinate to the exarch (supra, note to No. 12, first part). In this revolution, the progress of which we are now describing, these dukes were replaced by others elected by the cities which declared their independence of the emperor. That is the natural meaning of the words of Anastasius.

[3] "Cognitâ verò imperatoris nequitiâ, omnis Italia consilium iniit, ut sibi eligerent imperatorem, et Constantinopolim ducerent; sed compescuit tale consilium Pontifex, sperans conversionem principis." — Anastas. ubi supra, p. 1434.

God permitted the discovery of his designs; . . . and as he had sent an agent to Rome, with orders to put the pontiff and principal citizens to death, the Romans, who had been made acquainted with this meditated cruelty, determined to kill the envoy of Eutychius; and they would have done so, were it not for the prohibition of the pontiff. They also anathematized the exarch Eutychius, and bound themselves, one and all, by solemn oath, never to allow a pontiff so zealous for the faith either to be insulted or to be separated from them, and to die, if necessary, in his defence. The exarch, on his side, sent deputies to the king, and to the Lombard lords, to induce them, by the promise of rich presents, to withdraw their protection from the pontiff. But the Lombards, detesting the perfidy of the exarch, entered into close alliance with the Romans, and pledged themselves to die with glory in defence of the pope, to allow no one to give him any cause of annoyance, and, in fine, to support the Christian religion and the true faith, by every means in their power. In the mean time the pope redoubled his prayers, his alms, and his fasts, calculating much more on the protection of God than on that of men; and to testify to the people his gratitude for their generous dispositions, he pathetically exhorted them to persevere in faith and good works; but he warned them, at the same time, not to forget the attachment and allegiance they owed to the emperor. He thus soothed the hearts of all, and consoled them in their continual sorrows.[1] About the same time, the Lombards having taken possession of Sutri, a city in Tuscany, the pope obliged their king to restore this city; and this prince presented it to the holy apostles Peter and Paul. . . . Very soon after, the patrician Eutychius and King Luitprand formed a criminal alliance, engaging to combine their forces, that the king might reduce the kings of Spoletto and Beneventum to his sceptre, whilst the exarch made himself master of Rome, and executed the project which he had long since formed against the pope's personal liberty. The king accord-

[1] "Gratias voluntati populi referens pro mentis proposito, blando omnes sermone, ut bonis in Deum proficerent actibus, et in fide persisterent, rogabat; sed ne desisterent ab amore vel fide Romani Imperii admonebat. Sic cunctorum corda molliebat, et dolores continuos mitigabat." — Anastas. ubi supra, pp. 1434, 1435.

ingly came to Spoletto, where he received the oath of fidelity from the two dukes, with hostages as security. As he was approaching Rome, the pope went forth to meet him, and moved him so powerfully by his exhortations, that he threw himself at the pope's feet, and promised to do injury to no man. So deeply affected was he by the exhortations of the pope, that he stripped himself of his arms, and deposited before the body of St. Peter his mantle, his bracelets, his belt and gilded sword, with a crown of gold and a silver cross. Having then made his prayer, he besought the pope to admit the exarch also to peace; which was granted. The exarch having accordingly entered Rome, an adventurer named Tiberius, and surnamed Petasus, came to Mantura, in Tuscany, where he endeavoured to get himself recognised emperor, and even compelled the inhabitants of many cities to take an oath of allegiance to him. At this news the exarch was very much alarmed; but the pope encouraged him, and sent with him against the rebels a body of troops, accompanied by some of his principal clergy. Having arrived at Mantura, they put Petasus to death, and sent his head to Constantinople. Still the emperor's anger against the Romans was not appeased; he continued to give other proofs of his evil intentions towards the popes, so far as to induce all the inhabitants of Constantinople, either by seduction or by violence, to take down in all places the images of our Saviour, of his holy mother, and of all the saints, and to burn them in the middle of the city. It was on this occasion that Germanus, patriarch of Constantinople, was banished from his see, and replaced by the priest Anastasius, a partisan of the emperor."

21. *Remarkable Inferences from the Narrative of these Authors.*

These historical extracts from Paulus Diaconus and Anastasius we have thought it our duty to cite at length, not only because these two authors are the most esteemed of all those who have given a narrative of those facts, but still more because they supply in detail all the circumstances and the true causes of the revolution which happened in the West under Gregory II. From their testimony, it follows, in the first place, that the rising of Italy against the emperor at that time was provoked by the imprudence and the excesses of the emperor Leo and of his officers, who not only abandoned Italy as a prey to the fury of the Lombards, but deprived it of its best defence by declaring open war against the pope and against all the Catholics of that province. Secondly, that Pope Gregory II., far from favouring this rising of Italy against the emperor, and of profiting by it to establish his own sovereignty in that province, opposed the revolt with all his might, and used all his influence to preserve for the emperor and for his officers some portion of their authority. Thirdly, that notwithstanding all his efforts to maintain the emperor's authority in Italy, he was himself invested with a power almost kingly by the confidence of the people, who justly regarded him as their principal refuge against the fury of the Lombards, and the continual oppressions of the emperor and his officers.

22. *Greek Historians give a different Account of those Events.*

Having now given the history of this great revolution according to the most correct and trustworthy historians, we must not conceal that a very different account of these events is given by the Greek historians. If we believe Theophanes, an author of the eighth century, who is followed by more modern writers of the same nation, the emperor Leo having, in the ninth year of his reign (A.D. 726), issued an edict against the worship of images, Pope Gregory was not content with addressing very strong remonstrances to him on the subject, but *ordered the inhabitants of Rome and of Italy not to pay taxes to him.* The following are this author's words: "(The ninth year of the Emperor Leo.) This impious prince made his first attempt against the holy images, which he resolved to proscribe and to abolish. Pope Gregory having heard of it, forbade Rome and Italy to pay him any taxes, having previously addressed to him a dogmatic letter, announcing to him that it does not belong to the prince to make rules of faith, and to reform the ancient belief of the Church founded on the teaching of the holy fathers."[1] Four years later, according to the

[1] Theophanes's Chronographia, ann. Leonis Isauri 9, Parisiis, 1655, fol. p. 338. Our translation of this passage is somewhat different from P. Mamachi's (Origines et Antiq. Eccles. tom. iv. p. 208, n. 1). In our opinion, he either did not understand, or, at least, he has not correctly given, the sense of the passage. Our translation agrees perfectly with that of Baronius (Annales, ann. 726), and of Bossuet (Defens. Declarat. lib. ii. cap. xii.). See also Cedrenus, Chronic. art. on Leo the Isaurian; Zonoras, Annales, ibid. (apud Hist. Byzantin. et apud Baronium, ibid. n. 24, 26).

same author, the emperor obstinately persisting in his heresy, "the pope detached from his empire and from his obedience, both in the civil and in the ecclesiastical order, the city of Rome, Italy, and all the West."[1]

23. *Importance of discussing the Credit due to the Greek Authors on this Subject.*

This narrative of the Greek authors is cited with equal confidence by the defenders of two opposite opinions, one of which is as much opposed to the Holy See as the other is favourable, even to its most dubious and contested privileges. On the one hand, a class of modern authors adduce this narrative in support of the charge which they make against Gregory II. and his successors, of having dexterously turned events to their own aggrandizement in Italy at the expense of the emperors of Constantinople.[2] On the other hand, many theologians, especially not French, think they find in the same narrative a proof of the opinion which attributes to the Church and to the pope a "jurisdiction at least indirect over the temporality of princes;" and, as a natural consequence of that principle, they have praised Gregory II. for having renounced allegiance to an heretical prince, and for having caused a revolution in the state for the good of religion.[3] But before anything can be inferred from the narrative of Theophanes and of the Greek historians, we must first see what credit is due to them, and compare them with the Latins, who present the same facts in so very different a view.

24. *Paulus Diaconus and Anastasius agree in their Narrative.*

We have already seen that Paulus Diaconus, who wrote shortly before Theophanes, very far from attributing to Gregory II. the Italian rising against the emperor, on the contrary attributes it to the Italian troops themselves, who were so incensed against that emperor, "that they would have elected

[1] Theophanes's Chron. ibid. p. 342. Baronii Annal. ann. 730, n. 3.

[2] In the next chapter, art. ii. we shall discuss this accusation, which has been so often made against the popes of the eighth century by Protestant writers, and too easily adopted by some Catholics.

[3] See, among others, Bellarmin, De Rom. Pontif. lib. v. cap. viii.; Bianchi, Della Potestà della Chiesa, lib. ii. § 16; Mamachi, Origin. et Antiquit. Christ. tom. iv. p. 208; Rohrbacher, Des Rapports Naturels entre les deux Puissances, ch. xix.

another, had they not been restrained by the pope."[1] Anastasius, who wrote about the middle of the ninth century, confirms evidently this account; for he describes Gregory II. as opposing with all his might the revolt in Italy. "All Italy," he states, "having ascertained the impiety of Leo, resolved to elect another emperor, and to march with him to Constantinople; but the pope, who was hoping the conversion of Leo, prevented the execution of that design;" and though he neglected no means of confirming the attachment of the Italians to the Catholic faith, "he admonished them at the same time not to forget the attachment and fidelity which they owed to the emperor."[2] This author, it is true, appears at first sight to confirm the alleged fact of the refusal of taxes, by stating, a little higher up, "that the exarch Paul endeavoured, by the emperor's orders, to put the pope to death, because he was preventing the levying of taxes in the provinces."[3] But on an attentive examination of Anastasius's narrative, it will be seen, that he is stating in that passage not what St. Gregory did, but what he was charged by the emperor and the exarch with doing, as an excuse for their crime. So far from believing that pretext well founded, Anastasius states, in the end of that very passage, that Gregory II. opposed with all his might the revolt of Italy, and "neglected no means of retaining the people in that fidelity and attachment which they owed to the emperor." He adds, "that the pope, having heard the impious orders given by the emperor, for throwing down and destroying the images, prepared to resist him as an enemy;[4] but he soon explains the nature of that resistance by stating, that "the pope not only rejected the emperor's heresy, but wrote to the faithful in every quarter to caution them against the impious error;" from which it is manifest that the pope's resistance was confined to exhortations and to advice addressed to the faithful in every quarter, to put them on their guard against the impiety of Leo.[5]

[1] Paul. Diacon. De Gestis Longob. lib. vi. cap. xlix.

[2] Anastas. Bibliothec. Vita Gregorii II. (Labbe, Concil. tom. v. pp. 1434, 1435, supra n. 20).

[3] Anastas. Bibliothec. ibid. (supra, n. 20).

[4] See the text of Anastasius, ibid.

[5] It may not be useless to state here that Thomassin (ubi supra, ch. xxvii. n. 5) cites Anastasius as favouring the narrative of Theophanes; but the learned Oratorian, by a strange error, mistook for the text of Anastasius a passage of

25. *Impossibility of reconciling the Greek with the Latin Accounts.*

To reconcile the narrative of the Greek with that of the Latin writers, some modern authors have supposed that the refusal of taxes and the revolt of Italy mentioned by the former were subsequent by some years to the revolt mentioned by the latter; that Gregory II., in the hope of bringing the emperor round to sounder opinions, prevented at first the projected revolt of the people, but sanctioned it afterwards, to punish that prince for his obstinacy.[1] It is manifest, however, that these suppositions have no foundation in the Latin authorities, and that they are diametrically opposed to the Greek. The former, as we have seen, plainly state that the pope, far from favouring the revolt of Italy, used all means to suppress it. The latter do not record two different revolts, of which the first was suppressed, and the second sanctioned by the pope; on the contrary, they suppose that the pope, on learning the first measures of the emperor against holy images, "immediately prohibited the paying of taxes in Rome and Italy:" this is manifestly the meaning of Theophanes in the passage which we have cited.

26. *Contradiction between these Authors easily accounted for.*

We may add, that however surprising this contradiction between the Greek historians and the Latin may at first sight appear, it may be accounted for easily by the different circumstances in which both were placed.[2] The Greeks, seeing on the one hand the revolt of Italy occasioned by the imprudent conduct of Leo, and on the other the great influence of the popes in the public affairs of Italy, would be inclined naturally to attribute that revolt to him; and this impression would also be more and more

---

which he was only the translator. It is taken from the ecclesiastical history of Anastasius, which is merely a translation of the chronicle of Theophanes and of some others. (See on this subject, Bossuet, Defens. Declar. lib. ii. cap. xvii.; D. Ceillier, Hist. des Auteurs Sacrés et Eccl. vol. xix. p. 417; Cave, Script. Eccl. Hist. Litter. sæc. octavi.) Thomassin himself corrects his mistake by citing a little further on Anastasius's own text.—Thomassin, ibid. ch. xxvii. n. 8; ch. xxix. n. 2.

[1] This is the opinion of Baronius (Annal. ann. 730, n. 4, 5) and of Mamachi (ubi supra, p. 210, &c.). Cardinal Orsi, in his Dissert. already cited, admits that this supposition of Baronius has no foundation in the ancient Latin historians, and that on this point the Greeks are entitled to no credit (ch. i. pp. 5, 6. Edit. 8vo. 1688).

[2] Orsi, ubi supra, cap. i. p. 15, &c.

confirmed in course of time by the ever increasing hatred of the Greeks for the Latins, especially after Italy had contracted an alliance with the French.[1] The Latin historians, on the contrary, besides having a far better opportunity of knowing and verifying facts of so grave a nature and of so recent a date in that very country in which they were writing, had no interest either in disguising or misrepresenting them at a time when Italy had nothing either to fear or to hope from the emperor of Constantinople.

27. *The Narrative of the Greek Authors entitled to very little Credit.*

But whatever may be thought of the preceding observations, in the impossibility of reconciling the narratives by the historians of the two different nations, we, in common with the majority of critics, believe that the Greek narrative is of very little authority when weighed against the Latin, whether we consider both narratives in themselves, or judge of them according to the otherwise well-known character and principles of Gregory II.[2]

In the first place, considering the testimony of Theophanes in itself, we find that it cannot have very great importance. His frequent anachronisms, his want of accuracy and sound critical knowledge, are generally admitted by the learned.[3] These defects are specially observable in that part of his history which regards the affairs of the West; the difficulty of knowing and stating correctly facts occurring in a country so distant from that in which he was writing, obliged him frequently to depend on popular and groundless rumours. It is, moreover, natural to suppose that, notwithstanding his honesty, this author must have been sometimes influenced, unconsciously, by the prejudices which the Greeks had already conceived against the Latins, and which

---

[1] On the origin and progress of this alienation of the Greeks from the Latins, see Lebeau, Hist. du Bas-Empire, vol. xiv. book lxvi. n. 50, &c.; Thomassin, Anc. et Nouv. Dis. vol. i. book i. ch. x. &c.; De Héricourt's abridgment of the same work, part i. ch. iii. n. 2.

[2] Besides the authors already cited (n. 19, n. 1), see Launoy, Epist. lib. vii. epist. vii. (Oper. tom. x.); Natal. Alex. Hist. Eccl. sæc. 8, Dissert. 1. The author of the Annals of the Middle Ages, vol. vi. book xx. p. 169, appears at first to incline to the Greek account of these facts, but he corrects himself a little further on, book xxiii. p. 390.

[3] Cave, Scriptor. Eccl. Hist. Litter. sæc. 8. D. Ceillier, Hist. des Auteurs Eccl. vol. xviii. p. 261. Bossuet, Defens. Declarat. lib. ii. cap. xii. See also notes by P. Combefis on the work of Theophanes.

manifested themselves so signally not long after his death in the schism of Photius. These considerations, which render the testimony of Theophanes very suspicious in itself, apply with far greater force to the Greek historians Cedrenus and Zonaras, who have copied him on the affairs of Gregory II. These authors, who wrote in the twelfth century, and consequently more than 400 years after those events, were still more liable than Theophanes to be led astray by the prejudices of their nation against the Roman Church.

28. *It is contrary to the Principles and Character of Gregory II.*

What makes the testimony of those authors more suspicious, is its manifest opposition to the well-known character and principles of Gregory II. The Lombards had availed themselves of the troubles occasioned in Italy by the imprudence of the emperor to seize the exarchate of Ravenna, under the pretence of delivering it from an heretical prince. The pope wrote in the following terms to the doge of Venice: "Make the city of Ravenna be restored to the empire, and placed again under the sceptre of our lords the emperors Leo and Constantine, that by our fulfilling the duties of our holy faith, we may, with the divine assistance, remain inviolably attached to the state and to the emperors."[1] Candidly, now, is this the language of a pope disposed to shake off the yoke of the emperor, and to excite his subjects to revolt?

Two other letters of the same pope to the emperor Leo breathe the same submission and the same zeal for the defence of the empire.[2] These two letters are the more remarkable, as they

---

[1] "Quia, peccato faciente, Ravennatum civitas, quæ caput extat omnium, à nec dicendâ gente Longobardorum capta est, et filius noster eximius dominus exarchus apud Venetias (ut cognovimus) moratur; debeat nobilitas tua ei [*exarcho* scilicet] adhærere, et cum eo nostrâ vice pariter decertare, ut ad pristinum statum sanctæ reipublicæ, in imperiali servitio dominorum filiorum nostrorum Leonis et Constantini, magnorum imperatorum, ipsa revocetur Ravennatum civitas; ut *zelo et amore sanctæ fidei nostræ in statu reipublicæ et imperiali servitio firmi persistere, Domino cooperante, valeamus.*"—Gregorii II. Epistola ad Ursum, Venetiarum ducem (Baronii Annales, tom. ix. anno 726, n. 27; Labbe, Concil. tom. vi. p. 1447). Lebeau, Hist. du Bas-Empire, vol. xiii. book lxiii. n. 44.

[2] Baronius, Annal. ibid. n. 28. Labbe, Concil. tom. vii. p. 10. We suppose with Baronius, Bossuet, and the majority of modern critics, that these two letters were written by Gregory II., not Gregory III. The contrary opinion, which was held by some authors (Fleury, vol. ix. book xlii. n. 8, 9;

were addressed to the emperor at a time when he was violently persecuting the Church, and when the pope could resist him with the greatest facility, had he wished to use against an enemy of the Church any other arms than those of persuasion. The pope himself urged this point with great force in his first letter to the emperor: "You think you can terrify us by saying, 'I will send to Rome and break the image of St. Peter, and I will order Pope Gregory to be carried off in chains, as Constant did to Pope Martin.'[1] But know that the popes are the mediators of peace between the East and the West. We fear not your threats; at one league's distance from Rome, in the direction of Campania, we are secure. If you wish to try, you have only to come; you will find the Westerns well disposed to avenge the injuries which you have inflicted on the Easterns. The West offers to give to the see of Peter an effective proof of its faith. If you send any one to break the image of St. Peter, I warn you there may be blood shed. For me, I am innocent; and all the crime must fall on you."[2] This discourse was not for ostentation's sake from the pen of Gregory, for we have already seen[3]—and the course of history demonstrates more and more — what the attachment of

Annales du Moyen Age, vol. vi. book xxiii. p. 414), appears to be conclusively refuted by many critics, cited and analyzed on this point in Orsi's work (ubi supra, cap. i. n. 30, 31). Moreover, it is manifest that these two letters are not necessary to establish our opinion on Gregory's conduct. Whether they be his or his successor's, they must in any case be regarded as a signal testimony of the pacific temper of the Holy See to the emperor of Constantinople, at a time when the pope had the most just grounds of complaint against him.

[1] He alludes here to Pope Martin II. being carried off, in 653, by order of the emperor Constans II., who wished to compel that pontiff to subscribe the type or edict published by that prince in favour of Monothelism. See Fleury, Hist. Eccl. vol. viii. book xxxix. n. 1, 2.

[2] "At enim nos perterrefacis, aisque: 'Romam mittam, et imaginem sancti Petri confringam; sed et Gregorium illinc pontificem vinctum adduci curabo, sicut Martinum Constans adduxit.' Scire autem debes ac pro certo habere, pontifices qui, pro tempore, Romæ extiterint, conciliandæ pacis causâ sedere tanquam parietem medium Orientis et Occidentis, ac pacis arbitros et moderatores esse. . . . Quòd si nobis insolenter insultes, et minas intentes, non est nobis necesse tecum in certamen descendere; ad quatuor et viginti stadia secedet in regionem Campaniæ Romanus pontifex. . . . Quòd si hoc velis experiri, planè parati sunt Occidentales ulcisci etiam Orientales, quos injuriis affecisti. . . . Totus Occidens sancto principi apostolorum fidei fructus offert. Quòd si quospiam ad evertendam imaginem miseris sancti Petri, vide, protestamur tibi, innocentes sumus à sanguine quem fusuri sunt; verùm in cervices tuas et in caput tuum ista recident."—Gregorii Epist. i. versus finem (Labbe, ubi supra, pp. 19, 22).

[3] See supra, part i. n. 18.

the people of Italy was at that period to the Holy See, and how little disposed they were to bear with the violence of the emperor or of his envoys to the pope. But however favourable the opportunity was to Gregory II., had he wished to resist the emperor forcibly, he was content with using only exhortations and remonstrances. The greater part of his letters is taken up in proving by solid reasoning the worship of sacred images; and, far from thinking of diminishing in any manner the imperial power, he repeats and loudly professes the principles of antiquity on the distinction and mutual independence of the two powers. "You know, sire," he says, "that the decision of the dogmas of faith does not belong to the emperors, but to the bishops, who wish, consequently, to have liberty to teach them. For this reason the *bishops, being set over the government of the Church, do not meddle in political affairs; let not the emperors, then, meddle in ecclesiastical affairs; let them restrict themselves to their own.* Know, then, sire, the difference between the palaces of princes and the churches, between the empire and the priesthood: learn it for your salvation, and give not yourself up obstinately to controversy. *As the bishop has no right to extend his inspection to the palace, and to dispose of royal dignities, neither ought the emperor to extend his to the churches,* nor interfere in the elections of the clergy, nor consecrate nor administer sacraments, nor even receive them without the ministry of a priest. All of us ought to remain in that state to which God has called us."[1] The conduct of Gregory II. was always in conformity with these principles, and until the close of his life he laboured strenuously to sustain the authority of the emperor in Italy. The history of the revolt of Petasus, which we have given above from Anastasius, gives a

---

[1] "Scis, imperator, sanctæ Ecclesiæ dogmata non imperatorum esse, sed pontificum, qui tutò volunt dogmatizare. Idcircò *ecclesiis præpositi sunt pontifices, à reipublicæ negotiis abstinentes; et imperatores ergo similiter ab ecclesiasticis abstineant, et quæ sibi commissa sunt capessant.* . . . Ecce tibi palatii et ecclesiarum scribo discrimen, imperatorum et pontificum: agnosce illud, et salvare, nec contentiosus esto. . . . Quemadmodum pontifex introspiciendi in palatium potestatem non habet, ac dignitates regias deferendi; sic neque imperator in ecclesias introspiciendi, et electiones in clero peragendi, neque consecrandi, vel symbola sanctorum sacramentorum administrandi, sed neque participandi, absque operâ sacerdotis; sed unusquisque nostrûm, in quâ vocatione vocatus est à Deo, in eâ maneat."—Gregorii Epistolæ 1 et 2 (Labbe, ibid. pp. 18, 26).

convincing proof of this disposition.[1] That usurper having gained over many of the Italian cities to his party, and caused himself to be proclaimed emperor, the terror-stricken exarch found himself unable to take the field. Gregory encouraged him, and even sent a body of troops, which in a few days vanquished the rebels, Petasus himself being compelled to shut himself in a strong town, where he lost his imperial title with his life.

29. *The Conduct of this Pope approved by modern Authors who are beyond all suspicion of Partiality.*

From these facts, we must conclude that the conduct of Gregory II., in the difficult circumstances in which he was placed, was a perfect model not only of prudence and firmness in defending the faith, but also of the respect and submission which the Church has always professed in the temporal order even for the most wicked princes. Hence the conduct of this pope has been generally commended even by authors least inclined to flatter the Holy See, and who loudly condemn the conduct of his successors towards the emperors of Constantinople. "In one of the most critical conjunctures that ever existed,"[2] says one of these authors, "when on the one side heresy, armed with the imperial power, endeavoured to introduce itself into Italy, and, on the other hand, Italy seemed to have no chance of repelling heresy but by revolting against her sovereign, Pope Gregory II. discharged two duties equally well which then appeared incompatible. An intrepid head of the Church, he constantly opposed the execution of an edict contrary to the practice of Christianity; he used every effort to divert the emperor from his impious design; he confirmed the people in their determination of rejecting the orders which they could not obey without betraying their religion; but, at the same time, a faithful subject to his prince, he persisted himself, and kept the people, in due loyalty; he stifled the spirit of revolt; and, notwithstanding the dark plots which that prince hatched against his life, he, like a truly apostolical prelate, superior to every sentiment of vengeance as

[1] See the text of Anastasius, cited supra, part i. n. 21; Baronii Annales, anno 729; Lebeau, Hist. du Bas-Empire, vol. xiii. book lxiii. n. 48.

[2] Lebeau, Hist. du Bas-Empire, vol. xiii. book lxiii. n. 54. See, in confirmation of these views, Annales du Moyen Age, vol. vi. book xxiii. p. 391, 413, &c.; Daunou, Essai Hist. sur la Puissance temp. des Papes, ch. i. p. 23.

well as of fear, was generous enough to preserve for the emperor Italy, which he was on the point of losing."

30. *His Moderation imitated by Gregory III.*

If we believe some modern authors, the successors of Gregory II. did not imitate his respectful conduct to the emperors of Constantinople; and his immediate successor Gregory III. made no difficulty in openly renouncing the submission due to his legitimate sovereign.[1] But an attentive examination of the course of events, and of the difficulty of the circumstances, must convince us that the new pontiff conducted himself with the wisdom and moderation of his predecessor.[2] One of the first acts of his pontificate was to write to the emperors Leo and Constantine Copronymus, *exhorting them by wise remonstrances to adopt better opinions on the worship of holy images.*[3] A council held at Rome, not long after, by the same pope, decided that those who condemn that worship should be cut off from the communion of the Catholic Church. But there does not appear any act on the part of the pope contrary to the authority of the emperors in Italy: Anastasius even supposes clearly enough, that this province had not yet definitively renounced their sceptre; for he states, *that Italy addressed to them at the same time a petition for the restoration of the holy images;* which she would not do, if the authority of the emperors had been absolutely and permanently rejected.

---

[1] Lebeau, Histoire du Bas-Empire, vol. xiii. book lxiii. n. 63, p. 385. Annales du Moyen Age, vol. vi. book xxiii. p. 439. Velly, Hist. de France, vol. i. p. 336, &c. Daunou, Essai Historique, ch. i. p. 27. Vertot, Origine de la Grandeur de la Cour de Rome, pp. 18, 22, &c.

[2] Thomassin, Ancien. et Nouv. Discipline, vol. iii. book i. ch. xxix. n. 3. Bossuet, Defensio Declar. lib. ii. cap. xviii. xxxvii. Fleury, Hist. Eccl. vol. ix. book xlii. n. 8, 17, 24, &c. Daniel, Histoire de France, ann. 740. Annales du Moyen Age, vol. vi. book xxiii. p. 414, &c. Lebeau, Histoire du Bas-Empire, vol. xiii. book lxiii. n. 58, &c.

[3] "Idem sanctissimus vir [*ad Leonem et Constantinum*], ut ab hoc resipiscerent ac se removerent errore, commonitoria scripta, quemadmodum et sanctæ memoriæ decessor ipsius direxerat, misit per Georgium presbyterum.... Majore [*dein*] fidei ardore permotus, synodale decretum . . . decrevit, ut *si quis deinceps . . . adversus eamdem venerationem sacrarum imaginum . . . profanator vel blasphemus extiterit, sit extorris à corpore et sanguine Domini nostri Jesu Christi, vel totius Ecclesiæ unitate atque compage. . . . Post peractum igitur hoc synodale constitutum, . . . cuncta generalitas istius provinciæ Italiæ similiter, pro erigendis imaginibus, supplicationum scripta unanimiter ad eosdem principes direxerunt.*" — Anastasii Bibliotheca, Vita Gregorii III. (Labbe, Concil. tom. vi. pp. 1463, 1464).

31. *Leo the Isaurian by his excesses provokes Italy still more.*

In the mean time the emperor Leo, far from yielding to those pressing solicitations, redoubled his fury against the Catholics. He sent at first a considerable fleet to Italy, destined to plunder Rome, and many other cities, in punishment for their attachment to the worship of the sacred images. The commandant of the fleet had orders to seize the pope, and bring him bound hand and foot to Constantinople. The execution of the cruel project was prevented solely by the loss of the fleet, which was dispersed near Ravenna by a furious tempest. Irritated by this disaster, the emperor indulged in additional excesses against Italy, and especially against the pope; he loaded the people with new taxes, and ordered the seizure of the patrimonies of the Roman Church in Sicily and Calabria.[1] Conduct so outrageous confirmed the aversion of the people for the emperor, and gave, so to speak, the first blow to the imperial power in the West.

32. *Gregory III. calls Charles Martel to the aid of Italy.*

In fact, in this wretched position of affairs, the city of Rome was closely besieged by the Lombards, and reduced to extremity by King Luitprand. The Romans, having no hope of succour from the emperor, who, so far from defending Rome and Italy, openly declared war against them, saw no resource but in imploring the aid of the French. For that purpose Pope Gregory III. wrote many urgent letters to Charles Martel, who, under the title of Mayor of the Palace, governed France at that time in the name of King Thierry IV.[2] These first solicitations

---

[1] Theophanes, Chronographia, p. 343. We have seen above, that the annual revenue from these patrimonies was about 3½ talents of gold, that is, about £16,000.

[2] The two letters of Gregory III. to Charles Martel on this subject, may be seen in the collection of Councils of Père Labbe, tom. vi. p. 1472. These two letters are the first of the collection known as the Caroline Code, because it appears to have been originally compiled under Charlemagne. It contains twenty-nine letters, addressed principally to the kings of France and to the French, by Pope Gregory III. and his successors, from 739 to 791. It was published for the first time at Ingolstadt, in 1613, in 4to, by Gretzer. It is also given in vol. iii. of the Recueil des Historiens de France by Duchesne (Paris, 1641 and 1644, fol.). But the best edition is that found in tom. i. of Cenni's Monumenta Dominationis Pontificiæ; Romæ, 1760, 2 vols. 4to. The prefaces and notes to that edition throw great light on the history of the popes of the eighth century, and on the true origin of the temporal sovereignty of the Holy See. Henceforward this is the edition of the Caroline Code which we

not having produced any effect, the pope sent a solemn embassy to the mayor, in 741, to urge his petition more effectually.[1] The ambassadors brought with them magnificent presents for Charles Martel; but they were especially charged to offer him, in the name of the pope, and of the Roman lords and people, the dignity of consul,[2] provided that he assured them of his protection. In consequence of a decree adopted by the lords of Rome, the pope says in his letter to the French prince, "that the Roman people, renouncing the dominion of the emperor, besought Charles to come to their defence, and had recourse to his invincible protection."[3]

---

shall cite. On the two letters of Gregory III. to Charles Martel, see vol. i. of that collection, p. 1, &c.; Daniel, Hist. de France, vol. ii. anno 740; Hist. de l'Eglise Gall. vol. iv. anno 741; Annales du Moyen Age, vol. vi. book xxiii. p. 431, &c.

[1] Our ancient annalists do not omit observing, "that they had never before seen or heard of such an embassy" (see especially Annales de Metz, and the continuator of the Chronicon of Fredegarius). We cite the passages of these annals at length in the next page, note 2. Bossuet cites them in Defens. Declarat. lib. ii. cap. xviii. Anastasius (Bibliotheca), in his life of St. Stephen, appears to state the contrary; for he assures us that this pontiff "wrote secretly to Pepin, after the example of his predecessors, Gregory II., Gregory III., and Zachary, who had applied to Charles Martel for aid against the Lombards." (Labbe, Concil. tom. vi. p. 1622.) Anastasius may, however, be reconciled with the French authors, by supposing that Gregory II. only wrote to Charles Martel, and that Gregory III. sent him a solemn embassy. In fine, it is manifest that this discussion does not affect, in any important degree, the matter which we are now treating; for the same arguments which would justify the conduct of Gregory III. on this point, would apply with equal force to the defence of Gregory II.

[2] The title of consul, which in ancient times invested the person enjoying it with so much authority among the Romans, became under the emperors a mere title of honour, as those of duke, count, marquis, and many others, have become in later times among ourselves. It was suppressed by Justinian, who from the year 541 ceased to nominate consuls, as he had hitherto done according to the example of his predecessors. After that time, however, the emperors sometimes assumed this title, and gave it as an honorary distinction to some persons. We have numerous examples in the history of the eighth century. (Anastas. Bibliothec. Vitæ Gregorii III., Zachariæ, et Hadriani I. apud Labbe, Concil. tom. vi. pp. 1463, 1487, 1726, 1744.) Hence we may learn the nature and object of the *consulate* offered by the pope and by the Roman lords to Charles Martel. They by no means intended to recognise him as their sovereign, but simply to attach him to their interests by an honourable title, and to engage him to assist them the more effectually against the tyranny of the Lombards.

We deem it unnecessary to examine more in detail the opinions of the learned on this point. The reader may consult Ducange, Glossarium Infimæ Latinitatis, art. Consul; Pagi, Critica in Annales Baronii, tom. iii. anno 740, n. 6; Cenni, ubi supra, p. 4; Lebeau, Hist. du Bas-Empire, vol. x. book xlvi. n. 41; Daniel, Hist. de France, ed. Griffet, vol. i. p. 65, vol. ii. p. 219.

[3] "Eo tempore bis à Româ, sede sancti Petri apostoli, beatus papa Gre-

33. *This Measure easily justified by Circumstances.*

This conduct of the pope and of the Roman lords was certainly a bold measure; but it can be easily justified by the maxims of constitutional law, universally admitted.[1] A people abandoned by its former government, and unjustly oppressed by its neighbours, has unquestionably a right to elect a head who will be able to defend them; the natural law which, in a similar case, justifies a private individual in calling on the aid of his fellow-man, applies equally to a whole nation. "All admit," says Puffendorf, "that the subjects of a monarch, when they find themselves on the brink of ruin, without any help to be expected from their master, can place themselves under another prince."[2] "No part of the state," says Grotius, "has the right of detaching itself from the body, unless by not doing so it be exposed to manifest destruction; for all human institutions appear to suppose a tacit exception for the case of extreme necessity, which reduces all things to the law of nature."[3] In support of this assertion, Grotius cites a passage from St. Augustine, which is equally express. "Among all nations," observes that holy father, "submission to the yoke of a conqueror has been preferred to extermination by resisting to the last: it is the voice of nature."[4]

---

gorius claves venerandi sepulcri, cum vinculis sancti Petri, et muneribus magnis et infinitis, legatione, *quod antea nullis auditis aut visis temporibus fuit*, memorato principi [*Carolo*] destinavit, eo pacto patrato, ut ad partes [hoc est, consueto hujus ævi stylo, *à partibus*] imperatoris recederet, et *Romanum consulatum præfato principi Carolo sanciret*."—Fredegarii Chronicon continuatum, n. 110 (ad calcem Hist. Francorum S. Greg. Turon. ed. Ruinart; vol. i. of Duchesne's collection).

The Annals of Metz narrate, nearly in similar terms, the embassy from the pope to Charles Martel; to which they add as follows: "Epistolam quoque, decreto Romanorum principum, sibi [i. e. *Carolo principi*] prædictus præsul Gregorius miserat, *quòd sese populus Romanus, relictâ imperatoris dominatione, ad suam defensionem et invictam clementiam convertere voluisset*."—Annal. Metenses, anno 741 (vol. iii. of Duchesne's collection, p. 271).

[1] De Marca, De Concordiâ, lib. iii. cap. 11, n. 5, 6. Thomassin, Ancien. et Nouv. Discipline, vol. iii. book i. ch. xxvii. n. 8; ch. xxix. n. 1, &c. Bossuet, Politique Sacrée, book vi. art. 2, prop. 5. Pey, Autorité des Deux Puissances, vol. i. p. 210. Fleury, Hist. Eccl. vol. x. book xlv. n. 21. Orsi, ubi supra, cap. vi.

[2] Puffendorf, De Jure Nat. et Gent. lib. vii. cap. vii. § 4.

[3] Grotius, De Jure Belli et Pacis, lib. ii. cap. vi. § 5.

[4] "In omnibus ferè gentibus, quodam modo vox naturæ ista personuit, ut subjugari victoribus mallent, quibus contigit vinci, quàm bellicâ omnifariàm vastatione deleri."—St. Augustine, De Civitate Dei, lib. xviii. cap. ii. n. 1 (Oper. tom. vii.).

Even those authors who are most opposed to ultramontane principles, apply without hesitation these principles of natural equity to the circumstances in which Italy was placed after the pontificate of Gregory II. They do not, it is true, agree among themselves, either on the precise time at which the power of the emperors of Constantinople became extinct at Rome, and in the exarchate, nor on the nature of the power which the pope and the king of France exercised there subsequently; but they admit, or manifestly suppose, that these provinces, abandoned as they were by the emperors, after the pontificate of Gregory II., had a right to withdraw themselves from their allegiance, and to take another sovereign. "In the fall of the empire," observes Bossuet, "when the Cæsars could hardly defend the East, to which they were confined, Rome, abandoned for more than two hundred years to the fury of the Lombards, and compelled to implore the assistance of the French, was under the necessity of separating from the emperors. She endured much before she adopted this extreme measure; nor was it carried into execution until the capital of the empire was regarded by her emperors as a place given up to pillage, and left defenceless against its enemies."[1]

34. *Good understanding between the Pope and the Emperor during the Pontificate of Zachary.*

Charles Martel received with pleasure the proposal of Gregory III. He was even preparing to march to Italy, when he was suddenly surprised by death, a little after the departure of the ambassadors. The death of the emperor Leo III. and of the pope, which happened in the same year (741), induced the Romans to suspend their negotiations with the French, and the moderate conduct of Pope Zachary, successor to Gregory III., seemed for a while to restore the fortunes of the empire in Italy.[2]

The new pope had no sooner ascended the chair of Peter than he used all his influence to tranquillize Italy; to obtain the restitution of the cities and territories of the exarchate, which

---

[1] Bossuet, Politique Sacrée, ubi supra, p. 274. See also the authors cited n. 3, p. 213, supra.

[2] Baronius, Annales, tom. ix. anno 743, n. 12, 29, 30. Bossuet, Defensio Declarat. lib. ii. cap. xix. Fleury, Hist. Eccl. vol. ix. book xlii. n. 31, 38, 40. Annales du Moyen Age, vol. vi. book xxiii. p. 439. Lebeau, Hist. du Bas-Empire, vol. xiii. book lxiv. n. 2.

the Lombards had seized; to support against them the authority of the exarch, and consequently of the emperor, whose representative the exarch was. Success crowned the exertions of this pope; touched by his prayers and remonstrances, the king of the Lombards restored to him at first four cities of the duchy of Rome, and soon after many other cities and territories of the exarchate.[1] It must be remarked, however, that the pope, when soliciting the restoration of these places from the king of the Lombards, did not claim them in the name of the emperor, but in his own name, as chief of the Roman republic; that is, of the cities and provinces of Italy, which had freely elected him as their chief.[2] The king of the Lombards himself, yielding to the pope's remonstrances, made this restitution, not to the emperors, but to the Holy See and the Roman republic;[3] which clearly supposes that, in the opinion of all Italy, the whole power and authority of government in the duchy of Rome, and in the exarchate, was then in the hands of the pope.

But whatever was the case, it is certain that the emperor Constantine Copronymus, successor of Leo, appeared, though an adherent of heresy, perfectly satisfied with the conduct of the

---

[1] Anastas. Bibliothec. Vita Zachariæ (Labbe, Concil. tom. vi. pp. 1487, 1489). See the details which we have given above (part i. n. 12, note) on the geographical position of the exarchate, and of the duchy of Rome.

[2] The words "Roman republic," so frequently used by Anastasius, and other writers of this time, to designate the cities and provinces of Italy, which then acknowledged the pope as their head, do not imply that these cities and provinces then constituted a republic in the strict sense of the term, but generally a state, kingdom, or empire, according to the constitution of the government to which it was applied. (Muratori, Antiquit. Ital. Medii Ævi, tom. i. Dissert. 18, p. 987, &c.) The letter of Gregory II. to the doge of Venice, which we have cited above, gives a remarkable example of this fact (supra, p. 207, n. 1). It is in the general acceptation that it is used by Anastasius and by the authors of this period when they speak of the Roman republic; we find, in fact, from the whole tenor of history, that they speak of the inhabitants of that republic as being subjects of the pope; which supposes clearly that he was their sovereign. This observation shall be still better illustrated by the details which we shall give on the progress of the pope's power after the pontificate of Zachary.

[3] The following are the words of Anastasius on the restoration of the four cities of the duchy of Rome: "[Zachariæ] piis eloquiis flexus [Longobardorum rex], . . . prædictas quatuor civitates *eidem sancto viro*, cum eorum habitatoribus, *redonavit*; . . . . [quas] per donationis titulum, ipsi beato Petro apostolorum principi *reconcessit*." The same author employs similar expressions in speaking of the restitution of the cities and territories of the exarchate. "Ab eodem rege nimis honorificè susceptus [Zacharias], salutaribus monitis eum allocutus est, obsecrans . . . . ut ablatas Ravennatum urbes *sibi redonaret*. Qui prædictus rex, post multam duritiam inclinatus est, ... et duas partes territorii Cesenæ Castri *ad partem reipublicæ restituit*, &c."—Labbe, Concil. ibid.

pope, and gave him unequivocal proofs of that satisfaction by adding to the patrimonies of the Roman Church two considerable estates, situate in a part of Italy still subject to the empire.[1] This last fact is the more remarkable, as it shows clearly the pacific disposition of the emperor towards the pope, notwithstanding the great authority which the latter then exercised in Italy, like his predecessors Gregory II. and Gregory III.[2]

35. *Pope Stephen II. implores the Protection of Pepin against the Lombards.*

The good understanding between the pope and the emperor did not, however, save the authority of the latter from becoming every day weaker in Italy, by the natural consequences of the circumstances which we have explained, and especially of the troubles incessantly excited by the Lombards.[3] In the very year of Zachary's death, that is 752, they seized the province of Italy, Pentapolis, and the exarchate. The exarch Eutychius, being incapable of making any resistance, fled to Naples; and thus ended the exarchate, which had lasted during 184 years. After such success, Astolphus, king of the Lombards, seeing nothing but the city of Rome capable of checking the progress of his conquests, concentrated all his forces against it. Stephen II., successor of Pope Zachary, having no hope of succour from the emperor against these new attacks, first endeavoured to negotiate with Astolphus, the Lombard king. Far from blaming this conduct, the emperor sent deputies to the pope, imploring

---

[1] "Post hæc, requirens [*Constantinus princeps*] missum apostolicæ sedis, qui ibidem [*Constantinopolim*] in tempore perturbationis contigerat advenisse, eumque repertum ad sedem absolvit [i. e. *dimisit*] apostolicam; et juxta quod beatissimus pontifex postulaverat, donationem in scriptis de duabus massis [i. e. *fundis seu prædiis*], quæ Nymphas et Normias appellantur, juris existentes publici, eidem sanctissimo ac beatissimo Papæ sanctæ Romanæ Ecclesiæ, jure perpetuo, direxit possidendas."—Anastasius, ubi supra, p. 1491.

[2] In another place we shall examine the charges made against Pope Zachary for his answer to the consultation of the French on the deposition of Childeric III. See infra, ch. ii. art. ii. n. 92, &c.

[3] Anastas. Bibliothec. Vita Stephani II. (Labbe, Concil. tom. vi. p. 1620, &c.). Thomassin, Ancienne et Nouvelle Discipline, vol. iii. book i. ch. xxix. n. 6, &c. Fleury, Hist. Ecclés. vol. ix. book xliii. n. 4, 9, &c. Lebeau, Hist. du Bas-Empire, vol. xiii. book lxiv. n. 18, &c. 30, &c. Daniel, Hist. de France, vol. ii. ann. 752, &c. Annales du Moyen Age, vol. vii. book xxiv. Bossuet, Defensio Declar. lib. ii. cap. xix. Cenni, Monumenta Dominationis Pontificiæ, tom. i. pp. 11, 57, &c. Orsi, Della Origine del Dominio, et della Sovranità de Rom. Pontefici, cap. vi. Natal. Alex. Dissert. 25, in Hist. Eccles. sæc. 4, prop. 5.

him to take the interests of the empire under his protection, and to summon the king of the Lombards to restore the Italian provinces which he had usurped. At first these negotiations promised to be successful; but they soon were broken off by the perfidy of Astolphus, who, after signing a treaty of peace, returned almost immediately to the siege of Rome. In this extremity the pope, having solicited in vain succour from the emperor, saw no other resource for himself and his people than to implore the assistance of the king of France, after the example of his predecessors, Gregory II., Gregory III., and Zachary.[1] He wrote to him for that purpose, in 753, a very urgent letter, in which he asked both an asylum in the French kingdom, and protection against the Lombards. Pepin favourably received the pope's petition, promised him his protection, and invited him to take in France the asylum which he requested.

36. *Favourable Dispositions of Pepin—His first Expedition into Italy.*

Notwithstanding these invitations and these promises, Stephen II., before he went to France, determined to call on the Lombard court, and to make a last effort to obtain the restitution of Ravenna, of the exarchate, and of the other places usurped by the Lombards against the Roman republic.[2] Astolphus persisting firmly in his refusal, the pope retired to France, where he was received by Pepin with the greatest marks of honour and of respect. In a general assembly of the lords of the kingdom held

---

1 "Tunc præfatus sanctissimus vir, agnito maligni regis [Aistulphi] consilio, misit in regiam urbem [Constantinopolim] suos missos, . . . deprecans imperialem clementiam, ut, juxta quod ei sæpiùs scripserat, cum exercitu ad tuendas has Italiæ partes, modis omnibus adveniret, et de iniquitatis filii morsibus Romanam hanc urbem, vel cunctam Italiæ provinciam liberaret . . . *Cernens præterea et ab imperiali potentiâ nullum esse subveniendi auxilium;* tunc, quemadmodum prædecessores ejus beatæ memoriæ, Gregorius, et Gregorius alius, et Dominus Zacharias, beatissimi Pontifices, Carolo excellentissimæ memoriæ regi Francorum direxerunt, petentes sibi subveniri propter oppressiones ac invasiones quas et ipsi, in hâc Romanorum provinciâ, à nefandâ Longobardorum gente perpessi sunt; ita modò et ipse venerabilis pater [Stephanus], divinâ gratiâ inspirante, clam per quemdam peregrinum suas misit litteras Pippino regi Francorum, nimio dolore huic provinciæ adhærenti conscriptas."—Anastasius, ibid. pp. 1621, 1622.

2 "Conjungente verò eo [Stephano] Papiam civitatem, et præfato nefando regi [Aistulpho] præsentato, plura illi tribuit munera, et nimis eum obsecratus est atque lacrymis profusis eum petivit, *ut Dominicas quas abstulerat redderet oves, et propria propriis restitueret.*"—Anastasius, Vita Stephani II. p. 1623.

at Quierzy-sur-Oise, that prince solemnly promised to effect the restoration to the Holy See of the exarchate of Ravenna and of the other cities and territories usurped by the Lombards.[1] He drew up, moreover, an act of donation, or grant, signed by himself and by the princes his sons, binding themselves to place the Holy See in possession of the same cities and territories.[2] The pope, on his part, in order to encourage and reward this generosity, gave to him and to his two sons, Charles and Carloman, the title of Patricians of the Romans,[3] a title by which he invariably

---

[1] Anastasius, Vit. Steph. II. p. 1624.

[2] Anastasius, in his Life of Pope Stephen (ubi supra), mentions only the *promise* made by Pepin and the French lords, in the assembly at Quierzy, to restore those cities and territories to the Holy See; but he does not speak of the *donation* or grant of the said territories, which was signed in the same assembly by the king and by the princes his sons. This latter fact is given by Anastasius in his Life of Pope Adrian I. (ibid. p. 1738), when speaking of Pepin's deed of donation being read for Charlemagne, in 772, and the confirmation of that deed at the same time by another. Pope Stephen II. himself clearly supposes Pepin's donation in a letter written to that prince, in 754, after the assembly of Quierzy, shortly after Pepin's first expedition to Italy.—Cod. Carol. Epist. 7, alias 9; apud Cenni, Monumenta, tom. i. p. 81.

[3] It appears, from the Annals of Metz (ann. 754), that the pope conferred this title on the French princes during his sojourn in France; but he certainly does not give it to them in any of his letters before his return to Italy (see Pagi, Critica in Annales Baronii, ann. 755, n. 3; Cenni, ubi supra, pp. 12 and 60).

The dignity of patrician, which was created by Constantine in order to lessen and lower that of the prætorian prefect, was one of the most eminent in the empire of Constantinople. Of itself it had no special functions; but it was often combined with other dignities, such as the consulate, the prefecture of the prætorium, &c., and it gave the right of a seat in the council of the empire above that of the prefect of the prætorium.—Lebeau, Hist. du Bas-Empire, vol. i. book v. n. 11. Godefroy, Comment. sur le Code Théodosien, book vi. tit. vi. Naudet, Changements opérés dans la Constitution de l'Empire, vol. ii. p. 76, &c.

There were two sorts of patricians: one, purely honorary, enjoyed the honours and prerogatives of patrician without possessing any special authority annexed to that title. Thus Adalgisus, son of Didier, king of the Lombards, and Vitigez, king of the Goths, had in the court of Constantinople the rank and quality of patricians. (Hist. du Bas-Empire, vol. x. book xlv. n. 48. Annales du Moyen Age, vol. viii. book xxvii. p. 39.) Clovis, in the same manner, received, in 507, the title and insignia of this dignity, which was conferred on him by the emperor Anastasius, as a testimony of alliance and mutual friendship. (Hist. de l'Eglise Gallicane, vol. ii. ann. 508. Hist. du Bas-Empire, vol. viii. book xxxix. n. 12. Daniel, Hist. de France, vol. i. ann. 507; vol. ii. p. 219. Pagi, Critica, ann. 508.) Another sort of patrician had the right of defending or governing some province in the name of the emperor, who retained its sovereignty, properly so called; such were the patricians of Sicily, of Africa, of Rome, &c. The title of patrician of the Romans was always annexed to the exarchate of Ravenna, until that exarchate was destroyed in 752, a circumstance which led many writers, ancient and modern, to regard the titles of patrician and exarch as synonymous. (Anastasii Bibliothec. Vita Adriani,

addressed them afterwards in his letters, and which remained in the family until that of emperor was substituted for it by Charlemagne. In consequence of the promises made by Stephen II., and in compliance with the entreaties of that pontiff, Pepin immediately sent ambassadors to Astolphus, demanding the "restitution of the cities and territories taken by him or by his predecessors from the Roman Church and republic." [1] On the refusal of Astolphus, Pepin marched into Italy, in 754, at the head of a numerous army, annihilated the Lombards, and pursued Astolphus himself to Pavia, which he closely invested for several days. The Lombard prince, in fine, seeing no resource, offered to come to terms, and promised on oath to restore without delay to the Church and to the Roman republic the city of Ravenna and many others.[2] It was thus that Pepin established, or rather recognised and confirmed, the temporal sovereignty which long before, by virtue of the free choice of the people, the pope had enjoyed over the provinces abandoned by their former legitimate sovereigns. It must be remarked here, according to the narrative of Anastasius himself, from whom these facts are taken, that Pepin never pretended to make a grant or donation in the strict sense to the Church and to the Roman republic, but to restore to them what had been unjustly seized by the Lombards. The words

---

apud Labbe, Concil. tom. vi. p. 1736.) It is in this latter sense that Pepin and his sons received from the emperor the title of patricians of the Romans, which substituted the king of France for the exarch as defender of Italy. This is the idea which all the ancient authors give us of the patrician office of Pepin and Charlemagne. It is only in later times that some authors began to assume that the sovereignty of Rome and of the exarchate was attached to that title. In the following chapter, we shall see how groundless that opinion is, and how opposed to history. The reader may consult on the subject Ducange, Glossarium Infimæ Latinit. verbo Patricius; Alemanni, De Lateranensibus Parietinis, cap. xi.; De Marca, De Concordiâ, lib. i. cap. xii.; lib. iii. cap. xi.; Pagi, Critica in Annales Baronii, ann. 740, n. 6, &c.; Daniel, Hist. de France, ed. Griffet, vol. iii. p. 254, &c.; De Maistre, Du Pape, book ii. ch. vi. p. 257.

[1] "Porrò Christianissimus Pippinus, Francorum rex, ut verè beati Petri fidelis [i. e. *defensor*], atque jam tanti sanctissimi pontificis salutiferis obtemperans monitis, direxit suos missos Aistulpho, nequissimo Longobardorum regi, propter pacis fœdera, et *præfatæ sanctæ Dei Ecclesiæ ac reipublicæ restituenda jura;* atque bis et tertiò eum deprecatus est, et plura ei pollicitus est munera, ut tantummodò pacificè *propria restitueret propriis.*"—Anastasius, Vita S. Stephani, p. 1623.

[2] "Spopondit ipse Aistulphus cum universis suis judicibus [i. e. *magnatibus*], sub terribili et fortissimo sacramento, atque in eodem pacti fœdere per scriptam paginam affirmavit, *se illicò redditurum civitatem Ravennatium, cum aliis diversis civitatibus.*"—Anastasius, ubi supra, p. 1626.

"donation" and "restitution" are used indifferently both by Anastasius and by the ancient French authors who have treated of this subject, as we shall afterwards see.

37. *Rome again besieged by the Lombards—Urgent Letters of Pope Stephen II. to Pepin.*

Hardly had the king of France retired from Italy, when the king of the Lombards, instead of fulfilling his engagements, recommenced hostilities against the Romans, seized many of their fortified places, and ravaged all the environs of Rome, without sparing even the churches.[1] In this new extremity the pope wrote many urgent letters to Pepin, conjuring him to avert the ruin impending over religion and the people of Italy. To excite the imagination of the French more vividly, and to move their feelings more powerfully in his favour, he uses in one of those letters a rhetorical expedient, which the novelty of the circumstances might very naturally suggest to a pope so zealous for the good of religion, and for the relief of the people intrusted to his charge. It was in the name of St. Peter that he addressed the French king and his barons, putting into the mouth of the prince of the apostles the most moving supplications to obtain the succour so much needed in this great exigency of the Church and of the Roman people. We shall give here a literal version of the exordium, and of the most striking passages in this letter, which has been most malignantly interpreted by some modern authors: "Peter, called to the apostleship by Jesus Christ, son of the living God, and in me, the whole modern Catholic and apostolic Church, to you most excellent princes, Pepin, Charles, and Charlemagne, kings; as also to the bishops, abbots, dukes, and counts, to the French armies and people. I, Peter, apostle of God, to whom He hath deigned to intrust the charge of his flock, and the keys of the kingdom of heaven; I look upon you Frenchmen as my adopted children, and, relying on the love which you bear to me, I exhort and conjure you to deliver my city of Rome, my people, and that church in which I repose according to the flesh, from the cruelties which the Lombards are inflicting there.

---

[1] Anastasius, ibid. Codex Carolinus, Epist. 7—10 (Cenni, tom. i. p. 78, &c. Labbe, Concil. tom. vi. p. 1632, &c.). Daniel, Hist. de France, vol. ii. ann. 754. Hist. de l'Eglise Gallicane, vol. iv. ann. 754.

That cruel nation is oppressing cruelly the Church which has been intrusted to me. My dear children, do not doubt that I appear before you in person, conjuring you in these very urgent terms, because, according to the promise of our Redeemer, it is to you, O French nation, that we look especially among all the nations of the earth. The ever virgin Mother of God addresses to you the same request. She, with all the choir of angels, and all the holy martyrs and confessors, entreats and commands you to have compassion on the miseries of Rome. Protect it against the Lombards, lest those persecutors should profane my body, which was immolated in tortures for Jesus Christ; lest they desecrate the church in which it reposes. Hasten immediately to the relief of my people, that I, Peter, called by God to the apostleship, may in turn protect you in the day of judgment, and prepare for you places in heaven. It is well known that among all the nations under the heavens the French nation has manifested the greatest attachment to me, Peter the apostle; therefore have I, through my vicar, pointed out you as the deliverers of that Church which the Lord has confided to me. It was I that assisted you in your hour of need, when you had recourse to me; I that gave you victory over your enemies, and that shall give it again, if you fly to the assistance of my city."[1]

38. *The Language of the Pope in those Letters unjustly criticised by some modern Authors.*

A little reflection on the wretched extremities to which the pope and the Romans were reduced at this time by the tyranny of the Lombards, accounts naturally enough for the vivacity of the style of this letter, and for that bold figure by which the pope puts into the mouth of the prince of the apostles those urgent entreaties which he addresses to the French, in order to obtain their succour. "This practice of introducing the dead as speaking was familiar to the ancient orators," observes a famous historian;[2] and never perhaps had it been adopted on a more

[1] Cod. Carol. Epist. 10 (alias 3). Cenni, ubi supra, p. 98. Labbe, ubi supra, p. 1639.

[2] Gibbon, Decline and Fall, &c. vol. ix. ch. xlix. p. 306. After such an admission, it is not a little surprising to read in the same passage that the pope used that noble figure "with the bad taste of his age." It is not easy to see

important occasion; since the question at issue was nothing less than the deliverance of the head of the Church from ferocious enemies thirsting for his ruin.

Is it possible that judicious authors could have looked on that letter as a device or fiction unbecoming the gravity of the dignitary who had used it? If we believe Fleury, and other authors who have copied him, this letter which we have cited "is full of equivocal allusions, and by an artifice unparalleled in the whole history of the Church, motives of religion are there made subservient to affairs of state,"[1] as if the deliverance of the head of the Church, who was then persecuted by Astolphus, and of the Roman Church, then cruelly harassed by the Lombards, was merely a state affair, and not one of the most vital interest for religion. "The defence of Rome," observes an author not open to the suspicion of partiality, "was regarded as a religious war, because the Lombards were all either Arians or pagans."[2] This, too, we may add, is not the only occasion on which Fleury, and so many other writers, misled by his example, from not understanding properly the position of the popes of the middle ages, that is, their double character as spiritual pastors and heads of the Roman republic, which had intrusted them with its temporal interests, have attributed to a purely human policy measures which were imperatively necessary for the common good of religion and of the state.[3]

---

where the bad taste can be in using an oratorical form, which the author himself admits was familiar to the ancient orators. There is, in truth, nothing more common with orators, both modern and ancient, than that form of figurative language which personifies inanimate things, and the dead themselves, to impart more vigour and vivacity to language. Scripture abounds with examples of this kind. See especially Isa. xiv. 10; Jer. xxxi. 15; Ezek. xxxii. 21; Matth. ii. 18.

[1] Fleury, Hist. Eccl. vol. ix. book xliii. n. 17. These reflections of Fleury have been repeated by many modern authors, influenced, no doubt, by his example. See in particular Muratori, Annali d' Italia, ann. 755; Lebeau, Hist. du Bas-Empire, vol. viii. book lxiv. n. 28; Annales du Moyen Age, vol. vii. book xxiv. p. 58.; Michaud, Hist. des Croisades, vol. iv. p. 462; De Héricourt, Lois Ecclésiastiques de France, part iv. p. 185.; Daunou, Essai Hist. sur la Puissance Temporelle des Papes, vol. i. p. 33; vol. ii. p. 68, &c.; Gaillard, Hist. de Charlemagne, vol. i. p. 209.; Sismondi, Hist. des Français, vol. ii. part ii. ch. i. p. 194. On this point, as well as on many others, Receveur (Hist. de l'Eglise) may serve as a corrective to Fleury and the authors who have copied him. See especially vol. iv. p. 89, &c.

[2] Sismondi, Hist. des Républ. Ital. vol. i. ch. iii. p. 122.

[3] Fleury, ibid. book xliii. n. 15, 17, 31; book xliv. n. 17, et alibi passim. Annales du Moyen Age, ibid. p. 58, 72, &c. M. Ferrand, one of the most

39. *Second Expedition of Pepin to Italy—Donation made to the Holy See by Astolphus and Pepin.*

Moved by the entreaties of the pope, Pepin once more flew to his aid in 755. At the first rumour of his march, Astolphus raised the siege of Rome, which had then lasted three months. On his arrival in Italy, the king of France pushed on the siege of Pavia so vigorously, that he compelled Astolphus once more to sue for peace. Pepin granted it, but on conditions more severe than in the preceding year, and, to punish Astolphus for his treachery, he required the cession of the city and territory of Comachio, in addition to those cities and territories which Astolphus had engaged in the former year to restore to the Holy See. To insure the execution of this treaty, Pepin left in Italy Fulrade, abbot of St. Denis, who visited personally all the cities ceded to the Roman Church, and received their keys, which he afterwards deposited on the "confession" of St. Peter, with the act or deed of donation, by which the king of Lombardy himself made them over for ever to the Holy See. The possession of those cities and territories was thus guaranteed by two distinct deeds of donation; one drawn up by Pepin in the assembly at Quierzy in 754; and the other by Astolphus himself, on the demand of Pepin, in 755.[1]

---

severe among modern writers, in his censures on the popes of the middle ages, frequently cites Fleury in corroboration of his opinions, and pronounces his Ecclesiastical History as the best pilot to guide one through the rocks, to be encountered by the student in the history of the middle ages, with regard to the temporal and spiritual powers of the pope. Ferrand, Exposit. de l'Hist. vol. ii. letter xlii. p. 429.

[1] "De quibus omnibus receptis civitatibus, *donationem in scriptis*, à beato Petro et à sanctâ Romanâ Ecclesiâ, vel omnibus in perpetuum pontificibus apostolicæ sedis, [*Aistulphus*] emisit possidendam, *quæ usque hactenus in archivo sanctæ Ecclesiæ recondita tenetur*. . . . Prænominatus autem Fulradus, venerabilis abbas, ipsas claves tam Ravennatium urbis, quàm diversarum civitatum ipsius Ravennatium exarchatûs, *unà cum supra scriptâ donatione de eis à suo rege emissâ*, in confessione beati Petri ponens, eidem apostolo et ejus vicario sanctissimo Papæ, atque omnibus ejus successoribus pontificibus, perenniter possidendas atque disponendas tradidit."—Anastas. Vita Stephani II. (Labbe, Concil. vol. vi. pp. 1627, 1628).

Fleury, P. Daniel, P. Longueval, and the majority of modern historians, suppose that this deed of donation, which was placed by Fulrade on the confession of St. Peter, is the identical instrument drawn up by Pepin. This, however, appears to be a mistake: the text of Anastasius, which we have cited, states very clearly that the act of which we speak was drawn up and signed by Astolphus, who sent it to Rome, to be deposited on the confession of St. Peter. The text of Anastasius therefore supposes that the possession of those cities and territories of which there is question, was then secured to the

All the cities mentioned in this last donation, which are also mentioned by Anastasius, were in number twenty-two ; they included the greater part of the exarchate of Ravenna, with a part of Pentapolis and of the ancient Picenum. The greater number of them were situate on the shores of the Adriatic, or not far from those coasts, within a space of about forty leagues, from north-west to south-east. Thus the whole territory comprised in the donation was bounded on the north and west by the Po and the Tanaro ; on the south by the Apennines ; and on the east by the Adriatic Sea. This donation comprised also the city of Narno, in Umbria, which was a dependency of the duchy of Rome, and which the Lombards of Spoleto had seized.[1]

Holy See by two deeds of donation completely distinct ; one of them, drawn up by Pepin in the assembly held at Quierzy, in 754, as we have already seen (p. 219), and the other by Astolphus, in 755, on the demand of Pepin. It cannot be doubted, we may add, that Pepin, who reduced Astolphus to the necessity of making the deed of donation, had also dictated, or at least determined its provisions in detail. Viewed in that light, the donation of Astolphus may be considered identical with that of Pepin ; for it was in reality only a renewal and authentic confirmation of the former.

Some modern authors have fallen into a far more grievous error, by raising doubts on the authenticity of the donation of Pepin, because, they say, its provisions are not mentioned by any contemporary author, nor is the deed itself known to us earlier than from the pages of Anastasius the Librarian, whose work was not published until a century later. (Voltaire, Annales de l'Empire ; Essai sur les Mœurs, et alibi passim. Daunou, Essai Hist. vol. i. p. 34, &c.) The authors who proposed this difficulty did not know, we must presume, that the donation of Pepin, such as it is given by Anastasius, is found in MSS. more ancient than his time, in the opinion, at least, of many eminent critics, who inspected them personally, and cite portions of them. (Justus Fontanini Defens. 1ma Dominii temp. S. Sedis in Comachium, Italicè scripta, Romæ, 1709, 4to. pp. 242, 346. Bianchini, Proleg. ad Anastas. de Vitis Pontificum, tom. ii. p. 55.) But supposing even that Anastasius was the most ancient author that mentions those donations, on what probable grounds can his testimony be rejected, on a fact of such a nature, and for which he confidently refers to the documents then preserved in the archives of the Roman Church ? (Besides the passage of Anastasius, which we have cited in the commencement of this note, see also another, to which we have referred, supra, from the Life of Adrian, p. 219, note 2.) It is, moreover, certain that this fact is clearly supposed and confirmed by many subsequent deeds, and especially by a great number of letters of Stephen II. and of his successors, to Pepin and to Charlemagne. (Cod. Carol. Epist. 7, 8, 9, 15, 40, 42, 97 (alias 4, 6, 9, 19, 26, 36, 85). Cenni, Monumenta Domin. Pontific. tom. i. pp. 81, 85, 91, 144, 228, 239, 521, &c.) Accordingly, we have the authenticity of this donation of Pepin generally admitted, even by authors least favourable to the Holy See. See especially Gibbon, Decline and Fall, &c. vol. ix. ch. xlix. ; Hegewisch, Hist. de Charlemagne, p. 128 ; Guizot, Hist. de la Civilis. en France, 27e leçon, p. 316.

[1] On these geographical details, see supra, note, n. 12, part i. ; also Lecointe, Annales Eccles. vol. v. anno 755, § 17, &c. ; Annales du Moyen Age, vol. vii. p. 67, &c. ; D. Lieble, Mémoire sur les Limites de l'Empire de Charlemagne, Paris, 1764, 12mo. p. 42, &c.

40. *These two Princes never pretended that they were making a Donation, strictly so called, but a Restitution to the Holy See.*

But what must be especially noticed in the donation of Pepin, as well as in that of Astolphus, which was its consequence and its authentic confirmation, is, that those two monarchs, when guaranteeing to the Holy See the possession of all these cities and territories, never pretend that they are making a donation strictly so called, but rather "a restoration of the provinces usurped by the Lombards from the Church and republic of Rome." This was the title on which the pope and the king of France constantly claimed those provinces, and on which the king of the Lombards himself "restored them to the Holy See," as appears manifestly from the uniform testimony of ancient authors both French and foreign.[1] It was, in truth, very natural to regard as the property of the Roman Church and republic provinces long abandoned by their former masters, and which, in the extremity to which they were reduced, had of their own free-will placed themselves under the protection of the Holy See.[2]

---

[1] See the different passages from Anastasius which we have cited above, notes to n. 35, 37, 39.

The words of Eginhard agree perfectly with those of Anastasius on this point. "Pippinus," he says, "invitante Romano Pontifice, *propter erepta Romanæ Ecclesiæ per regem Longobardorum dominia, Italiam manu validâ ingreditur.*" And a little further on: "Haistolphus Longobardorum rex, quanquam anno superiore obsides dedisset, *et ad reddendum ea quæ Romanæ Ecclesiæ abstulerat,* tàm se quàm optimates suos jurejurando obstrinxisset, etc." Finally, he adds that Pepin, having made Astolphus surrender to him the cities of Ravenna and Pentapolis, and the entire Exarchate, delivered them himself to St. Peter: "*Redditamque* sibi *Ravennam,* et Pentapolim, et omnem Exarchatum ad Ravennam pertinentem, ad sanctum Petrum tradidit."—Eginhard, Annales, anno 755 et 756 (vol. ii. of Duchesne's collection, p. 235, &c.).

All these passages are cited in support of our opinion by P. Thomassin, ubi supra, ch. xxix. n. 6, &c.; Orsi, Del Dominio, &c. cap. vi. towards the end; De Maistre, Du Pape, book ii. ch. vi. p. 254.

[2] Some modern writers, either from not having perceived or perfectly understood the sense in which Pepin's donation could be considered a restitution made to the Roman Church, have suggested various explanations of the word "restitution," used by ancient writers on this subject.

P. Longueval suspects that those authors allude to the pretended donation by Constantine, which they believed was authentic. (Hist. de l'Eglise Gallicane, vol. iv. ann. 754, p. 376.) This conjecture supposes that Constantine's donation, such as we have it at present in the collection of councils, was in existence in the time of Pepin,—a supposition unfounded, improbable, and generally abandoned by the learned, as we have proved elsewhere. (See No. 1 of the Documentary Evidence at the end of this volume.)

Nat. Alexander, Cenni, and some others, convinced that this act did not appear before the ninth century, and consequently after the donations of Pepin and of Charlemagne to the Holy See, are at a great loss to explain the pro-

41. *Unavailing Protests of the Emperors against this Deed of Donation.*

The emperor of Constantinople, no doubt, did not omit putting forward his rights to the provinces usurped by the Lombards. He even sent ambassadors to Pepin, in 755, urging the restoration to the empire of the exarchate of Ravenna, and of all the cities and territories dependent on it.[1] But Pepin spurned the proposal, and protested that he would never tolerate the wresting of that province from the Roman Church. He added, even with an oath, that he had not been impelled by any human consideration to make his expedition to Italy, but solely by his love for St. Peter, and for the remission of his sins. This language of Pepin was as truly in accordance with the principles of equity, as it was with the sentiments of genuine piety. Would it, in truth, have been proper for this prince to march an army into Italy for the interests of an emperor who was evidently unable to defend his former possessions there, and who for so long a period had proved himself rather the declared enemy than the master of those provinces? Was it proper to restore to such a master a conquest so important? To make that conquest beneficial, should it not be ceded to him whom both the interests and the wishes of the conquered people evidently called to govern

---

priety of this word "restitution," applied by the ancient writers to this act. It may be explained, they think, by saying, first, that it is not applied to all the cities and provinces given to the Holy See by Pepin and Charlemagne, but only to the patrimonies of the Holy See, which the Lombards had seized; secondly, that the ancient authors might consider as a restitution made to the Holy See all those cities and provinces which had been given to it by our (French) kings, *after* the first donation of them made by Pepin in the assembly of Quierzy in 754, before his first expedition to Italy.—Nat. Alexander, Dissert. xxv. in Hist. Sæculi iv. art. i. prop. 6, obj. 3. Cenni, Monumenta Dominationis Pontific. tom. i. p. 76, note 5.

But these explanations cannot be reconciled with the language of the ancient authors; for, in the first place, it is certain that they apply the word "restitution" not only to the patrimonies of the Holy See which the Lombards had seized, but in general to all the cities and territories granted to the Holy See by our kings; secondly, it is equally certain, that before the assembly of Quierzy, held in 754, and consequently before they had given anything to the Holy See, that Anastasius represents the city of Ravenna, and many others which the Lombards had seized, as belonging to the Roman Church and republic; and on that title, he maintains, were they restored to them. In support of these positions the reader may see the testimony of Anastasius, cited above, pp. 216, 218, 220.

[1] Anastasius, Vita Stephani II. p. 1627. Fleury, Hist. Eccl. vol. ix. book xliii. n. 18. Annales du Moyen Age, vol. vii. book xxiv. p. 64. Cenni, Monumenta Dominat. Pontific. tom. i. p. 64. De Maistre, Du Pape, book ii. ch. vi. p. 255.

them ; to him who had acquired already, in a certain way, those provinces by the free choice of the people when abandoned by their legitimate sovereign, and by the generous protection which he had so frequently given to them in the greatest emergencies?

42. *From that period the Pope looked on himself as Sovereign of Rome and of the Exarchate.*

Such a combination of circumstances justified Pope Stephen II. and his successors more and more in considering themselves true sovereigns of Rome and of the exarchate. Accordingly, from that period the popes acted as sovereigns of those provinces, and believed themselves finally exempt from all allegiance to the emperors of Constantinople.[1] In many of his letters addressed to Pepin, from the year 754, Pope Stephen II. invariably claims his protection in the name of the Roman people and republic, whom he calls "his people and subjects," without any allusion to the emperor.[2] In another letter, he speaks of an alliance which he was after contracting with Didier, king of the Lombards; of the *restitutions* which that prince had promised to make not to the emperor but to St. Peter, to the Church, and the republic of Rome; in fine, of the peace which he has promised to keep with 'the pope's people or subjects."[3] Paul I., successor of Stephen II., supposes, still more clearly, in several of his letters to Pepin, the independent temporal sovereignty of the Holy See in the duchy of Rome and in the exarchate.[4] Not only does he speak of the many cities in those provinces as belonging to him, as subject to his dominion,[5] but he complains loudly of a design planned by

---

[1] Alamanni, De Lateranensibus Parietinis, cap. ii. Orsi, Della Origine del Dominio, &c. cap. viii. Cenni, Monumenta Dominat. Pontific. tom. i. pp. 12, 67, 68, et alibi passim. Pagi, Critica in Annales Baronii, anno 755, n. 6; anno 796, n. 11, &c. Nat. Alexander, Dissert. xxv. in Hist. Eccl. Sæculi iv. art. i. prop. 5, 6. Thomassin, Ancien. et Nouv. Discipline, vol. ii. book i. ch. xxvii. n. 8; ch. xxix. n. 1, &c.

[2] See Pope Stephen's Letters, cited supra, n. 37.

[3] "Longobardorum rex Desiderius, vir mitissimus, in præsentiâ ipsius Fulradi, sub juramento pollicitus est *restituendum B. Petro civitates reliquas,* Faventiam, Imolam et Ferrariam cum eorum finibus. . . . Et postmodum, per Garinodum ducem et Grimoaldum, *nobis reddendum spopondit civitatem* Bononiam cum finibus ejus, *et in pacis quiete cum eâdem Dei Ecclesiâ et nostro populo semper mansurum professus est.*"—Cod. Carol. Epist. 11 (alias 8) (Cenni, Monumenta, tom. i. pp. 109, 110. Labbe, Concil. tom. vi. p. 1642).

[4] Cenni, Monumenta Dom. Pontif. tom. i. pp. 12, 67, 68, 122, 131, &c.

[5] *Nostras civitates. . . . Nostram Seno-Galliam* (in Pentapoli). . . . *Nostrum*

the emperor, in concert with Didier, king of the Lombards, to recover the duchy of Rome and the exarchate; he conjures Pepin to oppose with all his might the execution of that project; and in this whole affair he never speaks of the emperor as his sovereign, but as the declared enemy of the Church and republic of Rome. "We have heard," he says to the king of France, "that the Greeks, those sworn enemies of the Church of God, those cruel persecutors of the orthodox faith, are plotting an expedition against us and against the exarchate of Ravenna. We, therefore, placing all our hopes in your protection after God and St. Peter, have recourse to you, our most excellent son; for the love of God and of St. Peter, save that province which you have delivered by your arms. We hope this the more confidently, because your excellency is convinced that the Greeks persecute us through hatred of the orthodox faith and of the traditions of the fathers, which they seek to destroy."[1]

Castrum Valentis (in Campaniâ).—Cod. Carol. Epist. 38, 39, 40 (alias 14, 24, 26) (Cenni, ibid. p. 218, &c.).

[1] Cod. Carol. Epist. 25 (alias 34). See also Epist. 18 (alias 15); Cenni, Monumenta Domin. Pontif. pp. 153, 175; Labbe, Concil. vol. vi. pp. 1676, 1684; Hist. de l'Eglise Gallicane, vol. iv. p. 421.

Fleury, in his Eccl. Hist. (vol. ix. book xliii. n. 31), censures severely the conduct and language of Pope Paul I. towards the emperor of Constantinople. This pope, he pretends, as well as his predecessor Stephen II., was always confounding the temporal and the spiritual, manifesting a greater repugnance to the Lombardian sway than the ancient popes ever had shown to the Heruli and the Arian Goths. . . . Nothing can be more groundless than such accusations. We have already observed, and the fact is notorious, that the deliverance of the head of the Church, and of his people, from the oppression of the Lombards, was not a merely temporal concern, but one of the deepest interest to religion (supra, n. 38). With regard to the pope's submitting to the Lombards, we are at a loss to know on what title they could claim it; for they had never obtained possession of Rome, and their conquests in Italy, especially in the duchy of Rome, and in the exarchate, were in reality acts of violence and of usurpation. Fleury should have been the last to reproach the popes of the eighth century with not submitting to the Lombards, for he considers that even at that period, the emperor of Constantinople was the true sovereign of Rome (Fleury, ubi supra). We may add, that on this last point Fleury is flatly contradicted by the very authorities which he quotes. To prove that the senate and people of Rome still continued to regard the emperor of Constantinople as the true sovereign of Rome, he produces two arguments; first, that the letters of Pope Paul I., as well as of the others, are dated according to the year of the reign of the emperors of Constantinople; second, that the Roman senate and people, writing to Pepin, never style him their lord, but their spiritual pastor and father. Now these two arguments, which of themselves are anything but conclusive, happen to be grounded on suppositions absolutely false; for, in the first place, most of the letters of Pope Paul I. are not dated by the reign of the emperor of Constantinople: only two in the "Collection of Councils" (vol. vi. p. 1689) are so dated; and even in one of

43. *This Opinion shared by the Roman Senate and People, and by the King of France.*

The senate and people of Rome, and the king of France himself, manifestly had the same persuasion as the pope regarding his temporal sovereignty in those provinces. From a letter of the Roman senate and people written to Pepin in the commencement of the pontificate of Paul I., we learn that the king of France, in his capacity as defender of the Church, had written to them, admonishing them "to persevere in the fidelity which they owed to St. Peter, to the holy Church, and to the sovereign pontiff Paul, their lord." They add, that corresponding with this prudent admonition, "they shall ever remain faithful to the holy Church and to Paul their lord, the sovereign pontiff and universal pope; because they revere him as their father and their excellent pastor, who never ceases to labour zealously for their salvation, like Pope Stephen, his brother, of pious memory, protecting and governing them as a human fold intrusted to their care by the Lord."[1] This language of the senate and people of Rome supposes clearly that in their minds the emperor of Constantinople was no longer sovereign of Rome and of the exarchate, and that all his rights in that respect had passed into the hands of the pope.

44. *Conduct of Pope Adrian I. in consequence of this Persuasion.*

The letters of Pope Adrian I. supply a great number of similar testimonies.[2] He always speaks of the city and duchy of Rome, of the cities and territories of the exarchate, as places subject to his dominion. He calls the inhabitants of those provinces his

---

those two it is given with the reign of Pepin also. (See a collection of the Letters of Pope Paul I. in Labbe's Concilia, and in Cenni's Monumenta Dom. Pontific. tom i.) Secondly, the Roman senate and people, in their letter to Pepin, which we shall cite in another place, style Pepin not only their spiritual pastor and their father, but also their lord. (Cod. Carol. Epist. 15 (alias 36), apud Cenni, ibid. p. 143.) In the next chapter we shall discuss more minutely the question of the sovereignty of Rome at this period.

[1] "Præcellentia vestra," say the senate and the people, speaking to Pepin, "nos admonere studuit, firmos nos ac fideles debere permanere erga B. Petrum, principem apostolorum, et sanctam Dei Ecclesiam, et circa beatissimum et spiritalem patrem vestrum, à Deo decretum *Dominum nostrum Paulum,* summum Pontificem et universalem Papam. . . . Nos quidem, præcellentissime regum, firmi ac fideles servi sanctæ Dei Ecclesiæ, et præfati Patris vestri, *Domini nostri, Pauli summi Pontificis,* et universalis Papæ consistimus, quia ipse noster est pater et optimus pastor, etc."—Cod. Carol. Epist. 15 (alias 36) (Cenni, ibid. p. 143).

[2] Cenni, ubi supra, p. 293.

subjects;[1] and, to express his temporal dominion, he uses precisely the same terms as he applies to that of the king of France over the territories and nations subject to his authority.[2] Moreover, he does not hesitate to implore the assistance of Charlemagne against the emperor of Constantinople, who had formed a league with some cities in Italy to take possession of Rome. "The dukes of Spoleto, of Beneventum, of Friuli, and of Clusium," he writes to the king of France,[3] "have combined in a malicious plot for soon uniting their forces with the Greeks and Adalgisus, son of Didier, to attack us by land and sea, *to take possession of our city of Rome*,[4] to pillage the churches of God, to carry away the rich ornaments of the altar of St. Peter, to lead ourselves (which God avert) into captivity, and to re-establish, in despite of you, the kingdom of the Lombards. I conjure you, therefore, most excellent king and very dear son, in presence of the true and living God, and of the blessed Peter, prince of the apostles, to come without delay, and as speedily as possible, to our assistance; because it is to you, under God, and by the order of God and of St. Peter, that we have intrusted the defence of the holy Church, of our Roman people and Roman republic. Come, therefore, speedily to the dwelling of the prince of the apostles, of St. Peter your protector, that you may reduce by your royal power all the enemies of the Church of God, that is, your enemies and ours, and may maintain the offering which you have made with your own hands to that holy apostle for the good of your soul." From these latter expressions, and others in the same letter, we find that it was subsequent to the destruction of the kingdom of Lombardy, and to the donation made to the Holy See by Charlemagne, extending and confirming the previous donation by Pepin.

45. *Temporal Sovereignty of the Holy See extended and consolidated by Charlemagne.*

Charlemagne had not only recognised and respected the pope's

---

[1] *Hanc nostram Romanam civitatem.... Nostros Romanos.... Civitas nostra Castelli Felicitatis* (in Tusciâ).... *Civitas nostra Centumcellensis* (in ducatu Romano).... *Territoria nostra.... Nostros homines*, etc.—Cod. Carol. Epist. 55, 57, 63, 83, 97 (alias 40, 59, 65, 84, 85).

[2] *Vestros fines,... Vestras partes,... Nostras vestrasque fines,... Vestros homines,... Nostros homines*, etc.—Ibid. Epist. 84, 97 (alias 85, 91).

[3] Cod. Carol. Epist. 57 (alias 59) (Cenni, ibid. p. 344, etc.).

[4] "Cupientes *hanc nostram Romanam* invadere *civitatem*."—Ibid.

sovereignty in Italy; he moreover extended and consolidated it by his victories over the Lombards, and by the total destruction of their monarchy in the year 773. Their obstinacy in persecuting the Holy See and in braving the arms of France was the true cause of this new revolution, which was not less advantageous to the king of France than to the Holy See, whose champion he had so generously become.[1] We shall give here briefly the principal circumstances of that event, which was at the same time one of the most important in the reign of Charlemagne, and one which contributed most to consolidate the temporal sovereignty of the Holy See.[2]

Adrian I. being assailed more vigorously than ever by Didier, king of the Lombards, in 772, implored the succour of the king of France, who he knew was devoted to the interests of religion and to the sovereign pontiff. Charlemagne having in vain attempted by negotiation to induce Didier to satisfy the pope, crossed the Alps in 773, and besieged him in Pavia, whither he had retreated. After a siege of six months, Didier, being compelled to surrender, was sent into France, where he died a holy death in the monastery of Corbie. Thus ended the kingdom of Lombardy, after having lasted more than two hundred years: from that time Charlemagne added the title of king of the Lombards to his hereditary title, king of the French.

During the siege of Pavia, this great prince having visited Rome, gave the pope the most affecting testimony of his respect and devotion. Not satisfied with confirming Pepin's donation, he ordered his chaplain Etherius to draw up a much more ample donation, securing to the Roman Church the exarchate of Ravenna, the island of Corsica, the provinces of Parma, of Mantua, Venice, and Istria, with the duchies of Spoleto and Beneventum.[3] The king signed this donation with his own hand, and ordered

---

[1] "Quoniam tuæ dulcissimæ Sublimitati, per Dei præceptionem et B. Petri, sanctam Dei Ecclesiam, et *nostrum Romanorum reipublicæ populum*, commisimus protegendum."—Ibid.

[2] Anastas. Vita Adriani, ubi supra, p. 1725. Fleury, Hist. Eccl. vol. ix. book xliv. n. 4, &c.; Hist. de l'Eglise Gallic. vol. iv. ann. 772. Lebeau, Hist. du Bas-Empire, vol. xiv. book lxv. n. 21, &c.; book lxvi. n. 49, &c. Annales du Moyen Age, vol. vii. book xxiv. ann. 774. Daniel, Hist. de France, vol. ii. ann. 772, &c.

[3] Anastas. ubi supra, p. 1738. On the extent of the possessions of the Holy See at this time, by the liberality of Pepin and Charlemagne, see Lièble's Mémoire sur les Limites de l'Empire de Charlemagne, pp. 42, 46.

it to be signed by the bishops, abbots, dukes, and counts who accompanied him ; he then deposited it on the altar of St. Peter, and swore with all his French lords to preserve for the Holy See all the territories mentioned in that grant.

46. *Solution of some Difficulties on this Point.*

It appears at first sight astonishing that Charlemagne included in that grant the island of Corsica, the duchy of Beneventum, and some other cities and territories over which he had as yet no right either of conquest or of sovereignty.[1] This is one of the arguments by which some persons have contested the authenticity of that donation, as far, at least, as it regards these provinces.[2] Still we may explain how they could be included in the grant by supposing that they were among that number of provinces which, during the pontificate of Gregory II., had given themselves to the Holy See to obtain its protection in the abandoned state in which they had been left.[3] There are strong reasons for believing that this was really the case with all those cities mentioned in Charlemagne's donation, over which he had not any right of conquest or sovereignty. For it is certain, in fact, that after the pontificate of Gregory II. many cities and territories in Italy surrendered themselves successively to the Holy See to obtain its protection against the Lombards. This the inhabitants of Spoleto and of Rieti certainly did in the pontificate of Adrian I., some time before the destruction of the kingdom of the Lombards, and perhaps even much earlier.[4] There are some grounds for the same

---

[1] It does not appear that at this time Charlemagne had any right to the island of Corsica ; and he did not obtain possession of the duchy of Beneventum until eight or ten years after the destruction of the Lombards. See Daniel, Hist. de France, vol. ii. ann. 774, p. 31 ; ann. 788, p. 61, &c. ; Cod. Carol. Epist. 91 (alias 88) ; Cenni, Monumenta, tom. i. p. 486 ; tom. ii. pp. 3, 60, 100.

[2] Lebeau, Hist. du Bas-Empire, vol. xiv. book lxv. n. 24. Annales du Moyen Age, vol. vii. book xxiv. p. 199. Hegewisch, Hist. de Charlemagne, p. 142. Daunou, Hist. Essai, vol. i. p. 38. Daniel, Hist. de France, vol. ii. ann. 774.

[3] See details on this subject, supra, n. 19, 32, &c.

[4] "Spoletini et Reatini, . . . antequam Desiderius, seu Longobardorum ejus exercitus, ad Clusas pergerent, ad beatum Petrum confugium facientes, *prædicto sanctissimo Hadriano Papæ se tradiderunt, et in fide ipsius principis apostolorum, atque prædicti sanctissimi Pontificis jurantes, more Romanorum tonsurati sunt* (*incisis nempe capillis et barbâ, in subjectionis signum*). . . . Et confestim ipse ter beatissimus bonus pastor et pater, cum omnibus exultans, *constituit eis ducem quem ipsi propriâ voluntate sibi elegerunt,* scilicet Hildeprandum nobilissimum, qui priùs cum reliquis ad apostolicam sedem refugium fecerat."—

conjecture regarding Corsica, and some other cities and provinces mentioned by Anastasius, according to the very grant of Charlemagne which he had then under his eyes.[1] This conjecture appears to be countenanced and even solidly established by the uniform language of the ancient authors, both French and foreign, who speak of Charlemagne's as well as Pepin's donation, as a restitution made to the Holy See of the provinces usurped by the Lombards. This is the language not only of the biographers of the popes, but also of Eginhard, who was so zealous for the glory of Charlemagne and of Pepin, and consequently so little inclined to depreciate the merit of the donations made to the Holy See by these two great princes.[2] Pope Adrian I. expresses himself in

---

Anastasius Biblioth. Vita Adriani I. (Labbe, ibid. p. 1735). Fleury, Hist. Eccl. vol. ix. book xliv. n. 4.

To understand this passage, we must observe that the Lombard fashion was to shave the hair on the back of their heads, and to let it grow long in front, as well as their beards. In the alliances which they contracted with the Romans or the Greeks, they adopted the usages of those nations, who wore the hair and beards much shorter; and they looked upon the reform as a mark of submission and dependence on their new masters or allies. In the letters of Adrian I. to Charlemagne (Cod. Carol. Epist. 91 (alias 88), apud Cenni, i. p. 488), an example occurs entirely similar to that mentioned here by Anastasius. Some other facts prove, that at this period there was, both among the Franks and Lombards, some kind of tonsure, regarded as a kind of alliance, or of adoption, by which the person whose hair was shorn acknowledged the authority of the person who had cut it. See on this subject Canciani, Barbarorum Leges Antiquæ, tom. v. p. 369, &c.; Muratori, Antiquit. Ital. tom. ii. Dissert. 23, pp. 298, 301; Ducange, Glossarium Infimæ Latinit. verbo Tonsura; Mabillon, Præf. in Ter. Sæc. Bened. § 1, n. 17; Thomassin, Anc. et Nouv. Discipline, vol. iii. book i. ch. xxix. n. 9; Lebeau, Hist. du Bas-Empire, vol. xiv. book lxxvi. n. 19.

A letter of Pope Stephen II. to Pepin, in 756, appears to suppose that the duchies of Spoleto and of Beneventum, which had been hitherto subject to the Lombards, had then expressed a wish, through the pope, to place themselves under the protection of the king of France, but that circumstances never enabled them to execute their design, or at least that it had no permanent results. For it is certain that both these duchies were subject to the king of the Lombards under the pontificate of Paul I. in 761. See on this subject Cod. Carol. Epist. 11, 18, 25 (alias 8, 15, 34) (Cenni, Monumenta, tom. i. pp. 110, 154, 176, 297, 298, 342).

[1] Thomassin, Ancien. et Nouv. Discipline, vol. iii. book i. ch. xxix. n. 8, et seq. De Maistre, Du Pape, book ii. ch. vi. p. 254.

[2] Charlemagne and his envoys, when demanding the cities and the provinces which he had taken from the Holy See, or delayed surrendering to it, invariably claim them as a restitution due to the pope and to the Romans. The following are the very words of Anastasius, which are repeated frequently in his Life of Adrian: "Ipsi Francorum missi, properantes cum apostolicæ sedis missis, declinaverunt ad Desiderium; qui et constanter eum deprecantes adhortati sunt, sicut illis à suo rege præceptum extitit, ut antefatas, quas abstulerat civitates, pacificè beato Petro redderet, et justitias parti Romanorum faceret; sed minimè quidquam horum apud eum obtinere valuerunt, asserentem

the same manner in a letter which he wrote to the emperor Constantine and to the empress Irene, to induce them, by the example of Charlemagne, to restore to the Holy See its patrimonies which were situate in Greece and in the East.[1]

47. *Charlemagne receives the Imperial Crown from Pope Leo III.*

Not satisfied with having solemnly recognised the temporal sovereignty of the pope, and with having delivered him from the tyranny of the Lombards, Charlemagne proved himself ever full of zeal for the glory of the Holy See, and for the maintenance of

---

se minimè quidquam redditurum. . . . Sed dum in tantâ duritiâ protervus ipse permaneret rex Desiderius, cupiens antedictus christianissimus Francorum rex pacificè *justitias beati Petri recipere,* direxit eidem Longobardorum regi, ut solummodo tres obsides Longobardorum judicum filios illi tradidisset, *pro istis restituendis civitatibus,* etc."—Anastasius, ibid. pp. 1734, 1735.

Eginhard uses similar expressions in his Life of Charlemagne: "Finis belli," says he, "fuit subacta Italia, et res à Longobardorum rege *ereptæ,* Adriano Romanæ Ecclesiæ Rectori *restitutæ.*"—Vol. ii. of Duchesne's Collection, p. 96.

These passages, and some others not less remarkable, are produced by the authors cited in preceding note.

[1] "Porrò et hoc vestrum à Deo coronatum ac piissimum poscimus imperium, ut, . . . sicut antiquitus ab orthodoxis imperatoribus, seu a cæteris Christianis fidelibus, oblata atque concessa sunt patrimonia beati Petri, apostolorum principis, fautoris vestri, *in integrum nobis restituere dignemini,* pro luminariorum concinnationibus, eidem Dei Ecclesiæ atque alimoniis pauperum. . . . Sicut filius et spiritualis compater noster, Dominus Carolus, rex Francorum et Longobardorum, ac patricius Romanorum, . . . per sua laboriosa certamina, eidem Dei Ecclesiæ, ob nimium amorem, plura dona perpetuò obtulit possidenda, tàm provincias, quàm civitates, seu castra et cætera territoria, imò et patrimonia, quæ à perfidâ Longobardorum gente detinebantur, brachio forti *eidem Dei apostolo restituit, cujus et jure esse dignoscebantur.*"—Concil. Nicæn. anno 787, act. 2 (Labbe, Concil. tom. vii. p. 119). Fleury, Hist. Eccl. vol. ix. book xliv. n. 25.

His knowledge of this point of history supplied M. Emery, superior of the seminary of St. Sulpice, a very simple means of answering a ridiculous pretension of Napoleon in 1810, who imagined that, as emperor, he had a right to deprive the pope of the temporal power which Charlemagne had conferred on him. The facts are thus related by M. Chevalier d'Artaud, in his Hist. de Pie VII., when speaking of a conversation of Napoleon with M. Emery, who was summoned to Fontainebleau, in November, 1809: "Napoleon having commenced to speak of his disputes with the pope, declared that he respected his spiritual power; but as for his temporal power, that it was derived not from Jesus Christ, but from Charlemagne; and that being emperor, like Charlemagne, he resolved to take away that temporal power, in order to give the pope more time to devote to his spiritual affairs. M. Emery, attacked on that point, denied that Charlemagne had given to the pope all his temporal possessions, some of them being very considerable so early as the fifth century; and that in any case the emperor ought not to touch these latter possessions. M. Emery was going to proceed with his discourse: Napoleon, who was not very well versed in ecclesiastical history, and who appeared never to have heard of this point, made no reply to it, but in a gentler tone passed suddenly to another topic."—Hist. de Pie VII. 2nd edit. vol. ii. ch. xxi. p. 256.

its temporal power against all its enemies, domestic and foreign. On his part the pope neglected no means to attach more firmly to the Church and to the Holy See so powerful a protection, and that was the true motive of the elevation of Charlemagne to the imperial crown in 800.[1]

Shortly after the election of Leo III., successor of Adrian I., a horrible conspiracy broke out by the intrigues of two nephews of Adrian, who aspired to the same dignity. The pope having with much difficulty escaped from the violence of these conspirators, retired to Charlemagne in France to implore his protection. The prince received the pope with respect, gave him a good escort to conduct him back to Italy, and marched to that country in person, in the year 800, to restore peace by bringing the conspirators to judgment. On the Christmas-day of that year, some days after the conclusion of that business, the prince coming into the church of St. Peter to hear mass, the pope placed on his head, while inclined in adoration before the altar, a precious crown; the people at the moment, as Anastasius informs us, burst out into unanimous acclamations, "To Charles Augustus, crowned by God, to the peace-giving emperor of the Romans, life and victory!"[2] Eginhard and some other French annalists add, that after the acclamation the pope was the first to give "adoration" to Charlemagne, that is, the expression of homage usually given to the emperors; he declared to him, at the same time, that henceforward, in place of the title, patrician of the Romans, which he had hitherto enjoyed, he should be styled emperor and Augustus.[3] The pope then anointed both the king and his eldest son Charles, who had not yet attained that title.[4] To this narrative Eginhard, secretary and confidant of Charlemagne,

---

[1] Anastas. Biblioth. Vita Leonis III. (Labbe, Concil. tom. vii. p. 1079, &c.). Eginhard, Annal. anno 800. Fleury, Hist. Eccl. vol. x. book xlv. n. 5, 10, 11, 21, &c. Daniel, Hist. de France, vol. ii. ann. 800. Lebeau, Hist. du Bas-Empire, vol. xiv. book lxvi. n. 52, &c. Annales du Moyen Age, vol. viii. ann. 800. Bossuet, Defens. Declar. lib. ii. cap. xxxvii. xxxviii.

[2] "Et ab omnibus constitutus est imperator Romanorum."—Anastas. ubi supra, p. 1082.

[3] "Post quas laudes, ab omnibus, atque ab ipso pontifice, more antiquorum principum, *adoratum*, atque, omisso Patricii nomine, Imperatorem et Augustum appellatum fuisse; ordinatisque rebus, Româ discessisse."—Annal. Met. Fuld. et alii (Recueil de Duchesne, vol. ii.; Bouquet, vol. v.). Bossuet, ubi supra, cap. xxxvii.

[4] See Documentary Evidences, No. 6, at the end of this volume.

adds a circumstance contested by many modern authors, but which can hardly be rejected after the positive testimony of so respectable an author.[1] He states that Charlemagne, when proceeding that Christmas morning to the church, had no knowledge whatsoever of the pope's intention; that when he was saluted emperor and Augustus he was both surprised and grieved at this conduct of the Roman people; and he protested that, had he had any suspicion of their intention, he would not have come to the church even on so great a festival. It is certainly difficult to conceive that Charlemagne was totally ignorant of the pope's intention; but he might very easily be ignorant of the intention to execute the design so promptly, notwithstanding the considerations which should induce the pope to defer it, namely, policy as regarded the court of Constantinople, or respect for the repugnance which Charlemagne himself manifested against accepting the new title which was offered to him.

But whatever may have been Charlemagne's repugnance at first to the title of emperor, it is certain that he assumed it immediately; for from the date of his coronation he always used that title in his official documents; addressed the emperors of the East as his "brothers," and joined to the dates of the years of his reign the date also of his empire. In fine, all the money coined at Rome from that time had on one side the name of the emperor, and on the other that of St. Peter or his image.[2]

48. *Conduct of the Pope on this Occasion easily justified.*

The conduct of the pope on this occasion must doubtless appear extraordinary to those who consider it without relation to the circumstances which had long since been accelerating and had even consummated the ruin of the Roman empire in the West. Nevertheless, it is unquestionable that contemporary authors regarded that conduct as fully justified by the state of

---

[1] Fleury, P. Daniel, P. Longueval, and the majority of historians, relate this circumstance on the authority of Eginhard. Lebeau, Gaillard, Hegewisch, and some others, here attribute to Charlemagne a dissimulation foreign to the character of this great prince, and which is only founded on malicious conjecture.

[2] Leblanc, Dissert. sur quelques Monnaies de Charlemagne, Paris, 1689, 4to. This dissertation, which was published by itself in 1689, was not added to the Traité des Monnaies published in the following year by the same author, but only to the Amsterdam edition, published in 1692, in 4to.

affairs at the time. Most of those authors take care to remark, that before Charlemagne received the imperial crown, his authority was already paramount in the greater part of the provinces of the Western empire, and especially in Italy, either by right of conquest or by the legitimate consent of the people, who, after being abandoned by their ancient masters, had selected him as their protector, giving to him, by the voice of the pope, the title of Patrician of the Romans. Though without the title of emperor, he possessed in reality all the authority which the emperors of Constantinople had gradually lost by their weak and imprudent conduct; hence some of the ancient annalists have observed "that it was no more than justice to give the title of emperor to the king of France, who really had the emperor's effective power."[1] The majority of modern historians adopt

---

[1] We shall cite only the Annals of Moissac, which have been copied almost literally by some others: "Anno 801, cùm apud Romam moraretur rex Carolus, nuntii delati sunt ad eum, dicentes quòd apud Græcos nomen *imperatoris* cessasset, et fœmineum imperium apud se haberent. Tunc visum est ipsi apostolico Leoni, et universis sanctis patribus qui in ipso concilio aderant, *seu reliquo Christiano populo,* ut ipsum Carolum, regem Francorum, *imperatorem nominare* debuissent; quia *ipsam Romam matrem imperii tenebat,* ubi semper Cæsares et Imperatores sedere soliti fuerant, seu reliquas sedes (putà Mediolanum, Trevirim et cæteras) quas ipse in Italiâ et Galliâ, necnon in Germaniâ tenebat; quia Deus omnipotens has omnes sedes in potestate ejus concessit; et ne pagani insultarent Christianis, ideo justum esse videbatur, ut ipse, cum Dei adjutorio, et universo populo Christiano petente, ipsum nomen haberet." —Annal. Mussiac. anno 801 (Recueil de Duchesne, vol. iii. p. 143; and Recueil de Bouquet, vol. v. p. 79). This passage is cited by Bossuet, ubi supra, cap. xxxvii. p. 543.

Some expressions used in this matter by our ancient annalists require some explanation, and give us an opportunity of making some important observations.

First. These authors suppose that Charlemagne, before his elevation to the empire, had already possession of the city of Rome, the capital of the old empire. He had, it is true, great authority there, as Patrician of the Romans; but we have already stated, and in another place we shall demonstrate at greater length, that he exercised no sovereign power there, strictly so called, and independent of that of the pope. The title of Patrician of the Romans, given to Pepin and to his children by Stephen II., did not of itself confer sovereignty, properly so called, but only the right and obligation of governing in the name of the legitimate sovereign, whatever provinces were intrusted to his care (supra, n. 36, note, infra, ch. ii. art. i. n. 65, 66, 82). It is in this sense that we must explain the power which our ancient annalists attribute to Charlemagne over Rome before his elevation to the empire; for otherwise they cannot possibly be reconciled with incontestable authorities which demonstrate that the pope was the real sovereign of Rome at that time.

Secondly. Among the reasons which induced the Romans to give the title of emperor to Charlemagne, the same writers insist especially on the honour of the Christian world, and the necessity of providing against the attacks of the pagans (ne pagani Christianis insultarent). These words may be naturally explained from an observation made a little before, as to the empire of Constan-

fully the same opinion. "Charlemagne," according to Fleury, "was already master of the greatest part of Italy after the fall of the Lombards, and he was in particular[1] sovereign of the Romans, for he received their oath of allegiance, and administered justice both by his deputies and in person, and in the case even of the pope himself. The Romans, moreover, were not without motives for conferring on Charles the title of emperor; they were abandoned by the Greeks, who, for a long time had given them no succour; and Constantinople was governed by a woman, whom they thought it shameful to obey; for a female reign was yet unprecedented. It was therefore proper to give the title of emperor to him who had its effective power; and it was so done by the pope, whose dignity gave him the first rank in Rome."[2] We may add, the emperors of Constantinople, notwithstanding the very great repugnance which they at first expressed and very naturally must have felt to recognise Charlemagne's new title, soon consented to admit it in several treaties made with that great prince after his elevation to the empire.[3]

49. *Increase of the Temporal Power of the Pope under the Successors of Charlemagne.*

This important revolution, which raised, so to speak, Charlemagne to the highest pitch of glory, was equally propitious for the temporal power of the Holy See, whose sovereignty in Italy

---

tinople being then governed by a woman; a thing entirely unprecedented, and which the Romans considered unworthy of them.

Thirdly. In fine, and principally, according to the narrative of our ancient annalists, as well as of Anastasius, Charlemagne was not elected emperor by the pope alone, as head of the Church, but by the pope, as the organ and representative of the Roman people, of whose interests he was the appointed guardian; by the pope acting in concert with that people, and approving and ratifying their pontiff's choice; so that from the uniform testimony of those authors, the pope's conduct or language by no means implies that he had attributed to himself, by divine institution, or in virtue of his sacred character, the power of disposing of the empire for the greater good of religion.

[1] Fleury, while adopting substantially the reflections of the ancient French annalists whom we have cited, goes much farther than they, and states roundly that Charlemagne was sovereign of Rome and of Italy since the ruin of the Lombards. This assertion must be reduced to its proper worth by our observations in the preceding note.

[2] Fleury, Hist. Eccl. vol. x. book xlv. n. 21. See also the authors cited above, n. 32, note 4.

[3] Eginhard, Annales, ann. 803. Daniel, Hist. de France, ann. 802, 811. Velly, Hist. de France, vol. i. p. 465.

was now guaranteed by the protection of the most powerful prince in Europe.[1] In accordance with the plan of our work, we close here the statement of facts connected with the rise of the pope's temporal power in Italy. We shall only remark, in conclusion, that the solemn act by which Charlemagne, after Pepin's example, had recognised and confirmed the temporal sovereignty of the Holy See, was frequently renewed by his successors. The diplomas of Louis le Débonnaire, in 817; of Otho I., in 962; and of Henry II., in 1020, of which we shall speak more in detail in the following chapter, are the most remarkable amongst these documents; and it is certain, that during more than two centuries after Charlemagne, the emperors were accustomed at their coronation to confirm by a solemn act all that their predecessors had done for the temporal sovereignty of the pope. Some[2] of them, after the example of Otho I. and of Henry II., not only guaranteed to the Holy See its ancient possessions, but even extended them. We shall omit here a detail of the accessions which the states of the Holy See received in the course of time before the donation of the Countess Matilda, the most extensive that had been made since the time of Charlemagne, and which lay principally in the dioceses of Mantua, Reggio, Parma, and Modena.[3]

---

[1] A correct estimate of Charlemagne's power may be formed from Lieble's Mémoire, already cited, Sur les Limites de l'Empire de Charlemagne (Paris, 1764, pp. 73, 12mo.). This Mémoire, which at present is very rare, was published in the Collection des Pièces Rares, concernant l'Histoire de France, by MM. Leber, Salgues, and Cohen, Paris, 1826-1842, 20 vols. 8vo. (See vol. ii. of that collection, p. 316.)

[2] Cenni, Monumen. Domin. Pontif. tom. ii. pp. 28, &c. 491, &c. In vol. ii. of the same work are found the texts of the diplomas above cited, with dissertations proving their authority, and solving the objections raised against them.

[3] This donation was made in 1077. At the present day it is difficult to fix its object or extent; it is certain, however, that the territories granted by it lay principally in the dioceses which we have named. See Cenni, ubi supra, tom. i. Præf. n. 33, &c.; tom. ii. p. 195, &c.

CHAPTER II.

CRITICAL DISCUSSION OF THE PRINCIPAL QUESTIONS RAISED BY MODERN AUTHORS ON THE ORIGIN AND TITLES OF THE TEMPORAL SOVEREIGNTY OF THE HOLY SEE.

50. *Question to be discussed in this Chapter.*

It is certain, and generally admitted, that from the fifth century, and especially from the establishment of the Lombard monarchy, in 572, the popes always exercised great influence in the temporal government of Rome and of Italy. But the nature and extent of that influence are a great subject of controversies among modern authors; and few historical questions have given rise to a greater diversity of opinion. Authors are not agreed either on the precise time at which the authority of the emperor of Constantinople ceased absolutely in the duchy of Rome and in the exarchate;[1] nor on the respective authority of the pope and the king of France in those provinces, after the emperor of the East had lost his ancient authority over them; nor on the real titles by which the pope exercised his authority there after that time.

51. *Chief Sources of this Difficulty.*

A modern historian has judiciously remarked that the chief difficulty in solving these questions arises from the fact "that the imperial power (in Italy) was not annihilated at once by a sudden revolution, but declined by little and little, and almost imperceptibly; it was a dying man, whose last moment was uncertain, and who was still breathing when his avaricious heirs believed him already dead."[2] By a natural consequence of this gradual decline of the empire in Italy, the authority of the popes was increasing every day in such a degree, that it is difficult to say at what time it became totally independent, and assumed the character of sovereignty, properly so called.

---

[1] By the exarchate, we mean in this chapter not only the exarchate properly so called, but also Pentapolis, which was one of its dependencies at the period when the authority of the exarchs was succeeded in Italy by that of the popes. See on this subject note 2, no. 12, part i.

[2] Lebeau, Hist. du Bas-Empire, vol. xiv. book lxvi. n. 52, p. 167.

52. *Plan of this Discussion.*

The succession of facts developed by us in the preceding chapter must, it is hoped, clear up most of those difficulties. To examine them in order, we shall divide this chapter into two articles. In the first place, we shall examine what date ought to be assigned to the origin of the temporal sovereignty of the Holy See both in the duchy of Rome and in the exarchate;[1] and, secondly, what are the grounds and primitive titles of that sovereignty.

ARTICLE I.

What Date is to be assigned to the Origin of the Temporal Sovereignty of the Holy See.

53. *Common Opinion of Foreign (not French) Authors.*

The common opinion of foreign authors, and especially of the Italians, who appear to have studied this question most carefully, assigns the rise of the temporal sovereignty of the Holy See under Gregory II. to that period when many of the Italian cities and provinces, abandoned by the emperors of Constantinople, and harassed by the tyranny which they had long inflicted on them, elected with the title of dukes, chiefs independent of the emperor, and placed themselves under the protection of the Holy See for combined resistance to their common enemy.[2] The advocates of

---

[1] We omit here some other provinces given by Charlemagne to the Holy See besides the duchy of Rome and the exarchate. The former he made only tributary to the pope, but reserved the sovereignty to himself. This was specially the case with the duchy of Spoleto, and that part of Tuscany which the authors of the time called Royal Tuscany. From the diplomas already cited of Louis le Débonnaire and Otho I. it is clear that the successors of Charlemagne retained, like him, for a long time the sovereignty of those provinces, reserving, however, the annual tribute which they were bound to pay to the Holy See. (Cenni, Monumenta, tom. ii. pp. 129, 130.) At the present day it is not easy to account for the true cause of the restriction placed on the pope's authority in those provinces, especially in the duchy of Spoleto, which had of its own accord submitted to the Holy See before the destruction of the kingdom of the Lombards, as we have already proved (supra, ch. i. n. 46). All we can find from these charters is, that there was on this subject a special convention between Charlemagne and Adrian I.—Cenni, Monumenta, tom. ii. pp. 130, 160.

[2] Nicolas Alamanni, De Lateranensibus Parietinis Dissert. Romæ, 1755, 4to. pp. 71, 95, 107, et alibi passim. This work, which was first published at Rome in 1625, in 4to., is also given in tom. viii. of Grævius's Collection, Thesaurus Antiquitatum et Historiarum Italiæ, Lugd. Batav. 1725, 45 vols. fol.; Cenni, Monumenta Dominat. Pontif. tom. i. p. 12, &c.; Orsi, Della Origine del Dominio, &c. cap. i.—viii. The common opinion of Italian authors

this opinion, however, generally maintain, that before Pepin's donation the popes, by exercising the authority vested in them by the free consent of the people, did not pretend to renounce definitively allegiance to the emperor, but rather regarded their authority as merely provisional, until circumstances enabled him to resume the exercise of his rights.

54. *State of the Question.*

This opinion, which we do not find rejected by any author of credit, and which is sustained by the mode of speaking of a great number even of those who do not expressly defend it, leaves completely unsolved the principal question to be discussed in this article,[1] namely, At what time did the popes commence to exercise definitively, in the duchy of Rome and in the exarchate, a sovereignty, properly so called, exempt from all dependence either on the emperor of Constantinople, or on the king of France? The different opinions on this subject may be reduced principally to three, which are, moreover, themselves subdivided by various modifications.[2]

---

on this point is adopted by some French writers. See, among others, Thomassin, Ancien. et Nouv. Discipline, vol. iii. book i. ch. xxvii. n. 8; ch. xxix. n. 1, &c.; De Maistre, Du Pape, book ii. ch. vi. pp. 249, 257; Receveur, Hist. de l'Eglise, vol. iv. pp. 83, 91, 208, 241, 285.

[1] See the authors cited above, note to n. 1 and 3, first part, and note 1, n. 30.

[2] In the eighth chapter of his work, already cited (Della Origine del Dominio, &c.), Orsi states and discusses these different opinions with great care. Many modern historians, and some even of the first rank, speak so lightly of this topic that they seem never to have seriously examined a question which has given rise to so many different opinions; nor do they appear to have even any fixed notion on the subject. Among these authors we may name especially the English historian Gibbon, in his Decline and Fall of the Roman Empire, a work which has been lauded so pompously for its erudition and critical discernment. In the 49th chapter of that work, where he gives in considerable detail a history of the great revolution effected in Italy at the close of the eighth century, he lays down, first as an indisputable fact, "that until the coronation of Charlemagne, the administration of Rome and of Italy was always in the name of the successors of Constantine" (vol. ix. p. 297, edit. 1828); an assertion which does not prevent him from supporting, a little farther on, with the same confident tone, that "the chiefs of a powerful nation [Pepin and Charlemagne] would have disdained servile titles and subordinate functions; that after the revolt of Italy [under Gregory II.] the reign of the Greek emperors was interrupted; and that during the vacancy of the empire, the French princes obtained from the pope and from the republic a more glorious mission [that is, as he explains himself, the sovereignty of Rome]. The Roman ambassadors [he adds] presented to the patricians of Rome [Pepin and Charlemagne] the keys of the church of St. Peter, as a pledge and symbol of sovereign power. . . . During the twenty-six years that elapsed from the conquest

5. *First Opinion—Sovereignty of the Emperor of the East in Rome, and in the Exarchate destroyed in the year* 754.

The first opinion maintains "that the jurisdiction of the emperor of Constantinople was completely annihilated in the duchy of Rome and in the exarchate after Pepin's donation in 754." This is the opinion of Alamanni, of Orsi, of Cenni, of P. Pagi, of P. Nat. Alexander, and of some other French writers.[1] These authors are not agreed about the respective authority of the pope and of the king of France in those provinces after Pepin's donation. The majority of Italian authors, whose opinions on

of Lombardy and the coronation of Charlemagne as emperor, he ruled as sovereign in the city of Rome, which he had delivered by his arms."—Ibid. pp. 312, 314.

Certainly it would be exceedingly difficult to reconcile these latter assertions with the first; for it is manifest, that if the administration of Rome and of Italy was in the name of the successors of Constantine, the French princes had not the sovereignty of Rome, but a title and functions subordinate to those of the empire.

This author appears not to have had clearer notions on the question relative to the sovereignty of Rome after the elevation of Charlemagne to the empire. At first he admits that the question appears to him to be involved "in great darkness," and he adopts as probable only the opinion which attributes that sovereignty to the emperor of the West (ibid. p. 333, note 1). But soon forgetting the reserved and hesitating manner in which he had expressed himself, he lays it down as a certain fact that "the sovereignty of the emperors was destroyed by the intrigues of the popes and the violence of the people; and that the successors of Charlemagne, content with the titles of emperor and of Augustus, neglected to maintain their jurisdiction" (ibid. p. 369). How can Gibbon assert so confidently that the sovereignty of the emperors was destroyed by the intrigues of the popes and the violence of the people, when he himself admits that it is very doubtful whether the emperors ever had that sovereignty?

The same confusion is observable in this author when he endeavours to assign the origin and titles of the emperor's sovereignty over Rome. He supposes both that Charlemagne reigned there "by right of conquest, and that the Romans, being at liberty to choose a master, conferred irrevocably on the French and Saxon emperors the power which had originally been only delegated to the patrician" (ibid. p. 368). See also chapter lxix. vol. xiii. p. 139. If Charlemagne was emperor of Rome by right of conquest, how could the Romans be at liberty to choose a master?

On this subject many other contradictions of a similar kind could be pointed out in Gibbon. Those which we have exposed are sufficient to justify the distrust with which everything in that work relating to the too famous contests between the popes and emperors in the middle ages ought to be read. A crowd of modern authors write on this subject with the same levity and the same contradictions. We shall name some of them in another note (infra, note 3, p. 246).

[1] Alamanni, De Lateranensibus Parietinis, cap. xi. Orsi, Della Origine del Dominio, &c. cap. viii. Cenni, Monumenta Dominationis Pontificiæ, tom. i. pp. 12, 67, 68, et alibi passim. Pagi, Critica in Annales Baronii, ann. 755, n. 6; ann. 796, n. 11, &c. Natal. Alex. Dissert. 25 in Hist. Eccl. sæc. 4, art. 1, prop. 5 and 6. Thomassin, Ancienne et Nouvelle Discipline, vol. iii. book i. ch. xxvii. n. 8; ch. xxix. n. 1, &c.

this point are adopted by Pagi, maintain that the pope alone was, properly speaking, sovereign of those provinces, and that the king of France, by virtue of his title as patrician, had no power therein except by the consent and under the direction of the pope. Natalis Alexander, on the contrary, maintains that the joint sovereignty of these provinces was vested in the pope and in the king of France, who exercised it in concert until the year 876; at which period, he says, Charles the Bold renounced it, leaving to the pope thenceforward complete and undivided sovereignty.[1]

56. *Second Opinion—This Sovereignty maintained until the close of the Eighth Century.*

According to the second opinion, "the emperor of Constantinople had the sovereignty of the duchy of Rome and of the exarchate until the close of the eight century." The advocates of this opinion contend that Pepin and Charlemagne, as well as Stephen II. and his successors, until the year 796, had no other authority in Italy but what was formerly exercised by the patricians or exarchs, who governed that province in the emperor's name.[2] M. de Marca and P. Lecointe, who are the principal supporters of this opinion, do not agree on the respective authority of the pope and the king of France in Rome and in the exarchate after the year 796. At that time, according to M. de Marca, the sovereignty of those provinces passed from the hands of the emperor of Constantinople to the pope and the king of France, who exercised it in common until the time of Charles the Bold. But, according to Lecointe, the sovereignty of those provinces was vested after that year, 796, exclusively in the kings of France, who allowed their administration, or *dominium utile,* to the popes until the year 824, when Louis le Débonnaire ceded them unreservedly to the Holy See.[3]

---

[1] This opinion of Nat. Alexander appears to be the same substantially as that of P. Daniel, Hist. de France (vol. ii. ann. 796, p. 95), and of P. Griffet, in his Observations on that History (vol. iii. p. 253, &c.).

[2] De Marca, De Concordiâ, lib. iii. cap. ii. n. 9, &c. Lecointe, Annales Eccl. ann. 796, n. 112; ann. 800, n. 31.

[3] Bossuet, Defens. Declarat. (lib. ii. cap. xix. xxxviii.) appears to adopt the opinion of P. Lecointe, with some modifications. He supposes that the emperor of Constantinople did not lose the sovereignty of Rome and of the exarchate before the year 800. It is uncertain whether Bossuet examined this question closely, and discussed carefully the different opinions to which it has given rise.

57. *Third Opinion—This Sovereignty destroyed, first in the Exarchate, in 754, and some time later in the Duchy of Rome.*

According to the third opinion, "the emperor of Constantinople first lost his sovereignty in the exarchate in 754, but retained it over the duchy of Rome at least until the destruction of the kingdom of Lombardy in 774, and, according to some, so late even as Charlemagne's elevation to the empire in the year 800. According to the advocates of this opinion, the sovereignty of the emperors of Constantinople, on its progressive extinction in those provinces, passed directly into the hands of the king of France, who left to the pope the administration, or *dominium utile*, but reserved to himself the sovereignty, or *altum dominium*, at first under the title of patrician, and afterwards of emperor, at least until the reign of Charles the Bold, and much later according to some authors. This opinion, which was first proposed by Melchior Goldast and by Francis Junius in the commencement of the seventeenth century, was revived by M. Leblanc in his dissertation on some coins of Charlemagne and his successors.[1] This dissertation, which has great pretensions to research and erudition, appears to have drawn most of the French authors who wrote on the subject since that time into the opinion of M. Leblanc; and we are not acquainted with even one who has attempted to refute it.[2] It has been revived in our days by celebrated authors, but with various modifications, a detail of which would be tedious and of very little utility.[3]

---

[1] See supra, last note, n. 47.

[2] Among the advocates of this opinion may be mentioned, in particular, Fleury, Hist. Eccl. vol. ix. book xliii. n. 31; vol. x. book lxv. n. 21; Lebeau, Hist. du Bas-Empire, vol. xiii. book lxiv. n. 32; Annales du Moyen Age, vol. vii. book xxiv. p. 74; book xxv. p. 246; vol. viii. book xxviii. p. 175; De la Bruère, Hist. de Charlemagne, vol. i. p. 121, &c.; Gaillard, Hist. de Charlemagne, vol. ii. p. 23, &c.; Maimbourg, Hist. de la Décadence de l'Empire de Charlemagne, pp. 8, 11, 16, &c.; Ferrand, Esprit de l'Histoire, vol. ii. Letter 28, p. 220, &c.; Lenglet Dufresnoy, Méthode pour étudier l'Histoire, vol. xiii. of the 12mo. ed. p. 230; Lelong, Bibliothèque Historique de la France, vol. ii. book iii. ch. v. art. x. § 1; Muratori, Annali d' Italia, ann. 800.

[3] See especially Sismondi, Hist. des Républiques Italiennes, vol. i. pp. 19, 20, 132, 135, &c.; Savigny, Hist. du Droit Romain, vol. i. pp. 234—238; Guizot, Hist. Générale de la Civilisation en France, vol. ii. Lesson 27, pp. 316—319. We must apply to these authors what we have said above of Gibbon (p. 244, note). They treat the question very superficially, and assume as certain some assertions which an attentive study of history would not, we are sure, justify them in enouncing so dogmatically. M. Guizot, for example, decides without hesitation that the system which attributes to the pope the administra-

58. *Importance of this Question—Its Solution reduced to Five Propositions.*

The very diversity of opinion which we have now stated is a sufficient evidence of the importance and the difficulty of the question which we now undertake to solve ; its importance must be still more deeply felt, when we reflect that the sovereignty of Rome was one of the principal causes of the exciting contests between the popes and the emperors during the middle ages, especially from the time of Frederick Barbarossa, who maintained his pretensions on this point with so much violence and ardour.[1] In all these controversies, the first opinion, such as it is explained by the greater number of Italian authors, appears to us best sustained by history. It can be even maintained confidently, we think, that most of the modern authors who have adopted the contrary opinion have been misled unconsciously rather by national prejudices than by an attentive examination of the facts and authorities which alone can point out the truth.[2] In order

---

tion alone of those provinces, and that which attributes to them the political sovereignty of them, are both alike untenable, "as being founded on a complete ignorance of the state of public opinion at the time ; because on questions of sovereignty, of powers, of rights, they had not then as defined, as precise notions as those which we have at present." (Guizot, ubi supra, pp. 317, 318.) This assertion must certainly astonish many readers ; for it is palpable, from the history of that period, that they had then, as now, very clear ideas on the distinction between the rights of a sovereign over his own states and those which he had over merely tributary states ; between the rights of absolute sovereignty and those of a mere *suzeraineté.* The terms used to express these different rights may have changed, but the thing was always the same. This is manifest from many facts already cited in the course of this work (Introduction, No. 80, and supra, p. 242, note 1). But if any doubts could remain on the subject, they must be completely removed, in our opinion, by M. Guizot himself, in his Essais sur l'Histoire de France (Essays 4 and 5), in which he explains the character and conditions of the feudal system.

[1] On the pretensions of Frederick Barbarossa, see Fleury, Hist. Eccl. vol. xv. book lxx. n. 23, 26 ; Maimbourg, Hist. de la Décadence de l'Empire, pp. 454, 465, &c. Many celebrated writers have remarked before us that these pretensions were one of the principal causes of the contests between the popes and the emperors. We have already cited in our Preface the testimony of Voltaire upon this point. See also Michaud, Hist. des Croisades, vol. iv. p. 467, &c. ; De Maistre, Du Pape, vol. i. book ii. ch. vii. art. iii. p. 298, &c.

[2] As it might be expected, national prejudices led German authors to support in this matter the pretensions of the emperors. Many French authors, also, were led into the same opinion after the contests of Philip the Fair with Boniface VIII., and of Louis XIV. with Innocent XI. As a matter of course, the same opinion is vehemently defended by heretical, schismatical, and infidel writers, whose principles inclined them naturally to censure and decry the popes. The common opinion of the Italians, which we adopt, has been admitted likewise by some French authors, mentioned in a preceding note, p. 242, n. 2.

to place in the clearest light the opinion which we intend to adopt, we shall reduce it to a few propositions, which appear to follow as the natural consequence of the facts explained in the preceding chapter.

I.—*The origin of the temporal sovereignty of the Holy See cannot be dated before the pontificate of Gregory II.*

59. *First Proposition—The Temporal Sovereignty of the Holy See cannot be assigned to any Period before the Pontificate of Gregory II.*

It is certain that before that period the popes never exercised in Italy any temporal authority in their own name, and independently of the emperor of Constantinople. It is true, that from the fourth century, and especially after the establishment of the monarchy of the Lombards in 572, they often had a very great part in the temporal government of Italy ; but they did nothing except in the emperor's name, as his officers and representatives, and for the purpose of maintaining his authority, and of retaining in their allegiance the people when inclined to revolt.[1]

II.—*The pontificate of Gregory II. must be considered as the true epoch of the temporal sovereignty of the Holy See in the duchy of Rome and in the exarchate.*[2]

60. *Second Proposition—The Pontificate of Gregory is the true Epoch of its Commencement.*

We have seen, in the preceding chapter,[3] that during the pontificate of Gregory II. many cities and provinces of Italy,

---

[1] See Nos. 7, 13, &c. of the preceding chapter.

[2] This is the opinion of the authors whom we have cited above, p. 242, note 2. See especially Orsi and Cenni. There is, however, a remarkable difference between the opinion of Orsi and that of Cenni. The former holds that the sovereignty of the pope was already established in the exarchate, as well as in the duchy of Rome, before Pepin's expedition to Italy in 754. (Orsi, Del Dominio, cap. i. v.) The second believes, that before that expedition the sovereignty of the Holy See was established only in the duchy of Rome, and that the emperor's sovereignty over the exarchate did not fall to the pope until Pepin's donation in 754. (Cenni, Monumenta Domin. Pontif. tom. i. pp. 15, 16, 76, 293, 294, 296.) The facts stated by us in the preceding chapter, appear to us to demonstrate Orsi's opinion.

[3] See supra, Nos. 20, 21, 32, 34, &c.

abandoned by the emperor, and disgusted with the vexations which he had so long exercised against them, elected with the title of duke chiefs independent of the emperor, in order to provide for their own liberty and that of the pope, whom they justly considered as their principal refuge in the abandoned state to which they were reduced. From that time the popes, though not assuming the insignia and titles of sovereign power, are seen constantly exercising all its rights in all the provinces and cities which had placed themselves under the protection of the Holy See, that is, principally in the duchy of Rome and in the exarchate.[1] They continued, it is true, to respect the emperor as much as circumstances allowed them; they even made exertions to preserve his authority in Italy; and there is every reason to believe that originally they had no intention of renouncing allegiance to him definitively and irrevocably.[2] But while still retaining all these professions of honour and respect, they really exercised in Rome and in the exarchate all the rights of sovereign power, and not in the name of the emperor, but as heads and representatives of the Roman republic, which had in the hour of its abandonment intrusted to them the guardianship of its temporal interests. By virtue of this free choice of the people, the pope regarded the duchy of Rome and the exarchate as his own states; he regarded the inhabitants of these provinces as his people and his subjects; reclaimed them on that title from the Lombards; called on the king of France to their assistance; and, in concert with them, gave him the title of patrician, or consul, to encourage them more in their defence.

---

[1] I say principally; for we have already remarked, that probably these provinces were not the only ones that placed themselves under the protection of the Holy See, after the pontificate of Gregory II. The same may very probably be said of some other provinces and cities of Italy, which were afterwards given to the Holy See by Charlemagne. See supra, No. 46; Thomassin, Anc. et Nouv. Discip. de l'Eglise, vol. iii. book i. ch. xxix. n. 8, et seq.

[2] This is substantially Orsi's opinion (ubi supra, cap. iv.), and also Cenni's (ubi supra, tom. i. pp. 14, &c. n. 21, 24, 58). The Abbé Pey, without pronouncing decisively, appears to incline to the same opinion (De l'Autorité des Deux Puissances, vol. i. p. 110).

III.—*Before Pepin's donation, in 754, whatever may have been the extent of the temporal power of the pope in the duchy of Rome and in the exarchate, it does not appear that they assumed definitively and irrevocably to renounce the dominion of the emperor of Constantinople.*[1]

61. *Third Proposition — Before Pepin's Donation, this Sovereignty was only Provisional.*

Though the popes were justified from that time, by the legitimate consent and free choice of those provinces, in regarding themselves as true independent sovereigns,[2] it does not appear, nevertheless, however just such an assumption would be, that they regarded themselves as such before Pepin's donation ; at least, all circumstances lead us to believe that they did not assume definitively and irrevocably the sovereignty of those provinces, but merely exercised over them a provisional authority, until circumstances should enable the emperors to resume their ancient rights. This opinion appears to account most naturally for the conduct of Popes Gregory III., Zachary, and Stephen II. The petition presented by Italy to the emperors in the pontificate of Gregory III. for the restoration of holy images ; the zeal of Pope Zachary to maintain against the Lombards the authority of the exarch, and consequently of the emperor whom the exarch represented ; the repeated applications of Pope Stephen II. to obtain the assistance of the emperor, before he called the king of France into Italy ; all these facts, and many others recorded in the history of those times, imply clearly enough that the popes had not then assumed definitively sovereign authority in the duchy of Rome and in the exarchate ; they exerted themselves on the contrary with all their might to maintain the sovereign rights of the emperor.

62. *Fourth Proposition—From Pepin's Donation, this Sovereignty was independent.*

IV.—*From Pepin's donation, in 754, until Charlemagne's elevation to the empire, the pope alone was sovereign, properly so called, in the duchy of Rome and in the exarchate.*

63. *This Proposition, so far as it regards the Exarchate, proved by Pepin's Donation.*

The first part of this proposition, with regard to the sovereignty

[1] See note 2, p. 249. [2] See supra, No. 42, &c. p. 228, et seq.

of the exarchate, can be easily proved by the nature and circumstances of Pepin's donation, and by the relations of the inhabitants of the exarchate with the popes after that donation. In fact, we have seen that from the pontificate of Gregory II., that is, about twenty-five years before Pepin's donation, the whole power and authority of the government of the exarchate was in the hands of the pope, in his capacity as head of the Roman republic; so that, though he had neither the titles nor the insignia of sovereignty, he really enjoyed all its rights.[1] Now there is no evidence that Pepin's donation made in this point any change whatsoever in the pope's position, except to consolidate his authority, and to make him definitively independent of the emperor of Constantinople. Pepin, when assuring to the Holy See the cities and territories of the exarchate, could and did intend to deprive the emperor for ever of the sovereignty of that province, to transfer it to the Holy See, without reserving over it any rights to himself. That he could deprive the emperor definitively of that sovereignty follows, as a matter of course, from his right of conquest;[2] the emperor could not reasonably expect that Pepin should restore so important a conquest to a master manifestly unable to defend it, and who for a very long period had acted rather as the declared enemy than as the master of those provinces. That the king of France really resolved to deprive the emperor of that sovereignty, is proved clearly by his absolute refusal to recognise the emperor's claims on the point.[3] Finally, it is equally certain that, when conferring those provinces on the Holy See, Pepin did not intend to reserve any sovereignty to himself. Such a reservation cannot be reconciled either with the testimonies of ancient authors, or with Pepin's own conduct; for the ancient authors speak of the donation made to the pope by that monarch as a restitution of provinces of which the Lombards had unjustly despoiled them;[4] and Pepin, when urged by the ambassadors from Constantinople to restore the exarchate to the emperor, declared, with an oath, that it was not from any human consideration he had undertaken his expedition into Italy, but solely from the love of St. Peter, and for the expiation of his sins. Such, assuredly, is not the

---

[1] See supra, 2nd assertion, p. 248, &c.

[2] See supra, n. 41.

[3] See supra, n. 41.

[4] See supra, n. 40.

language of a prince intending to reserve to himself a right of sovereignty over the conquered provinces. There is not the least proof that Charlemagne's dispositions on this point were different from those of Pepin; for his new donation merely confirmed and extended the former; and contemporary historians, both French and foreign, speak of those two donations as real "restitutions made to the Roman Church." [1]

64. *This Proof confirmed by the Conduct of the Popes.*

Finally, the conduct of the popes after Pepin's donation confirms our opinion; for from that period the popes, it is certain, exercised all the functions of sovereignty in the exarchate, without any acknowledgment of dependence on the emperor of Constantinople; and, so far from considering themselves as his subjects, they, on the contrary, openly denounced his pretensions to the exarchate, as those of a declared enemy.[2] Now this conduct of the popes would of itself be sufficient to establish our opinion. Not only were they authorized so to act by the legitimate consent of the people, but they were, moreover, it must be remembered, men eminent both for their virtues and intelligence. All ancient historians, and the majority of modern writers, even of those most prone to censure the political conduct of the popes of this period, have eulogized the prudence, the virtues, and the eminent sanctity of those particular popes. Even Lebeau, in his History of the empire of Constantinople, in which he represents Gregory III. and his successors as guilty of rebellion against the emperors of Constantinople,[3] afterwards passes the warmest panegyric on those very popes for their prudence and virtue. "Unhappily," he says, "for the emperors of Constantinople, the most eminent virtue, combined with the most enlightened prudence, was then sitting in the chair of St. Peter. During eighty successive years it was filled by seven popes not less respectable by the holiness of their lives than formidable to their sovereigns by their deepsighted policy. What a contrast between the wisdom of a Gregory III., of a Zachary, of a Stephen II., and, above all,

---

[1] See supra, n. 46.

[2] Ibid. n. 42, et seq.

[3] Lebeau, Hist. du Bas-Empire, vol. xiii. book lxiii. n. 63; book lxiv. n. 1; vol. xiv. book lxvi. n. 19, et alibi passim.

of an Adrian I., a man of commanding and comprehensive genius, worthy of the age of Charlemagne, and the levity and the pettish violence of Leo the Isaurian, and of Constantine Copronymus." [1] It is astonishing to find admissions of this kind in most of the authors who censure most severely the popes of the eighth century.[2] We shall cite only the testimony of Sismondi, whom no person can suspect of partiality to the popes. "The more," he says, "the Romans found themselves abandoned by the emperors, the more they attached themselves to the popes, who during this period were almost all Romans by birth, and who, from their eminent virtues, have been placed in the calendar of saints. The defence of Rome was regarded as a religious war, because the Lombards were either Arians or still attached to paganism; the popes, to protect their churches and convents from the profanation of those barbarians, employed all the ecclesiastical wealth at their disposal, and the alms which they obtained from the charity of the faithful of the West; so that the increasing power of those popes over the city of Rome was founded on the most legitimate of all titles, their virtues and their beneficence." [3]

65. *Proofs of the Fourth Proposition with regard to the Duchy of Rome.*

The second part of our assertion, which regards the pope's sovereignty in the duchy of Rome after Pepin's donation, seems at first sight not so easily demonstrable as the first, because the duchy of Rome was no part of the territories granted to the Roman Church by the king of France: independently, however, of that donation, the conduct of the popes from that period, and the relations of the French monarchs with the Holy See, are proofs sufficient of our assertion; for it is certain that, from Pepin's donation until Charlemagne's elevation to the empire, the popes constantly exercised all the rights of sovereignty in the duchy of Rome as well as in the exarchate, without any admission of dependency either on the emperors of Constanti-

[1] Lebeau, book lxvi. n. 51.

[2] Annales du Moyen Age, vol. vii. book xxiv. p. 67. Daunou, Essai Historique, vol. i. pp. 29, 30.

[3] Sismondi, Hist. des Rep. Ital. vol. i. ch. iii. p. 122. The author repeats these reflections substantially in his Hist. des Français, vol. ii. pp. 184, 186.

nople or the kings of France.[1] The latter, moreover, acknowledged plainly the pope's sovereignty in the duchy of Rome, both by receiving from him the title of patrician of the Romans, which could not be given except by the legitimate sovereign of Rome, and by acknowledging the papal sovereignty in the provinces of the exarchate, which had been wrested from the pope by the Lombards.[2] Is it not manifest that the king of France could not recognize this latter sovereignty without recognising also that which the pope exercised in the duchy of Rome, both being evidently grounded on the same title, namely, the free choice and legitimate consent of the inhabitants of those provinces abandoned by their ancient masters?

Besides, what title could the king of France pretend to the sovereignty of Rome? could it be a right of conquest? That right could apply only to the provinces recovered from the Lombards; and it is certain that they never obtained possession of Rome.[3] Could it be because he was patrician? But that title by itself certainly conferred no sovereignty. From the reign of Constantine until the fall of the Western empire, this title, even when not merely honorary, never conferred any jurisdiction independent of the legitimate sovereign. The patrician of Italy, like those of Sicily and of Africa, had no other power but that of governing his province in the name and as the representative of the emperor.[4] Hence it is generally admitted that the title of patrician of the Romans, granted to Pepin by Pope Stephen II., gave him no sovereignty before his expedition into Italy. We have not met even one author dating the sovereignty of the king of France over the duchy of Rome or the exarchate from the time when he received from the popes the title of patrician of the Romans. All the authors who allow any sovereignty to the French king in

---

[1] See supra, ch. i. n. 42. [2] See supra, ch. i. n. 46.

[3] Bossuet (Defens. Declarat. lib. ii. cap. 38. § 1), Fleury (Hist. Eccl. vol. x. book xlv. n. 21), and some other authors, suppose that Charlemagne was sovereign of Rome by right of conquest. We find nothing in history to prove that assertion. Hence the majority of historians, on the contrary, lay it down as certain, that the king of France was never sovereign of Rome before Charlemagne's elevation to the empire. (Lebeau, Hist. du Bas-Empire, vol. xiii. book lxiv. n. 32.) Consult also our observations on the subject at the end of the preceding chapter, supra, n. 48, text and notes.

[4] See supra, ch. i. n. 36, note 4.

Italy suppose it subsequent to that title, and rest it on a different ground.[1]

66. *The King of France, as Patrician of the Romans, had not the Sovereignty of Rome.*

From these observations we infer, that the title of patrician of the Romans, however honourable it undoubtedly was to Pepin and to Charlemagne, did not of itself invest them with any sovereignty, properly so called, over Rome and the exarchate, but solely made it their right and their duty to protect the Holy See against its enemies, and to regulate, in concert with the pope, all that regarded public order and tranquillity in his states. This consequence, which naturally follows from the facts already stated, is moreover confirmed by the manner in which the ancient authors usually speak of the patrician dignity of Pepin and of Charlemagne. The popes, the senate, and the people of Rome, and the king of France himself, far from attaching to that title the sovereignty of Rome, regarded it merely as synonymous with patrician and defender of the Roman Church.[2] The popes Paul I. and Adrian I., who themselves assumed the sovereignty of Rome and of the exarchate, style the king of France, indiscriminately, sometimes Patrician of the Romans, sometimes tutor, defender, or liberator of the Roman Church and of the people.[3] The Roman senate and people also use those expressions as synonymous in a letter to Pepin during the pontificate of Paul I.[4] Charlemagne had the same notion of the powers of the patrician; and it is very remarkable that in his letters and public acts he assumes indiscriminately the title of patrician and of defender of the Church, sometimes combining both titles; sometimes omitting patrician, and taking only that of defender, and always placing those titles after that of king of France and of the Lombards.[5] Is it credible that he would have constantly

---

[1] See the authors cited above, p. 246, note 2.

[2] See principally, on this point, Alamanni, De Lateranensibus Parietinis, cap. ii.; Pagi, Critica, ann. 740, n. 8; ann. 796, n. 3, &c.; Orsi, Del Dominio, &c. cap. viii. p. 126, &c.; Cenni, Monumenta Domin. Pontif. tom. i. pp. 294, 296; De Maistre, Du Pape, book ii. ch. vi. p. 257.

[3] Cod. Carol. Ep. 13, 17, 18, 30, 83, 93 (Cenni, Monumenta, tom. i. pp. 136, 150, 153, 189, 460, 500, et alibi passim).

[4] Cod. Carol. Ep. 15 (alias 36) (Cenni, ibid. pp. 142, 144).

[5] Caroli Magni Epist. ad Offam Regem; ad Fastradam Reginam; ad Angil-

used such a style had he regarded the sovereignty of Rome as annexed to his title of patrician of the Romans?

His letter to Pope Leo III., in 790, congratulating him on his accession to the papal throne, and soliciting a confirmation of his title as patrician of the Romans, is a decisive corroboration of these observations. "We send to thee," he says, "Angilbert our secretary, to whom we have given our instructions, that you may arrange between you all that you think necessary for the exaltation of the holy Church, for the support of your dignity, and the confirmation of our title of patrician. For as we maintained an alliance with your predecessor of happy memory, we desire to contract one as inviolable with your beatitude, that with the grace of God, and by the prayers of the saints, your holiness's apostolic benediction may ever accompany me, and that, with God's help, I may always defend zealously the Holy See of the Roman Church."[1] It certainly is exceedingly difficult to reconcile this letter with the opinion of modern authors, who attribute to the king of France, as patrician of the Romans, the sovereignty of Rome at that time. Far from assuming to himself that sovereignty, Charlemagne clearly recognises the pope as the true sovereign of Rome, both by applying to him for a confirmation of the dignity of patrician of the Romans, and by declaring expressly that the sole motive of that application was to contract an alliance with him, whereby he might efficaciously defend the Holy See against its enemies.

---

bertum; ad Leonem III. etc. (Baluzii Capitularia, tom. i. pp. 194, 255, 271, 272. Labbe, Concil. tom. vii. p. 1128, &c.). Ejusdem Capitularia, annorum 769, 789, &c. (Baluz. ibid. tom. i. pp. 190, 210).

[1] "Ad dilectionis pacificam unitatem, Angilbertum, manualem nostræ familiaritatis, Vestræ direximus Sanctitati, ... illique omnia injunximus, quæ vel nobis voluntaria, vel vobis necessaria esse videbantur; ut ex collatione mutuâ conferatis quidquid ad exaltationem sanctæ Dei Ecclesiæ, vel ad stabilitatem honoris vestri, *vel patriciatûs nostri firmitatem* necessarium intelligeretis. Sicut enim *cum prædecessore Vestræ sanctæ Paternitatis pactum inii*, sic cum Beatitudine Vestrâ ejusdem fidei et caritatis *inviolabile fœdus statuere desidero;* quatenus apostolicæ Sanctitatis Vestræ, divinâ donante gratiâ, sanctorum advocata precibus me ubique apostolica benedictio consequatur, et sanctissima Romanæ Ecclesiæ sedes, Deo donante, *nostra semper devotione defendatur.*"—Car. Mag. Epist. 1 ad Leonem III. (Labbe, Concil. tom. vii. p. 1128. Baluzii Capitularia, tom. i. p. 271). Fleury, Hist. Eccl. vol. x. book xlv. n. 5.

67. *The Pope's Sovereignty as absolute in the Duchy of Rome as in the Exarchate.*

To explain more fully the nature and extent of the pope's temporal sovereignty at this period, one important reflection must not be omitted. This sovereignty, some modern authors pretend, was less absolute in the duchy of Rome than in the exarchate; that in the duchy of Rome being limited by the powers of the Roman senate and people; while there was no such restriction in the other provinces subject to the Holy See. This difference arose, according to these authors, from the different titles of the Holy See to sovereignty in these provinces. In the duchy of Rome it was founded exclusively, they say, on the free choice of the Roman senate and people, who, in their submission to the pope, did not renounce, however, the exercise of those rights which they had constantly enjoyed under the emperors; whereas, in the exarchate, the sovereignty of the Holy See was not founded on the free choice of the people alone, but also on the liberality of the king of France, who recovered those provinces from the Lombards, and ceded them absolutely and unreservedly to the Holy See.[1]

We can discover nothing in history to justify this explanation; on the contrary, we find reasons for believing that the sovereignty of the Holy See was not less absolute in the duchy of Rome than in the exarchate. In both it was founded on the free choice of the people, who, in the abandoned state to which they had been reduced, placed all their interests in the hands of the pope, and intrusted to him all that authority which the emperors of Constantinople had formerly exercised over them through his representatives. The legitimacy of this title had been recognised by Pepin and Charlemagne themselves, by *restoring* to the Holy See the cities and provinces which had been wrested from it by the Lombards.[2]

68. *The Roman Senate and People had no Share in this Sovereignty.*

But can it be said that the Roman senate and people, by submitting to the authority of the pope, had not renounced the exercise of those rights which they had constantly enjoyed under

[1] Cenni, Monumenta Domin. Pontif. tom. ii. p. 108.

[2] See supra, n. 63, 65.

the emperors?[1] This objection supposes that the Roman senate and people had retained down to this period their ancient rights in the government of the state. But it is certain, on the contrary, and generally admitted, that by the successive increase of the imperial power they had long since been deprived of those rights.[2] The Roman senate, especially from the time of Constantine, was no more than a municipal institution, venerable, no doubt, from the associations of its character, but possessed of no jurisdiction outside the city walls, and without any political authority.[3] Its municipal rights were, it is true, in existence at the time when Italy renounced its allegiance to the emperor of Constantinople; and there are good reasons for believing that the municipal regime survived long after that epoch in Rome, as well as in many other Italian cities;[4] but this municipal government, which existed in the principal cities of the exarchate, as well as in those of the duchy of Rome, was limited to matters relating to the interests and public order of each city; and it in no respect diminished the rights of the sovereign in the government of the state.

V.—*From Charlemagne's election to the empire, the pope continued to enjoy exclusive sovereignty, properly so called, in the duchy of Rome (and of course in the exarchate),*[5] *as well during the Carlovingian as during the German dynasty of emperors.*

---

[1] Cenni, ubi supra.

[2] Mœhler, Manuel d'Hist. du Moyen Age, ch. i. § 3. Naudet, Des Changements opérés dans l'Administration de l'Empire sous Dioclétien et Constantin, vol. i. p. 289, &c.; vol. ii. ch. vii. Muratori, Chorogr. Medii Ævi, § 20 (Rerum. Ital. Script. tom. x.).

[3] We know that under the Roman emperors most of the cities in Italy were *communes*, or republics, having a kind of municipal government under the "altum dominium," or administration of the emperor. These republics had their own senate and magistrates, elected by themselves; and their own councils and laws, for matters connected with the order and interests of each city. (Godefroy, Cod. Theod. lib. xii. Præamb. in tit. i.; Comment. in tit. ii. n. 1, tom. iv. p. 289, &c. Muratori, Antiquit. Ital. Med. Ævi, Dissert. xviii. tom. i. p. 981. Naudet, ubi supra, vol. i. p. 49, &c.; vol. ii. p. 101, &c. Mœhler, ubi supra, p. 49. Guizot, Essais sur l'Hist. de France, essay i.) This order of things continued to exist under the Christian emperors; and traces of it remained under the Gothic kings, and even under the Lombards and Franks. (Muratori, ubi supra, pp. 982, 1007, &c.)

[4] Muratori, Antiquit. Ital. Medii Ævi, Dissert. 18, 45, tom. i. iii.

[5] I say, "of course in the exarchate," because, independently of those arguments which demonstrate equally the pope's sovereignty in both those pro-

69. *Fifth Proposition—From Charlemagne's Elevation to the Empire the Pope retains the Sovereignty of Rome and of the Exarchate.*

If we examine attentively the course of events relating to the temporal power of the pope subsequent to Charlemagne's elevation to the empire, we shall find that, by that great revolution, the sovereignty previously enjoyed by the pope in the duchy of Rome and in the exarchate was in no degree impaired; we shall find him from that period exercising in those provinces all the rights of sovereignty, without any dependence either on the emperor of Constantinople or on the new emperor of the West. Historians generally admit the pope's independence of the emperor of Constantinople after Charlemagne's election to the empire; and there can be no reasonable grounds, we are convinced, for questioning it. Long before Charlemagne's election to the empire, we have seen the emperors of Constantinople deprived of all their rights over the duchy of Rome and the exarchate by the legitimate will of the people of those provinces; and the pope himself, who at first had accepted the government of those provinces provisionally, had been definitively emancipated from all dependence on those emperors by Pepin's donation in the year 754.[1]

It is more difficult to decide whether the sovereignty of the pope in Rome was equally independent of the emperor of the West after the establishment of the new empire. The opinion, however, which maintains that independence appears clearly demonstrated by history, both under Charlemagne and under the successors of that great prince.[2]

---

vinces, the Holy See had additional titles to the sovereignty of the exarchate, by the donations of Pepin and Charlemagne. See supra, n. 63.

[1] See supra, Nos. 60, 65. From these observations we may infer that, correctly speaking, "the empire of the Greeks" was not transferred "to the French" by Charlemagne's elevation to the imperial dignity, as Baronius, Bellarmine, and many others, imagined. Long before that time the empire of the West had been destroyed, because the emperor had lost all his rights in the duchy of Rome and in the exarchate. Properly speaking, therefore, the Western empire was not transferred, but revived in Charlemagne; and the latter is the precise word found on many of his medals: "Renovatio Imperii." See on this point, D. Bouquet, Receuil des Historiens de France, vol. v. pp. 23, 53, &c.; Cenni, Monumenta Domin. Pontif. tom. ii. p. 17, &c.

[2] Cenni, Monumenta Domin. Pontif. tom. ii. Dissert. 1; De Leonis III. Epist. n. 2, 19, &c. Orsi, Della Origine del Dominio, &c. cap. ix. x.

70. *The Pope's Independence of Charlemagne proved by the Will of that Prince in* 800.

I. The independence of the pope with regard to Charlemagne, after that prince's elevation to the empire, appears to be clearly proved by the will which he made in the diet of Thionville, in 806, for the partition of his states between his children.[1] The emperor declares, in that instrument, that it is drawn up "in order to remove all grounds for dispute between his three sons, by dividing the whole of his empire between them." "We hereby make it known," he declares, "that we wish to leave our three sons, if it be God's will, heirs of our kingdom and of our empire. Not wishing, however, to bequeath that kingdom to them to be possessed conjointly and without any partition, an arrangement whence discord would arise, but to divide it into three parts, we hereby assign to each that portion which he is to govern and protect."[2] After this preamble the emperor assigns to each of his three sons a portion of his states, of which he gives a detailed enumeration, and among which he does not omit the Italian provinces, of which the Lombard monarchy was then composed.[3] But it is remarkable that in this partition of all his kingdom he entirely omits the duchy of Rome and the exarchate. He merely orders his sons "that they should all combine for the protection and defence of the Roman Church, after the example of Charles Martel, his grandfather; of Pepin, his father, of happy memory, and of himself."[4] Is it possible to imply more clearly that the duchy of Rome and the exarchate did not then form any part of his kingdom? If they did, would he have omitted them

---

[1] Baluze, Capitular. tom. i. p. 437. That document is given entire in the Annales du Moyen Age, vol. viii. book xxix. p. 267. Fleury also mentions it in his Eccl. Hist. vol. x. book xlv. n. 34. See Marchetti's observations on this subject, Critique of Fleury, vol. ii. n. 95. Orsi, Della Origine del Dominio, cap. ix. p. 154.

[2] "Non ut confusè atque inordinatè, aut sub totius regni dominatione, jurgii controversiam eis relinquamus; sed trinâ partitione *totum regni corpus* dividentes, quam quisquis illorum tueri vel regere debeat portionem distribuere et designare volumus."—Baluze, ubi supra, p. 439.

[3] This document supplies very useful data for fixing the limits and extent of the empire of Charlemagne. See on that subject, D. Lieble's Mémoire, cited supra, n. 49, note.

[4] "Super omnia autem jubemus atque præcipimus, ut ipsi tres fratres curam et defensionem Ecclesiæ sancti Petri simul suscipiant, sicut quondam ab avo nostro Carolo, et beatæ memoriæ genitore nostro Pippino rege, et à nobis postea suscepta est."—Baluze, ubi supra, n. 15, p. 443.

in the enumeration and partition of his territories? By omitting them, would he not have bequeathed to his children a great cause of discord by that very deed which he drew up for the express purpose of removing all grounds of quarrel between them?

71. *Letters of Pope Leo III. in support of this Proof.*

In support of this argument may be cited many letters written by Pope Leo III. to Charlemagne after his election to the empire, and which clearly imply that the title of emperor conferred on the king of France had in no degree impaired the papal sovereignty in the duchy of Rome and in the exarchate.[1] In these letters the pope gives to Charlemagne the title sometimes of emperor, sometimes of defender of the Church; and he uses both titles as synonymous, attaching to the word emperor the same signification,—defender of the Church,—which the title Patrician of the Romans had formerly implied.[2] Other letters of the same pope suppose that he was then exercising in the duchy of Rome and in the exarchate, without any protest on the part of the emperor, all the rights of sovereignty, appointing independently the dukes or governors of cities, and taking measures for the defence of the coasts against the Saracens.[3]

72. *The same Proof confirmed by a joint Deed of the Pope and Emperor.*

Another document of this period proves that the authority of the emperor was then subordinate to that of the pope in the duchy of Rome. In the Bullarium there is a deed, dated A.D. 805, by which the pope and Charlemagne secure to the monastery of St. Anastasius of the Three Fountains the possession of some property lying in the environs of Rome. In this document we find the pope named before the emperor both in the title of the charter and in the date, which gives the year of the pontificate of Leo, before the year of Charlemagne's reign; and also in the order of signatures, the pope's having the precedence.[4] Can it

---

[1] Cenni, ubi supra, n. 2.

[2] Leonis III. Epistol. ad Carol. Imperat. 2, 4, 5 (Cenni, ubi supra, pp. 51, 59, 62).

[3] Ibid. Epist. 4, 5, 8, pp. 60, 63, 74.

[4] For our purpose it is enough to cite the title, preamble, and conclusion of that charter:

"In nomine Domini Dei Salvatoris nostri Christi.

"Leo episcopus, servus servorum Dei, et Carolus Magnificus et præsens rex,

be reasonably supposed that an act of that kind, whose direct object was to secure the temporal rights of an important establishment, would have been so drawn up, if the pope's authority in Rome was subordinate to the emperor's? Does not that charter, on the contrary, manifestly prove that the emperor's authority in Rome was subordinate to the pope's?

73. *The Pope's Independence of the Successors of Charlemagne proved by the Charter of Louis le Débonnaire.*

II. The pope's independence of the successors of Charlemagne, both of the Carlovingian and of the German dynasty, is equally well established by history. To be satisfied of the truth of this position, we need only peruse attentively the charters of Louis le Débonnaire, of Otho I., and of Henry II., confirming the donations made to the Holy See by Pepin and Charlemagne.

The first of those charters, which was given by Louis le Débonnaire in 817, clearly supposes that the duchy of Rome and the exarchate had long been the property of the Holy See; the emperor declares expressly "that he does not pretend to assume to himself or to his successors any authority in them, except in case the pope should apply for his intervention." "I, Louis,[1]

---

hâc die, nullo prohibente nec contradicente, sed propriâ nostrâ voluntate, concedimus, tradimus, etc. . . . Actum est hoc traditum anno Dominicæ Incarnationis octingentesimo quinto, indictione decimâ tertiâ, et Domini Leonis summi papæ tertii anno decimo, Caroli imperatoris anno quinto.

"Ego Leo, episcopus Romanæ Ecclesiæ subscripsi.
"Ego Carolus rex, imperator augustus subscripsi."

This charter is given entire in tom. i. (p. 161) of the Bullarium Magnum Romanum, Romæ, 1739-1750, 28 vols. fol. It is also in Santelli's Italian Dissertation, entitled, Oltragio fatto a Leone ed a Carlomagno, in un Quadro ed una Stampa esprimenti l'Adorazione del Pontefice all' Imperadore. Roma, 1815, 4to. (p. 19).

[1] "Ego Ludovicus, imperator augustus, statuo et concedo per hoc pactum confirmationis nostræ, tibi beato Petro, principi apostolorum, et per te vicario tuo Domino Paschali, summo pontifici, et universali papæ, et successoribus ejus in perpetuum, *sicut à prædecessoribus vestris usque nunc in vestrâ potestate et ditione tenuistis et disposuistis,* civitatem Romanam cum ducatu suo et suburbanis atque viculis omnibus, etc. . . . Nullamque in eis nobis partem, aut potestatem disponendi, vel judicandi, subtrahendive aut minorandi vindicamus, nisi quando ab illo qui eo tempore hujus sanctæ Ecclesiæ regimen tenuerit, rogati fuerimus."—Privilegium Ludov. Imperat. apud Cenni, ubi supra, tom. ii. p. 125. Fleury speaks of this act in his Hist. Eccl. (ibid. book xlvi. n. 26), but very briefly and very incorrectly, as we shall see immediately. M. de Receveur's History of the Church may serve as a corrective on that and many other points (vol. iv. p. 209).

Emperor Augustus, decree and grant, by this deed of confirmation, to thee, blessed Peter, prince of the apostles, to your vicar the Lord Pascal, sovereign pontiff and universal pope, and to his successors for ever, the city of Rome, with its duchy and dependencies, as the same have been held to this day by your predecessors under their authority and jurisdiction."[1] Then follows an enumeration of the cities and territories in Italy that belonged to the Holy See; after which the emperor thus continues: "And we do not pretend to attribute to ourselves any right or power of governing or of judging in the said cities or territories; of diminishing or of taking anything from them, except when we may be solicited by him who for the time being shall hold the government of the holy Roman Church."

74. *Mistake of Fleury and some others regarding this Deed.*

After so formal a testimony, it is amazing to find Fleury, and some other modern historians, citing this document in confirmation of the opinion which supposes that Pepin and Charlemagne gave to the pope nothing but the "*dominium utile*," or administration, of those provinces, reserving to themselves and to their successors the "*dominium altum*," or sovereignty.[2] But the least examination of the context of the passage proves that these authors have entirely misunderstood its meaning; for Louis le Débonnaire, after confirming in the passage cited the donations made to the Holy See by Pepin and Charlemagne, confirms to it also some pensions and other revenues from the duchies of Spoleto and of Tuscany, with this remarkable proviso: "saving our

---

[1] In place of those words "sicut à prædecessoribus vestris," which is the reading in all MSS. the Decretum Gratiani, which has been followed by some modern critics, has "sicut à prædecessoribus nostris." But abstracting altogether from the authority of MSS., the last reading is palpably opposed to the testimony of history; for it is perfectly certain that the duchy of Rome, which is mentioned immediately after the disputed words, never was given to the Holy See by Pepin or Charlemagne, who never had any right of sovereignty over it. Louis le Débonnaire, therefore, could not say that his predecessors had it under their jurisdiction. On the contrary, it is certain, and could be truly asserted by Louis le Débonnaire, that the said duchy was under the jurisdiction of the popes, predecessors of Pascal, for they were its sovereigns from the year 754, and even earlier, as we have proved already. See on this subject, Cenni, Monumenta Domin. Pontif. tom. i. Præf. n. 26; tom. ii. Dissert. 1, n. 12, &c. and note 3, p. 125.

[2] Fleury, ubi supra. Leblanc, Dissert. sur quelques Monnaies de Charlemagne, ch. v. p. 30. D. Ceillier, Hist. des Auteurs Ecclés. vol. xviii. p. 618.

dominion over those duchies, and their subjection to us." [1] Now it is very clear that this proviso applies to the duchies of Tuscany and of Spoleto only, and not at all to those states of the Holy See which the emperor had previously enumerated. The authors whom we oppose appear, in truth, not to have read this deed attentively; for they cite the clause relating to the duchies of Spoleto and of Tuscany as if it applied to all the states of the Holy See, and omit altogether the other words of the charter, which clearly prove our opinion.

75. *Authenticity of this Deed.*

It must not be concealed that skilful critics have raised doubts regarding the authenticity of this deed; [2] still, in our opinion, it

---

[1] "Simili modo, per hoc nostræ confirmationis decretum, firmamus. . . . censum et pensiones, seu cæteras donationes quæ annuatim in palatium regis Langobardorum inferri solebant, sive de Tusciâ Langobardorum, sive de ducatu Spoletino; *sicut in suprascriptis donationibus continetur, et inter sanctæ memoriæ Adrianum Papam et dominum ac genitorem nostrum Carolum imperatorem convenit,* quando idem Pontifex eidem de suprascriptis ducatibus, id est Tuscano et Spoletino, suæ auctoritatis præceptum confirmavit; eo scilicet modo, ut annis singulis prædictus census Ecclesiæ beati Petri apostoli persolvatur; *salvâ super eosdem ducatus nostrâ in omnibus dominatione, et illorum ad nostram partem subjectione.*"—Privileg. Ludov. apud Cenni, ubi supra, pp. 129, 130. See above (n. 52, note), some observations on that passage of the diploma of Louis le Débonnaire.

[2] The authenticity of this document is contested principally by P. Pagi, and by Muratori. (Pagi, Critica in Annales Baronii, ann. 817, n. 7. Muratori, Annales Medii Ævi, tom. iii. p. 29. Idem, Piena Esposizione dei Diritti Imperiali, cap. iv. p. 42, &c.) It is ably defended by Gretzer, Defensio in Goldastum, p. 204. Idem, Apologia Baronii, cap. viii. p. 340. Cenni, Monumenta Dominat. Pontif. tom. i. Præf. § 3; tom. ii. p. 83, &c. See also Dissertation, by the same author, on Louis le Débonnaire's diploma, at the end of Orsi's work, Della Origine del Dominio, &c. Marini, Nuovo Esame dell' Autenticita de' Diplomi di Ludovico Pio, Ottone I. e Arrigo II. etc. Roma, 1822, 8vo. In support of his opinion, this last author (pp. 10, 11) cites many other Italian writers, who appear to have solidly examined this question.

The principal argument urged against the authenticity of the diploma of Louis le Débonnaire is founded on the rights which it attributes to the Holy See over Sicily, which then belonged to the Greek emperors, and over which the emperors of the West had no rights. To solve the objection, the defenders of the diploma observe, that the Holy See, which had long since been unjustly deprived by the Greek emperors of the extensive patrimonies which it possessed in Sicily and in Calabria (supra, ch. i. n. 31), was still exposed for many years past, to lose all hope of recovering them, in consequence of the excursions of the Saracens, who were threatening to seize those provinces. In such circumstances it was certainly lawful for the king of France to sustain the rights of the Holy See, both against unjust spoliation by the emperor of Constantinople, and against the equally unjust incursions of the Saracens, by assuring to it the possession of Sicily. There is every reason to believe that Charlemagne had taken the same means of securing the rights of the Holy See, since Louis le Débonnaire manifestly supposes that the Holy See *had*

may be confidently appealed to, both because its authenticity appears to us to be generally admitted and solidly vindicated by the majority of the learned, and because it is formally cited as genuine by many even of those whose opinions on the present subject of dispute it contradicts.[1]

76. *The Proof drawn from this Charter confirmed by those of Otho I. and of Henry II.*

We may add, that however decisive this document is, our opinion can be established without it; for it is certain that the same words and the same provisions are found in the charters given by the emperor Otho I. in 962, and by Henry II. in 1020, the authenticity of which is generally admitted.[2] In both these diplomas we find the same expressions as in that of Louis le Débonnaire, confirming to the Holy See the jurisdiction hitherto exercised by the popes in the duchy of Rome, and in the other provinces which then constituted the states of the Church.[3]

77. *The Pope's Independence of the Emperor proved by the Oath of Fidelity to the Emperors taken by the Romans.*

Independently of those diplomas, the emperor's authority in the government of those provinces is clearly proved to have been subordinate to that of the pope, by the oath of fidelity which the Romans took to the emperors who succeeded Charlemagne, at

---

rights over Sicily. See on this subject Cenni, Monumenta, tom. ii. Dissert. 1, n. 3; Dissert. 2, n. 20, note 14, p. 128, et alibi passim.

[1] See authors cited in note 2, p. 263.

[2] The text of those diplomas may be seen in Cenni's work, already cited, tom. ii. pp. 157, 187. The same author carefully discusses the sense and the authenticity of the same documents, ibid. tom. i. Præf. §§ 3, 4; tom. ii. p. 134, &c.

[3] Cenni, ubi supra, tom. ii. pp. 157, 187. It must be observed, 1st, that the reading "sicut à prædecessoribus vestris," which is disputed by some critics, in Louis le Débonnaire's diploma, does not occur in those of Otho I. and of Henry II.; 2nd, that in these two latter diplomas, as well as in the first, the clause "saving our rights over these duchies and their subjection to us," applies solely to the duchies of Spoleto and of Tuscany. Fleury and many other French authors, from not having read attentively the original documents, suppose that the same clause applied to all the states of the Holy See without distinction; whence they inferred, contrary to facts and even the express text of the diplomas, that the pope had only the "dominium utile" of those states, and that the emperor was their real sovereign.—Fleury, Hist. Eccl. vol. xii. book lvi. n. 1; book lviii. n. 46. Berault-Bercastel, Hist. de l'Eglise, vol. v. book xxix. p. 208.

least from the election of Pope Sergius II. in 844.[1] That oath, it is certain, never was taken except "by the pope's good pleasure," and "saving the fidelity due to him by the Romans." This is proved especially from the conduct of Pope Sergius II. to Prince Louis, son of Lothaire the First, in 844.[2] The latter having sent his son to Italy on account of some grounds of complaint which he had against the Romans, who had not awaited his consent for consecrating the new pope, the prince was not admitted by the pope into the church of St. Peter until he had protested in presence of the people, "that he had come with good intentions, for the good of the Church and of the state." [3] Some days after, "the French having asked all the Roman lords to take the oath of fidelity to Prince Louis," the prudent pontiff took care not to allow it, but answered with dignified firmness: "If you wish merely that they should take this oath to the emperor Lothaire, I consent and allow it; but to his son, Prince Louis, neither I nor the Roman lords can consent." [4]

---

[1] Cenni, Monumenta Dominat. Pontif. tom. ii. Dissert. 1, n. 25, &c. Fleury and some other modern writers suppose that a similar oath was taken by the Romans to Lothaire I. in 824. (Fleury, Hist. Eccl. vol. x. book xlvi. n. 53; Hist. de l'Egl. Gall. vol. v. ann. 824, p. 322. Receveur, Hist. de l'Egl. vol. iv. p. 241.) This assertion, however, rests exclusively on the testimony of an anonymous author, who continued Paul the Deacon's History of the Lombards; a testimony which appears very doubtful to the best critics. (See on this subject, Cenni, ibid. Dissert. 2, n. 35, 45; Dissert. 4, n. 21, &c.) We may add, that the formula of this oath, like that subsequently taken to the emperors by the Romans, contains the clause "saving the fidelity which I have promised to my lord the pope," which manifestly proves that the emperor's authority was subordinate to the pope's in the government of Rome. The whole formula of the oath is given in Cenni's work, already cited, p. 113, and in the Capitularia, tom. i. p. 647, of Baluze. It is certain, moreover, that the emperor Lothaire exercised no act of authority in Rome at that time without the consent and good pleasure of the pope. (Baron. Annal. tom. ix. ann. 824, n. 11, &c.; Hist. de l'Egl. Gall. ubi supra.)

[2] Anastasius, Vita Sergii II. (Labbe, Concil. tom. vii. p. 1793, &c.). Fleury, Hist. Eccl. vol. x. book xlviii. n. 16; Hist. de l'Egl. Gall. vol. v. ann. 844, p. 500. Daniel, Hist. de France, vol. ii. ann. 844, p. 346.

[3] "Tunc almificus præsul claudi faciens omnes januas beati Petri, . . . sancto Spiritu admonente, regi sic dixit: *Si purâ mente et sincerâ voluntate, et pro salute reipublicæ ac totius orbis, hujusque Ecclesiæ, huc advenisti, has ingredere januas, meâ jussione; sin aliter, nec per me, nec per meam concessionem, istæ tibi portæ aperientur.* Statim rex illi respondens dixit; *Quòd nullo maligno animo, aut aliquâ pravitate, vel malo ingenio advenisset.* Tunc, eodem præsule præcipiente, appositis manibus, prædictas januas patefecerunt."—Anastasius, ubi supra, p. 1794.

[4] "His igitur peractis, [Franci] à prædicto postulaverunt pontifice, ut omnes primates Romani fidelitatem ipsi Ludovico regi per sacramentum promitterent. Quod prudentissimus pontifex fieri nequaquam concessit, sed sic orsus est illis:

That the imperial power in the government of Rome was subordinate to the popes, is proved also by the formula of the oath of fidelity taken by the Romans to the emperor Arnolph in 896.[1] This formula was to the following effect: "I swear by all the holy mysteries, that, saving mine honour, my law, and the fealty which I owe to my lord Pope Formosus, I am and will be, all the days of my life, faithful to the emperor Arnolph, and that I shall contract no alliance against him with any person whatsoever."[2]

It is really difficult to conceive how so great a number of modern authors could undertake to prove the sovereignty of the emperors in Rome from the formula of this oath, which demonstrates so clearly the pope's independence of the emperor in that government.[3] The sequel of our inquiry will give us an opportunity of proving, that during the whole course of the middle ages the emperors themselves, at their coronation, took an oath of fidelity to the pope, which implied not only that the Holy See was independent of them, but that they were specially dependent on the pope.[4]

78. *Explanation of the Title of Emperor given to Charlemagne by Pope Leo III.*

If such were the case, what, it may be asked, were the effects of the coronation of Charlemagne by Pope Leo III., and of the title of emperor conferred on him on that solemn occasion?[5] I answer, that the pope wished to secure for himself more effectually the powerful protection of Charlemagne, by conferring on

---

Quia, si vultis, domino Lothario magno imperatori hoc sacramentum ut faciant, solummodo consentio atque permitto; nam Ludovico ejus filio ut hoc peragatur, nec ego, nec omnis Romanorum nobilitas permittit."—Anastasius, ibid. p. 1795.

[1] Cenni, Monumenta, tom. ii. Dissert. 1, n. 25, 26. Pagi, Critica in Baronii Annales, ann. 896, n. 3. Fleury, Hist. Eccl. vol. xi. book liv. n. 25. D. Ceillier, Hist. des Auteurs Ecclés. vol. xix. p. 460.

[2] "Juro per hæc omnia Dei mysteria, quòd, *salvo honore, et lege meâ, atque fidelitate Domini Formosi Papæ,* fidelis sum et ero, omnibus diebus vitæ meæ, Arnolpho imperatori, et nunquam me ad illius infidelitatem cum aliquo homine sociabo."—Luitprand, Hist. vol. i. ch. viii. (Duchesne's Collection, vol. iii.; Muratori, Script. Rer. Ital. tom. ii.).

[3] See among others, Fleury, Hist. Eccl. vol. x. book xlvi. n. 21, 53, &c.

[4] Second part of this Inquiry, ch. ii. art. 4.

[5] The various opinions of modern authors on this point are stated and discussed by Nat. Alexander, Dissert. 1, Hist. Eccl. sæc. ix. See also remarks of P. Roncaglia and Mansi on that Dissertation; Documentary Evidences, No. 6, § 3, at the end of this work; and supra, note 2, n. 69.

him a title pre-eminently honourable at that time in the opinion of all nations. However respectable was the title of patrician of the Romans, hitherto enjoyed by the king of France, that of emperor was much more so. Though it added no new territory to those previously occupied by Charlemagne, it gave him the first rank among all the princes of the West; it imparted an august character to royalty itself; and in some measure revived on Charlemagne's brow the halo of the ancient glories of Rome.

This explanation, which at first sight may appear extraordinary, is a natural consequence of the principles which we have established, and of the facts on which they are grounded. We have seen that Charlemagne's coronation by Pope Leo III., and the title of emperor then conferred on that prince, did not, properly speaking, deprive the emperor of Constantinople of the sovereignty of Rome and of the exarchate, for he had been deprived of it long before, at least since Pepin's donation in 754.[1] From our principles it also follows, that Charlemagne's coronation, in 800, had not the effect of transferring to the king of France the sovereignty of Rome and of the exarchate, because from that time the pope alone continued to exercise there all the rights of sovereignty, as he had constantly done since Pepin's donation.[2] What other effect, then, could Charlemagne's coronation, in 800, have but to attach him more closely to the defence and protection of the Holy See, by a title more honourable than that of patrician of the Romans, which he had hitherto borne?

This explanation of the title of emperor given to Charlemagne by Pope Leo III. is, we must add, not peculiar to the advocates of that opinion which we have embraced on the nature and extent of the pope's authority in Rome, after Charlemagne's elevation to the empire. Many even of the authors who do not adopt that opinion, believe that, before Charlemagne's elevation to the empire, he already possessed the sovereignty of Rome either in common with or exclusively of the pope.[3] From that opinion, as well as from ours, it follows necessarily that the title of

---

[1] Supra, n. 62, &c. [2] Ibid. n. 69.

[3] This is manifestly the opinion of M. de Marca, of Nat. Alexander, Fleury, and of many others whom we have cited above, n. 56.

emperor conferred by Leo III. on Charlemagne did not give him the sovereignty of Rome, but only a more august title, under which he was henceforward to exercise an authority which he had hitherto possessed as patrician of the Romans.

To establish more clearly the truth of our opinion, it may not be useless to examine here briefly the principal arguments urged in favour of other conflicting opinions by modern authors.

79. *Arguments urged for attributing to the Emperor of Constantinople the Sovereignty of Rome and of the Exarchate until the Close of the Eighth Century.*

I. Those who attribute to the emperor of Constantinople the sovereignty of Rome and of the exarchate until the close of the eighth century, urge, in the first place, that the popes of that period still dated their public acts very frequently by the years of the imperial reigns.[1] 2nd. That they still gave him in their letters and public acts the title of lord.[2] 3rd. That Pope Adrian I., when wishing to save the life of the chief of a faction, in order to give him time to do penance, wrote to the emperor, imploring him to give an asylum to the unhappy man in Greece.[3] 4th. That on a mosaic, still preserved in the Lateran palace, our Saviour is represented giving with one hand the keys to St. Peter, and with the other a standard to a prince named Constantine V.; whence it would appear to follow, that under the reign of that prince, that is, about the close of the eighth century, the pope still acknowledged the sovereignty of the emperor of Constantinople.[4]

---

[1] Bossuet and Fleury, besides others, regard this fact as a decisive proof of their opinion. (Fleury, Hist. Eccl. vol. ix. book xliii. n. 31. Bossuet, Defens. Declarat. lib. ii. cap. xix. p. 482.) Besides the letters of the popes, cited on this subject by Fleury, Bossuet produces a privilege, granted by Pope Stephen II. to Fulrade, abbot of St. Denis, and dated in the 38th year of the reign of Constantine Copronymus. (Labbe, Concil. tom. vi. p. 1647.) P. Longueval, in his Hist. de l'Egl. Gall. (tom. iv. ann. 757), throws some suspicion on the authenticity of that document. But his arguments do not appear conclusive against the authority of the MSS., which have led the majority of critics to maintain its authenticity. See Mabillon, Annales Ordinis Benedict. tom. iii. part. ii. p. 336; Fleury, Hist. Eccl. vol. ix. book xliii. n. 28; Félibien, Hist. de l'Abbaye de St. Denys, ann. 757; Gallia Christiana, tom. vii. p. 345; D. Ceillier, Hist. des Aut. Ecclés. vol. xviii. p. 189.

[2] Privileg. Fulradi, ubi supra. Adriani I. Epistola ad Constantinum et Irenem (Labbe, Concil. tom. vii. p. 99). Bossuet, Defens. Declar. lib. ii. cap. 19.

[3] Anastasius, Vita Adriani I. (Labbe, Concil. tom. vi. p. 1730). Fleury, Hist. Eccl. vol. ix. book xliv. n. 2.

[4] Ciampini, Vetera Monimenta, par. ii. cap. 21. Muratori, Annali d'Italia,

80. *Those Arguments not solid.*

These arguments, it must be admitted, are far from being conclusive; they must, in our opinion, appear very unsatisfactory on close examination;[1] for, in the first place, it is certain, from other examples, that public acts have been often dated from the reign of a prince, without admitting thereby any claim of his sovereignty. For instance, under the first race of French kings, many councils, held among the Franks, Burgundians, and Visigoths, are dated from the years of the consuls, whose authority was certainly not acknowledged by these nations.[2] Another council, held at Rome, in the year 743, by Pope Zachary, is dated the second year of the emperor Artabazus, and the thirty-second of Luitprand, king of the Lombards.[3] Can it thence be inferred that the Romans were at the same time subjects both of the emperor of Constantinople and of the king of the Lombards, it being unquestionable in history that Luitprand never exercised any authority in Rome? A privilege granted by Pope Paul I. to an abbot in Rome supplies another argument of the same kind; for it is dated by the year both of the emperor of Constantinople and of Pepin, king of France.[4] These examples prove conclusively that similar dates do not of themselves imply any subjection or dependence on the princes named, and that they are used purely as a chronological index of the year in which the document was drawn up.

2nd. The title of lord, given to the emperors of Constantinople after the year 754, is an equally inconclusive proof of their sovereignty over the duchy of Rome and the exarchate. Did not Popes Gregory II. and Gregory III. give the same title to Charles Martel, when he was only mayor of the palace? and can it thence be inferred that the popes acknowledged Charles Martel as their sovereign?[5]

---

vol. iv. ann. 798, p. 371. Lebeau, Hist. du Bas-Empire, vol. xiv. book lxvi. n. 52. Hallam, Europe in the Middle Ages, vol. i. p. 16, note 2.

[1] Pagi, Critica in Annales Baronii, ann. 796, n. 14. Orsi, Del Dominio, &c. cap. viii. pp. 121-123.

[2] Concil. Galliæ; passim in Inscriptionibus. See, among others, the titles of the Councils of Agde in 506; Orleans in 511; Epone in 517, &c. (Labbe, Concil. tom. iv.).

[3] Labbe, Conciliorum tom. vi. p. 1546.

[4] Ibid. p. 1694.

[5] Gregorii II. Epistola 2 ad Carolum Martellum. Gregorii III. Epistola

3rd. Pope Adrian I. could apply to the Greek emperor on behalf of an unfortunate fugitive without thereby recognising the sovereignty of that emperor over Rome and the exarchate. To ask a prince to do an act of mercy and to recognise his sovereignty are manifestly two very different things.

4th. The argument founded on the mosaic preserved in the Lateran palace supposes that the emperor Constantine represented on it is Constantine V.; but that supposition is too doubtful and too much disputed to supply a positive and conclusive argument. Many critics are of opinion that this tableau represents our Saviour giving with one hand the keys to St. Silvester, and with the other the standard to Constantine the Great. This explanation, which is adopted by Alamanni and P. Pagi, is at least as probable as the former, and it is not contested by any positive argument.[1]

81. *Arguments for attributing that Sovereignty to the King of France before the close of the Eighth Century.*

II. The authors who attribute the sovereignty of Rome and of the exarchate, before the close of the eighth century, to the king of France, either exclusively or conjointly with the pope, ground their opinion principally on the following argument: 1st. On the oath of fidelity which the Romans took to Charlemagne before his elevation to the empire.[2] 2nd. On the fact that Pope Leo III., after his accession to the pontifical throne, sent the Roman standard to Charlemagne.[3] 3rd. On Charlemagne's conduct in 799, in the trial of the conspirators who had attempted the life of the same pontiff.[4] On that occasion the king of France, they contend, acted as judge in a case between the pope and his subjects, a function which could not be exercised except by the sovereign of Rome. 4th. In support of their opinion, they cite, moreover, some expressions of Paulus Diaconus, an author of the

5 et 6 ad eumdem (Labbe, ibid. pp. 1439, 1472, &c.). Cod. Carol. Epist. 1 et 2 (Cenni, Monumenta Domin. Pontif. tom. i. p. 19, &c.).

[1] Pagi, ubi supra, ann. 796, n. 7, etc. Alamanni, De Lateranensibus Parietinis, cap. 9.

[2] Eginhard, Annales, ann. 796 (Duchesne's Collection, vol. ii. p. 248). Fleury, Hist. Eccl. vol. x. book xlv. n. 5.

[3] Ibid.

[4] Fleury, ibid. n. 20, 21.

eighth century, which appear to imply that Charlemagne, before his elevation to the empire, had the sovereignty of Rome. That author states, in his history of the bishops of Metz, that Charlemagne, after destroying the kingdom of the Lombards, subjected the city of Rome to his dominion.[1] Also in his dedication of the book of Pompeius Festus to Charlemagne, before that prince's elevation to the empire, he says: "In this book you will find the names of the streets, gates, and tribes of your city of Rome."[2] Similar expressions occur in the Annals of Moissac, and in some others of the same period.[3]

82. *These Arguments not conclusive.*

In our opinion it is very easy to show that these arguments are by no means conclusive. 1st. The oath of fidelity taken by the Romans to Charlemagne before his election to the empire proves unquestionably that they recognised in that monarch a great authority over them; but did they recognise him as *sovereign* of Rome and of the exarchate? This no person can assert in the face of our arguments, which have demonstrated the contrary. From our proofs, it inevitably follows that before his elevation to the empire he had no other power over the duchy of Rome and the exarchate than what he held as patrician of the Romans; a power which was limited to the defence and protection of the Holy See against its enemies, and to the regulation, in concert with the pope, of all measures relating to public order and tranquillity in the papal states.[4] The oath of fidelity which the Romans then took to Charlemagne referred solely to that authority which he had over them as patrician; but it was subordinate to that which they took to the pope as their true sovereign, and which they continued to take even after Charlemagne's elevation to the empire. It is certain, in fact, that even before that time the Romans took an oath of fidelity both to the pope and to the king of France. This is proved clearly, as M. de Marca observes,

[1] "Romuleam civitatem suis addidit sceptris."—Paul. Diac. Hist. Episc. Metens. (Biblioth. Patrum, tom. xiii. p. 331, col. 1).

[2] "Civitatis vestræ Romuleæ."—Annales Ordinis S. Bened. tom. ii. append. n. 36, p. 717, edit. 1704.

[3] Annales de Moissac, ann. 800 (D. Bouquet's Collection, vol. v. p. 79, col. 1). We have already cited this passage, ch. i. n. 48, note 1.

[4] See above, n. 66.

from a letter of the Roman senate and people to Pepin under the pontificate of Paul I., in which they acknowledge themselves subjects both of the pope and of the king of France.[1] Pope Paul I. supposes the same thing in a letter to Pepin, in which he complains of the bad treatment to which the king of the Lombards had subjected the duke of Spoleto and his officers, who had also "taken the oath of fidelity to the pope and to the king of France."[2] This language implies, no doubt, that the subjects of the pope were also, in a certain sense, subjects of the king of France; but not in such a sense that the sovereignty of Rome and of the exarchate belonged equally to both; for it follows clearly, from our proofs, that the pope alone then had the sovereignty, properly so called, of these provinces, and that the authority of the king of France in them was subordinate to that of the pope.[3]

---

[1] Cod. Carol. Epist. 15 (alias 36). Cenni, Monumenta Dominat. Pontific. tom. i. p. 143. We have cited in another place the expressions in that letter, by which the Roman senate and people acknowledge themselves subjects of the sovereign pontiff Paul, their lord (supra, n. 43). They use the same expressions in the same letter, acknowledging themselves subjects of the king of France, and they testify in the following strain their joy on receiving his recommendation to remain faithful to the pope: "O quantâ divinâ aspiratione interna viscerum nostrorum præcordia in nobis, vestris fidelibus redundant!" The word "fidelis," as is well known, means, in the language of that day, a subject or vassal, bound to his lord by an oath or promise of fealty. (See Ducange, Lexicon Infimæ Latin. verbo Fidelis.)

[2] "Comprehensum Albinum ducem Spoletinum cum ejus satrapibus, qui in fide beati Petri et vestrâ sacramentum præbuerunt, infixis in eis pessimis vulneribus, in vinculis detinet."—Cod. Carol. Epist. 18 (alias 15), p. 154.

[3] M. de Marca, and some other modern writers, think it may be inferred from the two letters which we have cited, that the pope and the king of France then exercised in common the authority of patricians, or of exarchs, in the duchy of Rome and in the exarchate. (De Marca, De Concordiâ, lib. iii. cap. ii. n. 6). See supra (n. 56), an exposition of that opinion. In truth, it appears from a letter of Adrian I. to Charlemagne, that the pope and the king of France both took the title of patrician, and exercised its authority in common for the government and the protection of the Roman people. (Cod. Carol. Epist. 97 (alias 95), apud Cenni, Monumenta, tom. i. p. 521. Labbe, Concil. tom. vi. p. 1773). But it must not be forgotten that the pope, besides being patrician, had moreover, in the duchy of Rome, and in the exarchate, a right of sovereignty, founded on the legitimate consent of the people of these provinces, who, after being abandoned by their ancient masters, had freely elected him as their chief,—a right which Pepin and Charlemagne themselves acknowledged, as we have proved, Nos. 63, 65.

These observations suggest a natural explanation of a passage in a letter of Adrian I., which suppose that the patrician dignity had been given to the pope by Pepin (a Pippino concessus); from which some modern authors have inferred that the pope derived that dignity from Pepin, as Pepin himself held it from the pope and from the Roman lords. (See Nat. Alexander, Dissert. 25,

2nd. The second argument urged against us is not more solid than the first. In order to make it conclusive, it should be proved that the sending of the Roman standard to Charlemagne was an admission of his sovereignty over the Romans; an inference which is by no means established; on the contrary, it is quite certain, that at this period the Romans used to pay that honour to the patricians or exarchs, who assuredly were not sovereigns, in the strict sense, of the provinces which they governed as administrators. We learn this fact from Anastasius in his Life of Adrian I., when he is describing the honours which that pontiff paid to Charlemagne in 774. "The pope," he says, "sent out to meet that prince the magistrates of Rome, followed by a numerous corps of troops, under the command of their officers, with standards and crosses, as was usual on the reception of an exarch or a patrician."[1]

3rd. The third argument must appear very weak, when we reflect that Charlemagne could exercise the function of judge, as he did in 799, between the pope and the pope's subjects, without being sovereign of Rome; he had a right to exercise that function either as patrician of the Romans, or on the solicitation of the pope, who had requested his protection against the conspirators.

4th. The expressions of Paulus Diaconus do not necessarily imply that Charlemagne had become sovereign of Rome after the destruction of the kingdom of the Lombards; they may be easily understood by applying them to the patricianship, which imposed on that prince the defence and protection of Rome, and the right

---

in Hist. Eccl. sæc. iv. prop. 6, initio; De Marca, De Concordiâ, lib. iii. cap. ii. n. 6.) The sequel of history, however, proves that the word "concessus" must not be taken in the strict sense; and that it must be understood in the same way as Pepin's *donation;* that is, as a restitution or confirmation of rights already acquired by the Holy See, and usurped by the Lombards. For, in fact, it is perfectly certain, that Pepin had no more right over the dignity of patrician of Rome and the exarchate than over those provinces which he restored to the Holy See. It is equally certain that the pope had not less authority in Rome and in the exarchate before than after Pepin's expedition. It is true that he was impeded in the exercise of that jurisdiction by the tyranny of the Lombards, from which he was not completely delivered before Pepin's expedition.

[1] "Obviam illi ejus Sanctitas dirigens venerandas cruces, id est, signa, sicut mos est ad exarchum aut patricium suscipiendum, eum cum ingenti honore suscipi fecit."—Anastas. Vita Adriani (Labbe, Concil. tom. vi. p. 1736. Fleury, Hist. Eccl. vol. ix. book xliv. n. 5).

of regulating, in concert with the pope, all measures relating to public order and tranquillity. In that view, the city of Rome, and all the provinces then subject to the Holy See, might, in a certain sense, be considered as parts of "the states of Charlemagne," and the Romans could be considered his subjects, though he possessed over them no sovereignty, properly so called, superior or equal to that of the pope. For it is manifest, from the history of the middle ages, that the word "subject" was applied not only to the subjects of a king or an emperor, but also to those of a duke, of a baron, and of many other lords, themselves subject to a sovereign, properly so called.[1]

83. *Arguments for attributing to Charlemagne, after his Elevation to the Empire, the Sovereignty of Rome.—First Argument, founded on the "Adoration" of that Prince by Leo III.*

III. We have now only to examine the arguments for that opinion, "which attributes to Charlemagne the sovereignty of Rome after his elevation to the empire."

The advocates of this opinion rely, in the first place, on the *adoration* or external homage which Pope Leo III., at the head of the lords of Rome, paid to Charlemagne in the ceremony of his coronation, whereby they seemed to acknowledge him as their sovereign,—"*à pontifice, more antiquorum princi pum, adoratus est.*" These are the expressions in the Annalia Francorum, which are commonly attributed to Eginhard.[2]

We could perhaps contest the truth of this fact, as it has not been mentioned by any contemporary author, French or foreign, even by those who give a detailed description of the ceremonies of the coronation.[3] Some critics believe that the silence of authors on so important a fact is a legitimate ground for questioning its truth; and that such silence is not sufficiently counterbalanced by the testimony of the Annals of France, attributed to Eginhard,

---

[1] Ducange, Glossarium Infimæ Latinit. verbis Regnum, Subditus. Pagi, Critica in Annales Baronii, ann. 796, n. 6. Dissert. on the meaning of "Regnum," in the Hist. de l'Acad. des Inscriptions, vol. i. 4to. p. 162.

[2] We have cited, supra, this text of Eginhard (ch. i. n. 47, note). On this subject there is an interesting dissertation, in Italian, by Santelli, which we have cited, supra, n. 72, note.

[3] Of these authors, the chief are Anastasius Bibliotheca and Paul the Deacon.—Santelli, ubi supra, p. 22.

but whose authenticity has itself seemed doubtful to some eminent critics.[1]

But admitting the truth of the fact, we see no argument that can be derived from it in favour of Charlemagne's sovereignty over Rome. Fleury, and some modern writers, it is true, when explaining that passage in the Annals of the Franks, suppose that the pope prostrated himself before the emperor, thereby acknowledging him as his sovereign. But an attentive and unprejudiced perusal of the passage itself proves that such an interpretation is conjectural and unfounded.

The passage, in the first place, does not imply necessarily that the pope prostrated himself before the emperor. Such a meaning cannot be sustained either by the proper sense of the word "adoratio," or by the ancient usage to which the Annals of the Franks refer; for, according to the style of the ancient authors, and especially of those of the middle ages, the word "adoration" frequently expresses no more than a simple tribute of respect given to a person distinguished by his character or his merit; for instance, by kissing his hands, by saluting him, or by wishing him good fortune, &c.[2] This appears to be the meaning of those expressions used by some ancient authors, and which we meet sometimes in the Theodosian and Justinian codes, "*adorare purpuram principis*," "*adorare serenitatem principis*," "*adorare diuturnitatem imperii*," &c.[3]

The ancient usage referred to in this passage of the Annals of the Franks does not require that the term "adoration," expressing the honour paid by Leo III. to Charlemagne should be taken in any other sense. It is, in the first place, highly improbable that these Annals should allude to the ancient usage of some oriental princes, who wished to be adored as gods, and who exacted from their subjects the homage of genuflection and prostration. It is more natural to suppose that the author of the Annals, who was a Frenchman, alludes only to some ancient usage observed towards the Frank kings. Now, it does not appear that such a custom was ever usual among them; not only is there no example of it in their history, but it is well known, moreover, that both

[1] Nat. Alexander, Lecointe, and many other authors, deny the authenticity of those annals.—Santelli, ubi supra, p. 30, &c.

[2] See the Dictionaries of Robert Stephen, Calepin, Facciolati, Ducange, and others, verbo Adorare. Diction. de Moreri, and Diction. Theol. of Bergier, at the word Adoration.

[3] Santelli, ubi supra, pp. 36, 54.

they and their subjects despised, as base and unworthy of a free people, the proud and domineering habits of oriental monarchs to the people subject to their authority.[1]

It may be urged, perhaps, that the author of the Annals alludes to the ancient usage among the Romans, who, in certain cases, genuflected and even prostrated themselves before their emperors. But besides the improbability of a French author making such an allusion, it must be observed that the practice of genuflection, or prostration, was not observed to all the Roman emperors.[2] Caligula, and some others who exacted it, had made themselves very odious, and most of the pagan emperors had constantly refused it. "The gods forbid," exclaimed the emperor Maximin I., "that men should ever adore me by prostrating themselves before me." [3]

From these observations, we may infer that the passage in question, taken in its proper and natural sense, means no more than that "the pope made a profound obeisance to the emperor, according to the ancient usage observed towards princes." It is in this sense that Montfaucon, Muratori, P. Daniel, and many others, understand the passage.[4]

---

[1] D. Ruinart, Præf. ad Opera S. Greg. Turon. n. 15. Santelli, ubi supra, p. 39, &c.

[2] Santelli, ubi supra, p. 49, &c. See also Godefroy, Comment. in Cod. Theod. lib. vi. tit. 8 et 13 ; lib. viii. tit. 7 (vol. ii. pp. 79, 94, 571).

[3] "Primus omnium (Diocletianus), post Caligulam Domitianumque, Dominum palàm se dici passus, et adorari se, appellarique uti Deum. Quis rebus, quantum ingenium est, compertum habeo, humillimos quosque, maximè ubi alta accesserunt, superbiâ atque ambitione immodicos esse."—Aurelius Victor, Hist. Rom. de Cæsar. cap. xxxix.

Ammianus Marcellinus, in relating the same fact, explains more clearly the rite of prostration, or genuflection, which was substituted by Diocletian for the simple salutation formerly in use : "Diocletianus, omnium primus, extero ritu et regio more instituit adorari, cùm semper antea ad similitudinem judicum, salutatos principes legerimus."—Ammian Marcellin. Histor. lib. xv. cap. v.

"Ipse" (Alexander Severus), says Lampridius, "adorari se vetuit, cùm jam cœpisset Heliogabalus adorari, regum more Persarum."—Lamprid. Vita Alex. Severi, cap. xviii. (Hist. Aug. Script. Lugd. Batav. 1671, 8vo. tom. i. p. 908).

Julius Capitolinus, in his Life of the two Maximins, tells us that Maximin I., though otherwise exceedingly odious to the Roman people, for his avarice and cruelty, would never tolerate any person prostrating himself before him. His son, whom he made his colleague in the empire, did not follow that example, and made himself thereby very odious : "In salutationibus superbissimus erat [Maximinus junior] ; et manum porrigebat, genua sibi osculari patiebatur, et nonnunquam etiam pedes ; quod nunquam passus est senior Maximinus, qui dicebat : "Dii prohibeant ut quisquam ingenuorum pedibus meis osculum figat." —Jul. Capitol. Vita Maximini Junioris, cap. ii. (ibid. tom. ii. p. 66).

[4] Montfaucon, Monuments de la Monarchie Française, tom. i. Muratori, Annali d' Italia, ann. 800. Santelli, ubi supra, p. 39, &c. Daniel, Hist. de France, vol. ii. ann. 800.

Finally, supposing that the pope had prostrated himself before the emperor, as a sign of his respect for his new dignity, it would yet remain to be proved, that by such testimony of respect he intended to recognise the emperor as his sovereign: now this latter supposition is even more gratuitous and more improbable than the former; for it is manifestly opposed to the documents which we have already cited in support of the opinion which attributes to the pope alone the sovereignty of Rome after Charlemagne's elevation to the empire.

We may add, that the explanation which we give of "the adoration" paid to Charlemagne by Pope Leo III. is not peculiar to the opinion which we have felt ourselves bound to adopt; it is also admitted by those authors who regard the sovereignty of Rome as having been possessed in common by the pope and the emperor, under Charlemagne and his successors. The pope and the emperor having, in that supposition, equal authority at Rome, it is utterly incredible that one of the two should have prostrated himself before the other, and thus acknowledged him as his sovereign.

84. *Second Argument founded on Charlemagne's Will in* 811.

In the second place, a difficulty much more plausible is proposed against our opinion. It is founded on Charlemagne's will, made in 811, for the partition of his treasures. By that act the emperor divides all his moveable property into three portions, and combining two of the said portions into one, he repartitioned it into twenty-one lots for the twenty-one metropolitan cities of his empire, at the head of which he mentions Rome and Ravenna. He therefore, it is contended, regarded these two cities as forming part of his kingdom.[1]

---

[1] "Omnem supellectilem atque substantiam suam, tam in auro quàm in argento, gemmisque et ornatu regio, . . . primò quidem trinâ divisione partitus est; deinde, easdem partes subdividendo, de duabus partibus 21 partes fecit; . . . ut quia *in regno illius metropolitanæ civitates* 21 *esse noscuntur*, unaquæque illarum partium ad unamquamque metropolim, per manus hæredum et amicorum suorum, eleemosynæ nomine, perveniat. . . . Nomina verò metropoliticarum civitatum, ad quas eadem eleemosyna vel largitio data est, hæc sunt: *Roma, Ravenna*, Mediolanum, etc."—Eginhard, Vita Carol. Magni (Baluze, Capitularia, tom. i. p. 487. Labbe, Concil. tom. vii. p. 1202, &c.). Fleury, Hist. Eccl. vol. x. book xlv. n. 50. Hist. de l'Eglise Gallicane, vol. v. book xiii. ann. 811.

Marchetti reproaches Fleury with having, by his own caprice, styled the

This difficulty would be really unanswerable if the word "kingdom" were taken in its literal and proper sense, for the states of a sovereign strictly so called. But it is certain that the authors of the middle ages use the word "kingdom" in a much vaguer sense for states subject to authority more or less restricted and subordinate to a sovereign authority. Thus in the law of the Bavarians, compiled in the fifth century by Thierry, king of Austrasia, and reformed in the seventh century by Dagobert I., the word "kingdom" is applied to the states of a duke.[1]

This being supposed, the will of 811 presents no difficulty against our opinion. An attentive collation of that act with the will of 806, and with other deeds which we have cited,[2] proves that the word "kingdom" (*regnum*) must be understood here in its general and more unrestricted sense for states generally. From some of those deeds, it follows inevitably that Charlemagne did not consider Rome and Ravenna as constituting part of his kingdom, that is, of those states of which he could dispose as a sovereign properly so called; that he never assumed to himself any authority over them, except in the case of the pope's applying for his protection. If, therefore, by the act of 811, he ranks Rome and Ravenna among the capital cities of his empire, it must be, in a general and improper sense, founded on the authority which the title of emperor gave him to protect and defend the states of the Holy See; an authority by which he neither could dispose of them at his will, nor govern them as sovereign properly so called; but solely execute in them, at the request of the pope and in concert with him, all acts necessary for the maintenance of public tranquillity in those provinces.

---

cities of Rome and of Ravenna as capital cities of Charles's kingdom. (Marchetti, Critique de Fleury, vol. ii. n. 95.) On this point, however, Marchetti's criticism is at fault; it is evident, from his manner of expressing himself, that he attended to the will of 806 only, of which we have already spoken (n. 70), and not to that of 811, of which there is question here.

[1] "Si quis filius ducis tam superbus vel stultus fuerit, ut patrem suum dehonestare voluerit per consilium malignorum, vel per fortiam [i. e. *per vim*], et *regnum* ejus auferre ab eo; . . . sciat se ille filius contra legem fecisse, et de hæreditate patris sui se esse dejectum."—Lex Bajuvariorum, tit. ii. cap. x. n. 1 (Baluze, Capitul. tom. i. p. 104. Canciani, Barbarorum Leges Antiquæ, tom. ii. p. 365). On the meaning of the word "regnum," in the writings of the middle ages, see supra, n. 82, para. 4, text and note.

[2] See supra, n. 70, &c.

85. *Third Argument.—The Acts of Authority exercised in Rome by Charlemagne and his Successors.*

In the third place, it is objected that Charlemagne and his successors performed certain acts of sovereign authority in Rome, by administering justice, holding courts, publishing regulations for the temporal government, judging causes between the pope and his subjects, requiring an oath of allegiance from the Romans, &c.[1]

These acts prove unquestionably that Charlemagne and his successors possessed great authority, and exercised very extensive rights in Rome. But were they rights of sovereignty,—of sovereignty independent of and superior to the pope? An attentive examination of history precludes the admission of such a conclusion. For, in the first place, it cannot be admitted, without contradicting all the authorities which we have already cited,[2] and especially that act by which Charlemagne partitioned his states in 806; the diplomas of Louis le Débonnaire, of Otho, and of Henry II., which confirm the donations made to the Holy See by Pepin and Charlemagne; finally, the formula of the oath of fidelity taken by the Romans to the Carlovingian emperors. All these acts clearly suppose, as we have proved, that the pope's sovereignty in Rome and in the exarchate, even after Charlemagne's elevation to the empire, was a sovereignty properly so called, independent both of the emperor of Constantinople and of the king of France. Secondly, the acts of authority on which this objection is grounded were exercised by the king of France before his elevation to the empire, by virtue of his title as patrician of the Romans, which gave him no sovereignty, properly so called, in the states of the Holy See, but merely the right of regulating, in concert with the pope, whatever concerned public order and tranquillity in his states. It was by virtue of this title that Charlemagne, on the demand of Pope Leo III., recently promoted (in 795) to the popedom, sent to Rome one of the principal officers of his court, to receive the oath of fidelity from the

[1] Fleury, Hist. Eccl. vol. x. book xlv. n. 20, 21; book xlvi. n. 53; book xlviii. n. 16. Daniel, Hist. de France, vol. ii. ann. 824 and 844, pp. 215, 346, et alibi passim. Berault-Bercastel, Hist. de l'Eglise, vol. iv. book xxiv. and xxv. passim.

[2] Supra, n. 70, &c.

Romans.[1] It was by virtue of that same title that this prince, who was always at the pontiff's command, marched to Rome, in the year 800, to restore public order, compromised by the conspirators who had plotted the murder of the pope.[2] Finally, the very circumstances of those facts which are objected to us, prove that Charlemagne, after his elevation to the empire, and all the emperors of his race after him, never pretended to exercise in Rome an authority independent of the pope's. When Charlemagne convicted those conspirators who had attempted the life of Leo III., he merely continued to exercise functions already commenced by him as patrician of the Romans, at the request of the pontiff.[3] The example of Lothaire I., in 824, is especially worthy of attention on this point.[4] The emperor Louis le Débonnaire having received intelligence of the election of Pope Eugene II. and of the troubles which it had occasioned, "resolved to send his son Lothaire into Italy to take, in conjunction with the new pope and the Roman people, those steps which circumstances might require."[5] Lothaire was received by the pope with all the honours due to his dignity, and immediately, "by the pope's good pleasure," made wise regulations to reform past disorders, and to prevent their recurrence.[6] For these objects he

---

[1] See the authors cited above, n. 47, note, especially Fleury, Hist. Eccl. vol. x. book xlv. n. 5.

[2] Fleury, ibid. n. 10, &c. Hist. de l'Eglise Gall. vol. v. ann. 800.

[3] Ibid.

[4] Eginhard, Annales, 824 (Duchesne's Collection, vol. ii. and vol. vi. of the Collection of D. Bouquet). Baronius, Annales, tom. ix. ann. 824, n. 31, &c. Hist. de l'Eglise Gall. vol. v. ann. 824, p. 320, &c. Fleury, ubi supra, book xlvi. n. 52, &c.

[5] "Cujus rei nuntium cùm Quirinus subdiaconus ad imperatorem detulisset, . . . ipse Lotharium filium suum, imperii socium, Romam mittere decrevit, ut vice suâ functus ea quæ rerum necessitas flagitare videbatur, *cum novo pontifice populoque Romano* statueret atque firmaret."—Eginhard, ubi supra (D. Bouquet's Collection, vol. vi. p. 185). Baronius (ubi supra) cites this passage, not as if from Eginhard, but from a Life of Louis le Débonnaire, by an anonymous author, known under the title of Astronomus. In this Baronius appears to be in error; Pagi, Bouquet, and the majority of critics attribute that passage to Eginhard. This dispute has, however, very little to do with the object of our inquiry. The annalists of that and of succeeding ages frequently copy each other; and the passage cited by us has been literally copied by the author of the Annals of St. Bertin, as D. Bouquet observes.

[6] "Statum populi Romani, jamdudum quorumdam perversitate præsulum depravatum, *memorati pontificis benevolâ assensione* correxit, etc."—Ibid. The words which we have marked in italics, in this and in the preceding note, should be specially attended to. It is strange how Fleury, who cites these

drew up some constitutions, which he published at Rome during his residence in that city. One of the chief objects of these constitutions was to maintain the authority of the pope in the government of his states, and in all parts of his administration.[1] It is also worthy of remark, that in all the articles of this very constitution which regard the authority of the pope and of the emperor in the government of Rome, the pope, as having the chief authority, is always named before the emperor.[2] The fourth article even expressly provides that the initiative in all the measures of government shall be taken by the pope or by his officers ; and that the emperor shall not interfere in the acts of the papal government, except at the request of the sovereign pontiff, to aid him in correcting the abuses which he may not be able by himself to correct.[3]

86. *Fourth Argument—The Money coined at Rome under Charlemagne and his Successors.*

It is urged, in fine, against our opinion, that the money coined at Rome under Charlemagne and his successors bore on one side the name of the emperor, and on the other that of the pope, or the figure of St. Peter. M. Leblanc especially, in his Dissertation on some coins of Charlemagne and his successors, regards these coins as the most decisive proof of the sovereignty of the emperor in Rome.[4]

It is surprising to see the confidence with which M. Leblanc and others urge this argument in support of their opinion. To make it available, it must, in the first place, be proved that when

---

very expressions, could say with such assurance, "that the emperor's sovereignty over Rome appears clearly from Lothaire's constitution, as well as from the oath which he made the Romans take." With regard to the oath, see the observations which we have made, supra, n. 77, note 1.

P. Daniel speaks with the same easy tone of assurance on this point (Hist. de France, vol. ii. ann. 824, p. 215). On this, as on many other questions, the Hist. de l'Eglise Gallicane may serve as a corrective for these two authors.

[1] The text of this constitution may be seen in the Concilia of P. Labbe, tom. vii. p. 1550.

[2] Lotharii Constit. art. 1, 4, 5, &c. (ibid. pp. 1550, 1551).

[3] "Decernimus itaque, ut primùm omnes clamores qui negligentiâ ducum aut judicum fuerint, ad notitiam Domini Apostolici referantur ; ut statim aut ipse per suos nuntios eosdem emendare faciat, aut nobis notificet, ut legatione à nobis directâ emendentur."—Ibid. art. 4, p. 1551.

[4] See pages 23, 40, &c. of that Dissertation, at the end of the Traité des Monnaies, by the same author. Amsterdam, 1692, 4to.

those coins were minted, the right of coining money was vested in sovereigns alone, to the exclusion of lords holding an inferior degree of power. Now, so far from that being the fact, it is certain, on the contrary, and admitted even by M. Leblanc himself, in his Traité des Monnaies de France, that at this period a great number of private lords enjoyed the right of coining money.[1] Under the first race of French kings this right was at first granted to some of the principal churches and to great abbeys; under the second race, and in the commencement of the third, the same privilege was granted not only to churches and abbeys, but to a great number of lay lords.[2]

This custom was not confined to France; it existed also in many other states, especially in Italy, in the eighth and ninth centuries, and even earlier. The cities of Pavia, Milan, Lucca, Trevisa, and some others, possessed this right under the Gothic and Lombard kings, and retained it for a long time under the French emperors, and even under the German.[3] With what probability, then, can the money coined at Rome in the name of Charlemagne and of his successors be urged as a proof of their sovereignty over that city? At a time when many private lords enjoyed the right of coining money, is it surprising that the emperors, though not sovereigns of Rome, should have used the same right there with the consent of the pope? Furthermore, may we not suppose, with very great probability, that this money was coined by order of the pope, who placed his own effigies with that of the emperor on it, either to honour the emperor, or perhaps to intimate the concert of the imperial and the papal power in the government of Rome?

So decisive do these replies appear to us against the objection proposed, that far from regarding it "as one of the strongest

---

[1] Leblanc, Traité des Monnaies de France, Paris, 1690, 4to. pp. 73, 143, &c. Daniel, Hist. de France, edit. by P. Griffet, vol. iii. p. 248. Ducange, Glossarium, verbo Moneta; observe especially §§ Moneta regia and Moneta baronum. Tobiesen-Duby, Traité des Monnaies des Barons, Paris, 1790, 2 vols. 4to. See, in the Preface to that work, a Dissertation on the origin and progress of this custom.

[2] Tobiesen-Duby, in his work already cited (tom. i. p. 79), gives a very long list of the prelates and barons of France who had enjoyed this right. On that list there are more than one hundred bishoprics, abbeys, or chapters.

[3] Tobiesen-Duby, ubi supra, p. 33. Muratori, Antiquit. Ital. Medii Ævi, Dissert. 27, De Monetâ, seu jure cudendi nummos, pp. 547, 581.

proofs of the sovereignty of the emperors in Rome," we think it cannot be urged with any confidence by persons acquainted with the facts which we have now stated. We are therefore inclined to believe that when M. Leblanc was writing the dissertation in which he proposed this objection, he was not acquainted with these facts, or, at least, that he had only vague and confused notions about them. We may remark, in truth, that his dissertation, which was published for the first time in 1689, was not republished by the author in the Traité des Monnaies, which he published the following year, and in which he acknowledges expressly the facts which we have now cited. There is every reason to believe that he proposed revising his Dissertation, in accordance with his subsequent researches; but it does not appear that he ever carried his design into execution. The Amsterdam edition of 1692, in which the Dissertation is given at the end of the Traité des Monnaies, appears to have been published without the author's consent. He died not long after (in 1698), without giving any other edition of his work.

ARTICLE II.

Foundation and Original Titles of the Temporal Sovereignty of the Holy See.

87. *State of the Question—Fundamental Principles in this Matter.*

To define more clearly and precisely the state of the question, which we are to examine in the second article, we shall, in the first place, lay down two principles which are generally admitted, and which must serve as a basis for all this discussion.

In the first place, we take it for granted, as an indisputable maxim *of law*, that ministers of religion are not by their sacred character disqualified for acquiring or possessing temporal property; and that their spiritual power is not of its own nature incompatible with temporal power. This principle, which was universally admitted in all ages and countries before the coming of Jesus Christ, has been as universally admitted since that time, even in the primitive and most glorious ages of the Church. This fact is demonstrated to evidence from the details given in the Introduction to this work, on the honours and temporal privileges granted to religion and its ministers by ancient nations, and especially under the first Christian emperors. Hence the principle which we lay down here has never been disputed except by a small number of heretics or of infidel philosophers, who were manifestly influenced by passion and partisanship in their declamations against the wealth and temporal power of the clergy.[1] In the second place, we suppose, as *a point of fact* equally indisputable, that the temporal sovereignty of the Holy See was not derived originally from Constantine's donation, as was very generally but falsely believed from the tenth to the fifteenth century. This question of fact, which is universally maintained by modern critics, is sufficiently demonstrated by the facts stated in the preceding chapter, on the origin and progress of the temporal sovereignty of the Holy See.[2] From that exposition, it clearly follows that, however generous Constantine and his successors were to the Holy See, they never gave it any sovereignty, properly so called, before the eighth century; and that even those popes who had taken the most prominent part in public affairs before that time, acted under the good pleasure of the emperor, and in concert with him as his officers or representatives in Italy.

---

[1] Among the heretics who denied to the Church and to her ministers the right of acquiring and possessing property, may be mentioned especially Arnold of Brescia, in the twelfth century; the Waldenses, in the thirteenth; Marsilius of Padua, in the fourteenth; and Wickliffe, in the fifteenth. Calvin and the first reformers, softening down somewhat the teaching of the ancient heretics, held only the incompatibility of temporal with spiritual power in the ministers of religion, at least under the new law. (Calvin, Instit. lib. iv. cap. xi. n. 8.)

Cardinal Bellarmine states and refutes solidly these different systems. (Controv. De Rom. Pontif. lib. v. cap. i. ix. x.; De Membris Eccl. lib. i. cap. xxvi. xxvii.) For a more detailed discussion of this question, see Dissert. sur la Grand. temp. de l'Eglise, in vol. i. Recueil de Pièces d'Hist. et de la Littér. by the Abbé Granet and P. Desmolets, Paris, 1731, 4 vols. 12mo.; and Carrière's Prælectiones de Jure et Just. tom. i. n. 94, p. 132, &c.

The true principles on this matter have been attacked in these latter times by some infidel philosophers and false politicians, whose errors have produced the most pernicious consequences in many states, and especially in France, in the revolution of 1798. The Encyclopædia, which had openly advocated these errors (art. Fondation), furnished the French revolutionists with most of the sophisms which they developed in the Constitutional Assembly on this subject, and which brought on the spoliation of the clergy. The work of M. Carrière, already quoted, gives a terse *résumé* of this discussion, and points out in great detail the principal authors to be consulted. To these we may add the Abbé Pey, De l'Autorité des Deux Puissances, vol. iv. p. 166, &c. We shall have an opportunity, in the course of our researches, of expounding more at length the true principles on this subject. See part ii. ch. iii. art. 2, § 3.

[2] Supra, ch. i. n. 6, &c. See also No. 5, among the Documentary Evidence at the close of this work.

88. *Various Opinions to be examined.*

These principles being supposed, we now have to examine the grounds and original titles of that temporal sovereignty which the Holy See acquired in the eighth century, and which it has ever since possessed. Modern authors are not less divided on this question than on the precise date to be assigned to the origin of the sovereignty itself.

1. Those who maintain that this sovereignty was anterior to Pepin's donation, assign as its title the legitimate consent of the people of Italy, who, finding themselves abandoned by their former master, intrusted, of their own free will, the guardianship of their temporal interests to the Holy See.[1] Some advocates of this opinion add that this conduct of the people of Italy was, moreover, authorized by the Divine law, which, they say, allows subjects to cast off the yoke of an heretical prince, at least after a sentence of the Church or the pope, declaring him deposed from his throne.[2]

2. The authors who maintain that the origin of the papal sovereignty was subsequent to Pepin's donation, generally regard that sovereignty as founded purely on the liberality of Pepin and of Charlemagne, who wished to testify their veneration for the Holy See by conferring on it a portion of those provinces which they had justly reconquered from the Lombards. This is the opinion commonly advocated or supposed by French authors.[3]

3. Some modern authors, without absolutely denying the legitimacy of Charlemagne's and Pepin's donations, accuse Pope Gregory II. and his successors of having dexterously relieved themselves by degrees from the yoke of the emperor of Constantinople, and of thus having paved the way to their temporal sovereignty by the intrigues of an ambitious and worldly policy. Of

---

[1] See the authors cited, supra, n. 53, note 1.

[2] Bellarmine, De Rom. Pontif. lib. v. cap. viii. (Oper. tom. i.). Baronii Annales, tom. ix. ann. 730, n. 4, 5. Orsi, Della Origine, &c. cap. v. Mamachi, Origines et Antiquit. Christianæ, tom. iv. lib. iv. cap. ii. § 4.

[3] De Marca, De Concordiâ, lib. iii. cap. xi. n. 5, &c. Nat. Alexander, Dissert. 25, in Hist. Eccl. sæc. iv. prop. 5. Bossuet, Hist. Univ. part i. ann. 755. Lebeau, Hist. du Bas-Empire, vol. xiii. pp. 292, 449. Velly, Hist. de France, vol. i. p. 363. Bernardi, De l'Origine et des Progrès, &c. book ii. ch. vi. p. 147. Magnin, La Papauté considérée dans son Origine, &c. part i. ch. x.

course, an opinion so disrespectful to the Holy See, and especially to many popes of eminent virtue, and honoured by the Church as saints, has been embraced by heretical and infidel writers; some of whom have pushed their opinions to the extreme already mentioned, of saying that temporal power was incompatible with spiritual, at least in ministers of the New Law.[1] But it is really surprising that the same opinion has been embraced by some Catholic authors sincerely attached to their religion, but not sufficiently on their guard against the prejudices nurtured and accredited in the world by the declared enemies of the Church and of the Holy See.[2]

4. Finally, under the influence of such prejudices, some modern writers go so far as to contest the legitimacy of the donations of Pepin and Charlemagne. If we believe the advocates of that opinion, those two monarchs, when making over to the Holy See the provinces which they had reconquered from the Lombards, disposed of what did not belong to them; as they could not, without injustice, deprive the emperor of Constantinople of that part of his dominions.[3] The advocates of this opinion, however, make no difficulty in admitting that, however defective in title the temporal sovereignty of the Holy See may have originally been,

---

[1] We have already remarked, supra, p. 285, note 1, that this opinion, which is so manifestly extravagant, was generally held by the first reformers. Modern Protestants appear in general to have renounced the absurdity; they nevertheless believe, for the most part, that the ambition and intrigues of the popes of the eighth century were the real causes and origin of the papal sovereignty. See, among others, Basnage, Hist. de l'Eglise, vol. i. p. 260, &c.; vol. ii. pp. 1347, 1598, &c.; Mosheim, Instit. Hist. Eccl. sæc. viii. part. ii. cap. ii. § 6, &c.; cap. iii. § 11; Gibbon, Decline and Fall, ch. xlix.; Hallam, Europe in the Middle Ages, vol. i. p. 11; Sismondi, Hist. des Républiques Italiennes, vol. i. ch. iii. pp. 123, 133; Hist. des Français, vol. ii. pp. 146, 186, &c.; Hegewisch, Hist. de Charlemagne, p. 56, &c.

[2] Vertot, Origine de la Grandeur de la Cour de Rome, pp. 10, 11. Lebeau, Hist. du Bas-Empire, vol. xiii. book lxiii. n. 54, 64; book lxiv. n. 1; vol. xiv. book lxvi. n. 19; Velly, Hist. de France, vol. i. pp. 336, &c. 361, 396, et alibi passim. Annales du Moyen Age, vol. v. book xviii. p. 244, et alibi passim. De Peyronnet, Hist. des Francs, vol. ii. book xii. ch. viii.

[3] This singular opinion was advocated in the commencement of the last century, by Muratori, in several writings published in defence of the imperial pretensions to the cities of Comachio, Parma, and Placença. It was solidly refuted by Fontanini, in several treatises on the same subject. In Moreri's Dictionary (art. Muratori, Fontanini), a list is given of all the works published on both sides during that controversy. Muratori subsequently published the same opinion, on the origin of the temporal sovereignty of the pope, in his Annali d'Italia. It is adopted by Sismondi, ubi supra, note 1 in this page.

it has long since been confirmed by undisputed possession, and recognised by all Christian princes.[1]

89. *The Question solved by the Facts already stated—The Solution reduced to three Propositions.*

From the series of facts already developed by us, we may form our estimate of those different opinions. From these facts, it follows manifestly, that the temporal sovereignty of the Holy See owes its origin neither to the ambition of the popes of the eighth century, nor to any power with which they believed themselves invested, to dispose of the temporalities of princes for the greater good of religion ; but that it was founded originally on the most legitimate titles, namely, the legitimate consent of the people of Italy, so solemnly recognised and confirmed by Charlemagne's and Pepin's donations. These inferences shall be illustrated more fully by the development of the three following propositions, in which our opinion may be stated.

I.—*The temporal sovereignty of the Holy See does not derive its origin from that theological opinion which attributes to the Church or to the sovereign pontiff the right of disposing of the temporalities of princes for the greater good of religion.*

90. *First Proposition—The Temporal Sovereignty of the Holy See does not derive its Origin from the Theological Opinion regarding the Divine Right.*

If we examine attentively the origin and progress of the temporal sovereignty of the Holy See, we shall find that the popes never claimed or exercised it by virtue of that theological opinion which we have just now stated ; but solely as chiefs and representatives of the people of Italy, who, in the abandoned state to which they had been reduced, had freely intrusted their temporal interests to the guardianship of the Holy See. This position is proved clearly from the facts which we have stated in the preceding chapter, and especially from the conduct of the sovereign pontiffs who succeeded Gregory II. When his immediate successor, Gregory III., to obtain the protection of Charles Martel, offered him the title of consul, he did so in the name of the

---

[1] Muratori : conclusion of the Annali d'Italia, cited by Orsi, Del Dominio, &c. Pref. p. xiii. note 6.

Roman people, and in virtue of a decree of the Roman lords.[1] Popes Zachary and Stephen II., when claiming from the Lombards the restitution of many cities and territories of the exarchate, and of the duchy of Rome, acted expressly in the name of the Roman republic, which had intrusted to them the guardianship of its interests.[2] Finally, Pope Leo III., when conferring on Charlemagne the title of emperor, acted in concert with the Roman people and the lords of Rome, who publicly announced their adhesion to that act.[3] In all the ancient documents we find the popes of the eighth century acting on these titles alone, which we have mentioned; and we defy our adversaries to point out a single passage in any of these documents, which supposes or implies in the popes of those ages the assumption of disposing of the temporalities of princes for the greater good of religion.

But independently of those decisive facts, our opinion could be demonstrated sufficiently by examining the principles then recognised and professed by the Holy See on the respective authority of the two powers. It is certain, that when the temporal sovereignty of the Holy See was first established, the principle of the distinction and mutual independence of the two powers was plainly professed by the sovereign pontiff, as it had ever been before. We have already seen the doctrine of antiquity on that point, stated with the greatest clearness and precision, by Popes Gelasius, Symmachus, and St. Gregory the Great.[4] We have also seen Pope Gregory II. expressing himself on the same subject, in a manner not less precise and energetic, in his letters to the emperor Leo the Isaurian, about the year 726; that is, at the very time when the temporal sovereignty of the pope was first established.[5] Can there, then, be the least semblance of plausibility in attributing the origin of that sovereignty to the theological opinion which asserts for the Church and the pope a power of disposing, "jure divino," of the temporalities of princes for the greater good of religion?

---

[1] See supra, ch. i. n. 32. [2] Ibid. n. 34. [3] Ibid. n. 47.
[4] Ibid. n. 9, 10, 14, 15, &c. [5] Ibid. n. 28.

II.—*The temporal sovereignty of the Holy See was not originally founded by the ambition or political intrigues of the popes of the eighth century.*

91. *Second Proposition — The Temporal Sovereignty of the Holy See was not founded originally by the Ambition or the Intrigues of the Popes of the Eighth Century.*

An opinion attributing to those pontiffs conduct so unworthy of their character is manifestly contradicted by history, which represents them, on the contrary, as models of disinterestedness, in circumstances the most delicate, and the most likely to suggest to men in general aspirations of grandeur and ambition. We have seen, in fact, that from the pontificate of Gregory II. the whole power and influence of the government, both in the exarchate and in the duchy of Rome, were centred in the pope, then considered as the head and representative of the Roman Republic, which had of its own free will intrusted to him its temporal interests; so that, without having the style and insignia of sovereign power, he yet was in reality the true sovereign of those provinces. We have also seen, that the consent of the people of Italy, who had intrusted this great power to the pope, was founded both on the natural law which justifies a people, when abandoned by its former masters, in choosing a chief capable of defending them; and on the invaluable services which the popes had conferred on Italy during more than two centuries. In circumstances so favourable to their ambition, the popes, far from seeking or eagerly grasping at sovereignty, used every means to decline it, and to maintain the emperors' rights in Italy; they exercised their authority in a provisional manner only, and from the unavoidable necessity of circumstances:[1] finally, they did not accept it definitively until the last extremity; that is, when the impossibility of the emperor's coming to the aid of Italy compelled them to appeal to the king of France to put a stop to the Lombard aggressions. Are there in this conduct of the popes the least grounds for charging them with that ambition so flippantly imputed to them by some modern writers? Is there, in all history, any instance of dis-

---

[1] See the details which we have given on this subject, n. 61, p. 250.

interestedness comparable to that of Gregory II. and of his successors?

As might be expected, most of the authors who maligned the memory of those pontiffs have fallen into the most glaring contradictions. What, in truth, can be more inconsistent than to attribute a long-sustained scheme of ambition and of intrigue to a succession of popes, who, these very authors themselves admit, were models of virtue and holiness? Now this inconsistency is inevitable in the opinion of all those who attribute the origin of the temporal sovereignty of the Holy See to the ambition and the intrigues of the popes of the eighth century. On the one hand, they accuse those popes of a deep-laid system of ambition and intrigue, designed to establish their temporal sovereignty at the expense of the emperors of Constantinople; on the other hand, they could not refrain from paying homage to the virtue and the eminent sanctity of the same popes. This appears manifestly by the remarkable admissions which we have already cited[1] from several authors not favourable to the Holy See. And is it not in fact impossible that qualities so opposite could be united in the same men? Had the conduct of these popes been guided by considerations of ambitious policy, should we not, instead of praising their eminent sanctity, be obliged to charge them with inordinate ambition, and with a spirit of rebellion and of hypocrisy, entirely unworthy of their high station, and of the sacred character with which they were invested?

92. *Objections against this Proposition founded on Pope Zachary's Answer to the French.*

The objections which may be proposed against us from the conduct of Popes Gregory II. and Gregory III. towards the emperor of Constantinople have, we trust, been satisfactorily

[1] See the testimony of Lebeau and Sismondi, cited above (n. 64, p. 252, &c.); also the authors cited in note 2, p. 287. Gibbon himself, who roundly accuses Pope Gregory II. and his successors of having prepared the way for the establishment of the temporal sovereignty of the Holy See by a spirit of ambition and of revolt against the emperors of Constantinople (Decline and Fall, ch. xlix. p. 284, &c.), afterwards expresses himself so moderately with regard to the conduct of the same popes (pp. 297, 300, 316, &c.), that he has been sometimes confidently cited as their apologist on this point. (De Joux, Lettres sur l'Italie, vol. i. Letter xx. p. 260.) We believe, however, that he would not have been cited so confidently if the contradictions into which, like many others, he has fallen on this subject, had been better known.

answered by the details which we have given on that subject in the preceding chapter.[1] But it may not be useless to examine here briefly the charges made against Pope Zachary, for his answer to the consultation of Pepin and the French lords on the deposition of Childeric III. Our ancient annalists state that, in the year 752, Pepin, in concert with the French lords, sent to consult Pope Zachary on the following question,—whether it was not better that the title of king should be given to him who had all the power of a king, than to a prince who had that title, but without any of its power? The pope replied that it seemed more suitable to give the title of king to him who had a king's power. In consequence of this answer, Childeric was tonsured and confined in a monastery, and Pepin was raised to the throne by the French barons.[2]

From this decision some modern authors have taken occasion to charge Pope Zachary, as well as his predecessors, with the ambitious views of a purely mundane policy. If we believe those authors, "Zachary, successor of Gregory II., but a deeper politician, without openly renouncing the allegiance which he owed to the empire, accelerated its doom in Italy. By his easy compliance with the wish which the French had conceived of placing a new race of monarchs on the throne, he attached them to the interests of the popes, and secured for his successors the co-operation of France in their defection from the sceptre of the emperors of Constantinople."[3]

93. *Injustice of the Charges made against this Pope—His Decision considered in itself.*

Nothing can be more groundless than the reproaches made against Pope Zachary on account of this famous decision.

---

[1] Supra, n. 29, &c.

[2] See Eginhard's Annals, the Continuator of Fredegarius, the Annals of Metz, and the other ancient annalists cited by Bossuet, Defens. Declar. lib. ii. cap. xxxiv. xxxv. A more copious series of authorities on this point may be seen in Serarius, Rerum Moguntinensium libri quinque; Moguntiæ, 1604, 4to. notes 38-44 in book iii. (The edition of this work given by Christian Johannis, Francofurti, 1722, fol. has some important additions.) See also Ellies Dupin, Traité de la Puissance Ecclés. p. 245, &c.; Fleury, Hist. Eccl. vol. ix. book xliii. n. 1; Annales du Moyen Age, vol. vi. book xxiii. p. 539; Daniel, Hist. de France, ann. 750; Hist. de l'Eglise Gall. ann. 752.

[3] Lebeau, Hist. du Bas-Empire, vol. xiii. book lxiv. n. 1. p. 395. Annales du Moyen Age, vol. vi. book xxiii. p. 536, &c. Hegewisch, Hist. de Charlemagne, p. 56, &c. De Peyronnet, Hist. des Francs, vol. ii. book xii. ch. viii.

Whether we consider that decision on its own merits, or consider the character of the pope who pronounced it, and the idea which history has bequeathed of his virtues, it is very easy to prove that the accusations preferred against him are groundless.[1]

In the first place, if we consider that decision in itself, it must be admitted that we do not know all its circumstances sufficiently to pronounce on it an unexceptionable opinion. Without pretending here to absolve Pepin of the charge of ambition, we yet may ask, is it quite certain that he ought to be regarded as an usurper of the crown of France? To answer that question, which must influence so decisively our judgment on Zachary's answer, we should have a far more profound knowledge than we at present have of the government and the constitutional law of the French monarchy under the Merovingian kings. Was the crown hereditary, then, or elective? How far was the king's power restricted by the rights of the general assembly of the nation? Did not that assembly enjoy, or believe it enjoyed, the right of deposing a prince or a dynasty which was useless to the nation, and incapable of governing it? Was not that right, however dangerous it may be in itself, universally admitted at the time by the French? Was not this general consent of the nation sufficient to establish that right at a time especially when the French had no written constitution? Granting even that this right appeared dubious, can the French barons be censured for inclining to that side of the question which would be most useful to their country, and for having solicited from Pope Zachary a decision conformable to their opinion? Finally, can the pope be censured for having solved the doubt submitted to him in the way most agreeable to the wish of the barons, and most conducive to the welfare of the nation? or, rather, was not that the decision which should, in the circumstances, be given on so delicate a question? After a little examination of these different questions, Pope Zachary's decision will not appear so surprising; and, far from censuring, we must perhaps regard it as a new proof of that rare prudence of which this pope's life has supplied so many incontestable examples.[2]

[1] See among the Confirmatory Evidence at the end of this work, note 7, on the authenticity of the decision attributed to Pope Zachary, and on the usurpation commonly charged against Pepin.

[2] See, in support of this observation, Bossuet, ubi supra, cap. xxxiv. xxxv.;

94. *His Character and Virtues.*

The accusations made against him on this point are the more outrageous, as they are manifestly at variance with the idea which history gives us of his character and virtues. What semblance of justice can there be in making such charges against a pope whom history proves to have been so respectful to the emperor, so zealous for the cause of the empire in Italy, and so eminent for all the virtues becoming his exalted station? All historians agree that at a time when Zachary had nothing to fear or to hope from the emperor, he exerted all his influence and authority to preserve for the empire the exarchate of Ravenna, which had been seized by the Lombards.[1] Is conduct so disinterested compatible with the ambitious views and the spirit of intrigue attributed to that pope? Historians are also unanimous in representing him as a man of eminent virtue. Even those authors who condemn so severely his answer to the consultation of Pepin and of the French barons, bear testimony on all other points, not only to his singular prudence, but also to the holiness of his life.[2] Can it be reasonably supposed that a pontiff of such a character could so far forget himself in his answer to the French as to sacrifice truth to the calculations of ambitious political intrigue?

95. *His Decision was not an Act of Jurisdiction in Temporal Matters.*

We may add, that whatever opinion we adopt on Zachary's conduct in this affair, it is important to bear in mind that his answer, such as it is represented to us by history, was not, properly speaking, an act of secular jurisdiction, which the pope assumed to exercise over the kingdom of France, but simply a doctrinal decision on a case of conscience which the French had voluntarily submitted to his tribunal. This is the clear and natural meaning of all the ancient annalists who have recorded this fact.[3] Nor can it be otherwise explained without attributing

Thomassin, Ancienne et Nouv. Discipline, vol. iii. book i. ch. xxix. n. 11; Receveur, Hist. de l'Egl. vol. iv. p. 80, note; De St. Victor, Tableau de Paris, vol. i. pp. 66, 69, &c.

[1] See supra, ch. i. n. 34.

[2] Lebeau, Hist. du Bas-Empire, vol. xiv. book lxvi. n. 51, p. 164. Annales du Moyen Age, ubi supra.

[3] See their testimonies cited and explained by Bossuet, Defens. Declarat. lib. ii. cap. xxxiv. xxxv.

to Pope Zachary a doctrine diametrically opposed to that of his predecessors, and especially to that which Pope Gregory II. had so manifestly professed some years before, on the distinction and reciprocal independence of the two powers.[1]

III.—*The temporal sovereignty of the Holy See was founded originally on the most legitimate titles.*

96. *Third Proposition—Temporal Sovereignty of the Holy See founded on the most legitimate Titles.*

From all this discussion, it clearly follows that the temporal sovereignty of the Holy See was founded originally on the legitimate consent of the people of Italy, solemnly recognised and confirmed by the donations of Pepin and Charlemagne.[2] This last title would of itself be certainly sufficient to establish the sovereignty of the Holy See, the conquests of Pepin and Charlemagne in Italy being perfectly legitimate ; conquests undertaken at the request of a people unjustly oppressed by its enemies, and abandoned by its former masters. But independently of that title, and before Pepin's expedition to Italy, the Holy See had already possessed there a real sovereignty founded on the legitimate consent of the people, who, in the extremity to which they had been reduced, freely intrusted to the pope all their temporal interests ; whence we must conclude that, properly speaking, Pepin and Charlemagne were not the founders but the guardians and protectors of the temporal sovereignty of the Holy See ; and that the result of their expeditions to Italy was not precisely to create that sovereignty, but to protect it, to consolidate it, and to make it permanently independent of the emperor of Constantinople.

This view could be confirmed by the admissions even of those modern authors who have proved themselves least favourable on this subject to the Holy See. Notwithstanding all their prejudices, they are compelled to acknowledge that the combination of circumstances which we have described was the principal cause of the great revolution which established the temporal sovereignty of the Holy See on the ruins of the imperial power in Italy. "Another cause," observes one of these authors, "prepared and even

[1] See the development of this subject, supra, p. 290.

[2] See supra, n. 33, 41, 63, pp. 214, 227, 250, &c.

justified the revolution which was now brewing in Italy against the Greek emperors; this was the state of almost utter abandonment in which the provinces possessed by them in that country had been left during two centuries. They kept no garrison in Rome; and that city, which was continually menaced by the Lombards, more than once solicited in vain, either through her popes or her dukes, the vigilance of the exarchs, and the power of the emperor; *abandoned by their masters,* the Romans were bound to attach themselves to their pontiffs, who at that period were nearly all Romans, and nearly all of praiseworthy characters. Fathers and defenders of the people, mediators between the great, chiefs of religion and of the empire, the popes united in themselves the various elements of influence and credit, which wealth, beneficence, virtue, and the high priesthood can confer."[1]

From these testimonies, and from all the facts developed in this first part, we conclude that the temporal sovereignty of the Holy See was founded on the most just and honourable titles; namely, on the legitimate consent of a people abandoned by their former masters; on the just conquests of the French, whom Italy had called to its assistance through the intervention of the popes; and on the invaluable services rendered to that country, during more than two centuries and in the greatest emergencies, by the prudence and generosity of a long succession of pontiffs. History presents, certainly, very few examples, perhaps not even one, of a sovereignty whose origin was so legitimate and so respectable; and though at the present day the Holy See needs no justification of a temporal sovereignty sanctioned by the prescription of so many centuries, it is not the least of its glories that it can produce in favour of that sovereignty, titles so honourable, and to which no other government on the earth can appeal.

97. *Establishment of this Sovereignty a visible Mark of God's Providence over His Church.*

Let us add, that this sovereignty, so legitimate in its origin, is likewise, in the opinion of all judicious and reflecting men, one of the most signal evidences of God's providence over his Church, and of that infinite wisdom which makes all human

---

[1] Daunou, Essai Hist. vol. i. pp. 29, 30. See also the authors cited above, n. 64, text and notes, and p. 287, note 2.

institutions subservient to the execution of his designs. After the fall of the Roman empire, and the consequent division of Christendom into different independent states, it was of the last importance for the good government of the Church that its head should not be the subject of any one monarch. Were the pope a citizen of London or of Paris, he would not be equally respected by both nations, nor would he always have free action in the duties of his administration. Voltaire himself justly observed, "that the popes of Avignon were too dependent on the will of the kings of France, and did not enjoy the liberty necessary for the good use of their authority."[1] The patriarchs of Constantinople, the mere puppets of Arian, Monothelite, Iconoclast, and Mussulman emperors, are the exact image of what the pope would, or at least might, have been in the course of ages, if they had not enjoyed this independent sovereignty. "So long as the Roman empire subsisted," as Fleury observes, "it embraced within its vast extent nearly the whole of Christendom; but when Europe was divided among many princes independent of each other, if the pope were the subject of any one of them, there might be reason to fear that the others would have some difficulty in recognising him as the common father, and that schisms might frequently occur. We may believe, therefore, that it was by a special dispensation of Providence that the pope became independent, and master of a state sufficiently powerful not to be easily oppressed by other sovereigns, in order that he might be more free in the exercise of his spiritual power, and might the more easily compel other bishops to discharge their duties. This is the reflection of a great bishop of our own day."[2]

98. *Bossuet's Opinion on this Point.*

The great bishop whose authority is here cited by Fleury in support of these reflections, is doubtless the bishop of Meaux, who proposed them confidently in many passages of his works, and especially in his Discourse on the Unity of the Church, delivered at the opening of the famous assembly of 1682. "God," he observes, "who willed that this Church, the common mother

---

[1] Voltaire, Annales de l'Empire, vol. i. p. 397.

[2] Fleury, Hist. Eccl. vol. xvi. Discourse 4, n. 10.

of all kingdoms, should not afterwards be dependent in the temporal order on any kingdom, and that the see in which all the faithful were to maintain their unity should be raised above those partialities which conflicting state interests and jealousies might cause, laid the foundations of this great plan by the hands of Pepin and of Charlemagne.[1] By a happy result of their liberality, it came to pass that the Church, independent in her head of all temporal powers, saw herself in a position to exercise more freely for the common good, and under the general protection of all Christian kings, her heavenly power of governing souls; and, holding in her hand the even balance in the midst of so many empires often at war, she maintains the unity of the whole, sometimes by inflexible decrees, sometimes by prudent compromises."[2]

99. *Remarkable Admissions of Protestant Writers.*

It is singular that these reflections of Bossuet are confirmed by the admissions of many Protestant writers, whom truth alone could have compelled to embrace on this point the opinion of a prelate justly regarded by them as the most formidable of their adversaries.[3] From many remarkable testimonies, we shall cite only that of a famous minister of our days, whose moderate opinions and candid admissions have made him justly estimable even in the eyes of Catholics. M. Hurter, in his History of Innocent III., fully admits the importance of a temporal jurisdiction, independent of all foreign influence, to secure the free exercise of the duties attached to the papacy. "The security," he says, "of the country and of the city, whence the sovereign pontiff was to watch over the preservation and interests of the Church in all other countries, was a condition indispensably required for

---

[1] We have seen above that Pepin and Charlemagne were not properly founders of the temporal sovereignty of the Holy See; but that they merely recognised and confirmed that sovereignty, already established in the pontificate of Gregory II. (See supra, ch. i. n. 36, 40, 46, &c.; ch. ii. n. 59, &c.)

[2] Œuvres de Bossuet, vol. xv. p. 529. This observation occurs again in a passage in the Defens. Declarat. (lib. i. sec. i. cap. xvi.), which we shall soon have occasion to cite. See also, in support of these reflections, some other testimonies cited by Feller, Catéch. Philos. (vol. iii. n. 511); Muzzarelli, Dissertation sur le Domaine temporel du Pape (pp. 33-42).

[3] In the Esprit de Leibnitz (12mo. vol. ii. p. 9, &c.), several remarkable passages occur on this subject. See also an extract from Hume, cited by Feller, ubi supra.

discharging the duties of so exalted a position. How, in truth, could the pope calmly survey and master so many complicated relations, give counsel and assistance, pronounce decisions on innumerable affairs of all the churches, watch over the extension of the kingdom of God, repel attacks against faith, speak boldly to kings and to nations, if he had no rest in his own house; if the conspiracies of the wicked forced him to concentrate on his own states the eye that should embrace the world, to fight in defence of his own safety and liberty, or to seek as a fugitive a retreat or protection from the stranger? Innocent knew from experience the dangers of such a situation."[1] "Had he not enjoyed this independence, the pope," M. Hurter adds in another place, "might soon become what the late emperor (Henry VI.[2]) had actually conspired to make him, a simple patriarch in the imperial court; and all Christendom would be delivered up to the caprices of that sovereign, as the Eastern Church already was delivered up to the caprices of the emperor of Constantinople."[3]

100. *Recent Experience in Support of these Observations—Wise Remonstrances of M. Emery with the Emperor Napoleon.*

The experience of our own times has more fully illustrated the truth of these reflections. Every one knows how much the Church had to suffer during the last years of Napoleon's reign, from his usurpation of the Roman states, and from the cruel captivity in which he kept the head of the Church. We cannot contemplate without horror the fatal consequences which would have resulted from those tyrannical measures, had not Providence soon after annihilated Napoleon's power. Abbé Emery had the courage to say so to the emperor himself, in respectful but energetic terms,

---

[1] Hurter, Hist. d'Innocent III. vol. ii. p. 216.

[2] Hurter himself explains a little higher up (p. 73) what he says of the project of the last emperor.

[3] Ibid. vol. i. p. 93. We seize with pleasure this opportunity of joining our voice to the merited praise given to M. Hurter by many Catholic writers, not merely for the extent of his research and erudition, but for what is far more precious, the spirit of honesty and candour which breathes, so to speak, in every page of his History of Innocent III. We shall only remark, that the author, not having been able to divest himself thoroughly of the prejudices in which he was educated, has allowed in the course of his work some assertions to escape him which grate harshly on Catholic ears. His singular sincerity will assuredly one day lead him to modify those assertions. See on this subject, Bibliog. Cathol. ann. 3, p. 295; L'Univ. Cathol. vol. xvi. p. 370, &c.

when interrogated by him in a session of the commission formed in 1811 for deliberating on the affairs of the Church. We take the details of this scene from the History of Pius VII. by M. Artaud de Montor, to whom we are indebted for so many valuable incidents illustrating the character and conduct of M. Emery in those difficult circumstances.[1]

The emperor, after having declaimed in the commission against the spiritual power of the pope, fell back, after some prudent reflections from M. Emery, and attacked the temporal power. "I do not dispute with you," he said, "the spiritual power of the pope, because he has received it from Jesus Christ; but Jesus Christ never gave him temporal power; Charlemagne gave it to him; and I, Charlemagne's successor, have resolved to take it from him, because he does not know how to use it, and because it prevents him from discharging his spiritual functions. M. Emery, what do you think of that?" "Sire," replied M. Emery, "your majesty respects the great Bossuet, and often cites him with pleasure. I can have no other opinion on the subject than that which Bossuet defends expressly in his Defence of the Declaration of the Clergy; namely, that the independence and perfect liberty of the head of the Church are necessary for the free exercise of his spiritual supremacy in our political system, such as it is, consisting of many different kingdoms and empires. I shall cite the passage literally, for I have carefully committed it to memory. Sire, these are Bossuet's words: 'We know that the Roman pontiffs and the sacerdotal order held by the concession of princes, and possess by the most legitimate titles, properties, rights, principalities (*imperia*), as other men possess them. We know that these possessions, as being dedicated to God, ought to be held sacred; and that without sacrilege they cannot be invaded, taken away, and given to laymen. The sovereignty of the city of Rome and other possessions have been given to the Apostolic See, that it might exercise with the greater liberty its power throughout the whole world. On this we congratulate not only the Apostolic See but also the universal Church; and, with all the ardour of our hearts, we pray that this sovereignty may ever remain, in all

---

[1] Supra, ch. i. n. 46, note 7.

respects, safe and inviolable.' "[1] Napoleon, after listening with patience, resumed in a gentle tone, as was his wont whenever he was openly contradicted: " I do not decline," he replied, " the authority of Bossuet; all that was true in his day, when Europe being under many masters, *it was not expedient that the pope should be the subject of any particular sovereign.* But what is the inconvenience of the pope being subject to me, now that I alone am master of Europe?" M. Emery was somewhat embarrassed, because he wished to avoid an answer which might be disagreeable to the emperor's personal pride. He merely replied, that possibly under the reign of Napoleon and of his successor the inconveniences predicted by Bossuet might not arise. He then added: " Sire, you know as well as I the history of revolutions; *what is now may not always be;* the inconveniences foreseen by Bossuet may again return. An order of things so wisely established ought not to be changed."[2]

[1] Bossuet, Defens. Declar. lib. i. § 1, cap. xvi. p. 273.

[2] Artaud, Hist. de Pie VII. 2nd edit. vol. ii. ch. xxii. p. 296.

CONFIRMATORY EVIDENCE.

ART. 40, 41, INTRODUCTION.

On the line of Policy adopted by Constantine and by the emperors his sons, with regard to idolatry.

ON this subject, there are two facts equally well attested by contemporary authorities, but which at first sight appear not easily reconciled. On the one hand Eusebius, and with him the most ancient ecclesiastical authors, expressly state that Constantine ordered the temples of the false gods to be closed, and prohibited all his subjects to offer idolatrous sacrifices.[1] On the other hand,

---

[1] Eusebius, Vita Const. lib. ii. cap. xlv.; lib. iv. cap. xxiii. xxv. Theodoret, Hist. Eccles. lib. v. cap. xxi. Sozomen, Hist. lib. iii. cap. xvii. Orosius, Hist. lib. vii. cap. xxviii. (tom. vi. Bibliothec. Patrum, p. 442).

In his fourth Memoir on the Pontificate of the Roman Emperors, M. de la Bastie gives an entirely different meaning to the first passage of Eusebius, which we have cited. He thinks that the law of which Eusebius speaks in that passage did not absolutely prohibit the exercise of idolatry, but only "whatever was most abominable in the worship of idols" (Mém. de l'Acad. des Inscriptions, vol. xxii. 12mo. edit. p. 378, &c.; vol. xv. 4to. edit.) M. Beugnot has adopted this interpretation in his Histoire de la Destruction du Paganisme en Occident (vol. i. p. 100). Supposing the truth of that exposition, the passage in question would refer solely to two laws published by Constantine in 319, against secret divination, as we have seen above (Introduc. n. 39). This exposition, however, which was first invented by M. de la Bastie, is generally rejected by critics (see the principal editions of Eusebius, particularly Heinichen's, Lipsiæ, 1830, 8vo. p. 115); nor can the text of Eusebius admit of it. The following are his words: "Afterwards, two laws were promulgated at the same time; the first prohibited *the abominations of idolatry* (τὰ μυσαρὰ τῆς εἰδωλολατρείας), previously practised both in the city and in the country." According to M. de la Bastie and M. Beugnot, these words of Eusebius, τὰ μυσαρὰ τῆς εἰδωλολατρείας, must not be taken in their unqualified signification, i. e. *abominable idolatry*, but, in a more restricted sense, for "whatever was most abominable in the worship of idols;" meaning exclusively the practice of secret divination. This interpretation cannot be admitted, we believe, by any critical Greek scholar. The generally received rules of syntax require, we are convinced, that the phrase used by Eusebius should be taken in the general sense (abominable idolatry); and that had he wished to restrict the prohibition to "the more abominable acts of idolatry," he would not have said τὰ μυσαρὰ τῆς εἰδωλολατρείας, but τὰ μυσαρώτερα, or μυσαρώτατα τῆς εἰδωλολατρείας. This is the opinion of a distinguished Hellenist, whom we have consulted on the passage; an opinion in strict conformity with the principles laid down on this point in the Greek Grammar by

Libanius states, not less formally, that, during the whole reign of Constantine, the pagans retained the use of their temples, and the free exercise of their worship.[1]

The difficulty of reconciling these contradictory statements has given great trouble to modern critics. Some defend the assertion of Eusebius in such a way, that they accuse Libanius of falsehood![2] others, preferring the assertion of Libanius, abandon altogether Eusebius and the ancient ecclesiastical authors who have followed him.[3] Others, again, believed that they could reconcile these statements either by softening down the expressions of Eusebius,[4] or by supposing that the prohibitory laws of Constantine against idolatry in general were not promulgated generally throughout all parts of the empire, or, at least, that they were not vigorously enforced in some places, and especially at Rome, where it would have been most difficult to carry them out.[5]

This last opinion appears to us the best for solving the difficulty; and, to illustrate it as fully as possible, we think that the three following positions can be established, which contain, we trust, a solution of all the objections that the question can give rise to.

I. It is certain that the public exercise of idolatry was tolerated both in the East and in the West by Constantine long after his conversion. This first point is hardly denied; and it is manifestly proved, first, by the unanimous testimony of both pagan and Christian authors, contemporaries of Constantine;[6] secondly, by the text of the laws published in 319 against secret divination;[7] and, thirdly, by many inscriptions of that epoch which prove that temples, statues, and altars were erected in honour of the false gods after the conversion of Constantine.[8]

Mathiæ (Paris, 1831-1842, 4 vols. 8vo. See tom. ii. §§ 320, 442). Moreover, this is not the only passage in which Eusebius states that Constantine issued a prohibition against idolatry in general; we have already cited two others, whose sense is not disputed.

[1] See supra, Introduction, p. 52, note 4.

[2] Godefroy, Comment. in Cod. Theod. lib. xvi. tit. x. n. 3.

[3] Quatrième Mémoire of M. de la Bastie, p. 378, &c. Beugnot, Hist. de la Destruc. du Paganisme en Occident, vol. i. pp. 98, 101, &c.

[4] H. de Valois, Notes on the different passages cited by us from Eusebius.

[5] Tillemont, Hist. des Empereurs, vol. iv. p. 203. Lebeau, Hist. du Bas-Empire, vol. i. book iv. n. 9.

[6] Eusebius, Vita Constan. lib. ii. cap. 56. Idem, Oratio ad Cœtum SS. cap. ii. See also the testimony of Libanius, cited in the Introduction, p. 52, note 3.

[7] Cod. Theod. lib. ix. tit. xvi. n. 1, 2. The text of these laws has been given above, p. 49, notes 1, 2.

[8] Beugnot, ubi supra, p. 106, &c.

II. Whatever be thought of the opinion that Constantine ever published a law prohibiting all his subjects the exercise of idolatry, it is a fact that idolatry continued to be exercised, at least in certain parts of the empire, and especially at Rome, during the whole reign of that prince. The testimony of Libanius [1] leaves no doubt on that fact, which is moreover confirmed by the unanimous testimony of ecclesiastical authors, who state that Constantine was the first that ordered the altar of Victory to be removed from the senate.[2]

III. There is every reason to believe that towards the close of his life Constantine promulgated a law prohibiting to all his subjects the exercise of idolatry.

This last position, about which alone any difficulty can be raised, appears to be established by positive testimonies, to which, in our opinion, no solid objection can be raised. First, the language of Eusebius on the point is so clear, that it does not appear susceptible of any other interpretation. He states and restates, in several passages of his Life of Constantine, that "this prince prohibited all his subjects in all parts of the Roman empire to enter the temples of the false gods, to erect statues, or to offer them sacrifices."[3] The most ancient ecclesiastical authors have also mentioned this general prohibition as an incontestable fact;[4] and there is no trace of any positive testimony to the contrary. The testimony of Libanius proves, it is true, that notwithstanding that general prohibition, the exercise of the pagan worship continued to be tolerated, at least in some parts of the empire; but such toleration is by no means incompatible with the fact of the general prohibition; for perhaps that prohibition was published only in certain parts of the empire, where it could be more easily enforced. It is certain, moreover, that among the Roman laws of that period many may be pointed out which were to be regarded merely as an expression of the personal wish of the head of the state, their enforcement being left to the discretion or the feelings of the local authorities;[5] and, especially with regard to the laws enacted by

---

[1] See note 2, supra, n. 40, Introduction. [2] Supra, n. 41, Introduction.

[3] Eusebius, Vita Constantini, lib. iv. cap. xxiii. xxv.

[4] See the works of Theodoret, Orosius, Sozomen, which we have cited above, p. 303, note 1.

[5] See Beugnot, ubi supra, pp. 138, 142. He cites, in support of his assertion, the laws promulgated by Constantine and Constantius against divination. These laws were, in fact, so feebly enforced, that it was frequently necessary to revive them. The persecuting edicts of the pagan emperors against Chris-

the first Christian emperors against idolatry, it is certain that it would not be always safe to enforce them rigorously at Rome, particularly where the ancient worship had still, both in the senate and in many distinguished families, numerous adherents whom it would not be prudent to offend.[1] The same state of things is found in the reign of Theodosius the Great, who enacted laws so severe, forbidding the people to enter the temples, to sacrifice victims, or to perform any act of pagan worship. Yet notwithstanding that express prohibition, it is certain, and now generally acknowledged, that the practice of idolatry was still tolerated for some time at Rome.[2]

Secondly, though the testimony of Eusebius and of the ancient ecclesiastical authors appears sufficient to prove the point in question, it can, moreover, be confirmed, we believe, by the text of the law published in 341 by the emperor Constantius, which we have cited above.[3] The emperor therein cites the example of Constantine in prohibiting absolutely all superstition and all sorts of sacrifices. If there be any obscurity or ambiguity in his language, it would be sufficiently cleared up by a law published by the emperor Constant not long after, prohibiting the demolition of pagan temples outside the walls of Rome. In that prohibition the emperor clearly supposes that *all pagan superstitions are prohibited.*[4]

---

tianity might also be cited. However severe these edicts were, they were not enforced with uniform rigour in all parts of the empire : at times they became so generally relaxed, that new edicts were required to stimulate the persecution. "It was by those revivals of oppression," as Bossuet observes, "that ecclesiastical historians count ten persecutions under ten emperors."—Bossuet, Hist. Univ. part i. an de J. C. 95 (Œuvres de Bossuet, vol. xxxv. p. 102).

[1] Beugnot, ubi supra, pp. 97, 151, 411, &c.

[2] Supra, n. 44, Introduction.

[3] Supra, n. 41, note 1, Introduction.

[4] It must be remarked, that even those Christian emperors who were most zealous for the Christian religion did not always think it advisable to demolish the pagan temples: frequently they believed it their duty to preserve them, either to consecrate them to the worship of the true God, or as an ornament for the cities, or for other motives of public interest. (See Godefroy, Comment. sur le Cod. Théod. vol. i. p. xxiii. book xv. tit. i. n. 36 ; book xvi. tit. x. n. 3, 25.) The holy fathers themselves were of opinion, that whenever these edifices were not an occasion of idolatry to the people, they should not be destroyed, but purified, and consecrated to the worship of the true God.—S. Greg. Naz. Epig. 226. S. Augustin. Epist. 47, ad Publicolam, Oper. tom. ii. S. Greg. Mag. Epist. lib. ii. ep. 76 (alias 71), (Oper. tom. ii.) In Beugnot's Hist. de la Destruction du Pagan. en Occident (vol. i. p. 259 ; vol. ii. p. 134, &c.), there is a very long list of the temples and oratories existing in Rome in the reigns of Valentinian I. and Honorius. But the author asserts, without authority, that under Valentinian I. "the greater number of the pagan temples in Rome were still dedicated to the service of the ancient worship" (vol. i. p. 268).

Some modern authors maintain that these two laws do not prohibit all pagan ceremonies indiscriminately, but only secret divination, described as *superstition*, a word which is always taken in a bad sense, and means, they say, unauthorized practices or ceremonies.[1] But this explanation, which was invented by some modern authors, as being indispensable for the support of their system,[2] appears evidently contrary to the literal and natural meaning of the word "superstition," as used in this law. It is, in fact, unquestionable that, in the language of the Christian emperors, as well as in that of all ecclesiastical authors, the word "superstition" means all pagan ceremonies generally. From the mass of authorities which might be cited in support of this assertion, we need produce only the first law of the emperor Constantine against secret divination: he there states expressly that those who wish to practise their *superstition* may do so in public.[3] In that passage the word "superstition" manifestly expresses not only the ceremonies of secret divination, but all pagan ceremonies in general.

From these observations, it appears that there are very slight grounds for the censures which M. Beugnot[4] passes on Eusebius, and on all ancient ecclesiastical authors, for attributing to Constantine the Great a general prohibition of idolatry. M. Beugnot had no doubt a fair right to propose his difficulties on the point, as so many other critics had done; but was it becoming to take so decisive and imperious a tone on a question which had hitherto been considered by them, and which still remains, so exceedingly doubtful?[5] He would have avoided these excesses and many other extravagances, if he had not adopted, as the basis of his work, a principle alike opposed to sound criticism, and to the example of the most enlightened historians; namely, that in order to write a good history of the fall of paganism, he should distrust Christian authors, and depend principally on the writings of their adversaries, and this, too, on the pretence that "we find in the former too much antipathy, prejudice, and hatred;"[6] as if pagan

---

[1] Quatrième Mémoire of M. de la Bastie, p. 383. Beugnot, ubi supra, pp. 100, 138, 139.

[2] M. de la Bastie was the first, as far as we are aware, to propose this explanation.

[3] Cod. Theod. lib. ix. tit. xvi. n. 1. The text of this law has been cited supra, n. 39, note 1, Introduction.

[4] Beugnot, ubi supra, pp. 98, 105, 107, &c.

[5] Heinichen, Notes on Eusebius, Vit. Constantin. lib. ii. cap. xlv. Lipsiæ, 1830, 8vo. p. 115.

[6] Beugnot, ubi supra, p. 4.

authors were not much more justly liable to such suspicions than Christians, in the opinion of all impartial and discerning critics.[1] "To refute this strange assertion," observes a judicious critic, "it is not necessary to make a long parallel between the historians of the two religions. Read the gravest, and apparently the most impartial of pagan historians, and say whether there is in Eusebius, or in Socrates, or in Sozomen, a single prejudice against paganism so bitter as those expressed by Tacitus against the Christians. He gives credit to popular rumours, to the most absurd calumnies, admitted as such by M. Beugnot himself, and by every sensible man. Have Christian historians reproached paganism, and especially its sacred mysteries, with a single abomination, whose existence is not demonstrated by pagan authorities themselves? On that question we may refer to M. Beugnot himself, and to the poets, orators, and historians of ancient times. What, then, are those prejudices of which he speaks? He is of opinion that at the epoch of the final struggle of paganism, 'it was supposed lawful to use against it something more than hatred.' Now, as history proves clearly the Christians never thought this *hatred* lawful, at least against individuals, and as they carried their toleration against errors as far as possible, even when defending truths highly calculated to inflame their zeal, what grounds are there for supposing that such men have been violently prejudiced historians? or, on the other hand, what grounds are there for supposing that the professors of a religion whose votaries had been during three centuries so unrelenting persecutors of the Church, and who afterwards remained so obstinate in their errors, are all oracles of truth, more faithful, more trustworthy? However strongly anxious to do so, we really cannot on this point reconcile our author's assertions either with themselves or with the facts which himself has not attempted to question."[2]

---

[1] See a review of M. Beugnot's work in the Ami de la Religion, ann. 1835, vol. lxxxvii. pp. 257, 305, 385, 465, 593; and in the Annales de la Philos. Chrétienne, ann. 1836, vol. xii. p. 7, &c. The judgment passed in these two publications on M. Beugnot's work has since been confirmed by a decree of the Congregation of the Index, July 4, 1837.

[2] L'Ami de la Religion, ibid. pp. 258, 260.

II.—Page 99.

On the value of Constantine's offerings to the principal churches of Rome and of the environs.

The difficulty of establishing on perfectly accurate principles the value of those offerings, and the great discrepancy of opinion on this subject among the learned, compel us to follow their example by proposing estimates merely approximative. A diligent perusal and collation of the authors who have already treated this subject has enabled us to correct, on some points, the estimates adopted by Fleury, and by many others who followed him, and to decide on one which, though not rigorously exact, is, at least, far more probable and more consistent.[1]

Agreeing with those authors who have studied the question most profoundly, we suppose, first, that under Constantine and his successors the Roman pound contained 12 ounces: secondly, that those 12 ounces were at most equal to 11 ounces of our *poids de marc:*[2] thirdly, that the pound of gold was in those days coined into 72 sous of gold: fourthly, that, according to information supplied at the Hôtel des Monnaies of Paris in the month of August, 1833, the price of the kilogramme of pure gold is 3,434 fr. 44 cent. (£137. 8s.); and of the kilogramme of pure silver, 218 fr. 88 cent. (£8. 15s. 3d.), which makes the actual price of a gold marc to be 840 fr. 60 cent. (£33. 13s.), and the price of the silver marc, 53 fr. 57 cent. (£2. 3s.):[3] fifthly, that, according to those

---

[1] The principal authors to be consulted on this subject are, Ducange, Glossarium Infimæ Latinit. verbis Libra, Uncia, Solidus, &c.; Leblanc, Traité Hist. des Monnaies de France, Paris, 1690, 4to.; Paucton, Métrologie, Paris, 1780, 4to.; Letronne, Considér. Génér. sur l'Evaluation des Monnaies Grecques et Romaines, Paris, 1817, 4to.; Idem, Eclaircissements Hist. faisant suite aux Œuvres de Rollin, Paris, 1825, 8vo. p. 1, &c.; Naudet, Des Changements opérés dans l'Administration de l'Empire, vol. ii. p. 319.

In the detail of our estimates we generally adopt Paucton's calculations, his work being much more complete than the others, and containing documents relating to all ages and countries. With regard to Greek and Roman coins, his valuations do not differ much from those of M. Letronne.

[2] According to Paucton, 12 Roman ounces were worth $10\frac{23}{24}$ ounces of French poids de marc; according to M. Letronne, they were equal to only $10\frac{3}{4}$ ounces; and according to Leblanc, to $10\frac{2}{3}$ ounces. To facilitate our calculations, without entering into an intricate, and not very useful discussion, we assume that the 12 Roman ounces were equal to 11 ounces French. All our calculations are based on this supposition.

[3] We assume as the basis of our valuations the price of pure gold and silver, whether there is question of ancient coins, or of works of art in gold or silver. Nevertheless, it is certain that the metal used in coins, and still more that used in works of art, was not always equally pure, but contained more or less of alloy. It being, however, impossible to determine the quantity of alloy in

principles, the golden sou was worth, under Constantine and his successors, about 16 fr. of French money (13s. 4d.).

These are the calculations according to which we have valued the different sums mentioned by Anastasius, whose text we have explained; and, summing up our estimates, we find, first, that the ornaments in gold and silver alone offered by Constantine to the church and the baptistery of Lateran were worth about 942 gold marcs, and 17,796 silver marcs: secondly, that the value of all those ornaments was more than 1,700,000 fr. (£45,500), the workmanship not included: thirdly, that the immoveable property given to the same church brought in an annual revenue of about 233,664 fr. (£9,345. 11s. 8d.): fourthly, in fine, that the possessions given to the other churches in Rome were worth 262,016 fr. annually (£10,480. 13s. 4d.).

There is a very considerable difference between this valuation and Fleury's.[1] According to him, the value of the gold and silver ornaments given to the church and baptistery of Lateran was one-fourth less; and the amount of annual revenue assigned to that church and to all the others which we have mentioned, one-half less than our valuation.

This difference between the two valuations arises both from the different readings in the work of Anastasius, and from the wrong principles on which Fleury appears to have made his calculation. We have already observed that he follows Labbe's edition of Anastasius, which differs on many points from the more correct editions of Bianchini and Muratori. He adopted, moreover, in his calculations, principles which we cannot admit, because even in his own day they were not correct, and, moreover, the price of gold and silver is very different now from what it was at that time.

Fleury assumes, first, that the Roman pound was equal to 12 ounces of French *poids de marc*: secondly, that in France, at the close of the seventeenth century, the gold marc was worth 450 livres Tournois, and the silver marc 30 livres: thirdly, that under

---

the metals used at different times, either for coins or for works of art, we are compelled to omit that item, and to assume the actual price of pure gold as the basis of all our calculation. This omission makes very little difference in the valuation of the ancient coins, which were of nearly the same material as in modern times. The difference is more considerable in the valuation of works of art, in which the quantity of alloy was both greater and more variable; but the error of our calculations, even here, in the valuation of gold and silver works of art, is nearly compensated for by the price of the workmanship, which we do not take into account at all.

[1] Fleury, Mœurs des Israël. n. 50. Hist. Eccl. vol. iii. book xi. n. 36.

the reign of Constantine and of his successors the gold sou was equal to 8 fr. 5 sous of present French money (6s. 10d.). In support of this valuation, Fleury cites the work of Leblanc; but he does not, we must say, follow precisely the principles of that author: whether from mistake or design, he abandons him on several points. Leblanc supposes, first, that the 12 ounces of the Roman pound were not equal to those of French *poids de marc*, but to only $10\frac{2}{3}$ of them:[1] secondly, that in 1689 the gold marc was 447 livres, 7 sous, 2 deniers Tournois; and the marc of fine silver 29 livres 7 sous:[2] thirdly, that under Constantine and his successors the gold sou was worth 8 livres, 7 sous, 10 deniers Tournois.[3] According to this valuation, we should adopt a lower estimate than that fixed by Fleury in his exposition of the text of Anastasius.

From this statement, it follows that the principal cause of the difference between our valuation and Fleury's is the variation in the price of gold and silver since the close of the seventeenth century. Many have explained the cause of these variations (so frequent in France as well as in other countries), and so necessary to be taken into account in reconciling or explaining the different authors, who in different ages have endeavoured to fix the value of ancient money compared with the money of their own day. On this subject the reader is referred to Leblanc's Traité Historique des Monnaies de France (Paris, 1690, in 4to.). At the close of that work, a detailed table is given of all those variations from the year 1113 to 1689. This table is continued to 1726, at the end of Abot de Bazinghen's Traité des Monnaies (Paris, 1764, 2 vols. in 4to.). For later times the reader may consult Paucton's Métrologie (pp. 333, 717, 939) and Corbaux's Dictionnaire des Arbitrages (2 vols. 4to. vol. i. p. 47, &c.). From these different works it appears that in 1689 the gold marc was worth 447 livres, 7 sous, 2 deniers Tournois; in 1692, 450 livres; in 1720, 600 livres; in 1726, 740 livres; in 1780, 793 livres 10 sous; in 1802, 828 livres 12 sous. The silver marc was worth, in 1689, 29 livres 7 sous; in 1706, 36 livres; in 1709, 40 livres; in 1720, 60 livres; in 1726, 51 livres 3 sous; in 1780, 54 livres 17 sous; in 1802, 53 livres 9 sous.

---

[1] Leblanc, Traité des Monnaies, p. 3.

[2] See the table at the end of Leblanc's work, already cited.

[3] Leblanc, ibid. p. 6.

III.—Page 114.

Of the 8,000 pounds of gold found in the treasury of St. John the Almoner's church.

This fact is recorded in the will of St. John the Almoner, preserved in his life, written by Leontius, a contemporary author, and by Simon Metaphrastes, who wrote about three centuries later.[1] According to the text of Leontius, the holy patriarch thanks God that at the hour of death he had only the third of a gold sou (*unus tremissis*); though, at his accession to the patriarchal see, he had found in the treasury of his church "about eighty centenaria of gold" (*circiter octaginta centenaria auri*). In place of these latter words, Metaphrastes reads "*circiter octo millia librarum auri*," which clearly implies that the *centenarium* of gold in the text of Leontius means 100 pounds of gold. Baronius has adopted the interpretation in his Annals.[2] In truth, it appears that these words, "*centenarium auri*" (κεντηναριον χρυσου), in the Latin and Greek writers of the middle ages always mean "a hundred pounds weight of gold."[3]

Adopting, therefore, Paucton's valuation of the Roman pound, and the value already assigned to a gold mark,[4] these 8,000 pounds of gold would be nearly equivalent to 11,000 marks of gold, that is, to 9,246,600 fr. (£369,864), a sum so enormous, that some authors have thence inferred that there must be some error either in Leontius's text, or in the interpretation given to it by Metaphrastes. Still, however amazing the sum mentioned by these two historians may appear, it will not be deemed incredible, when we remember the accounts preserved to us by profane history on the prodigious wealth of many ancient temples consecrated to celebrated gods. The treasures of Apollo's temple at Delphi, though so often rifled during the reign of Philip of Macedon, contained, at the time of the sacred war, which that prince undertook against the Phocians (about 350 years before Jesus Christ), a quantity of gold equivalent to more than 58,000,000 of francs (£2,320,000).[5] The gold

---

[1] Bollandus, Mens. Januar. vol. ii. pp. 515, 529.

[2] Baronius, Annales, ann. 620, n. 8.

[3] Ducange, Glossarium Infimæ Græcitatis, verbo Κεντηναριον; Glossarium Infimæ Latin. verbo Centenarium. Jac. Godefroy, Comment. in Cod. Theod. lib. xvi. tit. xxiii. n. 2.

[4] Supra, Confirmatory Evidence, p. 309.

[5] Supra, Introduction, n. 8.

ornaments alone in the temple of Jupiter Capitolinus at Rome, in the reign of Domitian, were worth, according to Plutarch, more than 12,000 talents, that is, more than 60,000,000 fr. (£2,400,000).[1] The treasure of the temple of Belus at Babylon was of equal value, according to Herodotus and Diodorus Siculus.[2] The great idea which ancient authors give us of the magnificence of many other celebrated temples in Greece, in Asia, and in the principal Italian cities, justifies us in assuming that their wealth was not inferior to that of those famous temples which we have mentioned.[3] But all of them were far surpassed by the temple of Jerusalem.[4] A vine in gold, adorning its columns and inner walls, which was carried off by Pompey about sixty years before Christ, was worth about 10,000 talents, that is, about £240,000. The treasures carried off from the temple by Crassus some years later were worth more than 100,000 talents, that is, about £2,400,000. Notwithstanding these losses, and many others, so great was still the quantity of gold in the temple at the time of its destruction, that in consequence of its pillage by the Romans, the price of gold and provisions fell one half in all Syria.[5] With these facts before us, can we wonder that the chief patriarchal see of the Eastern Church in the seventh century should have possessed a quantity of gold six times less than that in the temple of Delphi, and seven or eight

---

[1] Plutarch, Vita Publicolæ (p. 105, fol. edit. des Œuvres de Plutarque, Paris, 1624). Père Brotier, in his notes on Tacitus (Hist. lib. iv. cap. 53), values these 12,000 talents at 65,362,500 livres Tournois; but in Paucton's calculation they would amount to 72,000,000, as he makes the Attic talent equal to 6,000 drachms, or 6,000 livres Tournois.—Paucton, Métrologie, pp. 318, 366, 758.

[2] Herodotus, Hist. lib. i. cap. clxxxi. Diod. Siculus, Hist. lib. ii. n. 9. According to these authors, the wealth of the temple of Belus was about 6,300 Babylonian talents. On Paucton's valuation, the Babylonian talent was worth 7,500 Attic drachms, or 7,500 livres Tournois; the 6,300 Babylonian talents were worth 47,250,000 fr. (1,890,000*l.*).—Paucton, Métrologie, pp. 320, 359.

Rollin, in his Hist. Anc. (vol. ii. book iii. ch. i. § 2), estimates these talents at the enormous sum of 225,500,000 livres Tournois; Père Brotier, in his notes on Tacitus (4to. edit. vol. iv. p. 517), at 400,000,000; M. Letronne, in his notes on Rollin, at 662,000,000. It would be too tedious, and not very useful, to examine in detail the grounds of these different calculations, their result being, as M. Letronne observes, utterly incredible. M. Raoul Rochette, in his Cours d'Archéologie of 1835, adopts the sum of 54,000,000.—Annales de Philos. Chrét. vol. xi. p. 144.

[3] Père Brotier has collected curious information on this point, in his notes on Tacitus (4to. edit. vol. iv. pp. 476, 514); but some of these valuations need confirmation, especially those regarding the wealth of the temple of Belus.

[4] Brotier, Notes on Tacitus, vol. iv. pp. 549, 555, &c. 4to. edit.

[5] Joseph. De Bello Jud. lib. v. cap. v.; lib. vi. cap. xiii.

times less than that in the temple of Jupiter Capitolinus? Our supposition might, it is true, still appear improbable, if Leontius and Metaphrastes stated that all the quantity of gold was in coin; but we may suppose, without any violence to their texts, that it consisted principally of sacred vases, utensils, and other valuable things usually kept in church treasuries. Other contemporary accounts of the wealth of the Roman and Alexandrian churches corroborate our assertions.[1] The great authority enjoyed by these two churches, the extent of their jurisdiction, the considerable revenues possessed by them during many preceding centuries, their prodigious alms, all conspire to remove any suspicions of error or exaggeration in the statements of Leontius and of Metaphrastes.

These observations derive additional weight from a review of the conjectures offered by learned critics to correct the texts on the point in question. Fleury, D. Ceillier, Berault-Bercastel, and some others, suppose that they were 4,000 livres,[2] and not 8,000 pounds of gold; but they give no argument for this reduction, and we can discover none in its favour; for it manifestly contradicts the very text of the two authors whom it pretends to explain. Alban Butler supposes that they were not 8,000 pounds of gold, but 8,000 gold pieces.[3] This supposition seems as arbitrary and as groundless as the preceding. It is true that many centuries before John the Almoner, namely, under the reign of Heliogabalus, there was current in the Roman empire a gold coin called a "*centenarius aureus*," equivalent to 100 gold sous.[4] But the historian Lampridius, who mentions that money, states expressly that it was abolished by Alexander Severus, who issued an edict prohibiting its revival. Nor after the reign of that prince does any mention of that coin occur in history; whence the learned unanimously infer that in the Greek and Latin authors of the middle ages the "*centenarium auri*" always means a hundred pounds weight of gold, as Metaphrastes understood it in his interpretation of the text of Leontius.[5]

Some readers may perhaps propose to reduce those 8,000 pounds

---

[1] See details on this subject in our Introduction (art. ii. § 3). Similar details occur in the Lives of the Popes who succeeded St. Sylvester.

[2] Fleury, Hist. Eccl. vol. viii. book xxxvii. n. 12. D. Ceillier, Hist. des Auteurs Ecclés. vol. xvii. p. 608. Berault-Bercastel, Hist. de l'Egl. vol. iii. book xxi.

[3] Alban Butler, Lives of the Saints, January 30.

[4] Lamprid. Vita Alex. Severi, cap. xxxix. (vol. i. of the Collection, entitled Hist. Augustæ Script. Lugd. Batav. 1661, 8vo.).

[5] See notes by Casaubon, Salmasius, &c. on this passage of Lampridius.

of gold by supposing that Leontius and Metaphrastes do not mean the Roman pound of 12 ounces, but the Egyptian pound, which contained only 8 Roman ounces, that is, about $7\frac{1}{3}$ ounces of *poids de marc*. There certainly was this difference in the first ages of the Roman empire between the Roman pound and the Egyptian pound.[1] But there is no evidence that this difference was retained after the reign of Constantine; at least, we know no author who mentions it, nor any person having applied it to solve the difficulty in question. The learned generally assume that the pound weight mentioned in the Greek and Latin authors of the middle ages is always the Roman pound. This is also the opinion of a learned academician whom we have consulted on this question.

IV.—Page 118.

On the value of the three talents and a half of gold, the annual revenue taken from the Roman Church by Leo the Isaurian.

To fix the value of the three talents and a half of gold mentioned here by Theophanes, we must observe,

1st. That, according to the style of the Greek authors of the middle ages, the word "talent" is sometimes taken for the 100 pounds of gold;[2] sometimes for 1 pound of gold, as Ducange observes in a note on the Alexiad of Anna Comnena (p. 400); sometimes for a gold coin called a sou, a solidus, or besant.[3] In confirmation of these different significations, the reader may consult Ducange's Lexicon Infimæ Græcitatis, art. Τάλαντον, and his Dissertation on the Coins of the Middle Ages (No. 81), appended to his Glossarium Infimæ Latinitatis.

2nd. We have already seen,[4] that under Constantine and his successors, the pound of gold contained 12 ounces, which were nearly equivalent to 11 of French *poids de marc*. We have also seen that the pound of gold was divided at that time into 72 gold sous. A pound of gold was then worth about £48, and the gold sou about 13s. 4d., assuming, as we did, that the marc of pure gold is at present worth £33. 12s. 8d.

3rd. It is utterly impossible that Theophanes used the word

---

[1] Paucton, Métrologie, pp. 276, 303.

[2] Theophanes, Chronogr. ann. 9 Niceph. p. 414

[3] Ibid. ann. 1 Michael. Curopal.

[4] Confirmatory Evidence, No. 2, p. 309.

"talent" in this passage for one pound of gold, much less for one gold sou. For is it not incredible that the patrimonies of the Roman Church in Sicily and Calabria, which were considerable even in the time of Gregory the Great, would have been worth to his successors a century later only three pounds and a half of gold, that is, about £160. 16s.? Hence no one author, to our knowledge, understands the word "talent" in that passage of Theophanes in the sense of one pound of gold.

4th. There is, therefore, every reason to believe that "talent" in the passage cited means 100 pounds of gold, and that, consequently, the 3½ talents of gold were worth about 350 pounds of gold, that is, 404,530 fr. (£16,181. 4s.).

This calculation is confirmed, we believe, by P. Zaccaria, in his Dissertation on the Ancient Patrimonies of the Roman Church.[1] According to him, the 3½ talents of gold mentioned by Theophanes were worth, in 1781, 35,000 gold Roman sequins, that is, about 386,000 fr. (£15,440), on Paucton's estimate, that the sequin was then worth 11 fr. 4 cents, about 9s. 2½d.[2]

We must observe that Fleury computes the value of these 3½ talents of gold so low as 224,000 livres Tournois, and Lebeau at only 20,200 livres.[3] We have already seen, that when Fleury was writing, the marc of gold was one half less in value than at the present day.[4] As to Lebeau's calculation, we cannot see any argument for it; it is probable that the reading 20,000 livres in his text ought to be 200,000, an amount not differing much from Fleury's.

---

[1] Zaccaria, De Rebus ad Hist. et Antiq. Eccles. pertinentibus, tom. ii. Dissert. x. cap. ii. n. 9.

He merely follows on this point an opinion common among learned authors long before his time. See, among others, Nic. Alamanni, De Parietinis Lateranensibus, cap. xv. (p. 112, Roman edit. 1756, 4to.); Bianchini, Vitæ Roman. Pontif. tom. ii. p. 301; Cenni, Monumenta Domin. Pontif. tom. i. p. 13; tom. ii. p. 10. See also a note by this last author on chap. ii. of Orsi's work, Della Origine del Dominio e della Sovranita de' Roman. Pontef. (Romæ, 1788, 8vo. p. 19).

[2] Paucton, Métrologie, p. 865.

[3] Fleury, Hist. Eccl. vol. ix. book xlii. n. 17. Lebeau, Hist. du Bas-Empire, vol. xiii. book lxiii. n. 59.

[4] Confirmatory Evidence, No. 2, p. 309.

V.—Page 181.

On Constantine's donation to the Church of Rome.[1]

Constantine's donation, according to the edition of it preserved in the principal collections of the councils, is a formal deed whereby that prince concedes for ever to the Holy See the city of Rome, together with Italy and all the provinces of the empire of the West. The Latin text of this deed is taken from the collection of False Decretals, commonly attributed to Isidorus Mercator, and published, according to the more general opinion, in the ninth century, not long after the death of Charlemagne.[2] The Greek fragments of the same deed, which are appended to the Latin text in the collections of the councils, are taken from a commentary on the Nomocanon of Photius, compiled about the close of the twelfth century by Theodore Balsamon, patriarch of Antioch.[3]

After this deed had been inserted in the collections of the False Decretals, it was cited by a great many authors, who never suppose that there was the least reasonable doubt of its authenticity. It was first cited by two French authors; Æneas, bishop of Paris, in a Treatise against the Greeks, composed about the year 867;[4] and

[1] This deed is printed in Labbe's Collection des Concil. tom. i. p. 1530. For critical discussions on it, see Nat. Alexander, Dissert. 25, in Hist. Eccl. sæc. iv.; De Marca, De Concordiâ Sacerdotii et Imp. lib. iii. cap. xii.; Baronii Annales, ann. 324, n. 18, &c.; ann. 1191, n. 52, &c.; Morin, Hist. de l'Origine et des Progrès de la Puissance Temp. des Papes, fol.; D. Ceillier, Hist. des Auteurs Ecclés. vol. iv. p. 177; vol. viii. p. 145, &c.; Cenni, Monumenta Dominat. Pontif. tom. i. pp. 304-307; Zaccaria, De Rebus ad Hist. Eccl. pertinent. tom. ii. Dissert. x. cap. ii. n. 4, 5; Tillemont, Hist. des Empereurs, vol. iv. p. 142; Fleury, Hist. Eccl. vol. xvi. Discourse 4, n. 9; Recueil de Pièces d'Histoire et de Littérature (by the Abbé Granet and P. Desmolets), vol. ii. p. 137, &c.; Billuart, De Jure et Justitiâ, Digressio Historica, ad calcem Dissertationis.

[2] The most complete edition of the False Decretals is given in Merlin's Collectio Concil. tom. i. Paris, 1524, 2 vols. fol. The same edition was reprinted with some changes in Crabbe's Collection of Councils, Cologne, 1551, 3 vols. fol. Constantine's donation is given in both those editions. We know not why it has been suppressed in the edition of the False Decretals, subsequently published with the title Epistolar. Decretal. quæ vetustissimis Rom. Pontif. tribuuntur Examen, adversus Isidorum Mercatorem, Genevæ, 1635, 4to. For these bibliographical details the reader may consult Bibliothèque Choisie de Livres de Droit (n. 1664, 1715), appended to the Lettres sur la Profession d'Avocat, by Camus, 2 vols. 8vo.

[3] Theod. Balsamon, Scholium in Photii Nomocanonem, tit. vii. cap. i. (Justell. Biblioth. Juris Can. Veteris, tom. ii. p. 929).

[4] Æneas, Tract. adv. Græcos, quæst. 6, n. 209 (tom. vii. Spicilège de d'Achery, 4to.; tom. i. fol.). The passage referred to is cited in the Hist. de l'Eglise Gallicane, vol. vi. ann. 867, p. 200. See also Fleury, Hist. Eccl. vol. xi. book li. n. 14.

Hincmar of Rheims, in a Letter to the French Barons, written about the year 882.[1] Though neither of these authors cites the words of this document, they manifestly suppose its existence; and the former states that copies of it were preserved in the libraries of several French churches. Pope Leo IX. cites long extracts from it in his letter to Michael Cerularius, patriarch of Constantinople, in 1054, in order to establish against the Greeks the spiritual and temporal jurisdiction of the Holy See.[2] St. Peter Damian also cites some extracts from it in his Synodal Discussion, compiled about the year 1062.[3] Long passages from it are also found in a collection of canons, compiled about the same time by St. Anselm of Lucca; and also in the Decreta of Ivo of Chartres, and of Gratian, which appeared in the course of the following century.[4]

There are, nevertheless, reasons to believe, that though Constantine's donation was so confidently cited by those authors, its authority was not universally admitted; for it is not mentioned by many authors of the tenth and eleventh centuries, who could neither be ignorant of its existence, nor omit citing it, had they believed that its authenticity was unquestionable.[5] Even Gregory VII. himself does not cite it in many of those letters in which he collects so carefully all the arguments and authorities in favour of the extraordinary power which he claimed over sovereigns.

From these preliminary historical statements, three principal questions arise regarding this singular document. First, Is it authentic? Second, When and by whom was it forged? Third, How could it have so long enjoyed so great authority? We shall briefly discuss each of these questions.

FIRST QUESTION.

Is Constantine's donation authentic?

The insertion of this document in the Decreta of Ivo of Chartres, and of Gratian, naturally invested it with very great authority.[6]

---

[1] Hincmar, Epist. 14 ad Proceres Regni, de Institutione Carlomanni Regis, n. 13 (Oper. tom. ii.). This fragment is cited by N. Alexander, ubi supra, art. 2.

[2] Leonis IX. Epist. ad Michaelem Patriarcham C. P. n. 13 (Labbe, Concil. tom. ix. p. 954, &c.). Fleury, Hist. Eccl. vol. xiii. book lx. n. 2.

[3] S. Petri Damiani Opera, tom. iii. Opuscul. 4, p. 23 (Labbe, Concil. tom. ix. p. 1156). Fleury, Hist. Eccl. vol. xiii. book lx. n. 49.

[4] Ivo of Chartres, Decretum, part. 5, cap. xlix. Gratian, Corpus Juris, Distinct. 96.

[5] See details on this subject in the second part of this work, ch. iii. n. 173.

[6] The principal authors who controverted at this time the old opinions, are

From that period until the revival of learning in the fifteenth century, we find it generally admitted as authentic. But about the middle of that century many learned authors discovered that it was spurious, and proved their opinion by conclusive arguments. Thenceforward Constantine's donation was generally admitted to be apocryphal. Its spuriousness is, in truth, conclusively demonstrated not only by historical testimony, but still more by the silence of all authors anterior to the eighth century, and by many intrinsic evidences of forgery.[1] In another place, the first of those arguments has been stated in sufficient detail; it remains for us to state briefly the two others.

I. The silence of all authors anterior to the eighth century is of itself conclusive evidence against the authenticity of this document. No positive testimony of its existence can be cited earlier than the eighth century. Before that date, it is never mentioned even by those authors who should have best known it, and whom the subject of their works would have compelled to mention it, had they known it. Eusebius the historian, a contemporary of Constantine, and most diligent in collecting all the proofs of the respect and generosity of that great prince towards the Church, never even once alludes in any way to this pretended donation. Neither is it mentioned in any collections of canons compiled before the False Decretals, though these collections contain details much less important on the power and prerogatives of the clergy in temporal matters.[2] Moreover, Constantine's pretended donation is passed over in silence by many authors of the eighth and ninth centuries, who should have known and cited it, had they believed it authentic. Anastasius the Librarian never alludes to it in his Life of St. Silvester, which was compiled from another life much more ancient, and in which Constantine's liberality to the Roman Church is recorded in minute detail.[3] The same silence is observable in all the letters written about the year 865 to the emperor Michael by Pope Nicholas I., in which that pope collects *ex professo* all that could

---

Laurentius Valla, canon of St. John Lateran; Æneas Sylvius, afterwards Pope Pius II.; Jerome Paul, canon of Barcelona, and chamberlain to Alexander VI.; and Cardinal de Cusa. A detailed notice of their writings may be seen in the Dissertation of Nat. Alexander, already cited, art. 2.

[1] See the first part of our Inquiry, ch. i. n. 7, &c.

[2] Most of those ancient collections are given in Justell. Bibliothec. Jur. Can. Vet. tom. i.

[3] Some of these details are given by Fleury, Mœurs des Chrétiens, n. 50; Hist. Eccl. vol. iii. book xi. n. 36.

exalt in the estimation of the Greeks the dignity of the Holy See.[1]

II. An attentive inspection of the document itself reveals many intrinsic evidences of its spuriousness. A few of the principal ones shall be briefly pointed out.

First. The date of the document is false: it is dated "the third of the calends of April, Constantine being then consul for the fourth time with Gallicanus." Now, we know from history that Constantine, in his fourth consulate (A.D. 315), had Licinius, and not Gallicanus, as his colleague.[2]

Second. The author of the document mentions five patriarchal churches, including Jerusalem, which did not obtain that dignity until after the death of Constantine; and Constantinople, which was not at all in existence at that date, viz. the fourth consulate of Constantine in 315.[3]

Third. In the heading of that document Constantine is entitled Fidelis, Tranquillus, Beneficus, Alamannicus, Gothicus; and several other titles are attributed to him which he never assumed in his authentic decrees. In the latter, his sole style was either Augustus, or Victor, or the Very Great Augustus. At the close of this document, also, he is called Clarissimus, a style never used to emperors or princes of the empire, but to senators, to consuls, to governors of provinces, and to some other inferior dignitaries.[4]

Fourth. It gives Pope Silvester the title of Father of Fathers, and of Universal Pope, styles which were totally unknown at that time.

Fifth. In fine, it mentions the baptism of Constantine, though Constantine was not yet baptized (in 315), even in the opinion of those authors who maintain that he was baptized at Rome. Many other intrinsic evidences of the spuriousness of this document may be seen in the writers who have discussed the question at greater length.[5]

---

[1] Epistol. Nicolai Papæ ad Michæl. Imp. (Labbe, Concil. tom. viii. pp. 293, 326, &c.). Fleury gives an analysis of those letters, Hist. Eccl. vol. xi. book i. n. 41. D. Ceillier, Hist. des Auteurs Ecclés. vol. xix. p. 166, &c.

[2] See the Chronologie des Consuls, in the Art de Vérifier les Dates, Dictionnaire de Moreri (art. Consuls); Dictionnaire Historique de Feller, &c.

[3] On the origin of the patriarchates of the East, see note 3, supra, n. 113, Part 1.

[4] See in Godefroy's Comment. sur le Cod. Théod. the different passages indicated in the general Index Rerum, voce Clarissimi.

[5] See especially N. Alexander's Dissertation, art. i. prop. 1.

SECOND QUESTION.

When and by whom was Constantine's donation forged?

Though this document is unquestionably spurious, it would be difficult to determine with precision the date of its fabrication. M. de Marca, Muratori, and other learned critics, are of opinion that it was composed in the eighth century, before the reign of Charlemagne. Muratori, moreover, thinks it probable that it may have induced that monarch and Pepin to be so generous to the Holy See.[1] Natalis Alexander, D. Ceillier, Père Zaccaria, and many others, think it more probable that it was fabricated in the ninth century by the author of the False Decretals, or by some of his contemporaries.[2] Baronius, Binius, and others, assign to it a much more recent date; they hold that it was fabricated after the tenth century by some Greek author, through hatred of the Church of Rome.[3]

Without pretending to decide who was the author of this document, or when it was fabricated, we think we may confidently venture the three following assertions, which appear to be sanctioned by the majority of critics:—

I. *The opinion which assigns the fabrication of this document to a date subsequent to the Greek schism, is justly abandoned by all modern critics.*[4]

First. That opinion is clearly refuted by history, and by the very text of the document itself. It must have existed before the Greek schism, because it is cited by many authors of the ninth century, and it was included in the collection of the False Decretals, certainly published before the middle of that century.[5]

Second. The advocates of the opinion which we are now refuting suppose, without any grounds, that this document is opposed to

---

[1] De Marca, De Concordiâ Sacer. et Imp. lib. iii. cap. xii. n. 3, 5. Muratori, Piena Esposizione dei Diritti Imperiali sopra la Citta di Comachio, p. 26. Muratori is cited and followed in this point by Daunou (Essai Hist. sur la Puissance Temporelle des Papes, vol. ii. p. 39). P. Thomassin (Ancien. et Nouv. Discipline, vol. iii. book i. ch. xxix. n. 9), P. Longuevalle (Hist. de l'Eglise de France, ann. 754, book iv. p. 376), appear favourable to this opinion.

[2] Nat. Alexander, Dissert. ubi supra, art. 3. D. Ceillier and Zaccaria, ubi supra.

[3] Baronii Annales, ann. 324, n. 18. Notes of Binius on Constantine's Donation, in Labbe's Collection des Concil. vol. i. p. 1539.

[4] On this point, see especially De Marca, ubi supra, and Nat. Alexander, Dissert. art. 3.

[5] See the authors cited supra, p. 318.

the primacy of the Holy See; on the contrary, it expressly acknowledges that primacy as founded by Jesus Christ himself, and as having been the principal motive of Constantine's liberalities to the Roman Church.[1]

Third. It is utterly improbable that the Greeks, so rancorously opposed to the Roman Church after the schism of Photius, would have forged a document so favourable to the Holy See, and attributing to it prerogatives so great in the temporal and in the spiritual order.

II. *The opinion which maintains that this document was fabricated before the ninth century is unsupported by any proof, and entirely improbable.*[2]

This second assertion may be established by demonstrating the weakness of the arguments urged by the advocates of the contrary opinion.

Their principal argument is founded on a letter written to Charlemagne about the year 777 by Pope Adrian I., in which, they contend, that pope alludes to Constantine's donation. To induce the king of France to protect the Holy See against the Lombards, and to compel the restoration of the cities and territories which they had taken from the Roman Church, the pope reminds the king of the example of Constantine, who, "under the pontificate of St. Silvester, had so much exalted the Roman Church, and made it so powerful in Italy."[3]

An attentive perusal of this passage will, we are convinced, prove satisfactorily that it by no means implies the existence of Constantine's donation, such as it appears in the False Decretals, and in later collections. The pope merely states in his letter that Constantine had given great power to the Church of Rome in Italy;

---

[1] "Justum quippe est," says the emperor in this act, "ut ibi lex sancta caput teneat principatûs, ubi sanctarum legum institutor, Salvator noster, beatum Petrum apostolatûs obtinere præcepit cathedram. . . . Ubi principatus sacerdotum, et Christianæ religionis caput, ab imperatore cœlesti constitutum est, justum non est ut illic imperator terrenus habeat potestatem."—Labbe, Concil. vol. i. p. 1535 A, and 1538 C.

[2] See the authors cited, note 2, p. 321; also Cenni, Monumenta Domin. Pontif. tom. i. p. 304, &c.

[3] "Sicut temporibus B. Silvestri, Romani pontificis, à sanctæ recordationis piissimo Constantino magno imperatore, per ejus largitatem, sancta Dei catholica et apostolica, Romana ecclesia elevata atque exaltata est, et potestatem in his Hesperiæ partibus largiri dignatus est; ita et in his vestris felicissimis temporibus atque nostris, sancta Dei ecclesia, id est, B. Petri apostoli, germinet atque exultet, et ampliùs atque ampliùs exaltata permaneat."—Cod. Carol. Epist. 59 (alias 49). Cenni, Monumenta, tom. i. pp. 305, 352. Labbe, Concil. tom. vi. p. 1763.

and, in effect, history informs us that Constantine, who was so generous to all the bishops, was particularly so to the Holy See, and endowed it with numerous patrimonies.[1] This fact, which is generally admitted by historians, is abundantly sufficient to explain what *the power* was to which Pope Adrian referred; nor is there the least reason to suppose in *that power* any allusion to the exorbitant donation which afterwards appeared in the collection of the False Decretals. We might even go farther, and prove that such allusion is not only groundless, but utterly improbable, and opposed to the very words of the letter objected to us; for in Constantine's pretended donation he is represented as expressly declaring "that he concedes for ever to Pope Silvester and to his successors not only the Lateran palace, but the city of Rome, with all the cities and provinces of Italy and the Western regions."[2] Now if Pope Adrian, when writing the letter objected to us, had known this pretended donation as a genuine document, and alluded to it, how could he intimate clearly in that same letter that the properties of the Holy See in Italy had been conferred on her "gradually by Constantine and his successors, whose deeds of donation were still preserved in the archives of the palace of Lateran?"[3] Before we venture to impute so strange a contradiction to Pope Adrian, some express testimony should be produced, which certainly is not found in the passage objected to us from his letter.

Some advocates of the opinion which we are refuting reason

---

[1] See details on this subject in the Introduction to this work, art. 2. n. 73, &c.

[2] "Pro quibus [beneficiis a Deo acceptis], dedimus ipsis sanctis apostolis ac dominis meis Petro et Paulo, ac per ipsos beato Silvestro, patri nostro, summoque pontifici, et universali urbis Romæ papæ, omnibusque ejus successoribus summis pontificibus, qui ad mundi usque consummationem in cathedrâ beati Petri sedebunt, atque impræsentiarum tradimus; primùm quidem *imperiale palatium nostrum Lateranense*, quod præter omnia quæ in orbe terrarum sunt palatia in primis honoratur atque excellit. . . . . Quin et *Romanorum urbem, totamque Italiam*, et *occidentalium regionum provincias, loca, civitates*, sæpe jam dicto Silvestro, universali papæ, tradentes ac cedentes, hujus et successorum ipsius summorum pontificum auctoritate ac sententiâ, divino nostro hoc pragmatico decreto, administrari diffinimus, juri sanctæ Romanorum Ecclesiæ subjicienda, et in eo permansura exhibemus."—Donatio Constant. (Labbe, Concil. tom. i. p. 1530, &c.).

[3] After the words cited above (note 3, p. 322), Pope Adrian continues thus: "Sed et cuncta alia, quæ per diversos imperatores, patricios etiam, et alios Deum timentes, pro eorum animæ mercede, et veniâ delictorum, in partibus Tusciæ, Spoleto, seu Benevento, atque Corsicâ, simul et Sabinensi patrimonio, beatro Petro apostolo, sanctæque Dei et apostolicæ Romanæ Ecclesiæ concessa sunt, et per nefandam gentem Longobardorum, per annorum spatia, abstracta atque ablata sunt, vestris temporibus restituantur; unde et plures donationes in sacro nostro scrinio Lateranensi reconditas habemus, etc."—Adriani I. Epist. 59 (Cenni, ubi supra, pp. 305, 353).

from the fact that Pepin himself appears to suppose Constantine's donation, by demanding from the Lombards, as *restitution* due to the Holy See, the cities and territories which he himself subsequently conferred on it.[1] But it is certain that Pepin could claim these provinces as *restitution* due to the Roman Church, without supposing Constantine's donation; for, independently of that donation, the pope could then be considered as legitimate sovereign of those provinces which had voluntarily submitted to his authority in the state of abandonment to which they had been reduced. This assertion has been proved elsewhere by a simple exposition of the facts connected with the origin of the temporal sovereignty of the Holy See.[2]

III. *All evidences concur in proving that the donation was fabricated in the ninth century.*[3]

This third assertion follows naturally from the preceding; for, on the one hand, it seems unquestionable that no allusion to this document appears in history before the ninth century; and, on the other hand, it certainly was published among the False Decretals,[4] which were compiled, according to the more common opinion, in the ninth century, some years after the death of Charlemagne.

With regard to the author of this deed of donation, or his motives in forging it, we cannot hazard any conjecture; we shall only state briefly those proposed by other learned men. Some attribute it to the author of the False Decretals; others think that he borrowed it from some contemporary author.[5] The object of the fabricator, according to some, was to bring the imposing authority of Constantine against the pretensions of the Greek emperor on Italy and the other Western provinces which had shaken off their yoke.[6] M. de Marca even supposes that the author of the fabrication acted in concert with the pope and the king of France.

On a question so obscure, innumerable conjectures could, of course, easily be started; but they are all manifestly gratuitous. The last, in particular, appears to us utterly improbable. What probability is there that the French monarchs would have patro-

[1] Muratori, ubi supra. Hist. de l'Egl. Gall. ubi supra.

[2] See part i. of our Inquiry, n. 34, 40, &c.

[3] See works, already cited, of Nat. Alexander, D. Ceillier, Cenni, and P. Zaccaria.

[4] The opinion of D. Ceillier and of Cenni.

[5] The conjecture of P. Zaccaria.

[6] The conjecture of P. de Marca, and of P. Zaccaria.

nized a fraud, which, by investing the pope with all the provinces of the Western empire, made them all, France herself included, tributaries and even feudal subjects of the Holy See? What probability is there that the pope and the king of France should have promoted the fabrication of so extraordinary a document, to refute Greek pretensions, which could so easily be disposed of by other arguments?[1] What probability is there, in fine, that such a fraud should have been practised by princes like Charlemagne and Pepin, and by contemporary popes, whom history represents to us as men distinguished alike for eminent virtues and even saintly characters?

These observations are more than sufficient to expose the improbability of those conjectures, and consequently the injustice of many modern writers, who made these conjectures the pretext for their censures on the conduct of the popes of the eighth and ninth centuries; sometimes representing Constantine's pretended donation as the original basis of the temporal power of the Holy See,[2] sometimes openly accusing the popes of having been themselves the authors or the abettors of this fraud.[3] These accusations are the more rash, as, in the more general opinion of the learned, the pretended donation was fabricated after the reign of Charlemagne, and consequently after the establishment of the temporal power of the Holy See.

THIRD QUESTION.

How could this donation of Constantine enjoy so great authority during many centuries?

The document, then, being manifestly spurious, it is no doubt surprising that it could have enjoyed so great credit during many centuries; nevertheless, this surprise must diminish considerably when we reflect on the great temporal power possessed by the Holy See at the period of the publication of the document and during the following centuries. The pope was then exercising extensive temporal power not only in Italy, but in most of the Catholic states of Europe, by the ascendancy which his temporal

[1] See the first part of this Inquiry, ch. ii. art. 1.

[2] Bernardi, De l'Origine et des Progrès de la Législation Française, book ii. ch. vii. Daunou, Essai Historique, vol. i. p. 14; tom. ii. p. 67.

[3] De Héricourt, Lois Ecclésiastiques de France, part iv. edit. 1771, p. 180, note. Bernardi, ubi supra.

sovereignty, combined with the sacred character of his office, gave him in the estimation of princes and people. After the ninth century, this power insensibly increased to such an extent that the pope was generally regarded as the supreme judge of all Catholic sovereigns, many of whom expressly acknowledged themselves feudatories of the Holy See. It is manifest that in such circumstances, and at a time when historical criticism was so much neglected, Constantine's supposed donation must have obtained great credit. The traditional memory of that great prince's generosity to the Church, and the high estimate generally formed of his munificence, would naturally prepare men to believe that the whole temporal power of the Holy See was derived originally from this deed of donation.[1]

Moreover, it may be useful to observe here, that the consequences of the error of the middle ages on this point have been vastly exaggerated by modern writers. Fleury and many others suppose that on this error alone was grounded the grant of the isle of Corsica to the church of Pisa by Pope Urban II. in 1092,[2] as well as the grant of Ireland to Henry II. by Pope Adrian in 1156;[3] and the grant of the Canary Islands to Prince Louis of Spain by Pope Clement VI. in 1344.[4] All these suppositions, however, are very far from being unquestionable. Corsica, as it has been elsewhere observed, was part of the states *granted*, or rather restored, to the Holy See by Charlemagne;[5] and Gregory VII. supposes it as a notorious fact that the Holy See had retained down to his pontificate its ancient rights over that island.[6] We have also proved that Adrian IV. did not assume (as feudal lord—Ed.) to dispose of Ireland in favour of the king of England.[7] Of the grant of the Canaries to Prince Louis of Spain, it is enough to observe, that it was not a donation properly so called, but a decision by way of arbitration, in which the pope expressly declares that he does not intend to prejudice the existing rights of any person whatsoever.[8] This decision must be explained in the same sense as that of Pope Alexander VI. relating to cer-

---

[1] In support of these reflections, see Thomassin, Anc. et Nouv. Discipline de l'Egl. vol. i. book i. ch. v. n. 14.

[2] Fleury, Hist. Eccl. vol. xiii. book lxiv. n. 8.

[3] Ibid. vol. xv. book lxx. n. 16.

[4] Ibid. vol. xx. book xcv. n. 24.

[5] Supra, part i. n. 46.

[6] Gregorii VII. Epistol. lib. v. epist. 4.

[7] Infra, part ii. ch. iii. n. 203.

[8] Raynaldi Annales, ann. 1344, n. 39, &c.

tain islands and territories recently discovered in Africa and America.[1]

VI.—Page 236.

On some Circumstances relating to Charlemagne's Coronation in 800.

There are some difficulties raised about the history of Charlemagne's coronation in the year 800, which it may be well to discuss briefly in this place.

1. The first is "the royal unction given at that time to one of Charlemagne's sons," according to Anastasius. The majority of modern authors suppose that it was Pepin, king of Italy, and not Charles, eldest son of Charlemagne, who received the regal unction on this occasion from the pope. But the opinion which we adopt seems to be solidly established by M. de Bréquigny, in his Historical Inquiry on the Life of Charles, eldest son of Charlemagne.[2] The learned academician relies principally on a letter of Alcuin, addressed to "the young king Charles," which commences in the following strain: "I have learned that the pope, with the consent of the most excellent Lord David,[3] has conferred on you the title of 'king,' placing on your head the crown which symbolizes that dignity. I rejoice exceedingly for the honour which you have received, not only by the title but by the power attached to it."[4]

This clear passage helps to explain or correct the expressions of some ancient authors, who seem to suppose that it was on Pepin the pope conferred the regal unction on this occasion. That opinion, however, besides being irreconcilable with the statement of Alcuin, is, moreover, in itself exceedingly improbable; for, as early as the year 781, Charlemagne had certainly succeeded in having his two sons crowned by Pope Adrian I.—Pepin, as king of Italy, and Louis, as king of Aquitaine;[5] while Charles, his eldest son, though styled by many authors king after the year 800, is never styled so before that time.

It may be asked, what could have been Charlemagne's motive

---

[1] Infra, part ii. ch. iii. n. 221, &c.

[2] Mémoires de l'Académie des Inscriptions, 4to. edit. vol. xxxix. p. 617.

[3] The name commonly given to Charlemagne by Alcuin; he never styles him otherwise in his letters.

[4] Alcuini Opera, tom. ii. edit. Ratisbon, 1777.

[5] See Hist. Eccl. Fleury; l'Hist. de l'Eglise Gal.; les Annales du Moyen Age; and all the other historians, on this event, under the date 781.

for withholding so long from his eldest son a title which he had long before conferred on his other two sons? M. de Bréquigny suggests, very plausibly, that before Charlemagne became emperor, he did not think it prudent to give to his eldest son a title equal to his own over those dominions of which he retained the immediate administration in his own hands, and which he intended to bequeath to that son. The propriety of such reservation ceased as soon as Charlemagne received the title of emperor, which was superior to that of king; he had no grounds for apprehension in allowing another to govern as king under him the states which he himself governed as emperor.

2. The second difficulty regards "the oath taken by Charlemagne," according to some authors, "in the ceremony of the coronation," A.D. 800. Sigonius, who wrote in the sixteenth century, and some modern authors, suppose that the prince took on that occasion to Pope Leo III. the oath of fidelity, which the emperors afterwards took, and which was to the following effect, according to an ancient *Ordo Romanus:* "I, N. emperor, promise, in the name of Jesus Christ, before God and St. Peter, to protect and defend all the interests of the Roman Church to the best of my power and authority, with the blessing of God."[1] Fleury, P. Daniel, P. Longueval, and the greater number of modern authors, omit all mention of this circumstance, which, in truth, is neither well attested nor in itself probable. It is very difficult to conceive that Eginhard, Anastasius the Librarian, and the other historians of the day, who record in greater detail the history of Charlemagne's coronation, should have omitted so important a circumstance; nor does the ancient *Ordo Romanus,* cited by Sigonius for that fact, seem sufficient to establish it. This *Ordo,* published for the first time in 1561, by George Cassander, and afterwards by Hittorpius (Paris, 1569, in fol.), though for the most part very ancient, received, in the course of time, many additions of much more recent date; so that the most learned critics find it difficult to determine the antiquity of some parts of it, without recurring to other testimony.[2] The Sacramentary of St. Gregory, which

---

[1] Ordo Romanus ad Benedicendum Imperatorem; apud Hittorpium, De Divinis Officiis, fol. edit. 1624, p. 153 (Biblioth. Patrum, vol. xiii.). Sigonius, Hist. de Regno Italiæ, lib. iv. ann. 801 (Oper. tom. ii.). Baronii Annales, ann. 800, n. 7. Cenni, Monumenta Domin. Pontif. tom. ii. Dissert. 1, n. 45. Lebeau, Hist. du Bas-Empire, vol. xiv. book lxvi. n. 53. Hegewisch, Hist. de Charlemagne, p. 345.

[2] Mabillon, Musæum Italicum, vol. ii. Præf. p. 9.

was used in Rome and France during the ninth century, and which we have cited in another place,[1] proves, it is true, that an oath of fidelity to the pope was taken by some emperors in the course of the ninth century, but not that it was taken by Charlemagne himself.

3. The last difficulty regards "the title of emperor given to Charlemagne by Pope Leo III." The unanimous testimony of ancient authors, which on this point is generally admitted by the moderns, places it beyond doubt that the pope, when conferring that title on Charlemagne in the ceremony of his coronation, meant to confer on him a title of honour which he had not previously enjoyed. Charlemagne himself certainly thought so; for from that period he invariably assumed the title of emperor in his public acts, in which he had previously styled himself king of France, or patrician of the Romans.

Nevertheless, an author, who is justly esteemed for his researches on the history of France, asserts confidently "that the imperial dignity had been attached to the crown of France from the reign of Clovis; that the kings of the first, second, and third races had assumed the style of emperors; and that this title was given to them both by their subjects and by foreigners." A dissertation in favour of these positions was published by François Decamps, in the Mercure of the month of August, 1720 (page 50, &c.). On examining this singular dissertation, it appeared to us to be grounded principally on the ambiguity of the words "emperor," "consul," and of some other titles of honour, which in former ages were taken in many different senses. The name "emperor" was, in more ancient times, commonly given by the Romans to all generals of the army (from the Latin word *imperare*, which means "to command"). Afterwards it became a title of honour given by the soldiers or the senate to any general who had distinguished himself by some signal exploit. In later times Cæsar received this title from the Roman people, to express the extraordinary power which he had in the state; a power absorbing in itself all the functions attached to the different magistrates of the republic. It was in this latter sense that Augustus and his successors were called emperors. After the example of the Romans, they gave the same title, in a sense more or less general, to their sovereigns; whence it has resulted, that ancient as well as modern authors sometimes use promiscuously the words "king," "emperor,"

[1] Infra, part ii. ch. ii. n. 157.

"empire," "kingdom," and other similar expressions.[1] Hence it is manifest that the kings of France could be called in a general way emperors, and their kingdom an empire, before Charlemagne's coronation; though with propriety it could not be said that the imperial dignity was annexed to their crown, in the same sense as after Charlemagne's coronation in the year 800.

As for the title of consul given to Clovis by the emperor Anastasius, it is certain that this title was not inseparable from that of emperor, as François Decamps supposed in the dissertation already cited. We have proved in another place,[2] that under the empire it was nothing more than a mere title of honour, sometimes conferred by the emperors on distinguished personages.

We have thus proved that the title of emperor given to Charlemagne by Pope Leo III. was a title of honour, such as that formerly given to the emperors of the West. This new title made Charlemagne more respectable in the eyes of other sovereigns, and especially of the Romans; it conferred on him, moreover, a special authority in the government of Rome and of the exarchate. The nature and extent of that authority have been already explained.[3]

VII.—Page 293.

On Pepin's Elevation to the Throne of France, and on the charge of usurpation commonly made against him.

Two principal questions present themselves here: 1. Is Pope Zachary's decision concerning Pepin's elevation to the throne of France authentic? 2. What truth is there in the charge of usurpation made against that prince by so great a number of modern authors?

FIRST QUESTION.

The authenticity of Pope Zachary's decision was vehemently disputed at the close of the seventeenth century by Pères Lecointe

---

[1] See the articles *Emperor, Imperator,* in the following works: Robert Stephen, Thesaurus Linguæ Latinæ; Ducange, Glossarium Infimæ et Mediæ Latinit.; Facciolati, Lexicon; Moreri, Diction. Hist. See also Crevier, Hist. Rom. vol. xiv. p. 335.

[2] Supra, last note to art. 32, part i.

[3] Supra, part i. ch. ii. art. 1.

and Natalis Alexander.[1] It was recorded, they maintained, in chronicles of no authority, the most ancient of which were either invented or falsified by writers devoted to the Carlovingian dynasty.

This opinion was combated at once by Pères Pagi and Mabillon, and it never was embraced by many.[2] It was revived by a modern writer in a dissertation entitled, Pepin the Little and Pope Zachary; or, Proofs of the fidelity of the French to their legitimate Kings in the transition from the First to the Second Dynasty, by M. Aimé Guillon (Paris, 1817, 8vo.). This dissertation, however, never produced much effect among the learned; at least, we know no distinguished author of our own day maintaining it:[3] on the contrary, even after the publication of that work we see the authenticity of the fact under consideration manifestly supposed by these authors who have treated most accurately and at greatest length of the middle ages in general, and of France in particular.[4]

We are of opinion with these authors, and with the greater

---

[1] Lecointe, Annales Ecclesiastici Francorum, vol. v. ann. 752. Nat. Alexander, Hist. Eccles. Dissert. 2 in sæc. octavum. Tournely (De Ecclesiâ, vol. ii. p. 402, &c.) inclines to the opinion of these authors, without, however, openly adopting it.

[2] Pagi, Critica in Annales Baronii, ann. 751, 752. Mabillon, Annales Benedictini, tom. ii. lib. xxii. n. 43, 55. There is a special dissertation on the opinions of those authors in the first vol. of the Collection of Historical and Literary Papers (by the Abbé Granet and Père Desmolets), Paris, 1731, 4 vols. 12mo. Mamachi, Antiquitates Christianæ, vol. iv. p. 224, &c. Notes by P. Roncaglia and Mansi, at the close of the dissertation of Nat. Alexander, already cited.

[3] We have been informed, on the best authority, that the author of this dissertation, when aspiring to be elected member of the Academy, had presented this work, as a title to support, to one of the most influential members of the Institute. The Academy, however, after examining the dissertation, were of opinion, that so far from being a recommendation, it was rather a just ground for his rejection. The principal motives of this decision were, it appears, the cavilling, exaggerated, and prejudiced criticism, which the author displayed in that, as well as in some other works. See especially the review of his History of the Church during the Eighteenth Century, in the Ami de la Religion, vol. xxxvi. p. 385; vol. xxxvii. pp. 81, 321, 413; vol. xxxviii. pp. 49, 209, 413; Œuvr. de Fénelon; Notice Bibliog. vol. xx. p. lv. &c. The Abbé Guillon died in February 1842, aged 84 years.

[4] See especially Michaud, Hist. des Croisades, vol. iv. p. 462; Sismondi, Hist. des Français, vol. ii. p. 165; Idem, Hist. des Républiques Italiennes, vol. i. ch. iii. p. 132; Annales du Moyen Age, vol. vi. book xxiii. ann. 751; Châteaubriand, Etudes Historiques, vol. iii.; Analyse raisonnée de l'Hist. de France, second race, p. 1; De Peyronnet, Hist. des Francs, vol. ii. book xii. ch. viii. M. Receveur, in his Hist. de l'Eglise (vol. iv. p. 80, note), does not absolutely reject the fact in question; he merely represents it as doubtful. The arguments which he proposes in support of his opinion, appear to us to be very much weakened by the general observations which we are about to give in support of the common opinion.

number of modern critics, that this fact is attested by an historical tradition of the highest authority, and that none but absurd critics can question its certainty. In truth, it would not be easy to find in the history of that period a fact substantiated by a more ancient or general tradition; for, to cite none but the most ancient testimonies, we find this fact related by the continuator of Fredegarius, a contemporary of Pepin;[1] by the anonymous author of a note appended in 767 to the work of St. Gregory of Tours, De Gloriâ Confessorum;[2] by Eginhard, or the author of those Annals which go by his name,[3] and by a host of later annalists.[4] In every one of the different collections of the historians of France we meet a great number of testimonies corroborating the same tradition. These testimonies go back without interruption to the days of Charlemagne and of Pepin, thus forming an unbroken series from the middle of the eighth century until the close of the seventeenth, when some writers first began to contest it. What reasonable grounds can there be for disputing the authority of a tradition so ancient and so universal on a fact of such importance? Can it be disputed without perilling the certainty of the universally admitted facts of that period of our history?

And what are the arguments against this imposing tradition? The authenticity of some of the ancient testimonies which we have cited is called in question. But a detailed discussion of these testimonies is really not necessary to prove our opinion. For, omitting altogether the fact that the authenticity of these testimonies has been admitted by the majority of critics ever since this question first was raised, it must be borne in mind, in the first place, that the majority of those who dispute the authority of this tradition admit that it can be traced back to the time of Charlemagne:[5] secondly, that this ancient tradition was not contradicted

[1] Fredegarii Continuatio, ann. 752. This continuation is given at the end of the Hist. des Francs, by St. Gregory of Tours, in Ruinart's edition.

[2] Opera S. Gregorii Turonensis, ad calcem libri De Gloriâ Confessorum. The MS. of that work in which this note was found was formerly preserved in the abbey of St. Denis. It was communicated to Fathers Henschenius and Papebroch, editors of the Acta Sanctorum, who inserted it in the second volume of the month of March. Père Mabillon also published it in his great work, De Re Diplomaticâ, p. 384.

[3] Eginhard, Annales, ann. 750.

[4] A collection of these testimonies may be seen in Serarius, Dupin, and Bossuet, whom we have cited already (part i. ch. ii. n. 92, note 2). There are many more of them in the Recueil des Historiens de France, by Duchesne and D. Bouquet.

[5] M. Guillon alone refers the origin of this tradition to the commencement

positively by any person until the close of the seventeenth century: thirdly, that the authors who are charged with having inserted this fact in order to flatter the successors of Pepin, could have no interest in inventing it, since they could cite confidently in favour of that prince and of his dynasty another fact of the same nature, and incontestable; namely, the coronation of Pepin by Pope Stephen II. These arguments fully justified, in our opinion, the assertion of a celebrated historian of our time, who, when treating of the decision of Pope Zachary, pronounces it one of the best-attested facts in history. "There is, perhaps, no fact in history better attested than the part which Pope Zachary and his legate Boniface had in this affair." [1]

SECOND QUESTION.

With regard to the usurpation commonly charged against Pepin, it is very far from being certain: without undertaking to prove the contrary by direct evidence, we believe we can at least safely assert, that this charge of *usurpation is improbable in itself, and not sustained by any solid proofs.*

Before we propose the argument for these two assertions, we must not conceal that it was not without great hesitation we decided on opposing the common opinion of modern authors on this point. The number and the authority of its advocates appeared to us a legitimate and almost conclusive proof in its favour. It seemed to us extremely improbable that it could have received the sanction of so many judicious authors without solid arguments; and, notwithstanding the difficulties which it presented to us, we believed that a more attentive reconsideration would compel us to acknowledge that it was founded on at least very strong presumptive evidence. In this temper of mind we examined it; but that examination, far from making it more plausible, only increased the number and cogency of objections against it. We shall propose them here with the greater confidence, because they occurred before to learned authors, and were proposed in works now little known; nor has any solid answer ever been given to them to our knowledge, nor was there even an attempt to answer them at length.[2]

---

of the tenth century, because he denies the authenticity of all the more ancient testimonies: on this point his criticism is manifestly extravagant.

[1] Lingard, Antiquities of the Anglo-Saxon Church, ch. xiii. p. 544.

[2] The opinion which charges Pepin with usurping the crown of France was combated with great energy by Serarius, in his work entitled, Rerum Moguntinensium Libri quinque; Moguntiæ, 1604, 4to.; Francofurti, 1722, fol. See

I. The usurpation commonly charged against Pepin is improbable in itself: it seems utterly irreconcilable with the character which historians give us of that great prince, and with that of the principal personages who contributed to his elevation; and, finally, with the submission which the French barons invariably preserved to him during the whole course of his reign.

1. In the first place, those very historians who charge Pepin with the crime of usurpation, are compelled to acknowledge in him a combination of all the virtues and qualities required for a great prince. "He was," according to Père Longueval, "a prince in whom everything was great except his stature; whence he derived his surname of the 'Little.' Born a subject, his great qualities proved him so worthy of that throne on which he established himself, to the prejudice of the rightful heirs, that his ambition did not provoke the jealousy of the barons. So perfectly was he able to combine the virtues of a Christian and of a civilian with the excellencies of a soldier, that he was always the favourite of the people, the champion of the faith, and the terror of all the enemies of the Church and of the state. Son and grandson of heroes, he had also the singular happiness of being father of a hero, who eclipsed the glory even of his illustrious ancestors. To the highly honourable titles conferred on him by the pope, such as the 'second Moses,' 'liberator of the Church,' 'most Christian king,' 'greatest of kings,' we can only add that, a few failings excepted, he deserved them."[1] The opinions of our best historians agree perfectly on this point with Longueval.[2] Now can this be the character of an usurper, of a man capable, as it is said, of using all the appliances of religion and of the most astute policy to conceal from the people the crime of usurpation? Is it not a palpable contradiction to attribute to the same man the most exalted virtue and the most detestable intrigues of ambition? This contradiction, we are

especially note 40, on the third book of that work. Alban Butler, or his translator, in a note on the Life of St. Boniface, refers to that work of Serarius, as having cleared up satisfactorily the facts relating to Pepin's election (Vies des Pères, vol. v. June 5). In support of the opinion of Serarius, the following works may be also consulted: Notice Généalogique et Historique sur la Maison de France, Paris, 1816, n. 12; Gaillard, Hist. de Charlemagne, vol. i. pp. 194, 258, &c.; Clausel de Coussergues, Du Sacre des Rois de France, ch. iv.; De Saint-Victor, Tableau Historique et Pitt. de Paris, vol. i. p. 69; Mœller, Manuel d'Histoire du Moyen Age, ch. vii. § 1, ver. fin.

[1] Hist. de l'Eglise Gall. vol. iv. ann. 768, p. 452.

[2] Fleury and Bérault-Bercastel, in their Church histories, Père Daniel, in his Hist. de France, and with them the majority of historians both French and foreign, give the same high character of Pepin.

convinced, will appear more manifest the more closely we examine the whole history of Pepin, even in those writings which stigmatize him as an usurper.

2. The character of the principal personages who co-operated in his elevation appears also irreconcilable with the charge of usurpation. Characters the most respectable are represented as accomplices in the crime: Pope Zachary, who is described by all historians as a prelate of eminent virtue; Fulrade, abbot of St. Denis, one of the highest dignitaries in the church of France; St. Burchard, bishop of Wurzburg, a disciple of St. Boniface; St. Boniface himself, the apostle of Germany, who gave the regal unction to Pepin, after the decision of Pope Zachary. Now, how can it be imagined that so many persons distinguished for virtue and character could have all conspired to favour Pepin's usurpation; Fulrade and St. Burchard, by pleading the usurper's cause before the Holy See; Zachary, by deciding in favour of the usurpation; and St. Boniface, by investing it with a sacred sanction in the ceremony of coronation? Such a supposition, it must be admitted, is utterly devoid of probability.[1]

3. What confirms still more the improbability of this charge of usurpation against Pepin, is the respect and submission which he constantly received from the French barons and people during the whole course of his reign. Even those authors who charge him with usurpation are compelled to acknowledge that his conduct "did not even provoke the jealousy of the barons, and that during his whole reign there was neither insurrection nor faction against his authority."[2] Now is it credible that Pepin could have so speedily and so constantly obtained the respect and submission of the French barons and people if he had been guilty of usurpation?

---

[1] These observations may serve as a corrective for some passages in La Bruère's Histoire de Charlemagne, in which the author attributes to St. Boniface conduct unworthy of a saint, and especially of an apostle (vol. i. pp. 24, &c. 32).

[2] Père Longueval, Hist. de l'Eglise Gallicane, ubi supra. Daniel, Hist. de France, vol. ii. reign of Pepin, p. 267. Velly, Hist. de France, vol. i. p. 378.

M. Guillon, in his Dissertation already cited (p. 91), supposes, with the authors of the Histoire de Languedoc (D. Vaissette and D. Devic), that the revolt of Gaifre, duke of Aquitaine, which gave such trouble to Pepin, arose from that duke's opposition to that prince's usurpation. But, on the contrary, it is certain, as La Bruère remarks, that all the ancient historians speak of Gaifre as a rebel vassal, justly dispossessed by Pepin. (La Bruère, Hist. de Charlemagne, vol. i. p. 54.) Moreover, this individual case of revolt does not invalidate the assertion made by the authors whom we have cited, that the French lords were generally submissive and respectful to Pepin: the opposition of one duke cannot counterbalance the submission of all the others.

Could such a revolution have been effected so tranquilly? Surely it should have excited insurrections and factions, especially in those days, when, as is well known, the barons were generally so turbulent and so untractable.

II. The usurpation of Pepin, besides being improbable in itself, is, moreover, not attested by solid proof. All those usually proposed are derived either from the ancient constitution of the French monarchy, or from the testimony of some ancient authors, or from some circumstances in the relations between Pepin and the French barons. Now it is easy to prove that these arguments are inconclusive.

1. The charge that Pepin was an usurper derives not the least confirmation from the ancient constitution of the French monarchy; because it should be proved that, according to the then existing constitution, the French barons had no right either to depose Childeric III. or to elect Pepin: now neither of these points is by any means conclusively proved. In the first place, with regard to Childeric's deposition, it is certain, according to the more common opinion of modern authors, that the crown of France was elective, at least within the reigning family, under the first and second races of French kings,[1] and that in France, as well as in all other elective monarchies, the royal authority was very much limited by the general assembly of the nation; so that at present it would be difficult, perhaps impossible, to ascertain precisely the rights of that assembly.[2] As a necessary consequence of the obscurity in which that question is enveloped, it is impossible at this date to know what were the conditions made on the election of the sovereigns by the general assembly of the nation, and in what cases that assembly had, or believed it had, the right of deposing one sovereign and substituting another in his

---

[1] The Abbé Vertot adopts and proves this opinion, in a dissertation published in the Mémoires de l'Acad. des Inscrip. (vol. vi. of the 12mo. edit. and vol. iv. of the 4to.). Vertot's opinion appears to be generally admitted by the authors who have since written on the subject. See, among others, De St. Victor, Tableau Hist. et Pitt. de Paris, vol. i. pp. 62, 71; Hallam's Europe and Middle Ages, vol. i. pp. 175, 180, 284; Velly, Hist. de France, vol. i. p. 75; Gaillard, Hist. de Charlemagne, vol. i. pp. 151, 167, 184, 189, 258, et alibi passim; Notice Généalogique sur la Maison de France, § 3; Clausel, Du Sacre des Rois de France, ch. iv. and § 3, observations at the close of his work; Châteaubriand, Etudes Historiques, Préface, p. cxvi. 1st edit. and p. 93, 2nd edit. In the third volume of this last work, see the Analyse raisonnée de l'Histoire de France, first race, pp. 6, 7, &c.; second race, p. 1. Mœller, Manuel d'Hist. du Moyen Age, ch. iv. § 6.

[2] Annales du Moyen Age, vol. iii. book ii. p. 1, &c.

place. Nevertheless, it may be confidently assumed, that at the time of Pepin's elevation there was a general impression among the French that a prince "who was of no use" to the nation should not retain the title of king, and that the prince then enjoying that title was absolutely of no use whatsoever. All the French ancient annalists suppose, without exception, that this was the general impression; and they represent the incapacity or "do nothing" of Childeric III. as the true cause of his deposition.[1] This opinion, no doubt, did not appear so manifestly clear as to remove all scruple about Childeric's deposition; but it was sufficiently well founded to induce the French barons to desire and request a decision of the pope to set their consciences completely at rest on the point. From these observations, it may be inferred, we believe, that the conduct of the French barons to Childeric III. was not in reality so strange as it might at first sight appear. Hence it has been vindicated even in modern times by writers not less profoundly versed in French history than firmly attached to the conservative principles of society and of government. It was the opinion of Bossuet.[2] According to him, the excessive authority vested by the nation in the mayors of the palace, after Dagobert's reign, weakened to such a degree the royal authority, that it was gradually reduced to an empty title, and that the royal power was, in reality, placed in the hands of the mayors. "They became regular and permanent officers, invested with absolute power of deciding all affairs, and of commanding the army. Even the right of appointing this officer had not been reserved to the kings; he was elected by the chief men of the kingdom; and, once appointed, he decided all matters absolutely, without any reference to the king."[3] Struck with so palpable a defect in the constitution of the state, and with the inconveniences which would necessarily result from it in course of time, the French barons, at length, could find no other remedy than to take away the title of king from him in whom it was no more than a title, and to confer it on him whom the consent of the nation had already invested with kingly power. This was, in fact, the only means of remedying an anomaly gradually established by a defect in the constitution; and of pre-

---

[1] See the testimonies of our ancient annalists, cited by Bossuet and the authors mentioned in the first part of this work, n. 92.

[2] Bossuet, Defens. Declarat. lib. ii. cap. xxxiv. See also the authors cited already in support of Bossuet's opinion, part i. n. 93.

[3] Bossuet, ibid. p. 523.

venting all the disorders of anarchy, which sooner or later it must inevitably produce. The kingdom, it was manifest, could not continue long under two different masters, both of whom should alike claim the supreme power for himself, and on titles equally imposing.[1]

In the second place, supposing that the French barons had a right to depose Childeric, their subsequent election of Pepin cannot be proved contrary to the then existing constitution; for, as we have already observed, according to the more common opinion, the crown of France was at that time elective, at least within the reigning family;[2] and some eminent critics are of opinion that Pepin was of the royal blood of the Merovingians.[3] Even in our own days that opinion has appeared not improbable to some learned men; amongst whom may be reckoned especially D. de

---

[1] The conduct of the French lords could be more easily vindicated, if, as some say, Childeric, moved by the desire of consecrating himself wholly to God, had, with the consent of the lords, voluntarily abdicated the throne. (Jean de Paris, Tract. de Potestate Regiâ et Populi, cap. xiv. xv.; apud Richerium, Vindiciæ Doctrinæ Majorum Scholæ Paris. lib. ii. pp. 104, 108.) By this voluntary abdication, the right of electing another king naturally devolved on the French. This mode of justifying Pepin's election cannot, however, be well maintained; first, because Childeric's abdication is not satisfactorily proved. The unvarying narrative of the ancient annalists, who in this point are followed by the majority of modern historians, supposes that Childeric was placed in a monastery by order of Pepin and of the barons, not by his own free will: secondly, supposing even that Childeric had abdicated, it would be difficult to prove that, circumstanced as he was, his act was voluntary. It must moreover be observed, that this mode of justifying Pepin's election would be still more difficult in the opinion of those writers who maintain that the crown of France was strictly hereditary under the first race of kings. In truth, the Chronique de Fontenelle states, that Childeric III. left a son, who lived and died in that monastery; and this fact is admitted by the majority of historians. (Hist. de l'Eglise Gall. vol. iv. ann. 752, p. 354. Daniel, Hist. de France, ann. 750.) It appears also, that, besides this son of Childeric III., there were, long after Pepin's election, other princes of the royal Merovingian race. Several dukes of Gascony, sprung from that family, gave much trouble to Pepin, to Charlemagne, and to Louis le Débonnaire. (D. Vaissette, Hist. du Languedoc, vol. i. p. 413. L'Art de Vérifier les Dates; Chronologie Hist. des Rois de Toulouse et des Ducs de Gascogne. Annales du Moyen Age, vol. viii. book xxix. p. 331. Frantin, Louis le Pieux et son Siècle, vol. i. ann. 816, 819, pp. 38, 103, &c. De la Bruère, Hist. de Charlemagne, vol. i. p. 53, note.)

[2] See note 1, p. 336, supra.

[3] One of the principal advocates of this opinion was the Abbé Fr. Decamps, author of many curious dissertations on the history of France, a list of which is given in the 5th vol. of La Biblioth. Hist. de la France, by P. Lelong (Table des Auteurs, art. Decamps). See especially his Dissertation sur la Noblesse de la Race Royale des Français, in the Mercure de France, July, 1720. The author of this dissertation regards as certain the origin of the three royal races of France from the same stock (p. 13), and he proves his assertion at greater length in a manuscript dissertation, cited by Père Lelong (ubi supra).

Bévy, a Benedictine, and historiographer of France.[1] These authors trace in the following manner the genealogy of the French princes from Meroveus to Pepin and Hugh Capet: Sigebert, king of the Ripuari, brother of Childeric I.; Cloderic, killed by Clovis; Munderic, king in Auvergne; Bodegesilas, king in Austrasia; St. Arnould; Ansigises, mayor of the palace to Sigebert; Pepin d'Héristal. This Pepin had two sons, Charles Martel, the founder of the Carlovingians; and Childebrand, of the Capetians. The two were sons of Pepin by different wives, whom he married successively.[2] From Childebrand, who died in 753, descended Nivelon, Theodobert, Robert le Fort; Robert I., king of France; Hugh le Grand, and Hugh Capet. This system, it must be confessed, is considered by many learned men liable to very great objections; but even those who reject it believe that it cannot be refuted by decisive arguments.[3]

2. Neither can the testimony of ancient authors be cited in proof of Pepin's usurpation. The majority of them suppose that his elevation to the throne of France was effected by the consent of the French lords, combined with the decision of Pope Zachary, whom they considered themselves bound to consult on the subject.[4] Far from censuring that decision, they are generally lavish of their eulogy on Pepin and Zachary; they do not drop a single expression which could imply a charge of usurpation against Pepin; they do not even appear conscious that such a suspicion had ever been expressed. Theophanes alone, among all the ancient writers, asserts that Pepin had received from Pope Stephen II. absolution for his perjury, or the treason of which he had been guilty against his legitimate sovereign.[5] But the isolated testi-

---

[1] Unique Origine des Rois de France, by M. J. C. de Bévy, Paris, 1814, pp. 32, 8vo. Notice Généal. et Hist. sur la Maison de France, §§ 1, 2. See an account of this work in the Ami de la Religion et du Roi, vol. viii. p. 273.

[2] Many modern writers have questioned the legitimacy of the marriage of Pepin d'Héristal with Alpaïde, mother of Charles Martel. But grave authors assert it. Besides those cited in the preceding note, see in the Mémoires de l'Académie de Bruxelles (vol. iii. pp. 318, 320), a Memoir by M. Dewez, pour servir à l'Histoire d'Alpaïde.

[3] The opinion, it seems, of P. Daniel, in his History of Hugh Capet, and of P. Griffet, in his observations on that history (Hist. de France, vol. iii. pp. 264, 295, &c.).

[4] Serarius, ubi supra, n. 40, 43.

[5] "Pipinus primus extitit, qui, regio non oriundus sanguine, imperium in gentem illam [Francorum] obtinuit; ipse Stephanus eum à perjurio in regem admisso absolvit."—Theophanis Chronographia, ann. 8 Leonis, pp. 337, 338. This passage of Theophanes is also given in the Ecclesiastical History of Anas-

mony of this author, who was generally very little acquainted with facts connected with French history, cannot outweigh the testimony of so many others, having far better means of ascertaining the truth on this point.[1] His testimony was, therefore, generally rejected until the sixteenth century. Calvin, Illyricus, and some other disciples of the Reformation, were the first that presumed to assail on this point the character of Pepin and of Charlemagne, of whom they speak with sovereign contempt, through malign hatred of their generosity to the Holy See. From the new reformers such language is not surprising; but it is really surprising that an opinion so justly suspected, both from its novelty and from the character of its first defenders, should have found so many partisans among Catholic authors.[2]

3. Finally, some circumstances in the conduct of Pepin and of the French barons, which are sometimes cited as proofs of the usurpation, are equally inconclusive. It is objected, in the first place, that they used violence to Childeric by shaving his head and imprisoning him in a monastery for the rest of his days. Were Pepin's election unlawful, this conduct towards Childeric would be inexcusable; it would be a manifest crime of treason. But if

---

tasius Bibliothec., and in the continuation of the History by Paulus Diaconus. Both these works, however, on the history of this period, are nothing but translations of Theophanes; nor is there any proof that the translators adopted on this point the opinions of their author. Some modern writers believe that Anastasius Bibliothec., in his Life of Pope Stephen, corroborates the testimony of Theophanes; but there are no grounds for that assertion, as the slightest examination of the text of Anastasius proves that his meaning is entirely different from that of Theophanes. After having related the coronation of Pepin, and the miraculous recovery of the pope from a sickness under which he had been labouring during his abode at St. Denis, Anastasius adds: "Pippinus verò rex, cum admonitione, gratiâ et oratione ipsius venerabilis pontificis *absolutus*, in loco qui Carisiacus appellatur pergens, &c." (Labbe, Concilia, vol. vi. p. 1624, E.) Now manifestly there cannot be question in this passage of Pepin's absolution from the crime of treason; for Anastasius is speaking in this place of a fact subsequent to the coronation of Pepin and of his children, which he had already related; and it is incredible that the pope, had he believed absolution from treason to be necessary, would have deferred it until after Pepin's coronation. Hence Baronius, and the majority of critics, understand Anastasius in quite a different sense (Baronii Annales, vol. iv. an. 754, n. 6). They understand the word *absolvere* as equivalent to *dimittere*, a sense in which it is very often taken by writers in the middle ages, and by Anastasius himself in many other passages.

[1] See in the first part of our Inquiry (ch. i. n. 27) some observations on the authority of Theophanes in this matter.

[2] See in support of these observations our remarks, supra, n. 8, text and notes, Part First.

Pepin's election were legitimate, as we may well believe, his conduct to the deposed king was an act of prudence, rendered necessary by circumstances for the repose of France, and the prevention of those troubles which the discontented never fail to excite in similar circumstances.

But, it is asked, if the lords had a right to depose Childeric and to elect Pepin, why consult Pope Zachary on the subject?—Does not such conduct reveal the just remorse of their conscience?

It proves, certainly, that the French lords saw some difficulty in the question which they submitted to the pope. But there is nothing surprising in their being embarrassed on a matter of such moment, even supposing them by right competent to pronounce on it. It was a novel case of conscience, a singular one, and of the utmost importance, and consequently requiring of its own nature great intelligence, and an attentive examination. Embarrassment in deciding a question of that character by no means implies a wish to decide it against the dictates of one's conscience; it might rather arise from the difficulty of taking a decided opinion upon a question so delicate. Moreover, in this case the sincerity of the French lords is the less liable to suspicion, since before they undertook to depose Childeric, they wished to have the decision of the most venerable tribunal to which they could apply, and of a pontiff to whose virtue the unanimous voice of history bears testimony.

Finally, it is objected that Pepin himself, notwithstanding Zachary's decision, still regarded his authority as doubtful, since he wished to be crowned again by Stephen II. in 754, after Childeric's death.

This objection is not more solid than the preceding; for, admitting even, with the majority of historians, that Pepin had been already crowned by St. Boniface, it is not surprising that he should wish to be crowned again by the pope, to render his authority more sacred in the eyes of the French, and to confirm by a solemn act after Childeric's death the decision already given by Zachary during that prince's life. Legitimate kings have been often crowned more than once. In Scripture we find memorable examples in the person of David and of Saul; and in French history the same is recorded of Charlemagne and of his children.[1]

---

[1] Clausel, Du Sacre des Rois de France, 2nd ed. Paris, 1825, 8vo. ch. iv. and v.

In conclusion, we have no difficulty in admitting that we do not pretend to give direct and positive proofs of the legitimate title of Pepin; we merely believe ourselves justified in inferring from our arguments that his usurpation is by no means so incontestable a fact as modern authors commonly suppose; and that a grave historian ought not, without other proofs, to assume it as an unquestionable fact.

END OF VOL. I.

COX (BROTHERS) AND WYMAN, PRINTERS, GREAT QUEEN STREET.

www.ingramcontent.com/pod-product-compliance
Lightning Source LLC
LaVergne TN
LVHW010129110826
845151LV00002B/312

* 9 7 8 1 4 2 5 5 4 0 5 5 5 *